Changing Governance of Research and Technology Policy

Changing Governance of Research and Technology Policy

The European Research Area

Edited by

Jakob Edler

Fraunhofer Institute for Systems and Innovation Research, Germany

Stefan Kuhlmann

Fraunhofer Institute for Systems and Innovation Research, Germany and Utrecht University, The Netherlands

Maria Behrens

The FernUniversity/University of Hagen, Germany

Edward Elgar

Cheltenham, UK • Northampton, MA, USA

Published by
Edward Elgar Publishing Limited
Glensanda House
Montpellier Parade
Cheltenham
Glos GL50 1UA
UK

Edward Elgar Publishing, Inc.
136 West Street
Suite 202
Northampton
Massachusetts 01060
USA

A catalogue record for this book
is available from the British Library

Library of Congress Cataloguing in Publication Data

Changing governance of research and technology policy: the European research area/ edited by Jakob Edler, Stefan Kuhlmann, Maria Behrens.
    p. cm.
    1. Research – Government policy – European Union countries. 2. Science and state – European Union countries. 3. Technology and state – European Union countries. I. Edler, Jakob, 1967 - II. Kuhlmann, Stefan. III. Behrens, Maria.

Q180.E9C43 2004
338.94'06–dc22

                                                                2003049378
ISBN 1 84376 597 7

Printed and bound in Great Britain by MPG Books Ltd, Bodmin, Cornwall

Contents

Figures

Boxes

Tables

Contributors

Gabriele Abels is a senior researcher/lecturer at the Institute for Science and Technology Studies, Faculty of Sociology at Bielefeld University. Her main fields of interest are European integration and R&D policymaking, particularly in the areas of biotechnology, governance of science and participation.

Thomas Banchoff is Associate Professor of Government at Georgetown University. His publications include 'The German Problem Transformed: Institutions, Politics and Foreign Policy, 1945–95' (University of Michigan Press 1999), and (as co-editor and contributor) Legitimacy and the European Union: The Contested Polity (Routledge 1999).

Maria Behrens is Assistant Professor at the Department of International Relations and Comparative Politics at the Open University in Hagen. Since 2000 she has been speaker of the Committee on Politics and Technology of the German Political Science Association (DVPW). Her present research interests focus on issues concerning international trade policy and transatlantic relations. She has published numerous book chapters and articles in the field of global governance.

Peter Biegelbauer heads the research cluster 'Social Learning' at the Sociology Department of the Institute for Advanced Studies in Vienna, Austria. He is engaged in the Austrian Political Science Association, where he was Secretary General in 2000 and 2001. His research interests include social learning, the political economy of advanced industrial societies and the European integration process as well as political and economic theory since industrialization.

Paraskevas Caracostas has for the last fourteen years been involved in EU research policy shaping. He is currently Head of the 'Science and Technology Foresight' unit in DG Research, European Commission, Brussels. He has published numerous studies and papers in the field of industrial economics and science and technology policy.

Chris Caswill is currently Director of Research at the UK Economic and Social Research Council in Swindon, and Secretary to the Council's three Research Boards. In 2004, he will take up a Visiting Professorship at the University of Exeter. He has published a number of papers on science policy, on the use of principal agent theory and on interactive social science.

Ulrich Dolata is an economist and social scientist. During the 90s he worked at the University of Bremen, Department of Economics, and at the Hamburg Institute for Social Research. In 1999/2000 he was Senior Fellow and Visiting Professor at the Institute for Advanced Studies on Science, Technology and Society (sts), Graz/Austria. Since 1998 he has been a Senior Researcher at the Research Centre Work–Environment–Technology (artec), University of Bremen. Main research areas: economics of innovation, technology policy, empirical research on the economic and social development of biotechnology and the Internet.

Jakob Edler is a senior researcher at the Fraunhofer Institute for Systems and Innovation Research. He has conducted many studies in the area of innovation policies and innovation strategies. His main interests are in the field of international research and development and related policymaking and corporate knowledge management.

Johanna Hakala is a Master of Arts, a Master of Social Sciences and a researcher at the Research Group for Science, Technology and Innovation Studies at the University of Tampere. Her research themes include the internationalization of science and technology and the dynamics of academic research in different disciplinary and organizational contexts.

Jean-Alain Héraud is Professor of Economics at the Louis Pasteur University, Strasbourg, and member of the BETA research institute. His main fields of research are economics of innovation; research policy, particularly as a multi-level governance process; technological foresight; and recently the area of education/employment policies, as head of the BETA-Céreq regional center.

Peter Hilger is a social scientist and member of the Interdisciplinary Center for Social Research at the University of Hannover. He has conducted research in the fields of research co-operation, volunteering and local media. Presently he is writing his doctoral thesis on the organization of volunteering.

Hans-Willy Hohn is a senior researcher at the Research Institute for Public Administration, German University of Administrative Sciences in Speyer

(FÖV). He has conducted many studies in the area of labor-market policy, industrial relations, as well as research and innovation policy. At present his main interests are in the current reforms of the German innovation system.

Robert Kaiser is Assistant Professor at the Chair for Political Science, Technical University of Munich. His main interests are in the field of international political economy, innovation research and policy studies. Current research concerns the process of economic integration and its impact on federal states, innovation systems and policies, as well as political communication in digital media.

Stefan Kuhlmann is head of the department of Technology Analysis and Innovation Strategies at the Fraunhofer Institute for Systems and Innovation Research (ISI), Karlsruhe and Professor of Innovation Policy Analysis at the University of Utrecht, Copernicus Institute for Sustainable Development and Innovation, Department of Innovation Studies. He has published numerous articles and books in the area of innovation policy and policy evaluation.

Jürgen Lautwein is administrative director at the Max Planck Institute for the Study of Societies (MPIfG). His main interests are in the field of research management and research policy, as well as organizational development in scientific institutions.

Emmanuel Muller is Professor at the University of Applied Sciences, Heidelberg, and senior researcher at the Fraunhofer Institute for Systems and Innovation Research in the department of Innovation Services and Regional Development. He is involved in research, dealing mainly with regional development and innovation strategies, innovation processes within SMEs and KIBS and knowledge economics.

Michael Stampfer is currently managing director of the newly founded Vienna Science and Technology Fund (WWTF). He has over ten years experience in the field of research and technology, working for the Federal Ministry of Science and Research and the *Technologie Impulse Gesellschaft*. Michael Stampfer is author of a number of publications, member of several EU working groups and involved in EU projects. He is also co-ordinator of the Austrian Platform for Research and Technology Evaluation.

Andrea Zenker is a senior researcher at the Fraunhofer Institute for Systems and Innovation Research in the department of Innovation Services and Regional Development. Her research activities focus on regional innovation strategies, methodology in innovation research and knowledge economics.

Acknowledgments

This book grew out of an international workshop ' "European Research Area" or National Innovation Competition? Technology Policy in the European and Comparative Perspective', held at the Fraunhofer Institute for Systems and Innovation Research (ISI), Karlsruhe, in November 2001. The workshop, organized in co-operation with the Working Party 'Politics and Technology' of the German Political Science Association (DVPW), brought together scholars and policymakers from eight countries and from very diverse backgrounds to discuss at a very early stage the emergence of a – supposedly – new governance approach in research and technology policy at the European level. The lively debate during and after the workshop prompted us to compile a selection of contributions, amended by a couple of invited papers in order to broaden the perspective even further.

As always, both the scientific workshop and the compilation of the papers in this book would not have been possible without many supporting minds and helping hands. First of all, we are grateful to all participants of the workshop who are not represented in this volume but improved the content of the book through stimulating comments. We would also like to thank the speakers of the DVPW Working Party 'Politics and Technology' for their deep interest, organizational assistance, valuable feedback and, above all, their encouragement to produce this book. Furthermore, our thanks goes to an anonymous reviewer who impressed us by his very careful reading and his extremely valuable comments to each of the contributions. Thereby, the content and coherence of this book have benefited enormously.

Finally, we are very grateful to the staff of Fraunhofer ISI. Edeltraud Geibel and Meike Urresta have not only organized this workshop very efficiently, but provided for a pleasant and relaxed atmosphere. Without their help our academic endeavour would most certainly have drowned in organizational details. In addition, we would like to thank Chris Mahler-Johnstone for assistance in the language editing for a number of papers and to Rebecca Rangnow and Stefan Berwing for supporting the streamlining of the bibliographic references. Finally our warmest thanks goes to Sabine Wurst who – we do not know how – managed to make a thoroughly edited book out of a multitude of very diversely formatted papers.

The Editors

PART I

Changing Governance:
the European Perspective

1 Changing Governance in European Research and Technology Policy

Possible Trajectories and the European Research Area[1]

Stefan Kuhlmann and Jakob Edler

INTRODUCTION

Science, research, technology and innovations based on these play a significant role today in the economies of the industrialized countries and are a driving force in their international competition. Meanwhile national, and increasingly also regional, governments pursue, more or less explicitly, research, development and technology policies (R&D policies) or – more comprehensively – 'innovation policies'.[2] In January 2000, the European Commission challenged the current division of labor in innovation policymaking with its now famous document 'Towards a European Research Area (ERA)' (European Commission 2000b). This paper contained the first sweeping reform attempt in European R&D policymaking in the last 20 years and took the research community in Europe totally by surprise.

With this new approach, the European Commission claims to have overcome the existing multi-layer architecture of European R&D policymaking with three distinct research and technology policies on each governance level, with – for most European Union (EU) countries at least – a minor and complementary role of Europe as compared to the national level. Among other things, it attempts to build up a European research identity and enable more effective and strategically planned pan-European co-operation. Its major means would be:

1. better and more *flexible co-ordination of national R&D policies*;
2. *Networks of Excellence* (NoE), multi-partner projects aimed at strengthening excellence on a research topic by *networking* the critical mass of

3

resources and expertise around a joint program of activities, aimed primarily at creating a progressive and lasting integration of the research activities of the network partners;

3. *Integrated Projects* (IP), multi-partner projects to support objective-driven
research by bringing together a critical mass of resources to reach ambitions goals, where the primary deliverable is knowledge for new products,
processes, services etc.[3]

The aim of the two latter instruments is to establish self-organized, longer-
term co-operation across Europe that would replace the existing approach of
short-term, small-scale, centrally managed research projects. This would give
the supranational body European Commission more autonomy to initiate
projects and programs that directly affect national research actors and, in
addition, would take co-ordination of national policies more seriously.

The rationale behind this approach is that under the conditions of knowledge societies and knowledge economies Europe needs to exploit its potential
much more effectively. The ongoing and accelerating process of European
economic integration, in combination with the opportunities opened up by
future enlargement of the EU, and the growing challenges of economic and
technological globalization, therefore, functionally lead to an integrated R&D
– and even innovation – policy approach in Europe. Ideally, this would optimize the usage and development of critical research and innovation infrastructures in Europe, thereby exploiting the full potential of an integrated
Europe. Such a development would certainly mean a quantum leap in European governance of research, technology and innovation.

Recent developments are somewhat ambivalent, they both indicate first
successes in this direction and show signs of resistance and inertia. In March
2002, only two years after first mentioning the idea of ERA, the European
Commission issued a call for expressions of interest[4] as regards the usage of
the two major new instruments geared towards the research community itself,
Networks of Excellence and *Integrated Projects*. Altogether, 11 700 eligible
expressions of interest were sent to the European Commission (European
Commission 2002b). As each of these instruments requires a core group of
several participants, the number of research organizations and companies is
even far higher. The public and private research community in the EU – and
even beyond[5] – is on alert.

However, at the same time, national governments show signs of resistance.
For example, a large part of the budget of the new, Sixth Framework Programme (FP6) is still allocated towards small co-operation projects of the old
type. In addition, Commissioner Busquin, responsible for European R&D
policy, in October 2002 regretted that national governments are still slow to
move, especially regarding the necessary steps towards more co-ordination

(Busquin 2002). Thus, albeit the success of the European Commission in informing and mobilizing the research community might be interpreted as an important step towards a new ERA, the road towards an integrated policy is a long way off.

Therefore, it is still only the dim lights of a new 'ERA' dawning that we are seeing and it is far from clear how the governance structures of the multi-level policymaking in Europe will develop into the complex area of R&D and innovation policy. It is obvious that the neo-functionalist understanding of integration underlying the ERA initiative, faces a competing, disintegrative view, basically stating that the growing pressures from globalization and the growing divergence of national innovation systems due to enlargement would lead to a re-intensification of competition between national – and even re-gional – innovation systems. In other words, it is far from certain whether the processes of European innovation policymaking will experience a new level of intensified integration in the course of this decade – as ERA would have it.

Consequently, it is fair to say that European R&D policy is at a crossroads. The book at hand attempts to take a first, deeper look at the current attempt of the European Commission to lead Europe along a path of intensified and redefined integration. It does so by compiling a wide range of different con-tributions that regard the current developments and their implications from very different perspectives.

This chapter wants to be more than a traditional introduction to the whole volume. Before the idea and purpose of the book are specified and the various contributions introduced, it takes one step backward and tries to put the ERA process into perspective by speculating about the *possible* futures of Euro-pean R&D policy, regardless of the current process. This is motivated by two considerations: First, despite the initial success, the idea of ERA is far from institutionalized. In describing what other directions Europe might take, it will be stressed how delicate the development still is and what alternative roads might be taken. Second, the analytical exercise to define different future developments *before* analyzing and commenting on ERA helps us assess the potential value – and possibly drawbacks – of the whole endeavor in a more differentiated way. Therefore, this article is also meant to assist in exploiting the full value of the contributions of this volume.

The following section will first outline, very briefly, some theoretical con-siderations on the interdependence between, and co-evolution of, governance in the European political system, on the one hand, and the development of national and transnational innovation systems, on the other hand, and will outline the resulting governance challenges. Based on these theoretical con-siderations and taking advantage of existing heuristic tools to structure future-oriented analysis, the third section will sketch *three scenarios*:

1. an increasingly *centralized* and dominating European innovation policy arena, a scenario that resembles the ERA vision;
2. the opposite, i.e. a progressive *decentralization* and open competition between partly strengthened, partly weakened national or regional innovation systems and related policy arenas;
3. a centrally 'mediated' *mixture of competition and co-operation* between diverse national or regional innovation cultures.

Against the background of this potential spectrum of future developments, the fourth section will introduce the purpose, structure and content of the volume at hand more concretely by describing more broadly the ERA process, and the questions and interpretations of various contributions. Our introductory chapter concludes with some remarks on how the current developments towards ERA can be interpreted in the light of the three scenarios presented.

EUROPEAN POLITICAL AND INNOVATION SYSTEMS: CHARACTERISTICS AND CHALLENGES

In the following, two analytical systems concepts will be applied – 'political system' and 'innovation system': As a system we understand a conglomeration of actors, institutions and processes all functionally bound together, whereby certain characteristic core functions of each, form the demarcation criteria against other societal (sub)systems. The two concepts come from different theoretical angles: the one from American political science, and the other from innovation research, strongly influenced by evolutionary and neo-institutionalist economics. Both system concepts will be used in this paper with a pragmatic intention, thus helping to differentiate between fundamental societal functional areas – in the present case, the political system and the innovation system. The actual ways and mechanisms of policymaking within and between these systems shall be defined as patterns of governance (Marks et al. 1996). The topic of the chapter, therefore, can also be stated as speculation about the emergence of new patterns of governance in the field of innovation policy in Europe.

The Unique Political System of the EU

In the course of the 1970s the term *'political system'* developed into a generally acknowledged, basic concept of political science (e.g. Apter 1996, pp. 372–4; Almond and Coleman 1960, p. 7; Easton 1953), even in everyday speech. Among the most important elements of the political system of western democracies belong the constitutional legitimization of political rule. This is normally expressed as the institutionalization of the nation state, founded on the rule of law, with its guarantee of basic rights, democratic and parliamentary principles, the separation of powers – and the authorities derived therefrom – a comprehensive catalogue of state guarantees towards society and the economy, as well as more or less institutionalized forms of feeding back state actions to (mostly corporatist) socioeconomic interest groups or also 'new social movements'.

The system perspective can form an indispensable heuristic aid for the study and description of the growing international competition of the socio-economic effectiveness of competing political (especially politico-administrative) systems, since these systems can be understood as 'location factors' in the international economic competition, performing at least the functions of market-creating, market-sustaining, market-regulating and market-correcting (cf. Scharpf 1998, pp. 42–3). Regarding the ongoing economic and political integration of European countries, a systemic view may also reveal reciprocal dependencies on the achievements of diverse political systems and some transnational complementarity between them. Therefore, the category 'political system' not only shows its capabilities in the classical comparison of political national systems (e.g. Almond and Coleman 1960), it is also still useful in the analysis of transnationalizing innovation policy governance structures.

Analysts agree that, until recently, 'the study of politics has got stuck in an obsolete mind-set that sees nation states and societies as discrete units, which can safely be analyzed in isolation from others and in isolation from the basic structures of the international, or global, political economy' (Strange 1992, p. 308). For Western Europe this process has shown the most obvious consequences. There is no doubt that for half a century the integration of more and more European states has shaped a *European political system* (Kohler-Koch 1996), which is still further developing and extending sustainably over and into all participating national political systems – today visible e.g. as Brussels's 'comitology' and bureaucracy (see e.g. Bach 1997). One can hardly find any 'issue area that was the exclusive domain of national policy in 1950 and that has not somehow and to some degree been incorporated within the authoritative purview of the EC/EU' (Schmitter 1996, p. 124).

The debate about the related functions of the regional, national and transnational levels of political systems and the embedded 'state functions' (*Staatsfunktionen*) – not only referring to innovation policy – is in full swing, and the spectrum of the remaining, or even newly emerged, tasks of national policy bodies is still controversial. It is hardly contested that nation states remain indispensable for the present and near future: at least, they function as the 'local' guarantors of the rule of law, also as the legitimator for the growing number of transnational political arrangements (see Hirst and Thompson

1996, pp. 170–94; Streeck 1996, p. 314). Even in transnationally intermingled socioeconomic settings, national political authorities continue to fulfil crucial tasks.

Systems of Innovation

National '*innovation systems*' were discovered by the social scientists (first of all by economists[6]), as – with the increasing significance of international hi-tech markets – new explanations for the differing degrees of competitiveness of economies, especially of their 'technological competitiveness' and their ability to innovate, were sought. It was recognized that differing national and regional patterns of technological and/or scientific specialization and related 'innovation cultures' – each rooted in historical origins, characteristic and unique industrial, scientific, state and politico-administrative institutions and inter-institutional networks (Hollingsworth and Boyer 1997) – crucially affected the ability of economic actors and policymakers to produce and support successful innovations. Comparative empirical studies demonstrated this even on the level of individual technological developments (e.g. Jansen 1996).

The innovation system of a society encompasses, according to a current widely accepted understanding, the 'biotope' of all those institutions which are engaged in scientific research. They are responsible for the accumulation and diffusion of knowledge, which educates and trains the working population, develops technology, produces innovative products and processes, and distributes them. To this the relevant regulative bodies belong (standards, norms, laws), as well as the state investments in appropriate infrastructures. The innovation system extends over schools, universities, research institutions (education and science system), industrial enterprises (economic system), the politico-administrative and intermediary authorities (political system) as well as the formal and informal networks of the actors of these institutions. As a 'hybrid system' (Kuhlmann 1999) it represents a section of society which carries far over into other societal areas, e.g. through education, or through entrepreneurial innovation activities and their socioeconomic effects: the innovation system has a decisive influence on the modernization processes of a society.

Obviously, each innovation system is different, just as one society is not the same as the other. Sustainable innovation systems develop their special profiles and strengths only slowly, in the course of decades, or even centuries. The historical development, and present shape of a 'national' system of innovation, reflect, to a certain extent, the character of the related political system: centralist nations like France established an innovation system focusing quite clearly on its centrally constituted political system. By contrast, the innovation systems of federally constituted nations like Germany (or the US) are rooted in relatively strong regional infrastructures, institutions and related governance mechanisms. This heterogeneity is a framework condition for the European integration of innovation systems that cannot be underestimated.

Existing European Patterns of Innovation Policymaking: a Governance Gap

On top of the national and regional efforts and in parallel with Europe's economic and political integration, the emergence of an architecture and infrastructures of a European R&D and innovation policymaking system can be traced (see e.g. Peterson and Sharp 1998; Grande 1996; Guzzetti 1995). Its main pillar is the *Framework Programme (FP)*, the first of which was established in 1984 and concentrated on industrial technologies, information technology, telecommunications and biotechnology. Each subsequent FP has been broader than its predecessor in its scope of technologies and research themes, with correspondingly higher expectations of its impact on the economy and society. In addition to the target dimensions applied already in earlier FPs, the Fifth Framework Programme (FP5), covering nearly €15 billion, particularly emphasized social objectives that reflect the expectations and concerns of Europe's citizens. As a consequence, the rationales underlying the various specific Programs under each FP have become increasingly heterogeneous and even contradictory.

The EU R&D and innovation policy initiatives are – officially – restricted to, and concentrate on, the creation of 'European added value'. They are supposed to follow the principles of '*subsidiarity* and *European added value*'. These principles basically mean that each program, and indeed its projects, have to be justified through transborder co-operation that would not be effectively managed by national administrations and that promise synergy effects not attainable within national borders. Moreover, European Community (EC) research, technology and innovation programs and projects claim to contribute to the economy, science and technology in ways that will encourage the harmonious and sustainable development of the EC as a whole. This implies that projects should concentrate on areas in which there is expansion and therefore good prospects for growth, community businesses are supposed to become more competitive, and scientific and technological progress is expected to offer a medium- or long-term potential for dissemination and exploitation.[7]

Outside the FP, the European Commission also developed a number of own regional innovation policy initiatives. In 1993, for example, a pilot initiative called *Regional Technology Plans (RTP)* was launched which was to initiate the development of a regional innovation policy strategy. The projects in this initiative were to be undertaken in so-called 'less favored regions'. In terms of process the European Commission propagated instead a 'consensus-based' approach, where government agencies were to involve a large group of stakeholders to discuss strengths and weaknesses of regional innovation systems, define priorities, and set up (pilot) projects. Many public–private partnerships were established as a result of the RTP projects. Seven regions entered the experimental action and went through what was to become an ongoing Science and Technology (S&T) policy-planning process. The European Commission played a 'mentor role' in the background, the regions themselves were responsible for running the RTP projects (see Landabaso et al. 1997).

Finally, there are *intergovernmental* initiatives like COST (international co-operations in long-term, application-oriented research) and EUREKA, both of which are not institutions of the EU. In terms of innovation policy, EUREKA is the most important. It has always had a much wider membership than the EU, initially including the European Commission, the then European Free Trade Association (EFTA) countries and Turkey and later extending to the current 26 members, including Eastern Europe and Russia. EUREKA was launched in 1985 with the aim to strengthen the competitiveness and productivity of European industry through stimulation of co-operation between companies and research institutes in advanced civilian technologies. The positioning of EUREKA has always been understood to be nearer to the market than the FPs, though there is some overlap. Its policymaking approach is 'bottom-up' and (relatively) unbureaucratic with a very small secretariat (EUREKA 1999; Georghiou et al. 1999).

Despite these transnational efforts – and despite Article 130 of the Maastricht Treaty, which explicitly aims at a better co-ordination of genuine European, national and regional policy efforts (Caracostas and Muldur 1998, pp. 127 ff.) – the R&D and innovation policy of the large European Member States has not yet taken the step towards a conscious and comprehensive European integration and co-ordination of their measures. The majority of public initiatives is still mainly developed in national policy arenas, offered by national institutions, and addressed to national beneficiaries, borne by the implicit assumption that the research institutes, universities and enterprises involved carry out their innovation activities entirely, or for the most part, within national boundaries, or at least with a significant relation to the own economy. The EU programs in support of research and innovation have been increasing in volume and breadth of expertise since the end of the 1980s, their actual reach, however, was limited in the larger EU Member States (in Germany, the volume of expenditure of the EU programs up till now equaled ca. 4 per cent of the total national expenditure on research and development). Other European, transnational initiatives like EUREKA or COST occasionally attain an outstanding symbolic position in the concepts of the larger

European states, but in practical terms are treated as less prominent. Otherwise in smaller countries: there the instruments of transnational European innovation policy have been regarded for years as a constitutive element of national policy, not least, because large companies with headquarters in small countries are forced to act in international dimensions due to the small domestic market (like Philips in the Netherlands, or Nokia in Finland).

A '*governance gap*' emerges here: the presently applied 'division of labor' in R&D and innovation policy between regional, national and EU political levels and institutions is not yet systematically structured and determined. The subsidiarity principle has been working only as quite an abstract rule for practical policy decisions and their implementation. The present distribution of innovation policy responsibilities across the levels may, at best, be characterized as the result of an 'emerging strategy' between old and newly created institutions (Edler 2000). The arising European (innovation) political system still only partly reflects the economic and political activities within, between and across the national innovation systems.

Summing up, we can state:

1. that political systems are still nationally based, but European integration has brought about a European political system *sui generis* with a multi-layered division of labor as for classical state functions;
2. that innovation systems are nationally, regionally or sectorally rooted and have developed in very country-specific manners;
3. that both the political and the innovation systems are stirred up by 'globalizing' markets as well as by the increasing socioeconomic and political Europeanization;
4. in Europe, meanwhile, R&D and innovation policy initiatives are pursued in parallel on the national, the transnational and the regional level and this layer structure has left open a governance gap of poor integration and co-ordination.

Just in which direction this gap might develop is the subject of the remainder of this chapter.

POTENTIAL FUTURES IN EUROPEAN INNOVATION POLICY

Heuristic Tools

On a macro-level, i.e. beyond specific policy fields, social scientists have repeatedly attempted to sketch potential 'futures' of the ongoing European integration process: Philippe Schmitter, for instance, asking for the *future constitutional governance* in the European political system, has offered a matrix of two different principles of aggregation – the territorial and the functional (Schmitter 1996, p. 135 f.): the strongest case of political integration he calls *stato/federatio*. Typical elements are definitely fixed territorial boundaries, irreversible membership, an overarching hierarchy of authority and a fixed allocation of competencies among separate institutions within a cumulative division of labor. A *confederatio* 'would be a more loosely coupled arrangement in which the identity and role of territorial units would be allowed to vary, while the distribution of functional constituencies and competencies would be rigorously fixed ...'. In a *consortio*, national authorities of a defined number and identity agree to co-operate with respect to functional tasks that are variable and overlapping. They pool their capacities to act autonomously in fields that they can no longer control at their own level of aggregation. Eventually, the *condominio* would be the loosest way of integration since it allows variation in both territorial and functional constituencies. Instead of the present 'Eurocracy' accumulating organizationally distinct, but politically co-ordinated, tasks around a single center, there would be multiple regional institutions acting autonomously to solve common problems and produce different public goods.

Schmitter's models of governance in the EU provide helpful guidance when thinking about future developments of the 'constitutional' shape of Europe's future. The arenas of R&D and innovation policy, though, are also shaped by socioeconomic factors and actors, as discussed above. Another more specific 'forward thinking' experiment provides further insights, focusing explicitly on the relationship between *future socioeconomic developments and governance* structures, including the future of science and technology policy in Europe: the 'Scenarios Europe 2010' project of the European Commission's Forward Studies Unit developed 'five possible futures for Europe'. Bertrand et al. (2000, pp. 89–94) built their scenarios on alternative developments of *shaping factors and shaping actors* of European innovation policies, a concept that might also be fruitfully applied to R&D and innovation policy scenario-building.

First, one would have to identify the key *shaping factors*, processes and constitutive elements making up the innovation policy governance structure of the future, such as the dynamics of economic globalization, the present and upcoming technological regimes governing the dynamics, the competition and related patterns of specialization of national, regional or sectoral innovation systems (e.g. Lundvall and Tomlinson 2000), and – last but not least – the potential development of the European political system vis-à-vis national and regional systems (e.g. European Commission 2000b). The basic feature of all these factors is that they are important elements of the actors' environment. Causal or probabilistic effects could be better understood as potentially different reactions of actors to changing environments (economic, technological, political ...).

Second, one would have to define a set of *key shaping actors* affecting these elements and thus driving the development of innovation policy arenas and related governance structures, such as the actual orientations and strategies of multinational enterprises ('global players'), the specialization and internationalization strategies of higher education institutions, of (semi-) public research and technology organizations, of national or regional governmental bodies, and – last but not least – European institutions like the European Commission or the European Parliament.

Approaches like Schmitter's and the 'Scenarios Europe 2010' are helpful sources of inspiration when speculating about future developments. In the following, we shall speculate indeed and, while doing so, concentrate exclusively on the arenas of innovation policy. What are the patterns or governance in transnational multi-level, multi-actor political systems and in changing innovation systems? In the following sections, three different scenarios will be sketched. They should be read as subjects for debate, and as a point of departure for future research. In their present state, the scenarios are still mainly based on political institutional or constitutional design factors which are just one of the elements of R&D and innovation policy governance.

Scenario I: Concentration and Integration of European Innovation Policies in Transnational Arenas

Shaping factors in the political system: This scenario corresponds to Schmitter's 'stato/federatio' scenario (there is no obvious relationship to the 'Scenarios Europe 2010'). It assumes that the European political system stabilizes with a strong transnational governance structure based on generally acknowledged pan-European institutions, with a 'European state' and with the European Commission as the government at its core, governing major shares of public budgets, implemented and controlled by presumably centralized transnational bureaucracies. Correspondingly, the political autonomy of the national political systems would decrease. Nation states would hand over many of their responsibilities to centralist European authorities, in particular the European Parliament as legislative and the European Commission as executive bodies. Regional political authorities would probably be less affected by the transnational concentration of power, they might even take advantage of the decline of national powers by, simultaneously, gaining additional autonomy and accepting direct responsibility vis-à-vis the central European level – the 'sandwich effect' is a popular characterization in Europe of this governance model.

Shaping actors in innovation systems: Quite likely, an increasingly centralized and dominating transnational R&D and innovation policy arena would emerge. The shape of national, regional or 'sectoral' research and innovation infrastructures would now depend to a considerable extent on regulatory and investment decisions negotiated in transnational arenas and taken by strong transnational bodies. Consequently, the importance of national policy arenas would fade away. Formerly strong players in national innovation systems would either become marginal or try to establish strategic coalitions or to merge in order to strengthen their negotiating power: research universities, research councils and other basic research institutions would pool their interests in a body like the 'European Science Foundation', but significantly strengthened by comparison with its present role. Industrially oriented contract research organizations like the German Fraunhofer Society, the Dutch TNO, the Finnish VTT (Technical Research Center of Finland) etc. would amalgamate in a 'European Research and Technology Society', etc.

One can assume that, as a consequence, the diversity of the European landscape of innovation systems, often praised as a crucial source of vitality and innovation power of Europe's economy, would suffer from this kind of strong centralization – at least in the sense that long-standing 'national styles' of dealing with research, technology and industrial innovation could be leveled out or even disappear. Regional 'grass-root' initiatives, on the other hand, may evolve, driven by strong 'local' industrial and political forces, and develop – probably additionally fed by EU regional support programs – even more richly than in the old national innovation policy settings.

Evidence and future plausibility: Considering the historic development of the EU FPs for research and technological development, their growth in size, thematic breadth and their reach in the various national innovation systems since the mid-1980s, and extrapolating the present trend in a linear way, altogether this scenario does not look too implausible. As a matter of fact, the FPs grew steadily over the years (the First Framework Programme [FP1], 1984–87, covered ECU/€3.3 billion, the FP5, 1998–2002, amounted to nearly €15 billion and the FP6 to €17.5 billion), often at the cost of national efforts (in relative terms), in smaller Member States more clearly than in the bigger ones. In doing so, a considerable R&D and innovation policymaking bureaucracy developed, centralized in Brussels, formally differentiated from national institutions by the subsidiarity principle, but in practice, in many cases, competing with national policies[8] (as e.g. in the field of innovation support for SMEs).

On the other hand, there are a couple of reasons which suggest that the concentration and integration scenario will not come true. First of all, the degree of autonomy and the will for survival of important actors – in particular major research institutions as well as politico-administrative bodies – at national levels should not be underestimated. Secondly, for the time being and quite probably in the near future, it will be the national political systems and their democratic institutions which alone can provide the necessary legitimization of state action – also at transnational levels. It is hardly conceivable that, let us say, a €100 billion pan-European public research and innovation budget could be negotiated and decided only on the level of transnational stakeholder networks and by the European Parliament, without any involvement of national and regional 'innovation communities'. This legitimacy problem will, thirdly, become even more insurmountable the larger the EU grows: the vast number of organized actors in the innovation policy arenas of 25 Member States after 2004 will not allow a unilinear top-down innovation policymaking governance structure.

Scenario II: Decentralization and Regionalization of Innovation Policy Arenas

Shaping factors in the political system: The opposite scenario corresponds to Schmitter's *condominio* model and also to the 'hundred flowers' scenario of 'Europe 2010', assuming a decentralization and fragmentation, compared to the status the European political system had already achieved by the late 20th century: after the enlargement of the EU by ten central and eastern European countries in 2004, this capacious grouping of too many economically, politically, and culturally heterogeneous members states would no longer be able to maintain and further develop a joint political identity and related institutions. The governance of the EU and its Commission would progressively be retreating, its transnational institutions would be shrinking, concentrating now on the maintenance of the common European market and related regulation, supported by a certain concentration of foreign policies. The majority of other important fields of public policy, though, – like tax, social and innovation policy – would witness a continued heterogeneity of national or regional interests, political targets and strategies. The European polity would be suffering from an absence of co-ordination and a dismantling of already achieved pan-European regulation in many fields of socioeconomic policy. As a consequence, partly strengthened, partly weakened national or regional political systems and powerful corporatist actors in related policy arenas would compete harder against each other, seeking to increase their political autonomy and – with respect to economic development – to enlarge their share of foreign direct investment. Serious economic and, inevitably, political conflicts between regions or nations would thrive. Some groupings of regions and nations sharing similar interests may establish strategic coalitions seeking to strengthen their economic and political negotiating power against competing groupings within the policy arena of the now emerging '*condominio* of Europe'.

Shaping actors in innovation systems: An overcharging of existing centralized EU policymaking procedures around the year 2005 would lead to a
weakening of the genuine European R&D and innovation policy institutions
(in particular the related Directorates General of the European Commission),
or even their retreat from the EU policy arena. The competition of too many
contradictory regional, national or sectoral interests would create an intract-
able deadlock situation: the European FPs, suffering from an overload of
heterogeneous targets and expectations, would have to be terminated – the
Council of the EU and the European Parliament were unable to agree upon
the focus, shape, size and management of the Seventh Framework Programme
(FP7) (planned for 2006–10).

Instead, the competition between various national and/or regional innovation policies would increase. Smaller nations that had started to make significant investments in science, innovation and education already in the 1990s
(like Finland or Switzerland, the latter still not a member of the EU), attract
more and more international investment. The same holds true for some of
those regions which – while being part of a nation state – enjoy a high degree
of political autonomy. They used to afford and maintain strong research and
innovation infrastructures for many years and would now be keeping abreast
with the mentioned smaller nations. They may even establish inter-regional
transborder coalitions for concerted innovation policies, mutually matching
local strengths and weaknesses of innovation-related institutions. They may
also launch EUREKA-like 'bottom-up' inter-regional industrially oriented
innovation support initiatives – imagine e.g. an 'innovation belt' of regions
and nations surrounding the Alps, reaching from Bavaria, through Baden-
Württemberg (two federal states of Germany), Switzerland (independent),
Rhône-Alpes (French region), northern Italian regions like Lombardy to Slovenia (independent).

By contrast, many other regions in Europe might suffer from the new lack
of trans-regional and transnational efforts in regional economic and innovation development, thus experiencing a growing gap between economically
powerful and weaker parts of the continent. Not only would the EU's regional
initiatives have lost their thrust, but also long-standing and politically well
accepted mechanisms of intra-national compensation between rich and poor
regions (as were in force e.g. in Germany for decades) would be fading away.
Confronted with the challenges of increased international and global competition, the national governments of the larger EU Member States would have
agreed with major corporatist actors (leading research organizations, industrial associations etc.) to now concentrate their public policy efforts on
'promising regions' in their national innovation policy arenas. One can assume that, in particular, multinational enterprises would gain strong influence
by playing their games in this scattered landscape of European innovation

systems and related policymaking arenas.

Evidence and future plausibility: This scenario is borne by the assumption that the traditional, centralized R&D and innovation policy governance mechanisms at the national level – in particular larger countries struggling with the internationalization of research and innovation – and at the EU scale – at least after the enlarged membership of the EU 2004 – will be overburdened and experience a serious functional breakdown. Since no other integrative governance mechanism is available, strong (inter-)regional innovation systems, if effectively interwoven with political systems, would start taking command. European economic history provides evidence of the very strong role that the endogenous dynamics of the European regions have always played in economic development and industrial innovation. Many regional innovation systems are older than the nation states they presently belong to. Economically strong regions and related innovation systems, meanwhile, inter-connected by increasingly international and 'virtual' markets may survive and thrive, even with relatively weak political systems at the national and European transnational levels – but at the socioeconomic cost of the rest of Europe! In essence, this *condominio* scenario does seem less unlikely than many European policymakers may presently perceive.

Scenario III: Centrally 'Mediated' Mixture of Competition and Co-operation in Integrated Multi-level Innovation Policy Arenas

Shaping factors in the political system: The third scenario ranges somewhere between the previous two. It corresponds to Schmitter's *confederatio* or *consortio* scenarios and also to the 'shared responsibilities' scenario of 'Europe 2010', assuming a co-evolution of regional, national and European policy arenas towards an integration in, more or less, effectively working multi-level, multi-actor systems. All the three levels would undergo a re-distribution of tasks, thereby experiencing new functional and informational linkages, vertically and horizontally. Political power and policymaking competencies would not crystallize around one central European institutional core (like in the first scenario), nor would they slip away to some strong but scattered 'regional' domains. Instead, power and policymaking competencies would now be re-distributed throughout the European political system, consistently following the subsidiarity principle: in terms of political agenda-setting (regional, national or European thematic arenas), of decision-making and regulation (regional, national or European parliaments), and implementation (regional, national or European governmental institutions).

An important precondition is the general acceptance of the enduring co-existence of two, partly competing, overarching political targets:

1. The EU would continue to aim at a sustainable socioeconomic 'cohesion' of all European regions, i.e. political initiatives on all levels would have, in principle, to strive for the establishment of similar conditions of work and living, acceptable for all EU citizens, independent of their place of residence.
2. Interested groupings of regional, national or transnational authorities may seize at their own cost transnational strategic initiatives (regulation, funding, etc.) aiming at the creation of attractive and productive conditions for economic investments in 'their' parts of Europe or 'their' sectors – also if only a restricted number of EU Member States is willing to join such efforts. This concept has been entitled '*géométrie variable*' (in Brussels 'Eurospeak').

Another prerequisite – in particular for adopting policies of the *géométrie variable* type – is the effective functioning of vertical and horizontal, formal and informal networks of key actors, making use of visible, well-accepted platforms and intermediary institutions facilitating the exchange of strategic information and knowledge, allowing for 'mediated contestation' between representatives of conflicting interests. Governments on all three levels may perform mediating functions in a variety of policy fields.

Shaping actors in innovation systems: R&D and innovation policies would be based on a mixture of competition and co-operation between diverse but integrated regional or sectoral innovation systems and related policymaking arenas. While regional or national authorities would continue to improve the competitiveness of 'local' innovation systems, national institutions, and in particular transnational institutions like the European Commission – instead of running growing and cumbersome own funding programs – would be in a position to 'mediate' between the competitors and to 'moderate' their conflicts. Public investment in, and regulation of, research, technology and innovation would originate mainly from regional or national initiatives and sources – but it would have to be concerted and matched with any parallel activities throughout Europe. For example core competencies and research portfolios of publicly co-funded research institutions would have to be linked and matched across the continent in order to improve the effectiveness of efforts, national and regional funding schemes would have to be opened for applications from other parts of Europe, a variety of inter-regional or international, and where necessary, centrally developed initiatives would be disposable, normally following the *géométrie variable* approach.

The mediation of R&D and innovation policy would require appropriate arenas for negotiation, institutions and procedures (Caracostas and Muldur 1998, pp. 186–90). In today's political practice, though, hardly any 'postnational' arenas have been established hitherto. At best, a few 'provisional models' can be identified:

- in Germany, for example, the Federal Government–Federal State Commission for Education Planning and Research Promotion (BLK), which offers a model for aligning the various interests at the interface of regional and national actors. Here, nevertheless, alignment often means maintaining conservative positions or even deadlock with respect to institutional modernization;
- on the EU level, CREST (Scientific and Technical Research Committee) of the European Council, which provides a negotiating arena for the various national research policies. As far as general issues are concerned, however, CREST has also hardly progressed beyond the representation of national interests. A 'federal system of science' (Sharp 1999) is not yet in sight. New dynamics may however be sparked off by the growing involvement of the European Parliament, whose committee for Industry, Foreign Trade, Research and Energy is intervening increasingly in the innovation policy debate.

Contesting and negotiating actors in policy arenas use money, power and information as their main media. Various actors have different shares of these resources at their disposal. One important source of policy mediating authorities is the utilization of 'strategic intelligence'. *Strategic intelligence* activities may cover e.g. information gained from exercises like policy impact evaluation, from science and technology foresight efforts or from technology assessment (Kuhlmann et al. 1999). They may support:

- a more 'objective' formulation of diverging perceptions of (even contentious) subjects, offering appropriate indicators and information processing mechanisms, analyses of changing innovation processes, the dynamics of changing research systems, changing functions and likely effects of public policies;
- the organization of mediation processes and 'discourses' between contesting actors (or between representations of their views).

Mediating authorities like the European Commission – according to this scenario – would systematically facilitate the performance and the use of strategic intelligence, in particular by linking existing bodies of knowledge (and related institutions) on regional and national levels.

Evidence and future plausibility: Presently, there is no strong evidence for the realization of this scenario: in particular, proactive mediation efforts by the European Commission are still quite rare, although the EU's Maastricht Treaty explicitly requires an improvement of the co-ordination of the Member

States' innovation policies, envisaging the European Commission as a major co-ordinator. There is, on the other hand, some likelihood that the interest of regions and Member States in this *confederatio* mode may soon increase. While they are not ready to give away their power of allocating the lion's share of public investment in innovation, they might, nevertheless, become more interested in a mediation of conflicts among them: the transaction costs of contentious competition between scattered innovation systems may be too high in the long run. In essence, the probability of this scenario will depend on the 'policy learning' capabilities of major actors in the European innovation policy arena.

This is where the contributions of this volume take a deeper look from various angles and on various levels. Regardless of the perspectives and interpretations, the authors more or less agree on the assessment that the ongoing ERA process – provided the instruments materialize – at least *potentially* points in the direction of this last scenario, albeit elements of the other two scenarios will coexist for a long time to come. The following section will shortly introduce the idea and content of the book at hand.

THE IDEA AND THE CONTENT OF THIS BOOK

ERA: a Break in European R&D Policymaking?

Since the first announcement by the European Commission in early 2000 (European Commission 2000b) and the confirming resolution of the European heads of state at the Lisbon European Council in March 2000 (European Council 2000), the *European Research Area* has been evoking hopes and fears alike. The new approaches that European policymakers had presented would alter this architecture systematically, and national policymakers have been led to think anew about the whole architecture of R&D and innovation policy in Europe. Both the obvious tensions and the possible positive dynamics have not yet, however, received systematic attention from policy analysts, who have failed to reflect upon the challenges embedded in this new approach, both for the policy area and for European governance as such.

Why does the current debate deserve reflection? What is its meaning, what are the possible impacts of and hindrances for this approach to become a political success? Despite many attempts to reform the mode of operation, European R&D and innovation policy has remained relatively stable since its beginnings in the 1980s. The FPs of the EC for Research and Technological Development have supported cross-border co-operation research projects and mobility in topics of European interest. According to the European treaties, the EU initiatives are subject to the criteria of subsidiarity and 'European added value'. However, the responsibility for the long-term financing of research institutions and research networks has stayed at the national and regional level, and co-ordination and harmonization of national research and technology policies have remained a hollow treaty clause, never implemented. Thus, European policy in the field of research and technology has been characterized by a model of related, but largely separated, multi-level governance with a clear dominance of the national level.

Yet, if the ERA were successful, European R&D and innovation policy would allegedly take a qualitative step forward that could significantly change the relationship between the European and the national autonomy (European Commission 2000b; 2001a). It would, ideally, lead to complementary rather than parallel structures. On the one hand, it would be serious about the functional bundling, co-ordination and harmonization of national measures, oriented solely towards the greatest possible European effectiveness. ERA would take existing provisions of the Treaty, mainly Article 169, seriously, and would, for example, co-finance research that is financed nationally but integrated on a transnational scale within Europe. National programs could be co-ordinated and parallel, transnational structures would be built (European Commission 2001a).

On the other hand, ERA would complement its project-oriented, transnational research approach by European networks based on excellence, and respectively very long-term, comprehensive, large-scale projects (also European Commission 2002a). Practically speaking, a key player in the network of excellence would have complementary funds in addition to the basic funding received nationally. The European Commission would gain more direct influence on research institutions through a long-term financing of networks of excellence that would be built around specific issues, be highly flexible and largely self-organized, but always accountable to the European Commission.

This integrative European perspective advocated by the European Commission is highly contested since it confronts dominating national and regional governance schemes which are characterized by policy competition rather than integration. The members of the EU (as well as strong regions) compete for the leading role concerning research and technological innovation, not only within the EU, but also on a global level. Thus, from the perspective of governance theory, the structural integration of R&D and innovation policy in a European Research Area would enlarge the competencies and the room for maneuver on the EU level at the expense of the nation states.

At the same time, a growing number of large, and increasingly also smaller, companies operate in the transnational perspective. National policy is more and more threatened to be forced into a policy race by corporate interests that are fully dominated by economic considerations rather than reflecting comprehensive national policy concerns. In this perspective, a research and innovation policy that would be well-tuned throughout the whole EU and between the diverse national and regional authorities might be a means for public policy to *regain* room to maneuver.

Three Perspectives on the Meaning of ERA

A European perspective

The – potential – meaning of ERA can be analyzed from at least three perspectives. First, of, course, is *the European perspective – or the perspective of European governance*. All contributions in this volume looking at ERA from the perspective of European governance agree that the full implementation of ERA would mean a leap forward, a new kind of multi-level game in the area of R&D and innovation policy.

Pareskevas Caracostas[9] seeks to explain the rationale of a ERA in its global context, puts it in the long-term perspective of institution-building in R&D and innovation policy in Europe and describes and assesses what he calls 'shared governance' in European R&D policymaking. For Caracostas, the ERA – which he interprets as EIRA (European Research and Innovation Area) – is an ambitious multi-objective attempt: it seeks to increase the resources for research and innovation in Europe, to optimize the allocation and use of European knowledge resources and to strengthen a European identity as a Research and Innovation Area in the global context. The new instruments of the ERA – Networks of Excellence and Integrated Projects – are the major means to go in that direction and they must be, in Caracostas's functional reading, interpreted as a new step in the long history of institution-building in European R&D policy. This new institutional set-up would be characterized not only by stronger co-ordination of multi-level policies, but also by a reorientation of research institutes and companies alike towards long-term planning that would include European networking and co-operation strategically and much more self-organization. In this perspective, it is very important that many new tools of governance – such as common European indicators, benchmarking of policies, common foresight procedures – that support this institution building technically and cognitively have already been endorsed by the European Council and are being implemented. For Caracostas, to further develop these tools in close co-operation of European and national administrations is a major task to support ERA in a sustainable way.

However, it is far from clear if the ERA will succeed in the first place and which factors will hamper or push this success. Here, *Thomas Banchoff* is rather pessimistic, arguing that even a ERA, that had the backing of the Lisbon Council, could not overcome the inertia that has been characterizing European R&D policy for two decades now. The building up of a strong and, for many stakeholders meanwhile, important distributive system has placed

important actors at all levels in a conservative position, while national policymakers would defend their stakes against European orchestration. Potential
ERA losers might – in this perspective – succeed against winners. This esti-
mate, however, is opposed by *Chris Caswill*, who argues that a ERA could
very likely succeed just because it has taken all stakeholders by surprise and
has succeeded in getting high-level backing even before opposition could be
formulated. Caswill stresses the coalition building and structural adaptation of
potential winners at a very early policy stage, which potentially could overcome inertia. A somewhat mediating position is put forward by *Jakob Edler*.
He agrees with Caswill's 'surprise' theory. But by citing the historic example
of the genesis of EU R&D in the 1980s, he stresses that new approaches in a
complex policy arena need time to diffuse, and a '*coup d'état*' (Caswill) is of
limited value whenever 'money is not enough' and compliance by actors is
needed. Therefore, ERA is still open and – ironically – the initial success of
the European Commission – as political entrepreneur – at the highest policy
levels may have been too abrupt, leading to a Pawlow-like anti-reflex by
stakeholder groups and, above all, national policymakers and administrators.
Therefore, apart from all the dynamism evoked and dedication shown, the
logic of ERA needs patience and further active promotion.

A sub-European perspective
A second view of a ERA stresses the relationship between dynamics at the
European level on the one hand and national, respectively regional, R&D
policy and innovation systems on the other. In this complex, interdependent
multi-level governance system, *Michael Stampfer* focuses on the current and
future role of R&D programs and on the interrelationship between governance structures and such programs. His main conclusion is that changes in the
governance structures as regards R&D programs will be slow, that national
actors, albeit losing competencies, will remain the strongest players, that
national programs will prevail (but open up) and that the variety of programs
will increase. However, this increasing complexity caused by the coexistence
of different governance levels and program approaches is for Stampfer an
asset rather than a shortcoming of the future European governance structure.
In this perspective, a streamlined, fully integrated and common European
policy would not even be desirable.

Peter Biegelbauer, in contrast, takes a look at the policy processes underlying the European R&D. His comparative analysis of three country cases
shows the complexity and diversity of national policy debates and policy
formulation processes in R&D policy. The acceptance of a ERA at national
level has much to do with the readiness and flexibility in which national debates are able to integrate the ERA terminology and logic. This, in turn, is
partly determined by the openness of national discourse structures shaping

interest aggregation. As for the European policy debate, this openness is, as Biegelbauer shows, among other things dependent on the time of accession of the EU, i.e. the longer a country has been exposed to European R&D, the stronger the institutional – and cognitive – path dependencies that impede policy flexibility as demanded by the ERA.

The diversity of the relative importance of European policy structures and national R&D policy is shown by *Johanna Hakala* and her discussion of the Finnish national innovation system. Clearly, Finland has become a major R&D and innovation success in Europe and it appears strong enough to almost neglect the European discussion. However, while European R&D seems to play a relatively minor role in the Finnish success story, Hakala shows the co-evolution of policy approaches at the Finnish national level as well as at the European level and, indirectly, points to the potential impact the success of Finnish R&D policy approaches might have had on the European approach. The country may very well have had an integrative impulse on the European R&D policy style.

With respect to the discussion of accession countries and their relationship with a new R&D policy, *Peter Hilger* argues that a ERA can be an important chance as well as a potential threat. Since ERA aims at positioning the EU in the global innovation competition and aims at bundling European resources, large countries with strong R&D systems have more to lose than small countries which might be elevated to a higher level – through mobility schemes, integration into excellence networks and the like. However, on the other hand, a ERA is a very excellence- and size-oriented approach that might leave newcomers behind and put cohesion within R&D policy aside. The influence of these countries on the development of the clash between excellence and cohesion needs concerted bargaining efforts. Here Hilger is rather pessimistic, since the step-by-step approach of accession will foster disparities and heterogeneity among the accession countries rather than enable a strong group effort. For the whole group as such, the ERA might mean rather an impediment on their long way to catch up.

This line of reasoning is also followed by *Emmanuel Muller*, *Andrea Zenker* and *Jean-Alain Héraud* in their discussion of the meaning of ERA for the development of European regions. They introduce the results of an EU study on the typology of innovation needs of regions and conclude that a ERA – as foreseen – might enforce the divergence of regions. Regions with a higher level of innovation needs might be pushed even further and R&D capacity in Europe might be even more concentrated, while regions on a somewhat lower level of R&D and innovation capability might struggle even more. Although the European Commission has tried to calm those worries (European Commission 2001b), Muller et al. argue for a better awareness of the diversity of regional needs, and here they are in line with worries raised very early by the

European Parliament (2000). One might add that this is not only a conflict between the European and the regional level, since the nations with strong and weak regions alike face the challenge of taking on regional chances without aggravating disparities within their countries.

Hans-Willi Hohn and *Jürgen Lautwein* point to the highly interesting processes of institutional interdependence between the European and the national level and speculate about a possible reciprocal influence of European policy-making and deeply embedded national institutions. In the context of the ERA process – and after decades of inertia and stalemate – it now seems possible that a European 'collective research system' might evolve that combines elements of the Anglo-Saxon and the German collective research system. By looking in detail at the German collective research system offered by the German Federation of Industrial Cooperative Research Associations (Arbeitsgemeinschaft industrieller Forschungsvereinigungen [AiF]) the authors show that this possible development on the European level has been preceded by a change of the national system, as the AiF itself has been changing its own institutional setting and purpose quite a bit. In order to play the European game the Association has adapted more and more to a service institution mainly in order to assist their member enterprises and institutes in their efforts to participate at the European level. Therefore, a functional change at the national level has been accompanied by a structural change at the European level, as it 'does not appear impossible any longer that corporatist structures at the supranational level ... may evolve' (Hohn and Lautwein in this volume).

A sectoral perspective: the case of biotechnology

A last aspect in trying to make sense of ERA is to understand that this approach might mean different things in different sectors. Harmonization of national policies, variable geometry and large networks of excellence might be instruments with high added value in one sector, but might meet with much resistance in some other sector. In the context of this book, this dimension cannot be analyzed in a comparative way, as certainly should be the case in future analysis. However, one sector – biotechnology – is looked at as an example. *Ulrich Dolata*, *Robert Kaiser* and *Gabriele Abels* demonstrate the importance of certain sectoral and technological peculiarities for the potential impact of European schemes. Dolata and Kaiser, from different perspectives, both argue that while the biotech sector is highly dynamic and potentially could need transnational support schemes, especially in the competition against the US market, there are two reasons why European R&D support, and especially ERA, might not have the impact expected: the sector consists of a multitude of very small players for whom the European scale and the instruments foreseen might be too big, and second, the high and still not clearly foreseeable economic potential of this sector has led to a national competition within Europe that still fully defines the rules of the game. For this sector, ERA might come too early, respectively too late, or might be the wrong approach entirely. Abels sheds some light on the emerging European mode of governance, which is also reflected in the ERA process and which is especially pronounced for biotechnology. She stresses the importance of the contextualization of a policy issue and the procedural fit of the means employed by the European Commission to organize a consensus-building processes. However, Abels argues that these discursive instruments, that are part of what Caracostas has labeled 'shared governance', have serious pitfalls: first the openness of the consensus-building process goes along with less transparency and accountability and second, the European Commission frames not only the issues at stake, but also the consensus-building process itself, pointing at the instrumental potential of this allegedly democratic and inclusive governance style of ERA.

CONCLUSION

At the present stage it is far from clear to what extent the new instruments will take off and lead to the new ERA as it is sought by the European Commission. We will have to wait and observe what changes ERA will bring to the European governance system in R&D policymaking. However, what we know by now can be interpreted in the light of our three ideal-type scenarios presented above. The recent developments and the impact of the ERA debate that is already to be seen throughout Europe impinge upon the likelihood of these scenarios.

Most importantly, the current departure towards ERA seems to diminish the likelihood of the decentralization scenario (Scenario II). Although it is true that during the concrete negotiations for the FP6 the budget originally foreseen for the new approaches was downgraded to the benefit of traditional research projects. Moreover, the co-ordination of policies via Article 169 does not appear to take off broadly. However, the genie of a new governance giving the European level a new kind of relevance has left the bottle. Above all, the European heads of state have strongly endorsed ERA and even combined it with clear policy goals and new 'shared governance' activities (Caracostas in this volume), starting with the Lisbon Council in March 2000. Secondly, the European Commission's policy of mobilization has shown tremendous success. The orientation of thousands of European stakeholders in planning medium-term research strategies towards the European level, combined with dedicated budgets and European strategic intelligence systems will establish central program structures apart from, and independent of, national and regional policymaking.

Do these developments, in contrast, indicate a more likely road to centralization (Scenario I)? The answer – again – is most likely no. Models which assign a crucial role to the European Commission within a new division of labor between regional, national and global political authorities, have so far not progressed beyond conceptual suggestions (see on this Soete 1999; Sharp 1999; Peterson and Sharp 1998; Caracostas and Muldur 1998). The negotiations leading to ERA and the FP6 have very well shown that the diversity of 'national interests' for R&D policymaking, of national innovation system structures and of national governance schemes stand in the way of too much centralization. While the non-governmental stakeholders have followed the European Commission in order to stay in the game for funding, governmental actors have failed to react towards the demands for co-ordination and variable geometry (see above). Moreover, the European proponents of a ERA never claimed to take over the bulk of public money devoted to R&D from national governments. Even if integrative, the ERA is no kick off towards a common policy to the detriment of national approaches.

So is a ERA an important step towards the middle ground of the third scenario, of a centrally mediated mixture of competition and co-operation in integrated multi-level innovation policy arenas? Yes and no. The answer is 'No', since a ERA as it is likely to develop, lacks one dimension that is at the heart of our third scenario. It does not provide for a 'mediating' role of the European Commission in competing and conflicting national and regional policies. As the 'bottom-up' co-ordination of national and regional policies, through means like a re-enforced Article 169, may be born dead, this lack of central mediation – even in the context of the general willingness for a leap forward – indicates a structural limit on the way to the third scenario. The answer is 'Yes', since a ERA enforces and widens already existing transnational R&D structures. Even before and without a ERA, the EU could with some justification be described as an institutional structure, which at least forms a basis – albeit fragmented – of a system of 'postnational' European innovation policy governance: we have seen, at the same time, horizontally and vertically interwoven multi-level innovation policymaking arenas and we have noticed also some already quite sustainable transnational policy structures, going along with an issue-related European space of communication and orientation towards very similar goals. Now a ERA has certainly added a new momentum to this, as hundreds of European research organizations and companies have shown interest in linking parts of their research efforts with longer-term multinational projects or program-like structures. Moreover, the ERA has integrated the discourse on European R&D policy in a new way, it has triggered off a new mode of thinking. Even national policymakers have started to reflect more broadly about the role their policy can play in the future and how national and European policy can complement one another more effectively. Shared governance – which is largely based on common strategic intelligence – has already delivered results, as, for example, the benchmarking efforts and the streamlining of indicators for R&D activities have shown. A new kind of European orientation, along with the new instruments – strategic and self-organized – and the efforts for a common 'strategic intelligence' to provide the informational basis for a concerted effort at the European level, might reinforce each other and alter governance in European R&D and innovation policymaking towards new modes of integration. One of the most exciting questions will be just how exactly this new mode will take shape.

NOTES

1 This chapter largely draws on previous papers of the authors, in particular Kuhlmann (2001); Kuhlmann and Edler (2003); Edler (2002).
2 Innovation policy is understood here as the integral of all state initiatives regarding science, education, research, technological development and industrial modernization. Thus, innovation policy is a broad concept that contains R&D policy and overlaps with industrial, environmental, labor and social policies. Public innovation policy aims to strengthen the competitiveness of an economy or of selected sectors, in order to increase societal welfare through economic success.
3 The definitions of the latter two new instruments is taken from the European Commission; see: http://www.cordis.lu/fp6/instruments-print.htm.
4 Official Journal C 71/14 of 20 March 2002.
5 Twelve per cent of the submitting institutions (research organizations and companies) were from associated countries, 8 per cent came from non-EU countries (European Commission 2002b).
6 See in particular Freeman (1987); Lundvall (1992); Nelson (1993); Edquist (1997). Lundvall and Maskell (1999) provide a reconstruction of the genesis of the expression 'national innovation systems'. They all take as a theme, at least marginally, also the interface of markets and political systems (and, in particular, public policies by state governments) as a formative variable of innovation systems.
7 Cf. the criteria as modified by the European Council's Common Position on the FP5 based on Annex I of the European Commission proposal COM(97) 142 final, 30 April 1997.
8 See e.g. the example of the industrially oriented BRITE program which has been historically reconstructed by Edler (Edler 2000).
9 Caracostas works for the GD Research of the European Commission, however he is presenting his personal view here and not the view of the Commission.

REFERENCES

Almond, G.A. and J.S. Coleman (1960), *The Politics of the Developing Areas*, Princeton: Princeton University Press.
Apter, D.E. (1996), 'Comparative Politics, Old and New', in Goodin, R.E. and H.D. Klingemann (eds), *A New Handbook of Political Science*, Oxford: Oxford University Press, pp. 372–97.
Bach, M. (1997), 'Transnationale Institutionenpolitik: Kooperatives Regieren im politisch-administrativen System der Europäischen Union', in König, Th., E.

Rieger and H. Schmitt (eds), *Europäische Institutionenpolitik*, Frankfurt and New York: Campus, pp. 178–99.

Bertrand, G., A. Michalski and L.R. Pench (2000), *European Futures: Five Possible Scenarios for 2010*, Cheltenham, UK and Northhampton, MA, USA: Edward Elgar.

Busquin, Ph. (2002), *Un Nouvel Elan au Projet d'Espace Européen de la Recherche*, présentation de l'Association Leibniz, Brussels, 1 October 2002, http://europa.eu. int/rapid/start/cgi/guesten.ksh?p_action.gettxt=gt&doc=SPEECH/02/445|0|RAPID &lg=FR&display=.

Caracostas, P. and U. Muldur (1998), *Society, the Endless Frontier – a European Vision of Research and Innovation Policies for the 21st Century*, Luxembourg and Brussels: Office for Official Publications of the European Communities, EUR 17655.

Easton, D. (1953), *The Political System. An Inquiry into the State of Political Science*, New York: Alfred A. Knopf.

Edler, J. (2000), *Institutionalisierung europäischer Politik*, Baden-Baden: Nomos.

Edler, J. (2002), 'The "European Research Area" initiative. Reflections upon a potential take-off in European RTD policy', *Technikfolgenabschätzung. Theorie und Praxis*, **11** (1), 136–41.

Edler, J., F. Meyer-Krahmer and G. Reger (2000), *Managing Technology in the Top R&D Spending Companies Worldwide – Results of a Global Survey*.

Edquist, Ch. (1997), *Systems of Innovation. Technologies, Institutions and Organizations*, London and Washington: Pinter.

EUREKA (1999), http://www.eureka.be/home/index.html.

European Commission (1999), http://europa.eu.int/comm/dg12/fp5.html.

European Commission (2000a), *Governance and Citizenship in Europe: Some Research Directions*, conference proceedings, Brussels: European Commission, EUR 19313.

European Commission (2000b), *Towards a European Research Area*, communication from the Commission to the Council, the European Parliament, the Economic and Social Committee and the Committee of the Regions, 18 January 2000, Brussels: European Commission, COM (2000) 6.

European Commission (2001a), *The Framework Programme and the European Research Area: Application of 169 and the Networking of National Programmes*, Brussels: European Commission, COM (2001) 0282.

European Commission (2001b), *The Regional Dimension of the European Research Area*, Brussels: European Commission, COM (2001) 549 final.

European Commission (2002a), *Introduction of the Instruments Available for Implementing the FP6 Priority Thematic Areas*, internal speaking notes, 2 April 2002, Brussels: European Commission.

European Commission (2002b), *Report on the Analysis of Expressions of Interest 2002*, September 2002, Brussels: European Commission (EII.FP6.2002).

European Council (2000), Presidency Conclusion of the European Council of Lisbon, 23–24 March 2000, http://europa.eu.int/council/off/ conclu/mar2000/mar2000_en. pdf.

European Parliament (2000), *Report on the Communication from the Commission 'Towards a European Research Area'*, Committee on Industry, External Trade, Research and Energy, final A5, 0131/2000, 9 May 2000.

Freeman, C. (1987), *Technology Policy and Economic Performance: Lessons from*

Japan, London: Pinter.

Georghiou, L., O. van Batenburg, J.P. Chevillot, S. Kuhlmann, M. Oral and N. Reeve (1999), *Strategic Review of EUREKA – Building Europe's Innovation Network*, Brussels: EUREKA Secretariat.

Gerybadze, A., F. Meyer-Krahmer and G. Reger (1997), *Globales Management von Forschung und Innovation*, Stuttgart: Schäffer-Poeschel.

Grande, E. (1996), 'The state and interest groups in a framework of multi-level decision-making: the case of the European Union', *Journal of European Public Policy*, **3** (3), 318–38.

Guzzetti, L. (1995), *A Brief History of European Research Policy*, Brussels and Luxembourg: Office for Official Publications of the European Communities.

Hagedoorn, J. and J. Schakenraad (1990), 'Inter-firm Partnerships and Co-operative Strategies in Core Technologies', in Freeman, C. and L. Soete (eds), *New Explorations in the Economics of Technological Change*, London and New York: Pinter Publishing, pp. 3–37.

Hirst, P. and G. Thompson (1996), *Globalization in Question. The International Economy and the Possibilities of Governance*, Cambridge: Polity Press.

Hollingsworth, R. and R. Boyer (1997), *Contemporary Capitalism. The Embeddedness of Institutions*, Hollingsworth, R. and R. Boyer (eds), Cambridge: Cambridge University Press.

Jansen, D. (1996), 'Nationale Innovationssysteme, soziales Kapital und Innovationsstrategien von Unternehmen', *Soziale Welt*, **47** (4), 411.

Jungmittag, A., F. Meyer-Krahmer and G. Reger (1999), 'Globalisation of R&D and Technology Markets – Trends, Motives, Consequences', in Meyer-Krahmer, F. (ed.), *Globalisation of R&D and Technology Markets: Consequences for National Innovation Policies*, Technology, Innovation and Policy, series of the Fraunhofer Institute for Systems and Innovation Research (ISI), vol. 9, Berlin: Physica-Verlag, pp. 37–78.

Kohler-Koch, B. (1996), 'Catching up with change: the transformation of governance in the European Union', *Journal of European Public Policy*, **3** (3), 359–80.

Kohler-Koch, B. (1998), 'Regieren in entgrenzten Räumen', *PVS*, Sonderheft **29**, Opladen.

Kohler-Koch, B. (1999), The Evolution and Transformation of European Governance paper presented at the ECSA - Sixth Biannual International Conference, Pittsburgh, 2–5 June 1999.

Kohler-Koch, B. and J. Edler (1998), 'Ideendiskurs und Vergemeinschaftung. Erschließung transnationaler Räume durch Europäisches Regieren', in Kohler-Koch, B. (ed.), *Regieren in Entgrenzten Räumen*, Opladen: PVS Sonderheft 29, pp. 192–206.

Kohler-Koch, B. and R. Eising (2002), *The Transformation of Governance in the European Union*, London: Routledge.

Kuhlmann, S. (1999), 'Politisches System und Innovationssystem in "postnationalen" Arenen', in Grimmer, K., S. Kuhlmann and F. Meyer-Krahmer (eds), *Innovationspolitik in globalisierten Arenen*, Leverkusen: Leske + Budrich, pp. 9–37.

Kuhlmann, S. (2001), 'Governance of innovation policy in Europe – three scenarios', *Research Policy*, **30** (6), special issue 'Innovation policy in Europe and the US: new policies in new institutions', edited by Klein, H.K., S. Kuhlmann and Ph. Shapira, 953–76.

Kuhlmann, S., P. Boekholt, L. Georghiou, K. Guy, J.-A. Héraud, P. Laredo, T. Lemola, D. Loveridge, T. Luukkonen, W. Polt, A. Rip, L. Sanz-Menendez and R. Smits (1999), *Distributed Intelligence in Complex Innovation Systems*, final report of the Advanced Science & Technology Policy Planning Network (ASTPP), Karlsruhe and Brussels: ASTPP, http://www.isi.fhg.de/abtlg/ti/pb_html/final.pdf.

Kuhlmann, S. and J. Edler (2003), 'Scenarios of technology and innovation policies in Europe: investigating future scenarios', *Technological Forecasting and Social Change*, special issue 'Innovation systems and policies', guest editors Conceição, P., M. Heitor and G. Sirilli (forthcoming).

Landabaso, M., B.Å. Lundvall, P. Maskell and M.P.G. Feldmann (1997), 'The promotion of innovation in regional policy: proposals for a regional innovation strategy', *Entrepreneurship & Regional Development*, **9**, 1–24.

Lundvall, B.Å. (1992), *National Systems of Innovation: Towards a Theory of Innovation and Interactive Learning*, Lundvall, B.Å. (ed.), London: Pinter.

Lundvall, B.Å. and P. Maskell (1999), 'Nation States and Economic Development – From National Systems of Production to National Systems of Knowledge Creation and Learning', in Clark, G.L., M.P. Feldmann and M.S. Gertler (eds), *Handbook of Economic Geography*, Oxford: Oxford University Press.

Lundvall, B.Å. and Tomlinson (2000), *On the Convergence and Divergence of National Systems of Innovation,* paper presented at the Volkswagen Foundation Symposium on 'Prospects and Challenges for Research on Innovation', Berlin, 8–9 June 2000.

Marks, G., F.W. Scharpf, Ph.C. Schmitter and W. Streeck (1996), *Governance in the European Union*, London and Thousand Oaks: Sage Publications.

Meyer-Krahmer, F. (1999), 'Was bedeutet Globalisierung für Aufgaben und Handlungsspielräume nationaler Innovationspolitiken?', in Grimmer, K., S. Kuhlmann and F. Meyer-Krahmer (eds), *Innovationspolitik in globalisierten Arenen. Neue Aufgaben für Forschung und Lehre: Forschungs- und Technologiepolitik im Wandel*, Leverkusen: Leske + Budrich, pp. 35–65.

Nelson, R.R. (1993), *National Innovation Systems: a Comparative Analysis*, Oxford and New York: Oxford University Press.

Peterson, J. and M. Sharp (1998), *Technology Policy in the European Union*, New York: St. Martin's Press.

Scharpf, F.W. (1998), 'Globalisierung als Beschränkung der Handlungsmöglichkeiten nationalstaatlicher Politik', in Schenk, K.E., D. Schmidtchen, M.E. Streit and V.T. Vanberg (eds), *Globalisierung, Systemwettbewerb und nationalstaatliche Politik*, vol. 17, Tübingen: Mohr, pp. 41–66.

Schmitter, Ph.C. (1996), 'Imagining the Future of the Euro-polity with the Help of New Concepts', in Marks, G., F.W. Scharpf, Ph. Schmitter and W. Streeck (eds), *Governance in the European Union*, London and Thousand Oaks: Sage Publications, pp. 121–50.

Sharp, M. (1999), *The Need for New Perspectives in European Commission Innovation Policy*, paper presented at the European Socio-economic Research Conference, Brussels, 28–30 April 1999.

Soete, L. (1999), *The New Economy: a European Perspective*, paper presented at the European Socio-economic Research Conference, Brussels, 28–30 April 1999.

Strange, S. (1992), 'The Transformation of Europe from an International Perspective', in Kohler-Koch, B. (ed.), *Staat und Demokratie in Europa. 18. Wissenschaftlicher Kongress der Deutschen Vereinigung für politische Wissenschaft*, Opladen:

Leske + Budrich, pp. 308–10.

Streeck, W. (1996), 'Public Power Beyond the Nation State: the Case of the European Community', in Boyer, R. and D. Drache (eds), *States Against Markets. The Limits of Globalization*, London and New York: Routledge, pp. 299–315.

2 Shared Governance Through Mutual Policy Learning

Some Implications of the ERA Strategy for the 'Open Co-ordination' of Research Policies in Europe[1]

Paraskevas Caracostas

INTRODUCTION

In January 2000 the European Commission proposed the creation of a European Research Area (ERA).[2] At the Lisbon European Council on 23–24 March 2000 the Heads of State and Government of European Union (EU) countries fully endorsed this project as a central component of the establishment of a European knowledge-based society.[3] They set a series of objectives and an implementation timetable up to 2010.

Following on from the Conclusions of the European Council, the Resolution adopted at the Research Council on 15 June 2000 called upon the Member States and the European Commission to take the necessary steps to make a start on realizing this Area. Meanwhile, the European Parliament had strongly supported the project in a Resolution adopted on 18 May 2000. The idea of a European Research Area has also been warmly welcomed by the scientific community and industry. Several hundred companies, research bodies and individual researchers have sent in their comments, either spontaneously or in response to a wide-ranging consultation.

What made this call for a new step in EU research policy so attractive? What is the rationale behind this new European research policy? What makes it new? What went wrong in the past 15 years? What may be the new features of EU research and innovation policy in the period up to 2010? How this new policy might affect the respective roles of regional, national and EU policies?

This paper will attempt an answer to these questions by focusing on:

- the rationale behind the three interdependent dimensions of a European Research and Innovation Area in an age of globalization (Section 2);
- the lessons learned from 50 years of post-national institution building in the field of research in Europe for the interaction between the European and national levels of policymaking (Section 3);
- the shared governance of the ERA and the effects this shared governance might have in the future on the various research policy actors at all levels in Europe (Section 4).

The analysis will concentrate on the strategy presented in the above-mentioned January 2000 communication and the debate on its implementation through the 'open method of co-ordination' of national research and innovation policies and the Sixth EU Research Framework Programme (FP6) (2002–06).

THE THREE INTERDEPENDENT DIMENSIONS OF THE EUROPEAN RESEARCH AND INNOVATION AREA IN A GLOBALIZED AND COMPETITIVE WORLD

In the early 1980s voices were raised at national and European level warning against the risk of Europe falling behind the United States and Japan in the major fields of science and technology. Nearly 20 years on, knowledge is widely considered to be a central component of the economy and knowledge-based society developing worldwide. Seen as basic driving forces behind economic and social progress and a key factor in competitiveness, the dynamics of job creation and an improved quality of life, science and technology are also becoming central to the policymaking process.

While in the mid-1980s, Japan's emerging leadership in information and communication technologies was perceived by Europeans as the threat to their own competitiveness, today the United States constitute the new reference model for a majority of policymakers, industrialists, researchers and opinion leaders.

Europe is at the cutting edge of many areas of science, it has the proven capacity to turn ideas into innovative products and services, and its education systems are generally strong. At the same time, the European higher education and research system fails to attract enough people and investment, both from within Europe and worldwide.

Attractiveness is particularly important in the context of globalization. To be able to create or preserve jobs, to raise productivity, to improve quality of life, a country or a region of the world needs to attract qualified people, capital and knowledge services and to make the best possible use of its own human and financial resources. A few examples hereafter show that European countries are facing common challenges in this respect. In particular, under-exploitation of intellectual and human resources have been identified in the discussions preceding the launch of the ERA strategy:

- World-class centers of excellence exist in practically all areas and disciplines in Europe. Their exact specialties, however, are not always sufficiently well known outside the frontiers of the country in which they are established, especially by companies, which could usefully join forces with them.
- There are not enough women in research in Europe. Although they account for 50 per cent of university graduates and even exceed the number of men in some subjects (life sciences and technologies, for example), they are not found in the same proportions in the laboratories and research departments of companies. Their progress in a scientific career is slower than that of men and their numbers start to rarefy as we climb the ladder of responsibilities. At the top of the academic hierarchy in the EU, for example, there are on average fewer than 10 per cent women. Employment in high-tech sectors remains dominated by men, who account for almost two-thirds of total employment in these sectors.[4] Gender gaps in employment shares range from 25 per cent in Portugal to above 50 per cent in Greece, Belgium, the UK and the Netherlands.
- Every country in the Union is observing a disaffection for scientific study and a loss of interest among the young in careers in research. In Germany, for example, the number of physics students has dropped by half since 1991. In the United Kingdom the number of future teachers of physics slumped from 553 in 1993 to 181 in 1998. And in France the number of science students dropped from 150 000 in 1995 to 126 000 in 1999. This trend is even more worrying if one takes into account the aging of Europe's population which also affects the researchers population in many EU countries.

It is against this background that the question of a true European Research and Innovation Area can be discussed.

To be attractive, such an Area must show that it invests more than other parts of the world in research and education (commitment), that it optimizes its resources (optimization) and that it differentiates itself from its competitors (identity).

Increasing the Resources of the European Research and Innovation Area

Funding for research and education is still not sufficient in Europe, particularly from business sources in the case of research. The United States and Japan lead the EU in terms of investment in the knowledge-based economy. Figures speak for themselves:

- Average public spending on education in the EU as a percentage of GDP remained unchanged at 5 per cent between 1995 and 2000, even if that still resulted in an increase in the absolute amounts spent as EU economies have grown. Countries such as Denmark, Sweden, Austria and Finland and OECD countries such as the United States, Canada and New Zealand all invested more. Concerning third level education (university and non-university third level training), only Finland (32 per cent of the population) approaches the level reached in Japan (close to 40 per cent) or the United States (35 per cent).
- Governments and business in the EU still invest less of its GDP in research than the United States and Japan: 1.9 per cent for EU compared to 3 per cent for Japan and 2.6 per cent for the US in 1999. This investment gap is essentially due to lower investment by business. Moreover, the average annual growth of business research spending was still lower in the EU than in the US although it is slightly higher than in Japan during the second half of the nineties. In terms of research carried out in the public sector, the picture is rather different. In higher education research, Europe spends a similar proportion of its GDP as its two partners (around 0.4 per cent), while government research is higher in the EU and Japan than in the US.

The European Commission proposed in January 2002 that the European Council endorses action to strengthen the European area of research and innovation by setting a target of 3 per cent of GDP for the overall level of public and private spending on research and development by the end of the decade. Within that total, the amount funded by business should rise to around two-thirds against 55 per cent today.

The Heads of State and Government of EU countries endorsed this objective in March 2002 in Barcelona.[5] It is the first time that such a commitment to a quantitative target is made for research at such a high level.

Concerning the ways to reach such objectives, the policy debate so far has stressed the importance of a favorable economic and fiscal environment for R&D and innovation. The various public support mechanisms to stimulate private investment (subsidies, fiscal incentives, guarantee schemes, public–private partnerships, and those aiming at facilitating capital risk finance) need to be compared and assessed at European level as a means to improving their effectiveness and assessing their multiplier effect, individually and in combination.

Optimizing the Allocation and Use of European Knowledge Resources

The issue of better co-ordinating science and technology policies in Europe is not new. Going back to the European Atomic Energy Community (Euratom) Treaty at the end of the 1950s – which gave the European Commission the mission to co-ordinate national research programs – and to the original mandate of the Committee for Scientific and Technological Research (CREST) of the European Community (EC) in the mid-1970s, this is a recurrent theme in the European research policy debates.

More recently, at the end of 1994, the European Commission prompted also by demand from certain Member States, revived the debate on how to co-ordinate national and European research policies. The 1994 communication on 'co-ordination through co-operation' opened the way to the 'European Research Area' initiative by suggesting that more co-ordination was necessary at a number of levels:

- between national policies and European policy on the basis of joint analysis and information work (a shared knowledge base);
- between national and European activities (EC programs, other European programs and organizations, national programs) supporting research and innovation;
- between representatives of Member States and the European Commission in international fora and in the negotiation and implementation of global research programs involving e.g. the US, Japan and other non-EU countries.

A few years later, Caracostas and Muldur (1997)[6] were stating:

This revival of the theme of co-ordination has not as yet yielded any large-scale initiatives. ... Greater effectiveness of the diversified totality of systems of innovation in Europe will entail the pursuit of a limited number of key objectives. It may also be greatly improved by linking those objectives at three levels:

- between national and EC policies and actions;
- between European Intergovernmental schemes and the Union's Framework Programme;
- between research and innovation activity and other (structural) policies at national and European level.

Decompartmentalization and better integration of Europe's scientific and technological policies, resources and institutions is, after the European

Commission's January 2000 communication, now becoming the key message on a much greater scale:

> We need to go beyond the current static structure of '15 + 1'[7] towards a more dynamic configuration. This has to be based on a more coherent approach involving measures taken at different levels: by the Member States at national level, by the European Union with the framework program and other possible instruments, and by intergovernmental co-operation organizations. A configuration of this kind would make for the essential 'critical mass' in the major areas of progress in knowledge, in particular to achieve economies of scale, to allocate resources better overall, and to reduce negative externalities due to insufficient mobility of factors and poor information for operators.

The *European Research Area* strategy stems from the recognition by policy-makers and the various actors in the European research and innovation system of a 'systemic failure', i.e. a failure for European countries to jointly exploit their fragmented resources. This systemic failure combines many failures, e.g. failures:

- to develop regional and national policies on the background of a shared foresight and intelligence knowledge base;
- to plan, in a concerted manner, the setting up of new research and information infrastructures and facilities;
- to inform European and non-European firms about dispersed and under-sized nodes of excellence in research and technology in order to attract investments in Europe;
- to use, in a national or regional research and innovation context, the knowledge and expertise available elsewhere in the EU;
- to mobilize existing research capacities in virtual research centers capable of competing and co-operating with their US counterparts, etc.

Most of the issues related to the need to optimize the development and exploitation of Europe's research capacities are thus covered by the ERA strategy.

This is why the debate on the implementation of this strategy through the FP6 has been centered on the issue of the new implementation instruments proposed by the European Commission, the 'Networks of Excellence', the 'Integrated Projects' (see Box 2.1 below) and the use of Article 169 of the EC Treaty[8] that foresees the possibility for the Union to participate in the funding of a joint program initiated by Member States.

These new instruments aim at going beyond the '15 + 1' logic by incentivating the agglomeration and integration of national research efforts into 'virtual', network-based, European large-scale research organizations.

Box 2.1   Two main (new) instruments in the FP6

NETWORKS OF EXCELLENCE

The purpose of Networks of Excellence is to strengthen and develop Community scientific and technological excellence by means of the integration, at European level, of research capacities currently existing or emerging at both national and regional level. Each Network will also aim at advancing knowledge in a particular area by assembling a critical mass of expertise. They will foster co-operation between capacities of excellence in universities, research centers, enterprises, including SMEs, and science and technology organizations. The activities concerned will be generally targeted towards long-term, multidisciplinary objectives, rather than predefined results in terms of products, processes or services.
(…)
Subject to conditions to be specified in the specific programs and in the rules for participation, the Networks of Excellence will have a high level of management autonomy including, where appropriate, the possibility to adapt the composition of the Network and the content of the joint program of activities.

INTEGRATED PROJECTS

Integrated Projects are designed to give increased impetus to the Community's competitiveness or to address major societal needs by mobilizing a critical mass of research and technological development resources and competencies. Each Integrated Project should be assigned clearly defined scientific and technological objectives and should be directed at obtaining specific results applicable in terms of, for instance, products, processes or services.
(…)
Subject to conditions to be specified in the specific programs and in the rules for participation, the Integrated Projects will have a high level of management autonomy including, where appropriate, the possibility to adapt the partnership and the content of the project. They will be carried out on the basis of overall financing plans preferably involving significant mobilization of public and private sector funding, including funding or collaboration schemes such as EUREKA, EIB and EIF.

Source: Extracts from the Decision No. 1513/2002/Ec of the European Parliament and of the Council of 27 June 2002.

Moreover, because the projects that will be implemented through the use of these new instruments might cover many interface (with users and society at large) and other 'structuring' activities (training of young researchers, concertation and foresight, etc.), they require a much greater strategic preparation and involvement of the management of the organizations involved than with the 'old' instruments (which will coexist with the new ones for some time but in a 'phasing out' approach). This pressure on national (and European intergovernmental) research organizations for a more strategic commitment to joint European ventures is the counterpart of the flexibility and management autonomy they will gain in these new type projects.

Selected on the basis of calls for proposals, the new (large-scale) projects – either Networks of Excellence or Integrated Projects – will, in the approach shared between the European Commission and national governments, de facto materialize a restructuring of European research systems. The shift from a discussion between individual researchers to a 'marriage' between research organizations (or their departments) imply, for the latter, an ability to develop a long-term research strategy and to share parts of it with partners in other EU countries.

The organizational, budgetary and human resource implications for the research organizations involved are far from negligible. The discussions about the ERA strategy have highlighted so far the risks of over concentration of Europe's research excellence, of marginalizing emerging and atypical research teams, of transforming pre-project discussion from scientific to bureaucratic, etc. These risks exist but their taking into account by national and European authorities and the lessons gained from the experience of implementing the new instruments will be under constant scrutiny. The European Commission who is responsible for their implementation has, for example, repeatedly stressed the open character of Networks of Excellence and Integrated Projects which should constantly seek new participants to consolidate the initial core group of proposers.

Strengthening the Identity of the European Research and Innovation Area in the Global Context

In the global research arena, attractiveness of a particular zone also depends on the specific features of its research and innovation system. Specialization – in scientific, technological and economic terms – is therefore an important location factor for attracting ideas, human resources and capital investments.

Since the EU Framework Programmes have become an important instrument for stimulating co-operation between firms, research centers and universities within Europe, the issue of concentrating EU funds on a limited number of key research priorities has been at the core of the discussions between the Member States, the European Commission and the European Parliament.

The European Commission usually advocates the pursuit of concentration on the basis of both the principles of subsidiarity (i.e. focusing on what can be done best at EU level) and optimal use of fragmented European research resources (concentration means creating critical mass to compete internationally). Member States often defend priorities which they think make more sense if their specialization is to be strengthen through co-operation with their partners. The European Parliament (EP) pushes for priorities that, according to its role of transnational representation, correspond best to the aspirations and needs of European citizens.

Through the co-decision procedure which, on the basis of initial proposals be the European Commission, involves an agreement between the Council of Ministers and the EP, these points of view merge into a five-year EU Framework Programme.

The FP6 for Research of the EU (2002–06) will thus focus European partnerships on seven key priorities:[9]

- life sciences, genomics and biotechnology for health (advanced genomics and its applications for health, combating major diseases);
- information society technologies;
- nanotechnologies and nanosciences, knowledge-based multifunctional materials and new production processes and devices;
- aeronautics and space;
- food quality and safety;
- sustainable development, global change and ecosystems (sustainable energy systems, sustainable surface transport, global change and ecosystems);
- citizens and governance in a knowledge-based society.

Taking into account the fact that the new instruments described above will mobilize, through EU funding aiming at integrating national research activities, a much greater proportion of national resources than in past Framework Programmes, it is likely that the FP6 will have noticeable impact on Europe's research specialization. A 'European research identity' is in the making with sustainable development objectives (a better health and quality of life, sustainable energy and mobility systems, cohesion in the Knowledge society) pursued through co-operation in new research agendas.

Functional Reading of the January 2000 ERA Communication

If we attempt to present and re-interpret the various policy priorities deriving from the ERA strategy on the basis of our tridimensional functional classification illustrated above, it is clear that the priorities described in the European Commission's January 2000 communication mainly concern the level of resources and their optimal use in the ERA.

In addition, the issue of a 'European research identity' was, as analyzed previously, tackled through the proposed research priorities of the FP6. The latter has moreover introduced new ideas on how to create a bridge between the EU framework of co-operation and other intergovernmental co-operation frameworks such as EUREKA, the European Science Foundation or the European Molecular Biology Laboratory (see *National Shaping of a Post-national Research and Innovation System*). Strengthening this 'European research identity' will nevertheless require to go a step further by creating a policy framework encompassing both EU Framework Programmes and such intergovernmental schemes. The European Research Area strategy is clearly leading there[10] through the experimentation allowed for by the new instruments and structural actions of the FP6. It is indeed assumed that a better integration of these intergovernmental schemes into EU co-operation activities could, in the long run, promote a more strategic review of their collective interplay.

Now the rationale behind the ERA strategy has been analyzed, a look back at the history of post-national institution-building processes in Europe is necessary in order to address the issue of what type of interdependent research policies are likely to emerge in a post-ERA researchers Europe. This analysis is essential if one desires to assess the likely impacts of these new EU policy developments on national (and regional) policymaking.

A LOOK AT THE LAST 50 YEARS OF POST-NATIONAL INSTITUTION BUILDING IN THE FIELD OF RESEARCH AND INNOVATION

The development of European integration from the European Steel and Coal Community to the EU has led to the setting up of a number of original post-national institutions[11] which have contributed significantly to shaping the innovation process in the different European Member countries.

These institutions can be called 'post-national' on the one hand because they have created stable links between the main actors and existing organizations which have contributed to the fabric of National Systems of Innovation (NSI) and have been supported by specific new organizations and on the other hand because they have not replaced national institutions which continue to determine the specifics of NSI. The European institutions have combined elements of federalism (where sovereignty and the regulation of human interaction has been displaced at a supranational level) with elements of intergovernmental co-operation (where national institutions are interlinked while remaining truly autonomous).

This original institution building process has been the result of very diverse social, political and economic processes explaining its heterogeneity (if compared to national trajectories) but also its specific character (when evaluated vis-à-vis well-known explanatory/normative arguments).

National Shaping of a Post-national Research and Innovation System

Shaping post-national institutions is a complex, apparently ad hoc process. Many lessons can be drawn from a succinct historical review of European level institutions in the field of research.[12]

Firstly, post-national institutional building is not restricted to the EU framework. In the field of research, for example, many intergovernmental institutions and related organizations were created during the 1950s (CERN – European Nuclear Research Centre), the 1960s (the European Southern Observatory, the European Molecular Biology Organisation, the European Space Research Organisation, the Airbus consortium), the 1970s (the European Space Agency, the European Molecular Biology Laboratory) and the 1980s (EUREKA). Moreover, within the EC context itself, the tension between the federal and the intergovernmental approaches is perceptible with, for example, the support to the COST program or the way co-ordination of national policies is designed in the various versions of the EC Treaty. The 'subsidiarity' principle reflects also this tension by distinguishing areas where the EC has exclusive competence and those where competencies are shared between the EC and its Member States. Finally the Union as a whole is a hybrid concept covering both institutions mixing federalism and international co-operation and institutions completely outside any federal design.

Secondly, compatibility between institutions is a key issue at two interrelated levels: post-national EU institutions are defined in complementarity with national rules but also related to other EU rules.

Compatibility with national institutions was a major problem for the Euratom experiments in the 1960s. Sharp and Shearman (1987, pp. 29–30) describe the major problem of this early nuclear federalism:

> ... as an organisation and set of objectives it was the product of mistaken assumptions. The predicted fuel shortage in Europe failed to materialise. The novelty and potential of nuclear power ensured the growth of national programmes, and French military interests denied Euratom any effective role. Euratom was an institutional response to R&D needs which quickly became commercially oriented. Power plant firms were in strong competition with each other and preferred to exploit their historic links with US firms. They were also tied to deeply rooted patterns of national procurement, standards and regulation. Members had little incentive to pursue collective projects. Thus Euratom, by its own admission, failed to co-ordinate its members' activities.

For what concerns compatibility between EU institutions, it can be observed that institutional building has largely been incremental but with a set of radical innovations (the Single European Act, the Treaty on the EU) occurring when post-national institutions are redefined in all fields at the same time. But these important changes are always preceded by periods of intense institutional experimentation.

Thirdly, the ad hoc character of post-national arrangements makes it to some extent possible and essential to further develop institutional building. For example, EC research institutions (or quasi-institutions) such as the Research Framework Programmes were first tested by using the 'spillover' article of the EC Treaty, Article 235 (which stipulated that the Council can decide on any new EC action if there is no Treaty provision to underlie it). Well-known notions such as 'pre-competitiveness', and even more so the principle of 'subsidiarity', allowed for flexible and uncertain arrangements perceived beneficial by all Member Countries, often with different interpretations.

Thus the process of post-national institution building in Europe has been characterized by 'muddling through', by finding ad hoc arrangements in a slow and incremental institutional change process, sometimes spurred by the political attainment of radical new formal treaties, but where compatibility with national rules and routines are a constant problem.

One of the key issues relating to the debate on the history of European research institutions is the tension between a 'static economics of scale approach' (single market, relaxing competition rules, target strategic industries and big companies through R&D programs) and a 'diversity–connectivity–networking approach' (create a European institutional set-up which favors the emergence of international/interregional poles of specialization/growth beyond national and sectoral boundaries).

The two approaches underlining post-national institutional building in Europe since the 1950s were addressing different aspects of the economic fabric: industries where economies of scale play an important role are sometimes dominated by global oligopolies and the emergence of a European-based competitive pole (organized around alliances between European companies and between the latter and non European ones) may improve the competitive conditions at global level, but the 'diversity–connectivity' policy track is more adapted to the functioning of today's research and innovation systems, e.g. for exploiting the innovative (often locally generated) potential of SMEs.

European research and innovation policy has been a mix of the two logics but the second approach has not been sufficiently operationalized yet. It has remained a rather theoretical approach accompanied by a pilot phase of EU activity (i.e. the SPRINT program for supporting innovation and technology transfer at European level). The first approach has led to post-national institutionalization mainly outside the EU framework (e.g. JESSI in the EUREKA framework with debatable results or more successfully the Airbus and Ariane consortia), i.e. following a path of 'economic interdependency' rather than a coherent path of 'economic integration'. It is as if when independent nations decide to co-operate in sectors crucial for their security or economic independence, they prefer dedicated post-national institutional set-ups to comprehensive institutional building. Similarly, institutions defining a single European market have been developed on a full scale while those defining what is a European company or European industrial relations were stuck in endless debates, the first ones because of the second ones.

On a more theoretical level, the tension between scale and diversity in the European integration process has been analyzed by many authors. Matthews and McGowan (1992, p. 230), for example, state that 'any tendency to eliminate technological diversity represents diminution of the technological resource pool, even if, via such processes as gains from economies of scale, short term efficiency is increased by convergence'.

Gregersen, Johnson and Kristensen (1994) have described the rationale behind a European integration process for research and innovation: the 'single market' may be seen as both an extended home market where greater diversity in the potential demand may spur product and process innovation (leading to further diversity among firms and countries) and lead to convergence between firms, consumers and countries to the extent that it may stimulate diffusion of best practice across countries. Growth of multinational corporations through mergers and acquisitions across borders, which is a likely result of European integration, is often supposed to lead to better innovations performance since, in Schumpeterian terms, bigger firms in bigger and more specialized markets are better innovators. But the authors add their own critical assessment: 'On the other hand, (growing integration) might also hamper innovation processes and interactive learning in the long run, if established domestic linkages are broken'.

However, what is missing so far in many research contributions on these issues is the consideration of how institutional and learning diversity from the existence of NSI (or sectoral SI) is embedded in the post-national institution-building process. In other words, is this latter exogenous to the evolution of national and sectoral systems of innovation or does it evolve with them as part of the same process of integration and diversification?

On this last point, the German 'impact study' (see Reger and Kuhlmann 1995) has shown that German 'Länder', which are responsible, according to the Constitution, for science and research, see themselves being permanently affected by decisions in Brussels but do not feel adequately represented there. Similarly, the large science organizations in Germany fear that if EC R&D policy gains further importance, the tried and tested principles and mechanisms of self-organization in German science will be undermined, particularly since typical EC project support programs, similarly to the project support of their National Research Ministry, are shaped far more by 'political' criteria than institutional funding and are not predominantly determined by inherent scientific criteria. In order to defend an original national institution, they suggest that it should be established throughout Europe (through the establishment of an 'EU Science Foundation', more recently a 'European Research Council').

European Impact on National Research and Innovation Systems

The analysis of how post-national institutions have been shaped in Europe needs to be supplemented by an assessment of their impact on national institutions. A detailed analysis of the impacts of European institutions on national research and innovation systems is impossible within the context of this short contribution. The following observations draw from a series of studies carried out for the European Commission, the so-called 'national science and technology impact studies'[13] and other evaluation reports commissioned by EU and national institutions (see European Commission 1994 for a succinct review).

The following remarks are based on a distinction between the influence of EU funding on 'incentive funding' on one hand, and on 'infrastructure funding' on the other.

Incentive funding constitutes only a proportion of the total public R&D budget of each country (program or project funding beyond the routine or permanent financing of major research institutions). It appears that specific EC programs have had varying relative impacts and influences on national policies. In the field of environmental research and IT-related research (ESPRIT), EC activities were either the main resource for national research or influenced the design of complementary national policies (in the biggest Member States). The agro-food domain seems to have experienced the same situation in Denmark. Infrastructure financing was mainly channeled through the EC Structural Funds to those countries which are less advanced in research. The interaction between Framework Programme specific actions, Structural Funds and national policies was obviously important in those countries (Ireland, Greece, Portugal and, to a lesser extent, Spain and Italy).

Secondly, EC policy generally had only a slight influence on the structuring of national policy of the most advanced countries, while its impact was often very perceptible in the 'less favored' ones. In the latter, EC programs have inspired the design and adoption of similar national programs and procedures (e.g. for selecting projects): in Portugal, for example, reflections undertaken in connection with the preparation of the Framework Programmes together with activities related to SPRINT (a European innovation support scheme) and the Structural Funds have led to the creation of a national Agency for Innovation.

Thirdly, the networking effects of European committee and advisory structures are noticeable. The national experts participating in these structures meet regularly, get to know one another and learn through these contacts of the major stakes and technological trends. Moreover, it is often the same decision-makers and experts who participate in drawing up national and EC policies.

Finally, some worries concerning possible negative impacts of European policies on national policies have been voiced in the recent past:

- EC institutions may lead to a certain alignment of national policies with European policy resulting in a growing distance of national programs from national priorities.
- The promotion of European partnerships, a very positive goal in itself, could lead to a certain international sharing of tasks in the major technological fields. Countries with large companies would lead the way by using e.g. small companies of less favored countries as subcontractors. The larger countries would therefore benefit more from the possible economic repercussions, notably in terms of high skilled research jobs.

Post-national Institution Building and National Diversity: a Political Science Perspective

Borrowing some recent developments in the field of political science concerning European integration sheds some additional light on the embeddedness of diversity in the post-national institution-building process.

Muller (1994) has analyzed the transformation of public policies in Europe, what Andersen and Eliassen (1993) have called 'the Europeification of National Policy-Making'. He distinguished between three levels of interaction between the European integration process and the national policy system:

- the 'policy agenda';
- the representation of interest groups; and
- the decision-making process.

  a) The policy agenda is the sum of perceived problems at a given point in time which appear to be necessarily the subject for legitimate governmental intervention. The introduction of an issue on the agenda is a major element in the elaboration of public policies, and the target of strategic behavior for social and economic actors. Muller suggests that there is a transfer of some essential issues to the European policy agenda: the changes in agricultural policies or environmental directives before the Single European Act and, the most spectacular, the implementation of the Single Market are examples of this change. One could add today the Economic and Monetary Union (EMU) which constrains heavily national monetary, budgetary and economic policies. The various policies which constitute today industrial policy (e.g. competition, trade, regional policies to quote a few of them) are strongly determined at European level from the point of view of the issues discussed and the methods suggested for public policy implementation. Many authors explain this new phenomenon as a result of the cultural shock created by the creation of Single European Market and more recently the EMU.

In the field of research and innovation policy, the regular discussions of Framework Programmes are moments where a European policy agenda is defined through what Mazey and Richardson (1993) call a 'competitive agenda setting' process. Diversity of national science and technology structures and priorities is reflected in this lengthy process. Its results depend on the ability of national governments, other interest groups and political parties, as well as Committees and individual MEPs in the European Parliament to introduce new issues on the agenda.[14]

When the agenda has been set, it consequently influences national policy agendas. As Tsipouri and Xanthakis (1993) have shown it for Greece, the influence is greater in those Member countries where a structured policy-setting process is lacking. But, even for bigger Member States with a very broad science and technology base and a well defined policy process, the examples of ESPRIT show that European discussions and priorities can have a significant influence.

b) The second level of influence analyzed by Muller concerns the representation of interests. The situation here is more complex. The strengthening of European organizations (e.g. the Union of Industrial and Employers' Confederations of Europe [UNICE] or the European Round Table assembling major European multinationals) does not substitute to the activism of national bodies. These 'Eurolobbies' contribute to the integration of diverse national approaches vis-à-vis the initiatives of the European Commission and play a major role in distributing information to their national counterparts. But, even if there is no trend towards a monopoly power of these groups in the European policy system, their existence constitutes an additional uncertainty factor in the competitive agenda setting process referred to above which can destabilize national lobbying processes.

In the field of research policy however, given the fact that up to now the main emphasis has been on the initiation and implementation of common research programs rather than on regulation or co-ordination of national policies, the role of these 'Eurolobbies' has been much less important in shaping decisions than in other policy areas.

c) Finally Muller concentrates on a third level, the one of 'Europeifica-tion' of decision-making. He quotes Dan-Nguyen, Schneider and Werle (1993) for whom 'the policy networks of the European Community are hybrid mixes of national, supranational, intergovernmental, trans-governmental and transnational actors and relation systems', a reality which could be caught by the notion of a 'post-national' system. The model of 'government by committees' (see Sidjanski 1989) is an insti-tutional innovation required by the political necessity of producing, when a decision is elaborated, expertise that reflects European social and national diversity. Predecisional Committee work:

> constitutes, in the end, a powerful, more or less formalised, selection mechanism of an elite, both political-administrative and expressing 'civil society' (representatives of different professional or non-professional lob-bies), that will establish a whole ensemble of more or less stabilised net-works linked through conflictual relations or alliances.

And Muller develops a paradox: as rules are less precise, the decision-making system is more open than national systems which are characterized by a cer-tain degree of corporatism, but, because rules are less codified, the European system is less transparent.

Finally, the author concludes that these European processes tend to be replicated at national level. Reverse institutional borrowing is particularly visible in the field of regional and research policies where the 'partnership' discourse is invading national institution development:

> Beyond conjunctural uncertainties, an astonishing process – leading to the forma-tion of a common mediation space within which the fundamental norms around which our societies will interpret their relation to the world are defined – is taking place before us.

In the field of research, this hypothesis is confirmed by the analysis of trends in national policies in the mid 1990s (see European Commission 1994). First, the pressure on national R&D budgets, common to a majority of Member States, can be analyzed as an indirect effect of the EMU process.[15] Secondly, the regular debates at national level (White Papers, broad consultative proc-esses, foresight exercises etc.) on the direction to be given to the research system can be analyzed as the search for a new national policy legitimization in reaction to the double threat of 'Europeification' and 'regionalization' (a sub-national institution building process equally fuelled by a recent European regional policy revival). In this legitimization process, national institutions learn and borrow from each other with the help of the European 'common mediation space'.[16]

GOVERNING TOGETHER THE EUROPEAN RESEARCH AND INNOVATION AREA: TRENDS AND LIKELY IMPACTS

From government to governance, this shift in notions reflect both the new ways policymaking works in advanced democracies (participation of stakeholders in the preparation and the implementation of government decisions) and the complexity of articulating national (and increasingly regional) government policies into a post-national decision-making process such as the one characterizing the EU.

The notion of governance embeds the idea of policy convergence through diverse interaction and co-operation processes between policies and strategies carried out at different levels. As long as the EU treaty does not allocate a strong co-ordination mandate to the EU level of decision-making (Art. 165 is not imperative while in the past the Euratom Treaty was foreseeing a strong co-ordination role for the European Commission), the 'open method of co-ordination' allows to move in this direction. This section will attempt an analysis of the trends toward a shared governance of the ERA and a discussion of the implications it may have for national and regional research policies:

> It cannot be said that there is today a European policy on research. National research policies and Union policy overlap without forming a coherent whole. ... The European market of supply and demand in knowledge and technology still remains largely to be created. For it to develop and function a real European research policy needs to be defined.

These were key statements made by the European Commission communication of January 2000 on the European Research Area.

At the Lisbon European Council of 23–24 March 2000, the concept of 'open method of co-ordination' was introduced in order to better implement the long-term strategy for a competitive knowledge-based economy with more and better employment and social cohesion. This method is described in the conclusions (points 37 and 38):

> 37. Implementation of the strategic goal will be facilitated by applying a new open method of co-ordination as the means of spreading best practice and achieving greater convergence towards the main EU goals. This method, which is designed to help Member States to progressively develop their own policies, involves:

- fixing guidelines for the Union combined with specific timetables for achieving the goals which they set in the short, medium and long terms;
- establishing, where appropriate, quantitative and qualitative indicators and benchmarks against the best in the world and tailored to the needs of different Member States and sectors as a means of comparing best practice;
- translating these European guidelines into national and regional policies by setting specific targets and adopting measures, taking into account national and regional differences;
- periodic monitoring, evaluation and peer review organised as mutual learning processes.

38. A fully decentralised approach will be applied in line with the principle of subsidiarity in which the Union, the Member States, the regional and local levels, as well as the social partners and civil society, will be actively involved, using variable forms of partnership. A method of benchmarking best practices on managing change will be devised by the European Commission networking with different providers and users, namely the social partners, companies and NGOs.

This new method, a generalization of the approach developed in the field of the EU employment policy, is supposed to be more open to national diversity and variable geometry. In contrast with the policies aimed at building the single market the emphasis is here on mutual learning and discovering jointly appropriate solutions in those policy areas where a clear integrative role of the Union is not explicit or yet accepted.

Benchmarking National Research Policies

Notably, the Lisbon European Council recommended the benchmarking of national R&D policies. The European Commission and the Member States set up a partnership in the form of a High Level Group (HLG) of representatives of Ministers in charge of research. The initial task of the partnership was to propose relevant indicators and to elaborate the methodology for the five themes selected by the Research Council:

- human resources in R&D;
- public and private investment in R&D;
- impact of R&D on competitiveness and employment;
- S&T productivity;
- promotion of R&D culture and public understanding of science.

The European Commission subsequently established five expert groups to conduct the analysis of these themes. The High Level Group ensures the flow of information from national sources on statistical data and policy patterns. Together with the European Commission, it follows the work of experts and validates the analysis of data and issues. A progress report was presented in June 2001 together with the 'Key Figures 2001',[17] which concentrated on data and trends from the available indicators and outlined the issues to be examined.

A Working Document from the European Commission Services[18] presented in January 2002 first analyses of policy issues and trends. This document consists of comments about science and technology indicators and of a first review of policy measures in the five fields mentioned above. The five expert groups, which have been asked to study each of these five selected themes, completed their work by mid-2002. They notably aimed at:

- identifying good practices in terms of public policies for stimulating private investment in R&D, through competitive programs, indirect measures, the creation of appropriate business environments and regulatory frameworks;
- identifying the combinations of policy instruments most suitable to the specific context of individual countries or groups of countries;
- identifying the ways of developing a sufficient and sufficiently skilled research work force, matching the specific national needs and objectives;
- identifying the factors that contribute to S&T productivity, at the appropriate levels of comparison in order to draw policy lessons;
- studying the links between R&D inputs and outputs through, *inter alia*, the use of relative indices, in order to get a better understanding of national performances and their context.

Further issues studied by the expert groups include the following:

- a critical examination of the institutional set-up;
- some objectives of R&D policies not yet considered, such as support to the defense industry, which is especially relevant as Europe is building a common defense industry and launching a common policy for military procurements in some sectors;
- the contribution of regions, especially through regional or local networks;
- the service sector and intangible investments.

What is unclear as long as the analysis and comparison of best practices is carried out by experts and not by representatives of national Ministries is how will Member States engage fully in the process and progressively move to the joint reporting and national/regional implementation system foreseen in the 'open method of co-ordination'. Without this firm commitment, benchmarking will hardly achieve more than a regular exchange of views on commonly agreed indicators and thus fail to exploit the opportunities offered by the 'open method'. The European Commission Services allude to this risk when they describe the expected results of the first cycle:

> As soon as the expert groups have completed their work, there is a need to disseminate the results and turn the exercise to actions for policy making. This process will involve all stakeholders, namely government authorities, business enterprises, research community representatives and research users.

Policy workshops were organized during 2002, at the initiative of Member States, in order to discuss the recommendations of the expert groups in areas where policy action is urgently needed. A joint European Commission–Greek Presidency Conference took place in Athens in January 2003, with a double objective: the diffusion of the results from the first benchmarking cycle and the design of the next cycle.

The strong commitment of the research administrations of Member States in the benchmarking process will therefore be in the years to come a test of the full implementation of the 'open method' in the field of research policy. The joint follow-up of measures and policies decided at national and EU levels to reach the '3 per cent' Barcelona target is an area particularly fitted for this method. In addition, one can ask if a specific provision in the Treaties (a rewriting of the article which suggests a role for the co-ordination of national policies alongside the definition and implementation of EU Framework Programmes) could not be envisaged so as to institutionalize co-ordination and define the corresponding policy process and implementation instruments. If this occurs in the future (e.g. when Europe's Constitutional Treaty will be drafted), the 'open method' would have paved the way towards a renewed and more integrated EU research policy.

Sharing Visions of the Future: Policy Learning Through Co-operation in Foresight[19]

Alongside benchmarking, foresight activities carried out in a commonly agreed framework or jointly can also make an important contribution towards the promotion of the ERA. Indeed, foresight is precisely about identifying key social trends and leading edge technologies, mapping positions and then identifying priorities for investment. EU level foresight can help to identify those areas of emerging and strategic technologies where there is a requirement for pre-competitive joint responses to global developments in science and technologies, such as:

- common investments and exploitation of economies of scale in costly, large-scale facilities and infrastructures;
- the building-up of critical mass (in research expertise, approaches, learning

effects) especially in emerging or fragmented research fields;
- co-ordinated research approaches to complex issues such as environmental threats, individual privacy protection, food safety or nuclear safeguards, in particular in areas where EU policies are developed.

Foresight is also frequently orientated towards identifying strategies to build a competitive position for the future. In this respect European Member States, as well as regions within them, might be seen as entities competing with each other. But, even if Member States are competitors, a joint, co-ordinated foresight could help identify areas of industrial strength and research excellence that are based on common training infrastructures, market systems, regulatory structures. It could also help to raise awareness of areas of emerging technological opportunity in which the EU could become a leader e.g. by building interdependencies between existing areas of strength (e.g. in knowledge management, soft technologies or between embedded hardware and software technologies and mobile communications).

Europe has many common goals and priorities relating to areas such as knowledge-based competitiveness, innovation, establishing the ERA, cohesion etc.. Europe also faces many common and complex challenges, such as environmental crises, unemployment, infectious diseases, natural disasters, insufficient transport safety or energy efficiency, to name a few.

These challenges can only be addressed by co-operative action, across national borders and cultures. The same can also be said for research policies and programs. Policies and programs have traditionally taken place at national or regional level. Some issues, however, require a consistent position perhaps between neighboring countries or regions, at EU level or even global level. Examples include common security threats, averting environmental damage, the management of water resources, traceability of foodstuffs and global climate change. Foresight could also address emerging requirements for common approaches to regulations, standards, measurement and testing.

Such joint activities can moreover contribute to raising awareness and participation in political development. At the EU level, foresight can have a role in building solidarity and shared agendas by giving stakeholders a chance to contribute creatively to shaping a new Europe. Such vision creating and goal setting for Europe should be based on joint efforts and take into account different perspectives. As a long-range process, foresight also needs to be the subject of continuity in policies that will have to continue under changing national political administrations. European foresight processes are in a strong position, therefore, to make such joint vision and goal setting possible.

In short, foresight processes in Europe can help to:

- increase the strategic capabilities in the EU;

- improve communication and co-operation between actors from different sectors of society and between different policy levels on EU-wide issues; and
- contribute to the democratization of EU policymaking.

A Forward Look: How the Move Towards ERA May Alter the Interaction Between the Various Research Policy Levels in Europe

Before discussing the likely impacts of the ERA strategy on the respective roles of EU, national and regional levels of policymaking in the field of research and innovation, one needs to recall that the decision-makers at EU level are the Council of Ministers (of Research) and the European Parliament (through the co-decision procedure defined in the Treaty of the EU). It is important to recall this fundamental feature of the multi-level governance system of the EU to avoid any confusion about the possibility for the European Commission to take decisions that would be problematic for Member States policies. The European Commission proposes legislation or program funding decisions that are subject to co-decisions by the other two institutions.

This being restated at the outset, one can proceed in reflecting on the likely effects of decisions and policy developments shaped by the political will of national governments to co-operate at EU level both by using EU policy instruments they have co-decided (in this case the FP6) and by implementing the open method of co-ordination.

The analysis will proceed in two phases:

- first, the functional approach described above (see *The Three Interdependent Dimensions of the European Research and Innovation Area in a Globalized and Competitive World*) will be used in order to assess the respective roles of EU, national and regional policies and their interdependence;
- second, the likely impacts of the ERA strategy will be discussed against the background of the historical review presented (see also *A Look at the Last 50 Years of Post-national Institution Building in the Field of Research and Innovation*).

Based on our functional analysis, the following hypotheses can be made:

- the EU will have the more direct impact on national research organizations through the new instruments of FP6. These instruments are powerful means towards the end of integrating fragmented research resources in Europe. They will be used mainly in the fields of research covered by the seven key thematic priorities referred to above (see *Strengthening the Identity of the European Research and Innovation Area in a Global Context*). This can lead to the assumption that the EU will shape a significant part of national research priorities and related budgets. But if one recalls that EU priorities are shaped by co-decision between the Council and the European Parliament, this means that these priorities embed and transcend transnational approaches to what the EU should focus upon;

- moreover the call for expression of interest published by the European Commission in March 2002 may be considered as a way to allow the research organizations of Member States to contribute significantly to the shaping of the detailed work programs which translate the EU priorities into specific research agendas. In this process, national research organizations have been incentivated to indicate on which topics they are ready to join forces in long-term cross-border partnerships. These expressions of interest helped the European Commission program managers to define the first work programs needed to implement EU priorities;

- these work programs are regularly discussed with Programme Committees where Member States are represented, allowing them to voice their concerns;

- finally, on the basis of these work programs, calls for proposals are published, and proposals are evaluated and selected for funding.

The Networks of Excellence and Integrated Projects to be funded by the EU in the years 2003–06 will, as we have seen above, benefit from a much greater level of management autonomy than previous EU-funded research projects. This autonomy is reflected in the acceptance by the EU of their self-organization, provided that they pursue commonly agreed objectives and respect well-defined principles of integration and openness to outside players during their lifecycle.

For the part of the national research systems affected by this new type of Europeanization process, this will mean of course a greater interdependence with other Member States research organizations. How important will be this part for each Member State is very difficult to assess at this stage in so far the selection process will occur on a competitive basis (peer review system).

Another axis of the European Research Area strategy where the EU plays a leading role is the one dealing with the promotion of the mobility of researchers. But again the competitive approach that will be followed will provide researchers and research organizations in Europe many opportunities for learning from inwards and outwards mobility.

Finally, most of the remaining policy axes described in the European Commission's January 2000 communication show that the FP6 will support 'open co-ordination' and mutual learning for national and regional policies and programs through the support to various forms of benchmarking processes. In the absence of a research policy benchmarking process formalized in the EU Treaty, these measures will play a catalytic role for experimenting more 'open co-ordination' of national policies in many areas identified as critical to the success of the ERA strategy (e.g. science and society issues, research facilities, framework conditions for increasing private investments in research).

The second approach to assess the likely impacts of this strategy on national and regional policies consists in starting from the earlier remarks on national shaping of a post-national research and innovation system emerging at EU level and the impact of the latter on national systems, made above (see *A Look at the Last 50 Years of Post-national Institution Building in the Field of Research and Innovation*).

Firstly, the functional analysis performed above showed that the ERA strategy and its main implementation instrument, the FP6, were to a large degree shaped and will be shaped in the future by national approaches to Europeanization. The invention of this new institution, the 'open method of co-ordination' (OMC), for the EU employment strategy and its diffusion to other fields of EU policymaking such as research reflects the will of Member States to find new ways to enrich the European integration process:

> By agreeing to take part in the new process, States are also submitted to deep transformation in their preferences, perceptions and respective interests, in the framework of a reciprocal learning process, leading to greater convergence ... What is actually happening is a new development of the multilevel governance ... There is an increasing number of actors taking part in the multiple process of co-ordination and submitting themselves to continuous interaction that can lead to increased European inter-linking between the States and their political approaches. Governmental actors are to some extent obliged to work increasingly with each other within common institutions and to go beyond perceptions and actions which are strongly marked by national history (Telò 2002, p. 261).

In the case of the ERA strategy, the European Commission's Communication in January 2000 anticipated the formalization of the OMC in the course of the Lisbon European Council, two months later. The broad support to this strategy from Member States governments and research organizations stemmed out of the 'openness' of the ERA concept, i.e. the basic idea that the ERA will be built through a strong partnership between the EU and national (and regional) actors ('15 into 1' instead of '15 + 1') and that national specificities/aspirations – articulated in novel ways – will be the basis on which ERA will develop in the future.

Secondly, it is obvious that, with the new instruments of the FP6, the funding impact of European policy will go beyond 'incentive funding'.

Because national research organizations will decide to develop common programs of activities over a long period, the EU 'glue' funding (for supporting integration of these activities) might have a much greater impact than in the past.

Thirdly, the remarks of Muller concerning the representation of interests in EU policymaking (see above) do not seem to be relevant to the situation expected to be created by the ERA strategy so far. As long as open co-ordination of national policies is not yet formalized in the Treaty for research policy field, the role of 'Eurolobbies' in shaping decisions will probably not increase significantly in the near future.

CONCLUSIONS AND OPEN QUESTIONS FOR FURTHER RESEARCH

This paper has analyzed the logic behind the ERA strategy and attempted to provide some elements of reflection concerning the new collective governance model which is likely to emerge in the perspective of its implementation. Multi-level governance in this new context will probably not be based on clear cut distinctions between competencies to be exercised at EU, national or regional levels but rather on co-operation between these levels and mutual learning.

The combination of strong EC instruments such as the new ones introduced by the FP6 and 'softer' open co-ordination processes partially supported by EC financing will generate a process of self organization of this new multi-level governance in the making.[20]

A number of questions remain open that concern, for example, the likely direction and coherence of the whole process of opening and voluntary Europeanization of national and regional research policies: the democratic legitimacy of 'open co-ordination' processes combined with classical EC approaches; the question of time/synchronization of these various inter-related decision-making procedures; the necessity of professionalizing and Europeanizing the community of practitioners that prepare and inform the policy process at all levels.

The Direction and Coherence of This New Voluntary Europeanization Process

If one assumes that many bottom-up co-operative and mutual learning initiatives between the different levels of governance in Europe will emerge in the context of the ERA strategy, the first question concerns the overall coherence of these initiatives. In the employment field, the formalized benchmarking process introduced in the EC Treaty ensures a visibility and focus of the mutual learning between Member States. The well-codified reporting system which is, since Lisbon, also advocated for other fields of policy creates the necessary 'centralization' and 'codification' of the policy debate and facilitates the development of a commonly acceptable and understandable reference framework. After an initial period of experimentation, a similar formalization may be proven necessary for research and innovation policies as well in order to better prioritize issues for mutual learning and joint action at European level well beyond the FP instrument.[21] This, in theory at least, should be easier in this policy field where a strong EU competence is widely accepted.

Before this formalization occurs, one has to recognize that the Lisbon process (establishment of synthesis indicators at the central level, institution of the Spring European Council which monitors the state of progress of the strategy) paves the way:

> Indeed, to wager everything on decentralised governance alone, without improving the organisation of the central and formal government of the strategy would be inefficient. The approach is decentralised, but the Commission, the Council and the European Council will ensure the co-ordination and control of the follow-up (Telò 2002, p. 257).

The Democratic Legitimacy of the OMC

This raises immediately the question of democratic control over this complex multi-level governance system. Telò suggests two concrete measures for strengthening the role of the European Parliament in the Lisbon process:

- to establish an annual plenary session of the EP, devoted to the socio-economic strategy of the EU, before each Spring European Council;
- to establish the rule of regular contacts between the Presidency of the Council and the specialized Committees of the EP, with regard to the progress of the different chapters of the 'Lisbon Strategy' and the application of the OMC.

In fact, the President of the European Commission presents the Spring Report to the European Parliament at the beginning of the year and regular contacts exist now between the Presidency of the Council, the European Commission and the specialized committees of the European Parliament. The President of the European Parliament participates to each year's Spring European Council.

The question remains open though of how to improve the democratic control, at European level, over a complex strategic initiative encompassing many legal and budgetary decisions that are treated in the framework of separate legal and political processes and covering 'open co-ordination' processes as well.

The Synchronization of the Various Inter-related Decision-making Procedures

Mutual learning between EU, national or regional policies, supported by the OMC, can develop despite the asynchronous character of policy decisions and frameworks at these various levels. Nevertheless, one of the advantages of the EC method of regulation is that, after intense debate between Member States and between the Council and the EP, the implementation of agreed decisions takes place at the same time in all Member States (apart from exceptional cases of 'transition periods' allowed in some of them), at least in theory (the translation of EC law into national law takes sometimes longer in some Member States than in others). If it is true that once a year the Spring European Council highlights common targets and reports on progress achieved in meeting the ones defined previously[22], this process has no legal enforcement powers and a lot of action is left with the 'decentralized' policies of Member States. Delays in defining and implementing the specific measures needed to meet the targets in some Member States can diminish the effectiveness of the strategy in one or the other policy fields covered by the Lisbon strategy. New research into the interdependence of multi-level interconnected policy cycles is therefore called for in order to assess current problems and to design pragmatic policy solutions.

Professionalization of Policy Communities of Practice in a European Mutual Learning Context

The question of the professionalization of the science and technology policy practice has been analyzed recently by many scholars (see e.g. Caracostas and Muldur 1997; Teubal 1996). But, as the Europeanization of national and regional policymaking is likely to develop through a combination of European Community policies and OMC, mutual learning processes that this Europeanization implies need a knowledge base accessible to all and a certain level of codification as well as creative adaptation of this knowledge which will be generated in the process and applied in very diverse institutional settings. Mutual recognition of and mutual learning from others' specificities will progressively require interoperable or common policy 'languages'. How to define needs for new reference indicators, new policy targets and interdependent policy processes and instruments? What curricula and learning material/processes for a new profession of policy 'mediators' (between different policy contexts, between policy and policy research, between policy shaping and stakeholders aspirations)?

These are some of the questions that need to be addressed in the new context of European integration after Lisbon.

NOTES

[1] This paper updates the approach developed in a previous analysis of the evolution of EU research policy (see Caracostas and Soete 1997) and attempts a forward-looking approach of the issue of the governance of an emerging but rapidly developing European (structural) research policy. Views expressed in this paper are those of the author and do not reflect official positions of the European Commission.

[2] European Commission (2000), *Towards a European Research Area*, European Commission communication, 18 January 2000, COM (2000) 6.

[3] 'The Union has today set itself a new strategic goal for the next decade: to become the most competitive and dynamic knowledge-based economy in the world, capable of sustainable economic growth with more and better jobs and greater social cohesion.' (Point 5 of Lisbon conclusions).

[4] *Employment in Europe 2001. Recent Trends and Prospects* (European Commission 2001).

[5] Point 47 of the Spanish Presidency Conclusions: 'The European Council therefore agrees that overall spending on R&D and innovation in the Union should be increased with the aim of approaching 3 per cent of GDP by 2010. Two-thirds of this new investment should come from the private sector.'

[6] In *Society, the Endless Frontier* (Caracostas and Muldur 1997, pp. 186–7).

[7] '15 + 1' means the Fifteen Member States of the current EU and the European Commission acting as a separate actor.

[8] This article states that the European Commission may participate in research programs undertaken jointly by several Member States, including participation in the structures created for the execution of these programs.

[9] Funding co-operation in these seven broad fields of research represents nearly 70 per cent of the total budget foreseen for the FP6 of the EC (total budget 2002–06: €16 270 million), the rest being allocated mostly to activities aiming at 'structuring the ERA' and 'strengthening the basis of ERA'. Moreover a Framework Programme for atomic energy research (based on the EURATOM Treaty), totalling a budget of €1 230 million for the same period has been agreed upon.

[10] See Axis 2.2 (*Closer Relations Between Scientific and Technological Co-operation Organisations in Europe*) of the January 2000 Communication.

[11] 'Institutions' in the sense of 'humanly devised constraints that shape human interaction' and, more informally, of 'rules of a game in a society' (North 1990). Edquist and Johnson define institutions as 'sets of habits, routines, established practices or rules which regulate the relations between individuals and groups' (Edquist 1997).

[12] For most of the historical development analyzed below, see Guzzetti (1995) and Sharp and Shearman (1987). Guzzetti's work is a first step towards a comprehensive historical analysis of European research institutions.

[13] The results of the 'impact studies' quoted above – which were mainly based on a questionnaire survey of participating organizations, complemented by interviews of national experts in the R&D field – must be considered with caution as for all studies of that kind. But they can be used as a 'proxy' of an in depth research process still to be initiated on these issues.

[14] For example, the strengthening of renewable energies and the introduction of socioeconomic research in the Fourth Framework Programme (FP4) can be explained, at least partly, because of the strong push by the European Parliament to introduce these changes.

[15] Because governments, bound by a delicate equilibrium of many social and economic institutions, tend to reduce budgets in a linear way rather than to radically redeploy funding priorities.

[16] The example of 'technology assessment' institutions is striking. FAST, MONITOR, VALUE and the Targeted Socioeconomic Research Programme (successive EU programs with a strong TA component) have been institutional creations in reaction to which national institutions had or have to be built or strengthened in order to influence the European agenda and benefit from its likely results. But the institutionalization of technology assessment (TA) in European Community countries since the beginning of the eighties has had to some extent or can have in the future, in those countries which are lagging behind in this domain, consequences on national research institutions. The setting-up of new TA organizations and programs (e.g. in Belgium, the Netherlands, Germany) or the emergence of this issue in national policy agendas in Southern European countries are not completely independent from earlier European institution building in this field.

[17] SEC (2001) 1002: Commission staff working Paper *Progress Report on Benchmarking of National Research Policies.* 'Key Figures 2001' have also been published separately (ISBN 92-894-1183-X).

[18] Commission staff working paper *Benchmarking National RTD Policies: First Results,* Brussels (2002), SEC 129, 31 January 2002.

[19] See the report of the High Level Expert Group on the European dimension of foresight, *Thinking, Debating and Shaping the Future: Foresight for Europe,* April 2002, accessible at: http://www.cordis.lu/rtd2002/foresight/main.htm.

[20] The European Commission's communication on *The European Research Area: Providing New Momentum* published on 16 October 2002 provides an overview of progress made in reaching the objectives defined in January 2000 and proposes new mechanisms for moving forward (see European Commission 2002, p. 565 final).

[21] In an interview to the French magazine 'La Recherche' (N° 354, June 2002), Commissioner Busquin, in a forward looking statement, supports the view that, in a very long-term future where co-ordination of national research policies will have become routine, the need for a Framework Programme might well be questioned.

[22] An overview of European Council conclusions up to June 2003 has been prepared by the Greek Presidency, see http://europa.eu.int./comm/lisbon_strategy/pdf/thematic_lisbon_conclusions.pdf

REFERENCES

Andersen, S.S. and K.A. Eliassen (1993), The EC as a New Political System, in *Making Policy in Europe: the Europeification of National Policy-making*, London: Sage.

Caracostas, P. and U. Muldur (1997), *Society, the Endless Frontier*, Brussels and Luxembourg: European Communities Publication Office.

Caracostas, P. and L. Soete (1997), 'The Building of Cross-border Institutions in Europe: Towards a European System of Innovation?', in Edquist, C. (ed.), *Systems of Innovation – Technologies, Institutions and Organisations*, London: Pinter, pp. 395–408.

Dan-Nguyen, G., V. Schneider and R. Werle (1993), 'Networks in European Policy-making: Europeification of the Telecommunications Policy', in Andersen, S.S. and K.A. Eliassen (eds), *The EC As a New Political System*, London: Sage.

Edquist, C. (1997), *Systems of Innovation – Technologies, Institutions and Organisations*, Edquist, C. (ed.), London: Pinter.

European Commission (1994), *The European Report on Science and Technology Indicators 1994*, Brussels: European Commission.

European Commission (2000), *Towards a European Research Area*, Brussels, 18 January 2000: European Commission, COM (2000) 6.

European Commission (2001), *Employment in Europe 2001. Recent Trends and Prospects*, Brussels: European Commission.

European Commission (2002), *The European Research Area: Providing New Momentum*, European Commission Communication, Brussels: European Commission.

Gregersen, B., B. Johnson and A. Kristensen (1994), *National Systems of Innovation and European Integration*, paper presented to the EUNETIC conference on 'Evolutionary Economics of Technical Change: Assessment of Results and New Frontiers', Strasbourg: European Parliament, 6–8 October 1994.

Guzzetti, L. (1995), *A Brief History of European Union Research Policy*, Luxembourg: OPOCE.

Matthews, M. and F. McGowan (1992), *Reconciling Diversity and Scale: Some Questions of Method in the Assessment of the Costs and Benefits of European Integration 1992*, N° 59 1e tr. in N° Spécial de la Revue d'Economie Industrielle 'Technological Diversity and Coherence in Europe'.

Mazey, S. and J. Richardson (1993), *Lobbying in the European Community*, Oxford: Oxford University Press.

Muller, P. (1994), *La Mutation des Politiques Publiques*, N° Spécial de la revue Pouvoirs sur l'Europe de la Communauté à l'Union', April 1994.

North, D.C. (1990), *Institutions, Institutional Change and Economic Performance*, Cambridge: Cambridge University Press.

Reger, G. and S. Kuhlmann (1995), *European Technology Policy in Germany: the Impacts of European Community Policies Upon Science and Technology in Germany*, Heidelberg: Physica-Verlag.

SEC (2001), *Progress Report on Benchmarking of National Research Policies*, Commission staff working paper, Brussels: SEC (2001) 1002.

SEC (2002), *Benchmarking National RTD Policies: First Results*, Commission staff working paper, Brussels: SEC 129, 31 January 2002.

Sharp, M. and C. Shearman (1987), 'European technological collaboration', *Chatam House Papers*, **36**, The Royal Institute of International Affairs, London: Routledge & Kegan Paul.

Sidjanski, D. (1989), *Communauté Européenne 1992: Gouvernement de Comités*? N° 48, in N° Spécial de la revue Pouvoirs sur l'Europe 1993.

Telò, M. (2002), 'Governance and Government in the European Union: the Open Method of Coordination', in Rodrigues, M.J. (ed.), *The New Knowledge Economy in Europe*, Cheltenham, UK and Northhampton, MA, USA: Edward Elgar.

Teubal, M. (1996), 'R&D and technology policy in NICs as learning processes', *World Development*, **24**, N° 3, 449–60.

Tsipouri, L. and M. Xanthakis (1993), *Impact of the EC Science and Technology Policy on the Greek S/T Policy*, Athens: University of Athens.

3 Old Games, Old Players – New Rules, New Results

Influence and Agency in the European Research Area (ERA)

Chris Caswill[1]

INTRODUCTION

Science policy can be thought of as 'the actions, processes and institutions through which policy actors, individual or corporate, seek to shape scientific activity and outcomes' (Caswill 2001). Principal-agent theory and concepts have been used to explain these processes, the behavior of national science policy actors, and the relationships between different levels in science policy systems. They have been particularly useful in illuminating the relationship between funding agencies and the state apparatus which delegates the allocation of resources for scientific research to those agencies. (Braun 1998; Guston 1996; 2000).

Principal-agent theory has roots in discussions of regulation in the 1970s (Mitnick 1980). James Coleman provided the stimulus for the more recent use of these ideas in the study of science policy with his theoretical exposition of principal-agent transactions in *Foundations of Social Theory* (1990):

> This class of social transactions is fundamental, for it provides a means by which interests can be pursued far beyond the capacities of the original interested party. It is not the only such means but it is frequently used when an actor with interests to pursue has a sufficient quantity of resources, but not those of the appropriate kind to realise the interests (for example, has money but not the appropriate skills). He may then wish to use those resources to provide a kind of extension of self (p. 146).

Coleman rehearses the types of interdependence between actors, proposes laws of agency and discusses the types of relationships between principals and agents as part of his analysis of social relationships and systems of action.

The elaboration of principal-agent relationships as systems of delegation has provided the theoretical basis for a new approach to the study of science policy, which analyzes the resources used by principals such as Ministries of Science, or national Research Councils,[2] to pursue their interests by the recruitment of scientific actors for particular purposes. (Braun 1993; Caswill 1998; van der Meulen 1998).

Delegation relationships within science policy have been elaborated to show the 'moral hazard' which science policy principals experience because of the tendency of their actual and prospective agents to 'shirk' their responsibilities in pursuing their own interests. Moral hazard also flows from the asymmetry of the information available to principals and agents about the latter's social system and actions. The proposal that agents and principals will both want to maximize the realization of their own interests (Coleman 1990) and to minimize their dependence on each other (Braun 1993) has been extended to bring in the concept of principals and agents playing games (van der Meulen 1998).

Thus far principal-agent science policy literature has been concerned with science policy and resource allocation at the national level, within national systems of governance, where accountability can be clearly defined within the democratic nation state. This paper will consider the recent European Union (EU) proposals for a 'European Research Area' as supranational science policy in multi-level system of governance. Principal-agent concepts will be brought to bear in the analysis. This should provide an opportunity to assess how well the principal-agent perspective can be extended to supranational science policy issues. For example, how can the European Commission's relationship with the Member States be characterized? Braun (1993) has developed a tripartite Ministry–Agency–Research Institution model of science policy relations. Can this model be adapted to fit the complex multi-level science policy world of the European Union?

THE ARRIVAL OF THE ERA

The formal process of adoption of the ERA was remarkably swift. The European Commission published its proposals in January 2000 (European Commission 2000). The project was adopted by the EU Heads of State at their March 2000 European (summit) meeting in Lisbon. The European Parliament provided its strong support in a resolution agreed on 18 May 2000. This timetable would be extraordinary enough by European Union standards. It is all the more interesting because the ERA contains several radical proposals for the funding and organization of European research, with potentially large effects for both European and national research institutions.

In Lisbon, the Heads of State agreed to the main principles of the ERA 'project'. They called for more work to be done by the European Commission (in this case DG Research) on all the various details and instruments. Decisions taken by Heads of State at European Council meetings can often overlook important points of detail, as the British Prime Minister, Mrs Thatcher, discovered to her cost. The Lisbon Summit gave a remarkably strong push to the ERA. It provided the European Commission with an effective mandate to develop detailed proposals, and to incorporate many of those proposals into the upcoming Sixth Framework Programme (FP6).[3] In order to understand the significance of these events, and their causes, it is necessary first to review the background to the ERA and its key characteristics.

The idea of a European research space is not a new one. It has been at the heart of several earlier visions for European science, for example that of Ralph Dahrendorf in the 1970s (European Commission 1974; see also Banchoff in this volume). More recently Commissioner Ruberti returned to the issue (European Commission 1996). Ideas about co-ordination, co-operation and added value have been included in earlier FPs.

The European Commission's ERA proposals in 2000 differed from earlier attempts in several significant respects. They included several *fin de siècle* concerns – with the knowledge economy, with the utilization of science and technology, with the social contract between science and citizens. They did however share with earlier versions the sense that it is not enough just to identify the problems. Action was needed, and proposed. In this case, the call for action has borne fruit.

The ERA proposals arrived at a time when many key Member States had social democrat governments, positively engaged with these issues. The proposals included details and instruments which played well with the concerns of most, if not all Member States. They also played to current concerns about European Commission administration, by incorporating suggestions for the reduction of European Commission bureaucratic effort (and control), delegation of research award management to national research teams, reduction of process times, and building explicitly on national scientific and managerial capacity. The initial papers carefully avoided giving much attention to the awkward details, which were left for subsequent discussion.

The original authors of the ERA papers gave much emphasis to the novelty of their vision, going beyond the long standing rhetoric of competition and catch-up with the United States and Japan. The initial documents included a new emphasis on a partnership between the European Commission and Member States. This was a realistic recognition that European science policy is a long term and multi-layered process, in which DG Research and the next EU-FP would only be partial contributors. These were all important breaks with past rhetoric and ideology, which tended to emphasize the unique position of the European Commission as the guardian of the European element of science policy and the only effective European actor.

Historians and commentators with personal experience of the Lisbon Summit will in due course be able to unpack the processes at work in there. From this distance we can only look for plausible explanations. The drivers for the creation of the ERA proposal obviously lay within DG Research in the European Commission in Brussels. The original draft is believed to have been the work of a single hand within or close to the Busquin Cabinet. It was not the product of more conventional processes with the operational Directorates. Busquin himself was new to the job of Commissioner. Like all Research Commissioners, he must have found himself in a junior slot, looking for a way to enhance his role, station and impact. He will have been painfully aware of the fate of his predecessor, Mme Cresson, and anxious no doubt to put some distance between his leadership and hers. It is said that he has good connections to the Max Planck system in Germany, and this may have encouraged an approach which gave prominence to distributed and self-managed systems of national scientific excellence, and the idea of networks of excellent research groups which is one of the major ERA innovations.

The other powerful actors within DG Research are the Director General and the Directors. In the latter case, longstanding Directors with strong track records, business connections and national backing have in the past had a tight grip on DG Research policies. Their interests have been recognized in an important way by the identification of priority topics in FP6 which will provide continuing support for existing structures and power bases. It is interesting that DG Research will however lose some of its everyday powers through the delegation of project management to research centers and groups, which are inevitably located within national S&T systems. Opposition within DG Research to this radical change in delegation arrangements may have been weakened by a general weariness with the burden of micro-managing large and small projects, criticism by industry and Member States, criticisms by a series of internal reviews, and an eventual (if reluctant) recognition that DG Research could not develop and implement European science policy on its own. The ERA proposals seem to have found an inspired path through these internal minefields, adding credibility to the idea of an author experienced in local politics and thought processes.

After its adoption at the Lisbon Summit, the ERA proposals have been worked up in operational detail by DG Research and incorporated into the new FP (FP6). In this process, they have been subjected to the regular processes of negotiation with Ministries of Science in the Member States and with the European Parliament. In these discussions, the Commissioner and his DG Research colleagues pressed the point that the ERA project was both more ambitious and longer term than the FP, which can be seen as one of the instruments (albeit the largest one) for moving European science in new directions. The many actors who will contribute to the ways in which the European science system does move include of course the EU Heads of State, the EU Research Commissioner, his Cabinet, the Director General and the Directors within DG Research. Behind the Heads of State can be seen Ministers of Science and Ministry officials. European industry has well understood connections to DG Research and to national science policy actors.

European scientists are also influential actors. Although there is a perception that the FP is a very top-down process, scientists will have a large influence on FP6. All such programs are in any event shaped by the applications which are submitted by the best scientists, but in this case the influence is larger. The initial formal call was for the first time preceded by a 'pre-call' for Expressions of Interest in all the FP6 thematic priorities. DG Research have analyzed those inputs to see where academic research interests and strengths were clustered, and used this information for the development of the detailed work programs for the first call in December 2002.

In these processes there are signs of an increased sense of partnership between European and national levels, and between DG Research and the scientific community. As the commissioning of FP6 moves through its first phase, it still remains to be seen whether and how the European Commission, the national Research Councils, the European Science Foundation in Strasbourg and other funding agencies take up the ERA spirit of positive interaction.

THE ERA AS SUPRANATIONAL SCIENCE POLICY

The stated purpose of the ERA project is not only to shape the FP6 but also to influence science policy and scientific activity within European Union Member States (and associated countries). It explicitly recognizes that over 80 per cent of funding for science in Europe is provided outside DG Research. Its chosen paths are co-operation, delegation and co-ordination. It proposes at the same time to continue to fund new European science directly by means of the well-established FPs. Early adoption of the ERA in Lisbon allowed ERA principles and priorities to be included in the European Commission's proposals for FP6, which is formally took effect at the beginning of 2003.

This latest EU-FP is not only a response to the ERA. It has been created within the conventions, cultural practices and rules of European Union policymaking. The old familiar players have been engaged in the familiar games of negotiation, where the key actors pursue their different supranational, national, sectoral, scientific and corporate interests. At the same time, other actors have prepared proposals for scientific programs within rational and deliberate frameworks of consultation and scientific advice. This is a familiar EU policy mix.

The result is nevertheless a FP which differs from its predecessors in several important ways. It introduces new 'FP6 instruments', or mechanisms for funding research which reach in to national science systems in interesting ways, by co-opting national centers as managers of large-scale EU projects. It also includes at least two specific instruments for providing EU resources in support of national research programs and national science policies. In these important new ways, it has become not only a European science policy but a science policy for actors at multiple levels – a genuinely new kind of supranational science policy, consistent with the aims of the original ERA objectives. The new elements need now to be considered in more detail, in order to understand their likely effects.

ACTING ON THE ERA STAGE

There are many common elements between FP6 and its predecessor Programme. Many of the priority areas are continuations from the Fifth Framework Programme (FP5), for example information society, aeronautics, food, sustainable development and global change. Committee arrangements in Brussels look much as before, bringing together representatives of Ministries and other key national actors. Alongside these continuities, there are many new developments. Of these, the new mechanisms for funding the research, (instruments in Brussels terminology) are amongst the most visible. The European Commission has proposed and carried through a major reform of these funding instruments.

The Large Scale Instruments – Networks of Excellence and Integrated Projects

The previously dominant mechanism of 'shared-cost' research projects, which were normally modest scale research projects operating across three or more countries. In FP6, these are being superseded by two much larger-scale mechanisms, Integrated Projects and Networks of Excellence. The former are to be very large focused research projects, building on the idea of 'research platforms' in FP5. Integrated Projects will be led by a co-ordinating center to which the European Commission will make a substantial financial allocation to support the costs of managing the budget and the costs of co-operation between several research teams in different countries. It still remains to be seen how large Integrated projects will turn out to be – this is expected to vary across subject areas – but they will certainly be orders of magnitude larger in scale and ambition than shared-cost projects. Figures of tens or hundreds of millions of euros were quoted in early discussions.

Networks of Excellence are in many ways the more interesting of the two. Here the European Commission proposes support for joint programs of activity in networks of public and private sector centers of excellence with common work programs. Provision will be made for exchanges of staff and advanced use of electronic methods of work (European Commission 2000, op. cit.). These have been described as 'grants to support integration'. Funding is likely to be given for longer periods than in the past (probably five years) and awards are expected to be of several tens of millions of euros. The centers (or research groups) will need to be from at least three EU Countries.

In a radical break with the past, the European Commission proposes to make annual advance payments. The budget will be managed by the network, which will be required to include the competence for accountable self-management. Weight will be given in the evaluation process to management capacity as well as to scientific excellence. This represents a large increase in delegation from Brussels to national research centers.

Whilst this is a real increase in delegation to research teams, DG Research can be expected to pursue its goals by requiring Networks to act in some ways as agents of EU policy. It is likely, for example, to insist on their taking on a training role, to require them to set standards for communication with the public as well as other scientists, to insist on opportunities for researchers from accession states and on the implementation of EU gender policies within the networked centers. EU interests will in this way reach into the top national research institutions in completely new ways.

At the same time, Networks of Excellence may be attractive also for national Ministries of Science and Research Councils. They will foresee a European scientific agenda which is much more driven by the actual, current national priorities and leading edge capacities than by the internal policies of DG Research. Many Ministries and Research Councils will believe themselves capable of increasing their influence through contacts with national centers, by facilitating network building and through their own baseline funding of the centers in their own country.

Many individual actors will benefit from this innovation. Scientists in large high quality research centers in favored subject areas will have much to gain from this new mechanism. They will benefit from increased ability to move between institutes in different countries and from improved knowledge transfer. There will be less detailed contract and rule enforcement work for many European Commission officials, and opportunities for more direct engagement with science and its findings. New skills will be needed in DG Research, in research centers and in national agencies.

This will not, however, be a straightforward win–win situation. There are arguments about the use of the new FP6 instruments, about the effects of concentration on much fewer awards, about the selection and levels of aggregation of networks, about the delegation of management arrangements to research teams, about the inclusion of 'cohesion' criteria and accession country scientists – and of course about the ways in which the priority areas are being developed into detailed research programs.

This can be exemplified within the social sciences. Social scientists are already concerned about reduced availability of shared-cost projects and about the limitations of a funding mechanism based on centers and with high thresholds for minimum expenditure. EU funding opportunities are likely to be reduced, for example, for an anthropologist, historian or sociologist working in a small research group in a small country. The European Commission has had to concede some retention of shared-cost projects alongside the larger awards but the balance of opportunity (and power) has shifted towards larger-scale research activity.

Networking of National Programs

Early drafts of FP6 contained proposals for co-ordination and networking of national research programs which were both radical and contested. As has been seen, the ERA vision was innovative in its recognition that a ERA could not be constructed by action by the European Commission alone. It saw the need to draw in, and draw on, national programs of research as well as individual scientists. Obvious as this may now seem, DG Research had for decades pursued a combative unilateral policy based on the conviction that they alone spoke for Europe and ergo for European science. As a result the European Commission's scientific efforts outside the FP were for the most part limited to fruitless turf wars with national organizations, interspersed occasionally with time-consuming (and equally fruitless) attempts at co-ordination by committee and collection of information about national scientific programs.

Against this background, the ERA project was bold in its recognition of the need (and scope) for multi-level collaborative effort. In early policy manifestations, such as early FP drafts, much attention was given to a new form of support for co-operation between national research programs and the EU, which would depend on sophisticated parallel implementation of several Articles of the EU Treaty.[4] Of these, Article 169 was the most significant and this instrument has become known by that title. It is devised so as to allow FP funds to be used for the first time for the support of networked national program activity. The use of Article 169 for this purpose was endorsed by national science ministers in the European Research Council at an early stage (surprising many skeptical commentators), with the explicit requirement that this mechanism will be open to national Ministries of Science and agencies (e.g. national Research Councils) as well as to the European Commission. In practice, its use is severely limited by the fact that its origins in the Treaty articles make all Article 169 applications subject to co-decision by the European Parliament. As things stand, this leads to a long and complicated decision process and there are likely to be few takers unless the Parliament and the European Commission can agree on a streamlined process, which at the moment seems an unlikely prospect.

Faced with these difficulties, the European Commission has pursued the co-operative working agenda through another route. The more flexible if less ambitious ERA-NET proposal has been included within a small FP6 'Strengthening the European Research Area' budget line . Though the total €148 million allocated for ERA-NET is modest by comparison with other budget lines, ERA-NET may still bring about some large changes. Firstly, proposals can explicitly be limited to a small number of countries (three is the minimum), which may lead to use these funds in support of regional co-operation. This would be an important shift from previous insistence on EU-wide co-ordination activity. ERA-NET is also targeted at national research funding organizations such as Research Councils, which is completely new. It aims to bring about durable change in transnational co-operation in the support of research. It allows the co-ordination of pre-existing programs across countries, and the development of new parallel activities. Funds are available for networking for supporting studies, for improved co-ordination, for creating common intellectual property, and for opening up programs to researchers from other countries. Most importantly perhaps, one of the highest ERA-NET goals is the development of joint research priorities between several countries.

These proposals are particularly interesting because program co-ordination has been tried before without success – for example between European Social Science Research Councils such as the UK ESRC, the German DFG and the French CNRS, and between Nordic Social Science Councils. There are problems of differential timing, differing management styles, language and method. There have thus far been few incentives and many additional costs. The ambition of the European Commission now to be a partner with national Ministries and agencies may stimulate major changes in rules, decision-making, attitudes and behavior in national Research Councils and those national Ministries of Science which sponsor national science programs. Or it may be ignored. It is likely in any event to require similar changes of rules and attitudes within DG Research if it is to have the intended real and lasting effect.

THE ERA AS FP6

As has been seen, the European Commission promoted the ERA debate as a precursor to the debate on FP6. It also proposed the ERA as an ambitious longer term vision. The impact on the structure and operation of FP6 is now clearly visible, although this FP also has its roots in FP5, and in the familiar arguments and compromises between the usual actors.

If FP6 is the most significant practical manifestation of the ERA vision, the way in which it unfolds will determine whether new thinking within the ERA will have any significant impact on European science and science policy. The eventual down-stream implementation of the decisions on FP6 content, instruments, management arrangements and distribution of funds will have a large and possible crucial influence on which of the ambitions of the ERA can be delivered, and which are abandoned. It will in this way help determine whether the innovative co-operative vision of the ERA will survive beyond Commissioner Busquin and FP6. As a significant influence on the future organization of European science, FP6 is genuinely new.

NEW ACTORS ON THE STAGE

FP6 is also new in bringing some new actors on to the European science policy stage. In earlier versions of the FP 'games', national Research Councils have been the missing players. They have made only occasional appearances, or been curious members of the audience. These 'intermediary' organizations (Braun 1998) have until recently been marginal to European science policy – the missing links, so to speak. This began to change with the creation of the EUROHORCS (European Union Research Organisations Heads of Research Council) – a meeting of the Heads of many of the European Research Councils. The new FP6 instruments have begun to give more prominence to Research Council investments, as they will build upon national centers of excellence and national research programs. This offers Research Councils much bigger parts in the development of the ERA. Research Councils are also likely to be the main beneficiaries of the FP6 ERA-NET Programme, through which they are for the first time able to apply for Framework funds.

Any European future for national Research Councils will however be bound up with the fortunes of two other supranational institutions, namely the actual European Science Foundation (ESF) and the potential European Research Council (ERC). The ERA document calls for consideration of a European Council and the question of a supranational Research Council has already received much more serious attention than before, for example at the

Copenhagen Conference under the Danish Presidency in October 2002. In the meantime the ambitious but poorly-funded ESF has successfully bid for additional resources for building transnational research co-operation from within the same program which supports ERA-NET. It is making a strong bid for its place in the new ERA order. The national Research Councils have up until now been the main founders of the ESF, but again ERA-FP6 is disturbing the status quo in European science policy. It is not at all clear who will be left standing when the music stops.

WINNING AND LOSING IN THE ERA GAME

The implementation of the ERA through FP6 is changing the allocation of money for scientific research, and further downstream effects are clearly foreseen. As a result, there are gains and losses in sight for the main players in this new European science policy domain.

As the author of the ERA vision, the European Commission stands to get considerable benefit from the additional legitimacy which the ERA gives to the FP at Governmental level, and the outreach which it provides into national science systems. DG Research is becoming a visible and significant European science policy actor. The attention now being given to research at Head of State level must also give DG Research some restored credibility inside the European Commission. In practical terms, it will also benefit from the reduced operating costs of managing Networks of Excellence and Integrated Projects. On the other hand, it has had to accept very publicly that it is only one relatively small player among many in European science policy game.[5] The converse of its reaching out into national S&T systems is that it risks handing over its scientific agenda to the larger influence of the national agencies and scientific actors, who will tend to have closer links to their research systems than DG Research can hope to achieve.

At the national level, responses (and effects) will vary across countries and across the sciences. Large countries and large research institutions may get most financial benefit from the new FP6 instruments but will at the same time be most influenced by European Commission funding decisions. Smaller EU countries and accession states can be expected to worry about being marginalized in Networks of Excellence, excluded from significant participation in Integrated Projects and from co-ordination of programs through use of Article 169. This will be particularly serious for those countries like Spain and Portugal whose science polices have tracked FP priorities over the years. The cost and benefits for national Ministries of Science may then be the mirror image of those faced by the European Commission. The main recipients of money risk loss of influence, because of the new scope which the European

Commission will have to make new alliances at the national level, for example with Research Councils who are the Ministries' national agents, or with large and important national science centers. From public pronouncements however, it seems that many Ministries have not yet looked this far ahead and have confined their assessment of FP6 to welcoming the reductions in European Commission running costs and the move away from hands-on micro-management in Brussels which the new FP6 instruments will bring.

National institutions like Research Councils, whose objectives are focussed on support for high quality science in their countries, may also have grounds to be nervous of some of the ERA agenda – for example the co-ordination ambitions embedded within the FP6 instruments like Article 169 and ERA-NET allow the European Commission to begin to influence the shape of national Research Council decisions. Framework funding for Networks of Excellence will also begin to make national centers dependent on EU support for the maintenance of their international links and large-scale support through Integrated Projects will is bound to change patterns of national research. On the other hand, Research Councils who see themselves as international players may also welcome this as an opportunity to secure resources and incentives for co-operative research activity, leading to new advances in knowledge and better use of scarce resources. To achieve this, they will need be active and well informed if they are to be real beneficiaries of the new co-operative ERA vision.

Scientists are also likely to have mixed views about the changes in FP6 and to be less interested in the larger-scale policy debates. Though increased freedom from Brussels micro-management will be generally welcomed, the price for this is the additional and very demanding management tasks associated with leading (or even participating in) the new large-scale funding instruments. There is also concern that FP6 will contribute to further centralization of resources within a few privileged institutions. Those working in subjects which traditionally operate on a smaller scale may regret the eventual loss of the diverse networks financed by smaller-scale shared-cost projects which have helped to build up new European scientific co-operation (Redclift et al. 2000; Pohoryles 2002).

DG RESEARCH AS A SCIENCE POLICY PRINCIPAL

The ERA proposals can be seen as an attempt to disturb the relationships between the main actors in European science policy – Member States and their Ministries of Science, national funding agencies, scientific actors and of course the European Commission itself as represented by DG Research. Because of the ERA's influence on the structure and operation of the FP6, it has already introduced flows of influence and new types of social and political transactions. Delegation arrangements are being explicitly changed, new interests are being promoted and some of the old FP interests either abandoned or much reduced. As the institutional author of the ERA project, DG Research can seen in Coleman's terms as 'an actor with interests to pursue', with resources but not those of the appropriate kind to realize those interests (Coleman 1990, p. 146). In this principal-agent analysis, the ERA and FP6 are then the financial, policy and rhetorical resources which DG Research has used to pursue its interests by recruiting others to its purposes.

There are several specific examples of how these ideas of agency and principal-agent relationships illuminate the ERA story. The progress of the ERA project from an individual internal paper to European Commission corporate policy, to international science policy and an instrument of change in national science policies has been remarkable. It has moved rapidly across institutions and across the multiple levels of European governance. There are no doubt many complex reasons for this progress, which are beyond the scope of this paper. We can however look for the driving force for DG Research to push the ERA project in its need to enhance its autonomy from its formal principals, the EU Member States and the various European Councils. The ERA vision provides DG Research with new legitimacy as a quasi-independent European science policy actor. It has now for example enabled it to produce a report criticizing its principals for their slowness in implementing the ERA proposals. It seems certain to enable DG Research to exert new influence on national science systems by linking up with centers of research excellence and creating new dependencies on EU money.

As with all principal-agent relationships, however, this is by no means one-way traffic in terms of influence and interests. DG Research abandoned its close management of research projects, as part of its attempt to persuade Member States and other key actors to adopt the new FP6 instruments. In this it is increasing the ability of the national scientific actors to 'shirk' from their responsibilities to Brussels and oversight of the new arrangements will put substantial new demands on the small numbers of staff in Brussels. The outcome of the new instruments in terms of balance of influence is also not at all clear. Whilst DG Research is likely to become a bigger player in national funding systems, the dynamics of FP6 are such that DG Research now depends heavily on the research teams which have been set up by national finance and within national priorities. In that sense, DG Research also risks becoming the agent of national decision-making. The ebb and flow of those interests over the next few years will determine the outcome of the ERA, and will provide an important opportunity for the study of European science policy.

In another interesting innovatory development, the combination of the ERA and FP6 will bring the national Research Councils much more into the European science policy arena. The opportunities for use of Article 169 may be limited by process complexities but ERA-NET will promote new relationships between DG Research and national funding agencies. The ERA-NET scheme has clear ambitions to achieve durable change in transnational co-operation in priority setting and may turn out to be one of the unexpected stars of FP6. For national Research Councils it offers the opportunity to establish partnerships outside their normal relationships with the Ministries of Science who are their formal and very real principals, but may in the longer term produce another constraint on their ability to act independently in the setting of research priorities. The tripartite model of Ministry–Research Council–Scientific actor relationships (Braun 1993; Caswill 1998) needs to be adapted to a fourth dimension to take account of this new disturbance in the national systems.

There is another principal-agent concept which can shed new light on these events. One of the key elements in the principal-agent relationship is perceived to be the asymmetry in the information available to them. In brief, the principal has resources but is not well informed. This can be illustrated by the case of the science ministry and the Research Council, where the value and influence of the Research Council is much increased by the better information which it has about the current state of science, and about the scientific actors. Additionally the ministry is typically not well informed about the activities of the Research Council which it is attempting to use as its agent. DG Research is perhaps one of the most striking examples of an institution suffering from asymmetry of information, very distant from national systems, institutions and processes of science which are distributed over a large geographical area. It employs various mechanisms to reduce this asymmetry, including inviting scientists to Brussels, and paying detailed attention to project reports. In this analysis, the innovation of the pre-call for FP6 Expressions of Interest can be seen as a further imaginative step in to improve the information base. If DG Research uses its new networks of contacts with Networks of Excellence and Integrated Projects equally imaginatively, it could have an important new information resource, but it also risks losing contact with the more distributed levels of scientific activity (Pohoryles 2002).

In summary, we can see that the arrival and implementation of the ERA has disturbed the traditional picture of DG Research and the European Commission as the straightforward agent of the European Member States. It was the active author of proposals which seem likely to provide it with a new set of relationships with ministries, but also with national Research Councils (and their analogues) and scientific actors. There are some ways in which it is seeking to recruit those Research Councils and scientists and scientific institutions to act on its behalf. But the changes being made also allow those actors the possibility of more influence in European science policy, which makes for an uncertain future for the ERA vision. This uncertainty is increased by the likely departure of the Commissioner Busquin in 2004, by the debates around the European Research Council (which could become another major actor, and disturber of the new status quo) and the outcome of the Convention, which will also impact on the balance of influence in European science policy. These games will be played out in the development of the next FP, also destined to be 'new'.

CONCLUSIONS

This paper began with the assertion that the ERA is a science policy project. FP6 has emerged as an instrument for change, albeit with roots in the past. The ERA project has become a science policy with the potential for significant effect on the balance of interests and influence within European science. Although it was only launched three years ago, some tentative policy conclusions can be already be drawn from its early years. Firstly, the creation of effective science policy benefits from beginning with a vision for science which speaks to the needs of today as well as to the longer term future. Secondly, timing is crucial. The swift passage of the ERA from internal document to adoption by European Heads of State is an example of the windows of opportunity for effective new policy which open from time to time, when conservative forces are in some way neutralized or at least weakened. The story of the rapid adoption of the ERA also shows the importance of pitching policy at the right level and ensuring that it offers benefits to a necessary variety of key actors. Multiple visions and multiple interests need to be provided with provided with both space and opportunity. If science policy is a game involving many principals and agents (van der Meulen 1998), then policy will be best crafted if it allows for the interests of many principals to be accommodated, and for opportunities for active agents to exert some influence in the dynamic implementation of the policy detail. Effective delivery will be achieved by the incorporation over time of a variety of actors who expect to gain some benefit from policy implementation. Successful policy is a process rather than a one-off intervention.

This paper began with the intention to review the contribution of principal-agent to the understanding of science policy outside national systems of science. Principal-agent concepts have provided a useful analysis of supranational activities and relationships, but the one dimensional models used at the national level have been shown to need adaptation to cope with multiple principals and multiple levels of agency.

The ERA story is one of change and continuity, and of science policy operating at different levels of governance. Principal-agent analysis has illuminated this transnational and multi-level picture, bring out underlying processes of disturbance of institutions and the relationships between them. It has also pointed up the importance of continuing to study of the fate of Commissioner Busquin's ERA project.

NOTES

[1] UK Economic and Social Research Council, the views expressed are personal and do not reflect the view of the UK ESRC.
[2] The term 'Research Council' is used here to describe public sector non-departmental agencies tasked with funding scientific research, at arms length from Government, e.g. the German Deutsche Forschungsgemeinschaft, the UK Economic and Social Research Council, and the Academy of Finland.
[3] 'Framework Programmes' are the public research and development programs of the European Union, proposed and managed by the Directorate General for Research (DG Research, formerly DG XII) within the European Commission.
[4] Articles 163-2 (contextual regulations), 164 ('Framework Programmes'), 165 (policy coordination), 168 (programs complementary to the FP), and 169 (multilateral programs with or without European Community participation).
[5] This balance may change again after the European Convention, depending on the view taken there on responsibilities for R&D.

REFERENCES

Braun, D. (1993), 'Who governs intermediary agencies? Principal agent relations in research policy making', *Journal of Public Policy*, **13** (2), 135–62.
Braun, D. (1998), 'The role of funding agencies in the cognitive development of science', *Research Policy*, **27** (8), 135–62.
Caswill, C. (1998), 'Social science policy: challenges, interactions, principals and agents', *Science and Public Policy*, **25** (5), 286–96.
Caswill, C. (2001), 'Science Resource Decisions – Principals, Agents and Games', in Siune, K. (ed.), *Science Policy – Setting the Agenda for Research*, proceedings of the MUSCIPOLI Aarhus Workshop, 27–28 September 2001, Aarhus: Danish Institute for Studies in Research and Research Policy, pp. 13–17.
Coleman, J. (1990), *Foundations of Social Theory*, Harvard: Harvard University Press.
European Commission (1996), *Coordination Through Cooperation*, Brussels: European Commission.
European Commission (2000), *Towards a European Research Area*, communication from the Commission to the Council, the European Parliament, the Economic and Social Committee and the Committee of the Regions, Brussels: European Commission, COM (2000) 6.
Guston, D. (1996), 'Principal-agent theory and the structure of science policy', *Science and Public Policy*, **24** (4), 229–40.

Guston, D. (2000), *Between Politics and Science: Assuring the Integrity and Productivity of Research*, Cambridge, UK: Cambridge University Press.

Mitnick, B.M. (1980), *The Political Economy of Regulation: Creating, Designing and Removing Regulatory Forms*, New York: Columbia University Press.

Pohoryles, R.J. (2002), 'The making of the European Research Area: a view from Research Networks', *Innovation. The European Journal of Social Science Research*, **15** (4), 325–40.

Redclift, M., E. Shove, B. van der Meulen and S. Raman (2000), *Social Environmental Research in the European Union*, Cheltenham, UK and Northhampton, MA, USA: Edward Elgar.

van der Meulen, B. (1998), 'Science policies as principal agent games: institutionalisation and path dependency in the relation between government and science', *Research Policy*, **27** (4), 397–414.

Wilks, S. and I. Bartle (2002), 'The unintended consequences of creating independent competition agencies', *West European Politics*, **25** (1), 148–72.

4 Political Dynamics of the ERA

Thomas Banchoff

INTRODUCTION

At their Lisbon summit in March 2000, European Union (EU) leaders endorsed an ambitious goal: to make the EU 'the most competitive and dynamic knowledge-based economy in the world' by the year 2010 (European Council 2000). This was visionary rhetoric. But it was also more than that. While the ambition of surpassing the United States may or may not be realistic, European leaders are clearly committed to it in both word and deed. They continue to articulate the goal of being number one. And they have initiated a range of policies designed to bring the goal within reach – everything from the successful introduction of a single currency to competition policy reform and a range of Internet initiatives. This chapter examines a key part of this effort, the 'European Research Area' (ERA). Launched in January 2000 and endorsed in Lisbon, the ERA is an ambitious effort to pool European scientific and technological resources more effectively. This chapter seeks to explain the emergence of the ERA initiative, its initial successes in the face of considerable resistance, and its implications for both the study of European integration and EU efforts to compete with the United States.

The ERA is only the latest effort to co-operate on research matters within the EU. Since the 1960s a series of European leaders have called for the better co-ordination of national efforts to take on the American and Japanese competition. Those efforts have met with only limited success. EUREKA, an intergovernmental program in support of technological development, has grown since the 1980s. Within the EU framework, successive five-year EU Framework Programmes (FP) have provided increasing levels of funding to transnational networks of researchers in firms, universities, and public laboratories. The FP now constitutes the third largest item in the EU budget, alongside the Common Agricultural Policy (CAP) and the Structural Funds. Despite these achievements, however, national research policies still overshadow European-level efforts. EU expenditures only amount to about 5 per cent of public civil research spending within the Union, almost all state support flows to national researchers and institutions, and cross-national researcher mobility remains restricted. No integrated European space for science and technology exists.

The ERA, championed by Research Commissioner Philippe Busquin, aims to counteract national fragmentation and create such a space. It encompasses, but also goes beyond, a reform of the FP. Two new large-scale instruments, Integrated Projects and Networks of Excellence, are designed to break with previous FP's emphasis on smaller projects and create more 'European Added Value'. A third, more ambitious instrument is EU participation in research co-operation sponsored jointly by two or more Member States. Beyond the confines of the FP, the ERA involves a number of initiatives, including the benchmarking of national best practices, better cross-national researcher mobility, and improvements in research infrastructure. The overall goal, Busquin told a Berlin audience in January 2001 Berlin address, was to make the ERA 'in the research sector what the single market has been for commercial exchanges' (Busquin 2001).

Three years after its launching, the ERA has not yet fulfilled this ambitious agenda. Under pressure from entrenched interests – the smaller research networks that prospered under the previous FPs, and their allies in the European Parliament and national research establishments – the European Commission backed down from its initial insistence on the exclusivity of the new instruments. At least some funding was to flow through the established, more diffuse channels. The Member States represented in the Council of Ministers, or Research Council, gave a lukewarm reception to EU involvement in their bilateral and multilateral co-operation. Nevertheless, the Council did endorse the ERA and a modified European Commission proposal for the Sixth Framework Programme (FP6) (2002–06) at their December 2001 meeting. And while progress was slow in other areas, such as benchmarking and researcher mobility, High Level Groups of national civil servants went to work and began to share data and formulate recommendations. If the ERA was developing slowly, it was nevertheless moving forward.

What accounts for the launching of the ERA and its initial successes? After some discussion of the inability of intergovernmentalism and neofunctionalism to address this question satisfactorily, the chapter underscores the influence of three factors: policy ideas, structural conditions, and political entrepreneurship. The idea of closer research policy co-ordination at the heart of the ERA had a long history going back to the 1960s – a history of failure in practice. But under permissive conditions of the late 1990s, namely growing *national* concerns about a new 'technological gap' with the United States in the late 1990s, the European Commission was able to develop the co-ordination idea without encountering strong member state resistance. Political entrepreneurship – skilful efforts to push the ERA idea in the face of considerable institutional resistance from policy networks attached to the status quo – was a further necessary ingredient for initial successes. The absence of any of the three factors would have made the ERA unlikely. The presence of all three does not necessarily portend its success. But two years after its launching, the ERA has emerged as a central part of EU strategy to match and surpass the United States in the global knowledge economy.

EXPLAINING RESEARCH INTEGRATION

Neither intergovernmentalism nor neofunctionalism is well equipped to explain the development of EU research policy. Both conceive of integration as a shift of sovereignty from the national to the supranational level. The approaches differ over the likelihood of such shifts, and over what drives the integration process – national interests for intergovernmentalists, problem solving for neofunctionalists. These established approaches shed light on a variety of policy areas where shifts of sovereignty are clearly on the agenda, including trade, agriculture, and monetary policy. They are less adept in cases where sovereignty is shared between the national and supranational levels or vested mainly at the national level, such as social, cultural, environmental, or foreign and defense policy. Ambiguity in these and other issue areas has contributed to the rise of multi-level approaches that resist the national v. supranational categories that inform the leading theories (Marks, Hooghe and Blank 1996).

Both the strong national foundations of research policy and its institutional complexity militate against intergovernmentalism and neofunctionalism as explanatory strategies. In *France in the Age of the Scientific State*, Robert Gilpin argued persuasively as early as 1968 that science was becoming 'the most critical single factor in military power, economic growth, and public welfare' (Gilpin 1968). The strategic importance of science, evident in the rise of new industries of the post-war decades – nuclear energy, mainframe computer, and aerospace – made science and technology a strategic priority across the industrialized democracies. Different post-war scientific state rested on contrasting historical and institutional foundations from one country to the next. Different systems of national laboratories had grown up since the mid-1800s to tackle the exigencies of state-building. University-based science reflected very different national trajectories of higher education. And industrial research and development was framed by different patterns of corporate organization and government regulation. This institutional complexity, combined with considerations of national interest have tended to rule out major transfers of sovereignty from the state to a central set of European institutions.

It does not follow, however, that no integration can take place in the research sector. It can move along two paths. First, EU institutions can develop their own policy competencies alongside the nation state, giving rise to a situation of multi-level governance. This is evident in the case of the FPs, which have emerged since the early 1980s as sources of European funding alongside the national. Second, the EU can emerge as a context for the co-ordination of national policies in particular areas. Through use of its own policy instruments and appeals to a common European political interest, the European Commission can persuade Member States to exchange information, share best practices, and pursue common goals in order to strengthen the EU – and its constituent states – in the international arena. Such a regulatory strategy, while less ambitious, is better suited to the realities of entrenched national institutions and policies across a range of issue areas and to the dangers of over-centralization within a larger and more diverse Union. The Council of Ministers first adopted the principle of co-ordination in the area of unemployment at the 1997 Luxembourg summit. Since then, the Prodi Commission has incorporated a new emphasis on regulation and co-ordination into its 2001 White Paper on Governance. That emphasis is evident in the ERA project as well.

How can one explain the emergence of integration, conceived not as the transfer of sovereignty driven by national interests or functional imperatives, but as regulation and co-ordination at the European level? This chapter examines the interaction of ideas, structural constraints, and political entrepreneurship in the case of the ERA. As long as key actors conceive of integration as the transfer of sovereignty – and by extension, as a zero-sum game linking Member States and the EU – they are unlikely to shift to a co-ordination agenda. The turn to co-ordination requires a reconceptualization of the integration process. To be successful, however, that turn must also fit the operative structural constraints – the interests of the leading Member States. Where sensitive national interests are in play, governments are unlikely to press for more integration. But if co-ordination meshes with and reinforces policies pursued at the national level, co-ordination may muster the requisite member state support. Finally, to be successful, the co-ordination strategy requires successful political entrepreneurship. Any policy innovation engenders resistance from entrenched interests attached to the status quo – whether national bureaucracies, clients of existing EU programs, or civil servants within the European Commission itself. Political skill and leadership is necessary to overcome such opposition and institutionalize the new departure.

POLICY COORDINATION: AN IDEA WITH A HISTORY

The idea of policy co-ordination, a critical component of the ERA initiative, has a long history. Its roots go back to the 1950s, when first efforts were made to bring science and technology into the integration process go back to the 1950s (Peterson and Sharp 1998; Guzetti 1995). The European Atomic Energy Community (EURATOM), founded with the 1957 Treaty of Rome, was designed to pool European efforts in a cutting edge technology deemed central to the Community's economic development and modernization. Very quickly, though, conflicting national interests and France's determination to develop its own nuclear industry and military capacity reduced the scale of the EURATOM. What was to be an ambitious joint industrial policy project ended up as a loose network of European research laboratories dwarfed by their national counterparts. The reconstruction of science and technology in Europe took place on national foundations.

During the 1960s, concerns about a 'technology gap' with the US revived interest in closer European co-operation (Servan-Schreiber 1968; Layton 1969). Alarm about a 'brain drain' to the United States and an invasion of high technology American multinationals placed co-ordination on the Community agenda. Member states set up a committee in 1965 to recommend areas of joint action and ways to compare and co-ordinate national research policies. As it happened, these initial efforts lost political momentum with De Gaulle's 'empty chair' policy in Brussels, rejection of British Community membership, and rocky Franco-German relations. When Altiero Spinelli, appointed Commissioner for Industrial Affairs, General Research and Technology in 1970, floated the idea of a powerful European Science Foundation, he got a chilly reception. Research co-operation grew within Europe, but mainly on an intergovernmental, not a Community basis – through the European Center for Nuclear Research (CERN), the European Space Agency (ESA) and other arrangements.

After De Gaulle's departure, the idea of research policy co-ordination re-emerged. At their October 1972 Paris Summit, EU leaders supported the principle of 'co-ordination of national policies and the definition of projects of Community interest in the areas of science and technology' (Guzetti 1995, p. 52). Ralf Dahrendorf, who assumed leadership of the Directorate General for Research, Science and Education created in 1973, elaborated the idea in an 'Action Programme'. He called on Member States to 'harmonize national procedures relating to decisions on concerting R&D budget decisions' and provide 'systematic information' on their national own research policy initiatives (European Commission 1974, p. 10). The goal was the creation of a 'single area for European Science' through 'lowering national barriers in scientific research'. In the context of the oil shock and subsequent recession, the Council's response to these ambitious efforts was tepid. In January 1974 it authorized the creation of a Committee on Science and Technical Research (CREST) designed to monitor national policies and explore possibilities for co-operation. But CREST had no real power. Research policies continued to develop along different national paths.

The European Community's (EC) research policy that did take shape in the early 1980s in the context of the Single Market drive did not draw on Dahrendorf's ideas. In the context of concerns about the Japanese challenge, Etienne Davignon, Commissioner for Industry and later Education and Research, secured support for funds to assist European industry in high technology areas. In 1983, two of those programs, the European Strategic Programme for Research and Development (ESPRIT) for information technologies and the Research and Development in Advanced Communication Technologies (RACE) for communications technologies, were bundled with others into a multi-year FP later institutionalized within the Single European Act. As funding for subsequent FPs increased, the Community gradually emerged as an important source of research funds *alongside Member States* for re-searchers in industrial, university, and public laboratories. The underlying idea was distributive more than regulative – to increase overall funding rather than to foster research policy co-ordination across Member States. And over time, the FP became associated with a third value – cohesion, i.e. the reduction of differences in science and technological potential across the Community (Peterson and Sharp 1998, chapter 4).

The early 1990s saw a first attempt to revive the idea of co-ordination. On taking over as Research Commissioner in 1993, Antonio Ruberti argued that the EU should move from the 'simple juxtaposition' of national programs to the establishment of a 'truly European research policy'. He did not ignore the reality of the FP but argued that the co-ordination across national research programs could be fostered through EU funding and participation (Ruberti 1993). Ruberti formalized his approach in an October 1994 communication entitled 'Research and Technological Development: Achieving Coordination Through Co-operation' (European Commission 1994). The proposal called on Member States to identify strategic areas for multinational co-operation to which the European Commission could contribute and to set up a committee to explore the possibility of opening national programs to researchers from other countries. In keeping with Dahrendorf's approach, the European Commission was to assume an important regulatory role outside the distributive confines of the FP.

Ruberti's vision of a 'European scientific and technological space' did not materialize (André and Ruberti 1995). At their April 1993 meeting, the Research ministers called for better 'co-ordination between national R&D programmes and between national and Community R&D Programmes'. But in the context of fiscal austerity amid recession – and the political crisis that accompanied the ratification of the Maastricht Treaty – they were not inclined to support new policy initiatives. Both the German and French Council presidencies in late 1994 and early 1995 saw member state efforts to better monitor FP formulation and implementation – not to embrace a broader co-ordination agenda. National research bureaucracies were not inclined to cede power to Brussels. And program clients – groups of researchers who benefited from existing funding streams – were not supporters of change. By the time Jacques Santer replaced Jacques Delors as President of the European Commission and Edith Cresson took over as Research Commissioner in 1995, Ruberti's approach had achieved little.

Five years later, after Cresson's departure amid scandal and the resignation of the entire European Commission, Philippe Busquin and his closest advisors drew explicitly on the ideas of Dahrendorf and Ruberti in developing the ERA initiative. They acknowledged the FP as a starting point, but placed it within a broader context. Within the FP, Networks of Excellence were designed to link up *national* centers of excellence, providing a framework for the exchange of researchers and the sharing data and facilities. Integrated Projects, a break with the FP's focus on smaller projects, were to bring large research teams together from the private and public sectors in at least three countries together to develop strategic technologies. In accordance with Article 169 of the Maastricht Treaty, which explicitly allowed for research policy co-ordination, the European Commission hoped to co-sponsor intergovernmental research projects and open national funding streams to researchers from other countries. Outside the FP, the European Commission revived the idea of sharing information on national programs, comparing best practices, and lowering barriers to researcher mobility, a co-ordination agenda that harkened back to the views of Dahrendorf and Ruberti. In marked contrast to the earlier failures, these ideas now fell upon fertile ground.

PERMISSIVE STRUCTURAL CONDITIONS: NATIONAL REFORM DRIVES

The evolution of EU research policy indicates that European Commission initiatives have traditionally risen and fallen with the support and opposition of Member States. First efforts to co-ordinate research policy in the mid-1960s coincided with a wave of national concern about a transatlantic 'technology gap', while Dahrendorf's efforts foundered as governments grappled with the recessions of the 1970s. Ruberti's 'co-ordination through co-operation' initiative, elaborated amid renewed concerns about European competitiveness, did not secure member state support in a context of fiscal austerity, recession, and post-Maastricht crisis in the early 1990s. For policy innovation at the European level to take place – in the research policy area or others – member state *initiative* is not a necessary condition. The European Commission can take the lead. But to win the support of Member States and take effect, EU-level innovation must reinforce, or at least not contradict, the interests of key states.

Such a constellation was in place in 2000–02. Busquin launched the ERA at a time when the three leading scientific powers – Germany, Great Britain, and France – were engaged in reforms of national research policies. In light of concerns about national competitiveness in science-based industries dominated by the United States – information, communication, and biotechnology in particular – all three governments endorsed changes in two directions: more competition within the public research sector and more co-operation with the private sector in strategic technology areas. Busquin's new instruments had the same underlying logic: Networks of Excellence to foster collaboration between the best research institutions, mainly in the public sector, and Integrated Projects that would focus on large-scale technological collaboration across public, university, and industrial labs. Other aspects of the ERA, such as the systematic comparison of 'best practices', had the potential to reinforce reform at the national level. The compatibility between European co-ordination and national reform, addressed below in the key cases of Germany, France, and Great Britain, constituted a permissive structural constraint for the ERA initiative.

Germany

As Germany emerged out of its post-reunification recession and grappled with the fiscal constraints of the drive for monetary union, concerns grew loud about its relative position within the global knowledge economy. Overall research and development spending fell from 2.9 per cent of GDP in 1989 to 2.4 per cent in 1995. While still Europe's overall scientific leader, the Federal Republic ranked behind Great Britain, France and the United States in papers and citations per unit of scientific expenditure, as well as papers per researcher (Higher Education Funding Council of England [HEFC] 2000). Furthermore, the German share of leading science-based industries declined in 1995–97 – biotechnology from 17.8 to 14.8 per cent and information technology from 7.9 to 6.8 per cent (Bundesministerium für Bildung und Forschung [BMBF] 2000). Against this backdrop, the Ministry of Education and Research claimed that 'the international competitiveness of German research was in jeopardy'. On coming to power in late 1998, the government of Gerhard Schröder pledged to address the problem.

Schröder and Edelgard Bulmahn, his Education and Research Minister, initiated a series of reforms designed to improve the competitiveness of the public sector and spur more co-operation with industry. Public sector reform focused on universities and the Helmholtz institutes, major research facilities that devoured 20 per cent of the ministry's budget. In an effort to stanch the flow of scientific talent to the United States and trim the power of the German professoriate within the state-financed university system, the government created Junior Professorships, a partial approximation of the US 'Assistant Professor' model. By giving young scientists more autonomy and resources, the reform aspired to energize a university research enterprise dominated by 'the patriarchal tutelage of the old professorial system'. Bulmahn pitched the model to German postdocs in the United States, urging them to return home with the promise that 'in future the motto will be "sink or swim" in Germany, too' (Bulmahn 2001). Reforms of the 'Big Science' Helmholtz Institutes also sought to spur competition. In 2000–01, government reduced the guaranteed funding of the individual institutes and compelled them to compete with one another for project-based research support.

The 'reordering of the research landscape' (Bulmahn) included efforts to spur more co-operation between public sector and industry research in developing cutting-edge technologies. In 2001 the government transferred a set of information technology institutes from Helmholtz to the Fraunhofer Society, a network of public laboratories that worked closely with industry to translate scientific and technical knowledge into new products and processes. Other initiatives included new funds for collaboration between public laboratories and industry in 'future areas' (Bulmahn) – the life sciences, information and communications technology, microelectronics, and nanotechnology. And in March 2001 the government moved to facilitate the exploitation of scientific research through greater protection for intellectual property. These efforts, flanked by related initiatives at the level of Germany's federal states, marked a break with the cautious incrementalism of the early and mid-1990s.

France

A parallel reform drive unfolded in France in the late 1990s. On coming into power in early 1997, Prime Minister Lionel Jospin argued in his first address on science and technology that 'the international competition of the next century will be a battle of intelligence' (Jospin 1997). His government commissioned a series of reports to gauge France's position within the global knowledge economy and recommend policy changes. One influential report underscored a decline in the proportion of French GDP committed to research and development – from 2.45 per cent to 2.26 per cent between 1993–96 – and the country's weak position in new strategic sectors, ICT and biotechnology. It also noted France's proportionally large and inflexible public research sector and comparably low levels of corporate investment in research and development (Cohen 1999). Jospin's two ministers for science and technology, first Claude Allègre and then Roger-Gérard Schwarzenberg, sought to strengthen France's research capacity as the principal motor of competitiveness, growth, and employment.

As in Germany, efforts to reform the public sector emphasized more competition among laboratories and more opportunities for young scientists. Allègre's effort to reform the massive National Center for Scientific Research, a network of public laboratories with some 12 000 researchers in 1200 laboratories, ran up against considerable opposition. The rank and file, represented in strong unions, impeded government efforts to set research priorities from above and shift funds to competitive university-based funding. A more successful effort to spur competition was the creation of 'National Science Funds' to distribute funding not to institutions, but to high quality projects. Between 1996 and 2001 the government more than quadrupled the funds to about FRF1 billion. As in Germany, efforts to increase the competitiveness of the public sector also targeted young researchers. More – and more attractive – posts were designed to counteract the emigration of young scientists educated in France. The country's educational institutions, Schwarzenberg insisted, should not operate 'for the benefit of big foreign countries which, more and more, are our rivals in international scientific, technological, and economic competition'.

Efforts to reform the public sector were flanked by measures to increase co-operation between public and university laboratories, on the one hand, and industry, on the other. The 1999 'Law on Innovation' was a milestone. It included legislation to facilitate movement personnel between public institutes and corporations and back again, and funding streams to encourage joint research projects across the public–private divide. The law also set up venture capital funds for high technology start ups and created a legal framework for the commercialization of scientific knowledge developed within the public sector. Related efforts included the 'National Technology Funds', designed to foster co-operation between public labs and industry in strategic sectors, which saw its funding double to FRF1 billion by 2002. As in the case of the Federal Republic, it is too early to evaluate the overall impact of these efforts. But they mark the most sustained effort to reform the French scientific state in two decades.

Great Britain

Reform was also on the agenda in Great Britain. Here, a key juncture was the 1993 White Paper, *Realising Our Potential: A Strategy for Science, Engineering and Technology*. The paper noted Great Britain's traditionally low levels of investment in science and technology – under 2 per cent of GDP – and its weak position in the ICT field in particular (White Paper 1993). On taking office in 1997, Tony Blair insisted that Great Britain should 'live up to the challenge of the knowledge economy' and 'reverse the decades of decline that we suffered in the twentieth century and become one of the world's most successful economies in the twenty-first century' (Blair 2001). His government commissioned another White Paper in 2000 which painted a mixed picture of Great Britain's global position. In it, Stephen Byers, Minister for Trade and Industry noted the strength of British science – per capita publication rates that surpassed those in the US, France, and Germany, and traditional strengths in the bio-medical sector. But he warned that Great Britain should better mobilize its science and technology resources, both public and private, in an increasingly competitive global environment (White Paper 2000).

In pursuit of this goal, the Blair government continued efforts initiated in the early 1990s to increase competition within and across public laboratories and British universities. The network of public laboratories attached to the British Research Councils continued to decline in importance, as some were privatized and others had their funding cut. The overall trend was away from public labs and toward more competitive project funding for university-based science. The government also pushed ahead with the Research Assessment Exercise, a controversial conservative innovation which linked institutional funding to research performance. And, like the German and French governments, it moved to funnel support to young and promising researchers and stop the flow of talent abroad, mainly to the US. In 2000 the government partnered with the Royal Society and a private foundation, the Wolfson Foundation, to create a fund to bring 50 leading scientists from around the world to Great Britain.

The Blair government also implemented a parallel set of reforms designed to improve co-operation between the public and private sectors. A centerpiece was the 'Higher Education Innovation Fund', stocked with £675 million to encourage universities to co-operate with business in joint research projects. Other measures, including the 'Enterprising University Initiatives' to support knowledge transfer to local corporations and 'University Challenge Competition' designed to spin off companies from university laboratories. The government also increased support for an established program – Faraday Partnerships – that bring university researchers and corporations together with the specific goal of developing new products and processes. A revision of intellectual property rights was designed to stimulate the commercialization of research findings.

Both the conceptualization and direction of reforms in Europe's three leading scientific powers were broadly compatible with the European

Commission's ERA departure. From its rhetoric through its specific provisions, the ERA initiative mirrored reforms unfolding at the national level in Europe's leading scientific states. Busquin, too, painted a pessimistic picture of the situation viz. the US. 'The average research effort in the Union', he argued, 'was only 1.8 per cent of Europe's GDP, as against 2.8 per cent in the United States and 2.9 per cent in Japan' (European Commission 2000a, pp. 4–5). He proposed instruments that dovetailed with national efforts to increase the competitiveness of the public sector and enable more interaction with industry in cutting edge fields. And he argued that steps to overcome national fragmentation through a broad co-ordination agenda would serve the common interest. 'Fragmentation, isolation and compartmentalization of national research efforts' had, in his words, lowered the EU's 'global investment in knowledge'(European Commission 2000a, p. 7). Still, the political task remained: to persuade national governments of the synergy between the ERA and their own reform efforts.

POLITICAL ENTREPRENEURSHIP AND THE STRUGGLE AGAINST THE STATUS QUO

The appeal of the idea of policy co-ordination and the existence of reform drives at the national level are not sufficient explanation for the initial success of the ERA initiative. The European Commission also had to secure the support of two other key actors in the policy process, the Council of Ministers and the European Parliament. Both were initially receptive. In its November 2000 communiqué, the Research Council welcomed efforts 'to develop an open method of policy co-ordination' and was even amenable to 'the gradual voluntary opening-up by the competent authorities of national research programmes' (Council of the European Union 2000). It set up High Level Groups of national civil servants to map areas of excellence, benchmark best practices, and study barriers to researcher mobility. The Parliament, too, gave its initial, if conditional assent in May 2000. As the European Commission settled down to the difficult work of preparing the FP6 (2002–06), it had succeeded in changing the terms of the debate.

This quick start was enabled by Busquin's assumption of the mantle of reformer. After the allegations of misconduct precipitated the fall of the Santer Commission, Busquin – a Belgian politician with a scientific background and relative outsider to the EU system – seized the opportunity to set a new tone. He criss-crossed the continent to engage members of the European research community, and encouraged criticisms of European Commission proposals through an open consultation process. He acknowledged a history of too much bureaucracy and micromanagement within the European Commission, and parts of the ERA addressed the problem. Once a Networks of Excellence and Integrated Project award was made, for example, participating researchers would have unprecedented autonomy in their internal governance and distribution of funds. Furthermore, Busquin streamlined DG XII in 2000, reworking an organization centered on the FP management, and introduced a political wing charged more flexibly with the implementation of the ERA. This theme of decentralization dovetailed nicely with a reform impetus of the European Commission under President Romano Prodi – a strategy designed to address ongoing legitimacy problems, fiscal constraints, and the complexities of managing an enlarged EU from the Center.

As the new FP proposal took shape, however, Busquin ran up against complex procedural hurdles and entrenched interests. Under the co-decision procedure set out in the Maastricht Treaty, FP approval required a unanimous Council vote and a Parliamentary majority, first on the Programme as a whole and then on its specific provisions. This cumbersome procedure allowed interest groups ample opportunity to influence the process. As successive FPs had grown, the number of program partners in public, university, and national laboratories rose from thirteen to more than 18 000 between the Second Framework Programme (FP2) (1987–91) and the Third Framework Programme (FP3) (1990–94) (European Commission 1998, p. 46). National organizations representing different research communities developed contacts in Brussels. Some of them combined to form an Informal Group of Liaison Offices (IGLO). Natural alliances were forged within the European Commission bureaucracy and with a wide range of committees of scientific experts and national civil servants charged with the selection and oversight of research projects. Interest groups found a natural ally in the European Parliament, which consistently backed larger research budgets. And they could appeal through their national governments to shape the FP as well.

In early 2001, the European Commission's specific proposals for the FP6 (2002–06) began to come under scrutiny. They concentrated more than €16 billion around seven thematic areas: biotechnology, information technologies, nanotechnology and advanced materials, aeronautics and space, food safety and health, the environment, and the 'knowledge-based society'. Familiar haggling over distribution – concerns about the particular selection of strategic priorities, for example – combined with confusion and concern with the new proposed instruments (Research Europe 2001b). For the Parliament and its allies, concerns that Integrated Projects and the Networks of Excellence might marginalize particular disciplines, industries, and countries was paramount. European business leaders cautioned against a focus on basic research at the expense of technological development, while university leaders articulated the opposite fear (UNICE 2000; Research Europe 2001b). Some of these concerns reached the ears of national research ministries, which were hesitant about opening up their programs or opening intergovernmental arrangements to EU participation, as proposed by the European Commission under Article 169. By mid-2001, the legal and procedural demands of the FP, complicated by the introduction of new instruments, had undermined the political momentum for the ERA accumulated over the previous year.

In the face of opposition through 2001, Busquin and his allies compromised on certain aspects of the ERA. At their June meeting in Luxembourg, the Council of the EU rejected the European Commission insistence on the exclusivity of the new instruments and expressed little enthusiasm for the implementation of Article 169 (Council of the European Union 2001). In the months that followed, as the European Commission's proposals went through a first reading in Parliament, Busquin backed the further utilization of established instruments centered on smaller research projects (while calling for their review in 2004) and downgraded Article 169 to the status of a pilot program. The openness of Integrated Projects to a variety of partners, including the accession countries, was emphasized, and the concept of 'Stairway to Excellence' was endorsed to underscore that Networks of Excellence would not be limited to elite players. The Council adopted these changes at its December 2001. Its amendments included the addition of an eighth priority for small- and medium-sized enterprises (SMEs) and explicit reference to the FP6 (in order to emphasize the novelty of the ERA, the European Commission's draft had referred simply to 'Framework Programme').

As the FP legislation headed into its second reading and approval by late 2002, the European Commission could claim an overall success. While certain aspects of its original ERA framework had not survived, its basic thrust was intact. The FP was to be centered on larger projects with more obvious 'European Value Added'. And EU research policy won a regulative as well as a distributive dimension. While national civil servants conferring as High Level Groups had not reached consensus on an ambitious co-ordination agenda, they had initiated wide-ranging consultations and made first recommendations. In a Union where the very idea of 'best practices' and 'centers of excellence' had long been anathema to many, this represented genuine progress.

CONCLUSION

The initial success of the ERA, this chapter has argued, cannot be reduced to overlapping national interests or functional imperatives. It depended on the interplay of policy ideas, structural conditions, and political entrepreneurship. Had the European Commission continued to conceive of integration in distributive terms, on the model of the FP, the ERA would have had scant chances for success. Furthermore, the initiative, no matter how persuasive as an idea, could hardly have flourished had it clashed with national reform efforts. Member states remain the key players in research policy. The absence of national opposition was not, however, sufficient to get the ERA off the ground. European Commission entrepreneurship was necessary to steer the reform over legislative hurdles against the opposition of entrenched interests wedded to the status quo.

A multidimensional explanatory approach like the one deployed in this chapter is well suited to the contemporary phase of integration. At the turn of the new century, EU leaders faced with legitimacy problems, fiscal constraints, and the daunting challenges of enlargement have begun to recast integration in more modest terms. Co-ordination, not transfers of sovereignty to the center, has become a watchword. From this perspective, the EU provides a framework for sharing best practices and setting joint goals – a way to regulate the interaction of states with overlapping interests. As EU leaders rethink integration along these lines, scholars should rework theories that conceive of integration as a shift of sovereignty to the center. The multi-level governance literature acknowledges the reality of shared sovereignty but in a descriptive rather than an explanatory idiom. An approach centered on the interplay of ideas, structure, and entrepreneurship constitutes an explanatory strategy with potential applications beyond the sphere of research policy.

What are the ERA's implications for the goals set out in Lisbon? In isolation, the ERA will certainly not revolutionize the European Union's position in the global knowledge economy. Innovation depends not just on scientific research and technological development, but also on capital markets, intellectual property rights, and a host of other factors. But to the extent that the ERA can concentrate resources more effectively, create stronger research networks, and foster mobility within the Union, it will reinforce the Lisbon process. If the EU does meet the American challenge successfully, it will be not as a federal state with a central science and technology policy, but as a set of scientific states competing with one another and, within the context of the ERA, collaborating more effectively to joint advantage.

REFERENCES

André, M. and A. Ruberti (1995), *Une Espace Européene de la Science*, Paris: Presses Universitaires de France.
Blair, T. (2001), *Address of 11 September*, www.number-10.gov.uk.
Bulmahn, E. (2001), *Address of 18 January*, www.bmbf.de.
Bundesministerium für Bildung und Forschung (BMBF) (2000), *Zur Technologischen Leistungsfähigkeit Deutschlands. Zusammenfassender Endbericht 1999*, Bonn: BMBF, Appendix, Table A11.

Busquin, P. (2001), *Address of 18 January*, Brussels: European Commission, http://europa.eu.int/comm/commissioners/busquin/speech/sp18012001fr.html.

Cohen, R. (1999), http://www.missioncoheledeaut.org/pages/section3/pages/rapport.zip.

Council of the European Union (2000), *2305th Council Meeting – Research – Brussels, 16 November 2000*, Press Release, 13084/00, 16 November 2000.

Council of the European Union (2001), *2363rd Council Meeting – Research – Luxembourg, 26 June 2001*, Press Release, 9932/01, 27 June 2001.

European Commission (1974), *Research, Science and Education: Scientific and Technical Information*, Brussels: European Commission.

European Commission (1994), *Research and Technological Development. Achieving Coordination Through Cooperation*, 19 October 1994, Brussels: European Commission, COM (94) 438.

European Commission (1998), *Second European Report on S&T Indicators. Key Figures*, Brussels: European Commission.

European Commission (2000), *Making a Reality of the European Research Area: Guidelines for EU Research Activities (2002–2006)*, 4 October 2000, Brussels: European Commission, COM (2000) 612.

European Commission (2000a), *Towards a European Research Area*, communication from the Commission to the Council, the European Parliament, the Economic and Social Committee and the Committee of the Regions, 18 January 2000, Brussels: European Commission, COM (2000) 6.

European Commission (2001), *Proposal for a Decision of the European Parliament and of the Council*, 21 February 2001, Brussels: European Commission, COM (2001) 94.

European Council (2000), *Presidency Conclusions*, Lisbon European Council, 23–24 March 2000, Press Release, Nr. 100/1/00, 24 March 2000.

European Parliament (2000), *Report on the communication from the Commission to the Council, the European Parliament, the Economic and Social Committee and the Committee of the Regions 'Towards a European Research Area'*, 9 May 2000, European Parliament, A5 – 0131/2000.

Gilpin, R. (1968), *France in the Age of the Scientific State*, Princeton: Princeton University Press.

Guzetti, L. (1995), *A Brief History of European Union Research Policy*, Brussels: European Commission.

Higher Education Funding Council of England (HEFC) (2000), *Review of Research*, Report 00/37, http://www.hefce.ac.uk/Pubs/Hefce/2000/00_37d.doc, Annex D, Table D2.

Jospin, L. (1997), *Address of 25 August*, http://www.premier-ministre.gouv.fr.

Kowi-Aktuell (2001), 'Diskussionsforum bei Kowi-Brussel zum Kommissionsvorschlag zum 6. Forschungsrahmenprogramm', *Kowi-Aktuell*, **47** (30 March 2001).

Layton, C. (1969), *European Advanced Technology: a Programme for Integration*, London: Allen & Unwin.

Marks, G., L. Hooghe and K. Blank (1996), 'European integration from the 1980s: state-centric v. multi-level governance', *Journal of Common Market Studies*, **34** (3), 341–78.

Peterson, J. and M. Sharp (1998), *Technology Policy in the European Union*, New York: St. Martin's Press.

Research Europe (2001a), *Industry Rejects FP6 Devolution Plan*, 3 May 2001.

Research Europe (2001b), *MEPs Will Not Be Rushed on FP6*, 12 April 2001.

Research Europe (2001c), *Universities Fear for Basic Research in FP6*, 12 April 2001.

Ruberti, A. (1993), *L'Avenir de la Recherche Communautaire*, Washington: European Institute, 20 May 1993, Cordis News Service, 24 May 1993.

Sandholtz, W. and A. Stone Sweet (1998), *European Integration and Supranational Governance*, Oxford: Oxford University Press.

Schwarzenberg, R. G. (2000), http://www.recherche.gouv.fr/discours/2000.htm.

Servan-Schreiber, J.-J. (1968), *The American Challenge*, New York: Atheneum.

UNICE (2000), *Towards a European Research Area*, 25 February 2000, Brussels: UNICE (Union of Industrial and Employers' Confederations of Europe).

White Paper (1993), *Realising Our Potential: a Strategy for Science, Engineering and Technology*, London: Her Majesty's Stationery Office.

White Paper (2000), *Excellence and Opportunity: a Science and Innovation Policy for the 21st Century*, http://www.dti.gov.uk/ost/aboutost/dtiwhite.

5   Change in European R&D Policy as a Complex Consensus-building Process

Experiences from the Past and What They Can Teach Us for the Present

Jakob Edler

INTRODUCTION

To the surprise of observers and stakeholders alike, a new quality of European policy regarding Research and Technological Development (R&D policy)[1] is emerging. For the first time since the beginning of the current approach of the European R&D policy with the first co-operative programs back in the early 1980s, a serious attempt is underway to upgrade and restructure the European programs. The major idea is to let Europe exploit its potential in the knowledge economy more comprehensively, by creating a European Research Area (ERA) in which the main features are mobility, the bundling of excellence across Europe, the upgrading of co-operation from specific, targeted research projects to larger networks, longer-term institutionalized co-operation and self-management by the European actors. In addition, although this seems more or less to be a long-term project, national R&D policies should become more co-ordinated and should join forces more flexibly within the European Union (EU) (variable geometry, opening up of programs).

This article does not judge the quality of the change we are witnessing, it does not try to speculate about possible output or outcome of the ERA approach. Rather, it wants to step back and analyze the conditions for, and nature of, the process of policy change in R&D policy at the European level *in general*. It does so by looking back onto a historic process of Europeanization of R&D policy in the mid 1980s. Then, after more than a decade of various failed attempts, the European Commission finally succeeded in formulating and implementing supranational R&D programs that put the European

Commission for the first time in the position to allocate a fixed amount of money in fixed technological areas, provided the recipients co-operated across borders. The lessons learned from the analysis of this first leap forward in European R&D policy will be confronted with what we – up to now – know about the driving forces that led to a first, if somewhat limited success of the ERA. The idea behind the historical analysis is that the lessons about the conditions for, and nature of, R&D policy change might serve as an analytical framework to guide our – preliminary – assessment of the most recent process of change and reveal both similarities and differences.

Starting point for the analysis will be the observation that R&D policy is a special policy area characterized by a high degree of uncertainty about causal relationships, the principle role of the state and the effectiveness of policy measures. Moreover, there are a multitude of different actor groups to be integrated, and thus a high demand for consensus under the conditions of uncertainty. This is even more true at the European level, at which stakeholders with very different national and institutional backgrounds have to be integrated. Consequently, under these circumstances a variety of very diverse stakeholders must be reconciled with the conceptual reasoning for the policy. In such a setting, policy ideas must be convincing and appeal to the broad variety of stakeholders in order to overcome policy stalemate. The historical analysis of the paper will show that policy change under these circumstances can be defined as a process of institutionalization, driven by the interplay of:

- conceptual *ideas* that are convincing and appeal not only to (national) policymakers, but also to the broad range of stakeholders;
- *functional discursive interactions* of stakeholders; and finally a
- strong *central actor* who moderates and heads the discourse towards a common policy.

The analysis presented in this article deliberately concentrates on the conditions for consensus-building in the early phases of policymaking, and it does so by utilizing a specific analytical approach that stresses the cognitive, normative and social dimension of policymaking. It must be stressed that with this approach no comprehensive analysis is intended or even could be provided. Rather, the focus of analysis and the specific theoretical concept are deliberately chosen in order to highlight a dimension of policymaking in Europe that is too often neglected, however – as will be shown – that is extremely important, especially for R&D policymaking.

Although the analysis of the current debate is – by nature – rather abridged and speculative, it will be argued that both back in the 1980s and during the ERA debate these three factors were and have been driving the process, but that their meaning and weight in the last two years has been somewhat different from the 1980s. Most importantly, the role of the European Commission has recently become even more proactive and self-defined than 20 years ago. The main, if somewhat speculative, conclusion is that the European Commission has learned from the past and utilized its special provisions as a central actor in the European policy process, instrumentalizing existing policy ideas and shaping – in a very structured way – the discourse on policy ideas from the very beginning. However, this strategy has not only borne fruit but also created resistance, mainly within national administrations and some stakeholder groups, as the European Commission has asked too much of them in too little time.

The following section will characterize the policy area and its special features, especially at European level. Then, the theoretical perspective to analyze policy change in this area at European level will be introduced very briefly. Section four will tell the story of the 'historic' leap forward, i.e. the genesis of thematic collaborative programs in the 1980s in analyzing the underlying ideas, the functional interaction and the role of the central actor, the European Commission. In the light of the conceptual framework and the lessons learned from this analysis on the nature of policy change at the European level, the article concludes with a preliminary analysis of the process that led to the implementation of a ERA.

R&D POLICY IN EUROPE: A VERY SPECIAL CONSENSUS DILEMMA[2]

In order to understand the discussion and perspective of this article, a characterization of the policy area is crucial, since the features of R&D policy, especially at the European level, are the most important variables for structuring the processes of its change.

As regards the optimization of the general welfare, research and development are governable only to a limited extent (Mayntz and Scharpf 1995). Knowledge and new technological developments are quasi-public goods with distinct external effects, the optimal production of which as demanded by society is generally not the outcome of the utility maximizing behavior of private and public actors. At the same time, public R&D policy cannot simply 'order' actors to produce knowledge and technology and to change behavior in a socially desirable way. Therefore, there must first be a *consensus* on what is socially desirable and how the behavior of actors involved must change in order to reach these individual and social goals. Second, if policy wants actors to change their behavior in doing research in a sustainable and socially desirable way, what is needed is *compliance* by the very diverse actors involved. As Scharpf showed almost two decades ago (Scharpf 1983), only if actors are convinced that what they are supposed to do in participating in incentive programs is in their long-term interest, will they actually adjust their behavior in a sustainable way that conforms with the intention of the program – rather than simply free-riding and maximizing short-term profits through taking advantage of the subsidy provided.

However, the preconditions for this consensus, and thus public policy, are especially problematic in the R&D area. Cause and effect relationships are ill-defined and amorphous, and research and technology develop faster than the theories to explain the change itself. The complexity is increased, given the high number of different actor groups playing important roles, ranging from basic scientists in some forefront university laboratory (exploring the frontiers of knowledge) to the development unit of an SME (small- and medium-sized enterprise) in the manufacturing sector (developing technologies in an entirely market-driven manner). In addition, there are enormous differences in scientific disciplines, technological areas and economic sectors. Finally, the different political systems have different polities and policy traditions. Thus, R&D policy is characterized by extremely diverse identities, intrinsic and extrinsic motivations, the competitive contexts, time frames and, above all, the very understanding of what policy should do.

Furthermore, administrations in R&D policy are highly fragmented (e.g. Grande 1994, p. 191). In most countries, the responsibility for policies that influence research and technological development is divided among at least two ministries. In many cases these national ministries show very different policy concepts, based upon very different policy rationales.

At the European level, complexity increases. The precondition for the successful formulation and realization of a new European policy is a consensus of national policymakers that a new policy will serve not only European, but also the national needs. Given the poor hierarchical power of the European Commission and the consensus principle in the European Council, a new EU policy necessitates a broad agreement on 'ideas and doctrines' (Wallace 1983, p. 49), the Europeanization of a policy in the European multi-level system is characterized by the 'imperative of consensus' (Jachtenfuchs and Kohler-Koch 1996).[3] While all this is true, *regardless* of the policy area, what has been said above about the need for consensus in R&D policymaking still adds to this imperative.

In sum, the preconditions for European R&D policymaking, and especially for pushing through new approaches in R&D policymaking, can be labeled as a consensus dilemma, stemming from an especially high demand for consensus and at the same time especially complicated structures and actor constellations to generate it.

What does this mean? Above all, it means that policymakers and stakeholders alike need some kind of intellectual and normative guidance. They need assistance in order to make sense of this complexity, in order to assess the conditions and consequences of their actions, in order to recognize possible alternatives; in short, in order to define their interests and choices. Therefore, R&D policymaking – and this is truer than in policy areas with less diverse actor groups and with more hierarchical policy leverage – is highly dependent on policy concepts and ideas that are shared by the majority of actors involved. R&D policymaking is a classical case of 'politics of expertise' (Peterson 1995), as the experts are the ones to provide conceptual ideas. Scientific and – to some extent – distinguished industrial experts not only provide insights, data and interpretation of cause and effect relationships in order to make sense of the complexity at hand, they also formulate new policy options (Braun 1993). However, as Peterson has pointed out (Peterson 1995, p. 407), the role of the experts is limited, given the complexity of technological and economic development, as the expertise itself is highly contested and experts differ on basic assumptions as well as interpretation.

Therefore, the analytical question is what are the processes and the driving forces that make some ideas and concepts prevail and others die? In the context of the EU R&D policy: how does a concept come into existence and mobilize sufficient consensus throughout the fragmented and heterogeneous policy arena in Europe? Before presenting some empirical evidence, an appropriate theoretical perspective is shortly sketched.

THE THEORETICAL PERSPECTIVE

The assertion that the driving mechanism of political change is based upon the building of consensus is reflected by a specific understanding of the political process. This cannot be elaborated in full within the framework of this paper.[4] The main theoretical premise is the constructivist claim that politics rests upon the interpretation of reality and that all definition of interest is dependent upon the construction of what is perceived as being real (Berger and Luckmann 1967). This has three consequences. *First*, it means that actors' interests – and even identities (Wendt 1992) – are not exogenous, rather they are constantly reproduced through cognitive processes of coming to grips with the constant flow of *new information and ideas*. In other words, the interpretations of problems and concepts that lead to interests are derived from a supply of ideas.

Two forms of ideas must be distinguished:

1. *Causal ideas* help define the current situation and explain what action leads to what outcome; and

2. *normative ideas* suggest where one should head and what is perceived as legitimate.

Therefore, while power games and bargaining on the basis of interests remain important in the political process, it is ideas which shape these interests in the first place. Consequently, which ideas are taken up in this process and perceived as being legitimate and valid is one crucial determining factor. The analysis of a political process, especially under the conditions of EU policy-making, must not neglect the ideational dimensions, rather, this should be the starting point. This is even truer the greater the uncertainty of stakeholders involved and the greater the complexity of the policy areas.

In strong policy concepts, causal and normative policy ideas need to fit. If so, one can speak of a 'policy guiding idea' (*Leitidee*). Such a *Leitidee* directs stakeholders' actions and orients them towards a shared normative goal (Göhler 1994). The better causal and normative ideas of a policy concept match and the stronger the causal ideas are oriented towards a norm widely shared by stakeholders, the stronger the *Leitidee* will be. A strong *Leitidee* is the most important prerequisite for intrinsic policy consensus.[5]

The *second* consequence of our constructivist premise is that ideas only become meaningful if they are exchanged and transferred through the relevant sociopolitical subsystem. The conditions and characteristics of the processing and exchange of ideas and information are crucial. The most obvious and influential way to exchange ideas is through *social interaction*, thereby, one way or another, constructing social reality. Therefore, to understand the mechanism by which social interaction results in political action and decision, one must keep in mind what, in turn, shapes interaction.

Thirdly, while interaction might be more or less spontaneous, it still has to be managed one way or another. It can be observed that in most policy discourses, out of a mix of motivations related to interest and institutional responsibilities, this organization is driven by one *central* institutional respective corporatist *actor*. Fully spontaneous interaction – triggered by ideas and guided by existing rules and procedures – is not realistic, rather there must be at least one actor proposing and shaping the agenda, carrying the organizational burden of bringing people together, filtering ideas and enabling targeted communication. What is important in the context of this paper is to bear in mind that the very institutional setting, rationale and capabilities of such a discourse-moderating actor influence to a large degree the style and character of the moderation and the likelihood with which different ideas are taken up and different actor groups are integrated in the process. We shall call an actor, who is willing and able to shape ideational interaction, the process manager or the *central actor* of the political discourse in which ideas are institutionalized.

In sum, our theoretical perspective rests basically on three pillars, first on *ideas as strong forces shaping policy concepts as well as interests*, second on the meaning of *interaction* for the diffusion and processing of political ideas and third on the meaning of a *central actor* who – to a large extent – shapes interactions and inserts and carries further ideas in order to enable consensus and binding decision-making.

For the analysis, it follows that it is crucial to identify the interdependence of these three variables. For example, it is clear that the scope and composition of the relevant *interaction* strongly influences *what* ideas and concepts are dealt with – and what ideas are excluded – and what, *a priori*, the various expectations within the discourse are. At the same time, the political *idea* defines who is relevant for the discourse and who is only a peripheral player. The power with which political ideas exert influence, in turn, differs considerably and depends on many variables, such as their origin (scientific context, administration, interest groups etc.) or the existence of some sort of crisis. By the same token, the institutional context of the central actor – ranging from its normative goal function to its organizational capabilities – determines the ability to formulate or bundle ideas, to widely communicate them and to call on others to interact.

As for the effect of ideas, there is a – theoretical – scale ranging from entirely spontaneous interaction mainly driven by the power of the underlying ideas themselves, at the one end, and an instrumental interaction entirely dominated by a powerful interaction moderator – lining his interest with the content and outcome of the discourse – at the other. Therefore, every analysis of the power of new policy ideas must define the degree of spontaneity – or instrumentality– of the ideational interaction.

The following sections analyze the relationship of the three core variables ideas, interaction and central actor in the process of change in European R&D policy.

EUROPEANIZATION OF R&D POLICY IN THE EARLY 1980s: MULTI-STAGE CONSENSUS BUILDING

New Policy Ideas

Since a Council decision in 1974, the mission of the European Commission and the General Directorate for Research DG XII[6] was twofold: to *co-ordinate* national policies and to formulate and design a *common European R&D policy*. However, until the 1980s, not much had happened (e.g. Kalka 1984; Schneider and Welsch 1990; Guzzetti 1995).

National policies had not been co-ordinated. On the contrary, until the mid-1980s the catchword for the approach in the Member States of the EC had been the strategy of 'national champions'. A genuine European R&D policy, with a relevant budget and a clear-cut added value, had not been developed. There was no explicit legal basis for European R&D policy.[7]

In addition, especially in Europe, private actors in traditional industries had not yet discovered trans-border co-operation in R&D as a strategic means to speed up innovation, the number of trans-border technological co-operations before the mid-1980s is negligible (Meyer-Krahmer and Walter 1982; Narula 2000).

However, in the early 1980s, a new trend of technological co-operation in traditional industries emerged. Specific programs such as the sectoral programs European Strategic Programme for Research and Development (ESPRIT) and Research and Development in Advanced Communication Technologies (RACE) as well as the horizontal program Basic Research for Industrial Technologies in Europe (BRITE) were agreed upon in the Research Council. These programs had a couple of new features, which are taken for granted nowadays as core elements of modern innovation policymaking. In the mid-1980s, however, several new characteristics marked a paradigm change:

- obligatory co-operation across country borders;
- co-operation between industrial companies, even competitors, and between industry and research institutes;
- trans-sectoral and interdisciplinary co-operation (especially BRITE);
- European Commission as organizer of the thematic consensus-building of the thematic programs and as the organizers of the allocation of money to individual co-operative projects – with national administration playing a formal role of having the last say through program committees.

What were the underlying conceptual ideas behind this sweeping change? In the late 1970s, new theoretical paradigms in the area of innovation and technology policy emerged in the transnational arena. Based on a number of empirical studies and conceptual thinking, innovation experts started to come up with a new understanding of the very nature of industrial and public R&D, of their potential benefit and the way to influence industrial progress. From the enormous amount of literature on the innovation process, three lines of reasoning can be analytically identified, the first rooted in an intensive macro- and techno-economic discourse, the second and third emerging from innovation theory.

1. *R&D as a basic driving force of economic growth within supply-side economics*: The 1970s saw a new type of macroeconomic crisis labeled

stagflation – the combination of stagnation and inflation. Low productivity was perceived as being its major reason. Higher productivity was needed, and this was tightly linked to innovation and to efficient and effective R&D processes. But as studies showed, the reaction of private actors towards the crises was counter-productive, since the expenditure on R&D decreased in almost all industries (Boyer 1979; OECD 1980; Freeman, Clark and Soete 1982). Therefore, R&D became a central pillar of economic policy and gradually turned into the key to trigger innovation and growth as directly and as widely as possible.[8]

2. *Interdependent, recursive understanding of the innovation process*: A new model of technological progress emerged, replacing the old linear model of succession of different stages by a model of feedback loops and recursion between the different stages of the innovation process. In this understanding,[9] basic science cannot be separated anymore from applied science and development, not even from marketing and procurement (von Hippel 1978). Consequently, effective and efficient innovation requires intensive interaction, first between the actors of the various stages of the innovation process, second between producers, clients and suppliers.[10]

3. *Generic technologies*: Related to the first line of ideas, the growing importance of a few key technologies, most of all microelectronics, was recognized. These so-called generic technologies were identified as being influential for innovation and growth, not only in one core industrial sector, but across a range of sectors. This made integration of the R&D process instrumental, both for the generic technology and the technologies applied in a whole range of industrial sectors.[11]

The combination of these three lines of reasoning led to a *paradigm shift* in R&D and innovation policymaking, that was shaped by experts from both sides of the Atlantic and step by step established new innovation and R&D policy rationales, with the following main *causal* ideas of this concept:

- The role of innovation: Innovation was seen as being crucial for competitiveness for companies and national economies.
- The role and shape of R&D: The message for industrialists and policymakers alike was that enhanced productivity was the key to growth; R&D the key to enhanced productivity; increased co-operation across R&D stages, disciplines and sectors the key to effective R&D and fast and broad diffusion of technologies.
- The role of the state: The state had to provide incentives and the best environment possible to enable actors to interact and co-operate.
- The role of Europe: There was an added value through European policy as

the area for potential sensible co-operation significantly widens as compared to national approaches.[12]

Functional Interaction

Ex post, the consensus for this new paradigm is obvious, however the interesting question is, how these ideas were synthesized into a concept and how this concept became consensual within the EC.

Transnational discourse of experts

The new problem definition and the new understanding of the role of R&D and R&D policy emerged gradually, with input from different corners of the globe. The first level of interaction to put forward these ideas was not bound to the EC, but rather was even more transnational. These kinds of interactions were to some extent spontaneous and not mediated centrally. However, facing stagflation and the need to find new policy concepts, the Organisation for Economic Co-operation and Development (OECD) started to bundle and push the discourse towards the end of the 1970s. In 1977, the OECD called together a transatlantic group of first-rate experts to produce a study on the link between 'Technical Change and Economic Policy'. The OECD picked experts who were most recognized in the field of innovation and R&D policy, they were the core of the relevant transatlantic 'epistemic community' (Haas 1993).[13] This linked the discussion in the United States to the European context and introduced the 'technology gap' discussion. The ad hoc experts within the OECD themselves perceived their role as being providers of data and ideas, without the ambition and responsibility to represent national interests (Delapalme 1980). Moreover, the analysis of the experts was accompanied by a series of conferences linking the expert group to a wider scientific and administrative community.[14] The experts were highly active in other contexts and involved in various other fora, on national level and – more importantly – on the European level.[15]

The OECD report mainly laid down the new thinking as described above (OECD 1980). The influence of the report and the interaction it caused cannot be overestimated. The report was clearly the most often cited source in the discussion in the early 1980s, and among the many policymakers influenced were also those members of DG XII who had to work on new concepts for European R&D policy.[16] Moreover, it became the basis of a resolution within the Council of Ministers in the OECD and the core of its argument was even put forward by some of the members of the expert group at the world economic summits in Versailles (1982) and Williamsburg (1983).[17]

The transnational expert discourse put forward by the OECD had various consequences:

- A *new problem* was defined and put on the agenda of political decision-makers, problem definitions and concepts to solve them converged transnationally.
- The *new ideas*, once they were formulated within the institutional context of the OECD, were attributed with high *legitimacy*.
- Since the institutional rationale of the OECD is to foster *economic development*, the discourse within the OECD helped to frame R&D policy as *industrial* policy to foster growth very directly. This, however, fitted well into the institutional logic of the European Commission in general, since the most important leverage of the 'promoter of integration' is the economic efficiency attributed to its proposals.
- Since the level of analysis and deliberation had been *transnational*, the conclusion to react beyond a national level seemed logical. The *supranational* setting of the EU looked like a perfect arena to give it a try.

Why was it that the OECD deliberation became so relevant? The reason lies in its institutional shape which is very well suited for ideational discourse. The organization does not have operational leverage and authoritative decision-making powers, neither 'carrot nor sticks' to make its members follow the deliberation coming out of the OECD discourse (Bayne 1987). To advance its ideas, it has rather to convince by the power of its arguments, which most importantly rest on the reputation of the experts involved and the enormous amounts of comparative data gathered. The technical character of its expertise depolitizes and legitimizes its deliberations. In addition, the OECD has a standing committee for R&D policy that on a *regular and permanent* basis serves as a forum for national R&D policymakers and experts alike, thus building common understanding on the administrative level (Henderson 1993; Federal Ministry for Research and Technology [BMFT] 1984).

Functional interaction on the European level
Although the OECD was not the only organization shaping the international discourse, it was clearly the most influential international body to put forward and legitimize new thinking in R&D policymaking. However, it was a complex, multi-level interaction on the European level that resulted in the formulation of a *European* approach in R&D policymaking. This functional discourse moderated by the European Commission soon took a different shape for different technological programs such as ESPRIT, RACE and BRITE.

The following summary concentrates on the program for traditional industries BRITE, mainly because the prerequisites for consensus were most problematic for this horizontal program, as it was geared towards traditional industries that, first, had a very low R&D intensity and, second, were important for each member country of the EC. However, the consensus production at this stage can be observed for other programs as well. As regards ESPRIT, for example, the discourse reflected the almost oligopolistic structure of the information technology sector. Commissioner Davignon, who was responsible for DG III (industry) at the time, organized a discussion group 'Round Table' (Sandholtz 1992). It included the leaders of the twelve most important European companies in the sector (ibid. Grande 1994). In this discourse, Davignon was interested in setting up a substantial research program and thus turning the EC into an important industrial policy player, while the industrialists involved sought financial support in order to counter the extra-European IT companies that had – at the time – a strategic competitive advantage. Thus, all parties involved were fully interest-driven, however, their interest definition and the processes they embraced in order to achieve them changed during and because of the political discourse at the European level. The analysis of the minutes of the Round Table meetings (Edler 2000, pp. 283–9) clearly shows that Davignon was very well aware that the only possibility to set up a large-scale R&D program for the sector was to integrate the idea of trans-border co-operation that had already become common sense in the academic world. The minutes also show that the industrialists were – at the beginning of the talks – not at all willing to join forces with their competitors – not even if this was the precondition to get funds. However, after having met a couple of times and after having learned from some pilot projects launched in 1982, they gave up opposition to the thought that co-operation, not only because of extra money would make sense. They literally bought the idea and started broad co-operation efforts. Thus, the consensus-building process at European level had a catalytic effect on the growing inclination to co-operate. The idea of co-operation then spread into the world of national policymakers. Once the companies could credibly prove this willingness, they were successful in supporting Davignon in his attempt to convince national governments. This last step, however, was facilitated by a normative leap towards more and intensified integration in general that was under way to overcome *Eurosclerosis* (see below).

As for BRITE, the process was more complicated, as the arena is bigger and more heterogeneous. First of all, there was an *industrial European discourse* mostly organized and fed by the European Commission and centered around a newly established Committee. In parallel to the epistemic discourse on OECD level, the European Commission, which for BRITE was DG XII had turned to a more industry-focused approach in its R&D policy. In the second half of the 1970s, a new form of interaction with industry emerged, starting with conferences and informal contacts moderated by DG XII and the European industrial federation UNICE (Union des Confédérations de l'Industrie et des Employeurs d'Europe). UNICE already had a permanent committee to discuss technology policy matters that consisted of representatives from national federations responsible for R&D in their respective organizations. In 1978, the European Commission installed the Industrial Committee CORDI (Comité Consultative pour la Recherche et le Developement Industrial) which was to become the source of the industrial R&D program BRITE. It consisted of representatives of European industrial federations, a majority of which came from UNICE. In addition, the European Industrial Research Management Association (EIRMA) was included. This is important, since EIRMA had been a forum for European industrial discussion on R&D matters since 1966 and in the late 1970s and early 1980s one can find industrial co-operation in R&D as a prime topic in documentation of EIRMA conferences and in EIRMA studies (EIRMA 1978; 1982a; 1983a; 1983b). Thus, CORDI, which in 1984 became IRDAC (Industrial Research Advisory Committee), was a forum for a specialized and broadened discourse on the new R&D ideas.

CORDI is regarded even today as the most influential body for the formulation of BRITE,[18] most importantly because of its functional structure which already showed the networking and inclusive discourse organization that was to become the trademark of European policymaking. As one of the responsible members of DG XII put it:

> CORDI committee was a *framework*, all the subgroups and so on, were very effective when we brought people together, because it enabled us to invite people to Brussels ... We had working groups, subgroups, specialist groups and studies and gradually this thing [BRITE] evolved.

One of the working groups ('Basic Technological Research') had the explicit task to formulate an industry-oriented policy concept. Like all working parties, it was very flexible, enabled a very wide discussion, with hundreds of experts involved, and provided the transmission of the transnational ideas on the European level and back to the national interest groups participating in the European discourse.[19]

In addition to the standing committee CORDI and the flexible and permanent interaction it provided, the European Commission organized a number of big conferences, and through high level representatives, played an outstanding part in international conferences organized by universities, business federations, the OECD expert group or the European Commission. According to interviews and to the documentation of participants and contributions, two key conferences took place in Paris and Strasbourg (Fusfeld and Haklisch 1982; European Commission 1982). Both conferences intensively discussed the necessities for European industry to co-operate in R&D. The first linked the US discourse to the European context, the second – organized by the European Commission – explicitly discussed the OECD deliberations and gave shape to a concrete European concept (Colombo et al. 1982).[20] Strasbourg especially was a break-through. It indicated the direction for the DG XII and it gave the discussions within its advisory body CORDI a new momentum and new analytical basis. It is interesting to note that after the Strasbourg conference the statements coming out of CORDI and DG XII (European Commission 1980; 1981a; 1981b) and out of UNICE (UNICE Monthly Report 11/1980) had literally taken up the expertise of the OECD expert group and thus the common understanding of the epistemic community.

After the outline of a new program for industrial R&D was constructed, DG XII started a new discourse, *targeting the scientific experts in the technological fields* which the new program was supposed to support (especially in materials technologies and advanced production technologies). In several countries and for several disciplines, DG XII commissioned central, widely acknowledged nationally based scientific institutions to conduct studies (European surveys and interviews) on the need for a European program.[21] These studies not only identified and specified the scientific and industrial priority areas for the program, their function was also to spread the idea of trans-border co-operation across the Community and to link monetary incentives to a demand for a new kind of behavior.

To sum up: the various activities at European level unfolded a virtuous circle of interaction and conceptualization. Interaction between DG XII and industry, loosely started in the mid-1970s, was institutionalized in CORDI, was linked to scientific expertise ranging across country borders, was accompanied by intensified industrial discussion on R&D matters, and finally – once the concept of BRITE was formulated – made industrialists not formerly involved in the discourse turn towards the DG XII. In this process – and just like within the more closed discussions of the ESPRIT Round Table – parts of industry had changed their attitudes towards co-operation. While the first internal UNICE reports of the CORDI discussions clearly indicated that industry started out with demands for indirect support through tax incentives, the demolition of obstacles for technologically sensible goods, the co-ordination and harmonization of national policies and so on,[22] company representatives had started to formulate their interest in a European policy in a new fashion.

Moreover, during the newly established interactions DG XII itself had been developing a sense of what was feasible with European industrialists and how far it could go in demanding a certain change in industrial R&D strategies. More importantly, as DG for research, the interaction with industry opened up new needs and possibilities to incorporate 'industrial thinking' into its own institutional rationale. It is fair to say that the processing of new paradigmatic ideas (linking science and industry through co-operation) and the interaction with experts and industrialists alike let the institutional identity of

DG XII develop from being dominantly oriented towards research and re-search institutions also towards industry and its R&D needs.

Inter-administrative interactions
Only *after* the processes of mutual learning and common conceptualization of European Commission, industrialists and scientists had unfolded, was this concept lifted to the national political and administrative level, mostly by bilateral consultations. Here, the consultations clearly had the character of marketing, of selling the new program approach, of convincing. There were essentially two leverages:

- *first*, of course, that the concept was accepted in industrial and scientific circles throughout Europe through the previous interactive construction with nationally based industry and science;
- *second*, the match to several national attempts for new concepts in innova-tion policy, since the new thinking had reached nation-states as well.

Thus, national ministries, although showing a reflex of defending their own national room to maneuver, did not have a very high level of resistance. Not in the small countries, of course, but not even in the big ones with programs of their own.

The German administration, however, was a special case, and this case il-lustrates the power of consensus already reached in European interaction. In Germany, two different kinds of ministries had to be convinced, the Ministry of Research and Technology (BMFT) and the Ministry of Economics (BMWi).[23] Only the BMFT was involved in the international flow of con-ceptual ideas and showed policy rationale similar to the DG XII. By and large, it shared the logic of what by now was called the 'technology commu-nity'. The Research Ministry quite easily acknowledged the European Com-mission's approach.

The Ministry of Economics, on the other hand, could not be convinced. This is due to its deeply rooted ordo-liberal, non-interventionist institutional philosophy. Moreover, actors of this ministry were not integrated into the specific transnational discourse. For them, the European program was a cen-tral, industrial interventionist policy to be opposed. This attitude could not be reconciled with the interventionist approach of the European Commission, but the new consensus was too broad and too pervasive, the BMWi remained the odd man out, however, too peripheral to stop the successful institutionali-zation of the new ideas.

A European approach: the normative uplift of economic causal ideas
The combination of various causal ideas into a feasible and acceptable

concept of governance for industrial R&D in Europe is a necessary condition for a new European policy, but it is not sufficient. As said above, what is needed is a *Leitidee* that gives *orientation* beyond the causal effectiveness of a policy concept. In the case of European policy, a causal concept must prove that it serves *the norms* of the European treaty, most of all European integration and economic growth. The more conclusive this normative match, the more convincing a new *European* policy concept. The *Leitidee* of the European R&D policy in the 1980s, in short, is that broader and more interactive R&D throughout Europe, with the EU playing the role of a catalyst for cross-border R&D co-operation, fosters *both* economic growth *and* integration in Europe. The build-up of this strong *Leitidee* was a process parallel to and interdependent with the consensus-building process described above. The last open question therefore is, how and why did the ideas processed and formulated with administrators, industrialists and scientists turn into a *European* policy?

The documents produced by the heads of state of the European Community and the integration discourse by foreign secretaries indicate that the broad debate about industrial productivity, technological gap and appropriate R&D concepts slowly reached top level politics in Europe. A first momentum was built up after the European Commission launched the results of the Strasbourg conference of October 1980 – which connected the 'neutral' causal ideas with the European level as locus of governance (see above) – into the European Council. In December 1980, the European Council accepted this paper and for the first time the heads of state and government officially made a comprehensive statement on innovation (European Council 1980, p. 138). They basically instructed the European Commission to further prove how the fragmentation of the European Market could be overcome and the incentives for innovation and diffusion of results throughout Europe could be improved. From now on, the European Council repeatedly included technological matters in its summit talks.

Several impulses led the heads of state finally to turn towards explicitly embracing the concept of co-operation of European companies. First, as stated above, the heads of the 12 leading information technology companies in Europe approached the national governments and demonstrated their willingness to co-operate throughout Europe. This active lobbying, although concentrated in one sector with clearly defined interests, once again heightened awareness for technological co-operation and, more importantly, for the first time gave the debate on '*Eurosclerosis*' (Dahrendorf 1983; Kaiser 1983; Moravcsick 1991) an optimistic twist. Secondly, in March 1982, the European Council shortly after the resolution of the OECD research ministers who had adopted a resolution based on the report by the OECD expert group (OECD 1980) for the first time linked the European dimension to the development of an industrial strategy and a technology and innovation policy (European Council 1982, p. 150). Thirdly, in April 1983 the expert group 'Technology, Growth and Employment (TGE)' of the economic world summit in Williamsburg – which included some members of the OECD group and of DG XII – stressed the issue of technology-driven growth and R&D cooperation and linked it to the issue of employment (Working Party TGE 1983). Three months after the official adoption of this document in Williamsburg, the European Council followed this approach and – again for the first time – stressed the need for European companies to co-operate in R&D (European Council 1983, p. 170). Fourth, the European Council formally recognized the effective and instrumental interaction between industrialists and European institutions (European Council 1984, p. 175). Therefore, not only the content and scope of the new concept, but also the processes by which it had been constructed, had its effect at the highest European level.

This development indicates the integrative appeal of the concept constructed in a complex European discourse that was more and more organized and shaped by the European Commission. This integrative appeal can be well illustrated by the argumentation put forward by the German Foreign Ministry (AA, *Auswärtiges Amt*). Traditionally, this ministry has been pushing for further European integration and been eager to embrace policy concepts which serve European integration (Kohler-Koch 1998). For example, in the years leading up to the adoption of ESPRIT (1984), BRITE (1985) and, more generally, the article on European technology policy in the Single European Act, there were a number of statements coming out of the AA that emphatically welcomed the European Commission's approach (Genscher 1984; Grewlich 1981; 1984; 1985; Seitz 1985)[24] and elevated the question of technological development in Europe to a 'matter of survival for the EC'. Most importantly for the genesis of BRITE, the German Foreign Ministry stressed the potential value of integration in a concept including all industries and not only IT industries (Genscher 1984, pp. 5 ff.; Grewlich 1984, p. 231). It is interesting to note that the AA was very much aware of the underlying theoretical ideas of the new concept for a European R&D policy. Even more telling, the AA had taken notice of the complex web of interaction of industrial and scientific actors as well as the European Commission and welcomed this consensus-building as a prerequisite for effective R&D policymaking.[25]

The dynamism with which R&D policy gained relevance in the integration discourse is impressive. The relaunch of the integration dynamic was started by Genscher and his Italian colleague Colombo in 1981. In their joint paper, however, there is no single sign for R&D policy at all. But when the transnational discourse of experts, mostly through the moderation of the European Commission, was tailored towards the European level, advocates of integration captured the concept and normatively endorsed it, demanding the establishment of a 'technology community' (Dooge-Committee 1985), a phrase which for a short while served as the chiffre for the *Leitidee* that had been developed. R&D policy that had not been on the top European agenda at the beginning of the 1980s at all, was one of the least controversial articles of the Single European Act. This is an indication of the power growing out of continuous, broad interaction to produce consensus on new ideas at European level.

The European Commission as the Agent of Change

The analysis so far could be interpreted as a success of the political entrepreneur European Commission. Indeed, the European Commission has shown institutional strength in pushing through a new policy which rested on 'strategies of inclusion' (Kohler-Koch 1998), communication and convincing. Interestingly, the institutional ability to do so is in fact caused by a structural weakness. Since the European Commission lacks certain hierarchical powers of a national government (Wallace 1983; Cram 1994; Mayntz and Scharpf 1995), it has no choice but to concentrate on the function of a 'process manager' and 'idea broker' (Mazey and Richardson 1996) of European policy-making. This functionality of the DG XII in the genesis of the specific programs can be explained by – and reflect – the institutional features of the European Commission:[26]

- right to initiate (including the exclusive right to draft the text of new initiatives), veto power, agenda-setting powers;[27]
- leading role in the preparation of decisions within bureaucratic, supposedly depoliticized contexts (comitology etc.);
- horizontal administrative knowledge, power of expertise (Peterson 1995);
- designing specific networks of administrations and stakeholders, organizational capacities, consultation with highly differentiated administrations, a high degree of autonomy of internal staff, leading to the formation of 'functional elites' and complementary, 'technical' perspectives on issues at stake (March and Olsen 1989, p. 109; Bach 1995);
- creation of issue-specific relations to practices and analyses of other international institutions (OECD, WTO, World Bank etc.) by means of integration into working groups as well as exchange of experts and documents.

It is true that the European Commission, more concretely DG XII (and DG III for ESPRIT), applied all these abilities. However, although ex-post this might look like a well-defined strategy from the very beginning, the European Commission itself was subject to the influence of ideas that gained legitimacy elsewhere. The process of formulating and spreading the new ideas began slowly and was *not driven* by DG XII. Rather it was initiated and driven by a somewhat heterogeneous epistemic community, which came to complementary conclusions. The DG XII, on the other hand, closely watched this process and accompanied it with its scientific and industrial committees, always waiting for ideas to adopt for its institutional interests. In other words, the European Commission did not act as a political entrepreneur from the beginning of the whole consensus-building process. In contrast, only by observing, influencing and interacting with experts and hundreds of industrialists, the DG XII *adjusted* to the new ideas it was exposed to. Founded as a science-oriented DG in the early 1970s, DG XII became a more focused and industry-oriented administrative body. The final norm of the BRITE concept, to support application-oriented R&D to foster economic growth, did not really fit the initial institutional rationale of DG XII. Only after a gradual shift in its identity, did DG XII succeed in linking the scientific ideas to its institutional interest. The more clearly the new thinking emerged, the more the European Commission became its 'advocate' (Kingdon 1984) and developed into an 'entrepreneurial leader' (Young 1991).

THE ERA PROCESS IN LIGHT OF THE LESSONS LEARNED

In order to better grasp what has been happening in the process that led to the – somewhat limited – acceptance of the ERA idea, this process will finally be confronted with the major lessons of the historical process of *R&D policy change* at the *European level* as they can be derived within the theoretical perspective that has guided the analysis. To sum up, the lessons learned can be summarized as follows:

1. European R&D policy is characterized by a special *consensus dilemma*: First, there is a high demand for consensus, as stakeholders must believe that what they are supposed to do in incentive programs serves their long-term interest. Second, there is a high threshold for consensus, given the uncertainty and heterogeneity in this policy area.
2. To understand how this dilemma can be overcome and sufficient consensus on a new R&D policy within the EU can be built up, three sets of variables and their interplay have to be considered:
   a) **Ideas** (*Leitidee* as fit of causal and normative policy ideas):
      • *Causal ideas* must be able to explain the existing crisis and suggest 'reasonable' lines of action. They must be diffused throughout the whole European[28] area of scientific and industrial research and attributed with legitimacy.
      • Success of a causal concept in the multi-level European policy

system necessitates a *convincing link* to the basic European *normative ideas* (economic wealth through integration), a European *Leitidee* is needed.

- The demands of a *Leitidee* in European R&D policymaking are manifold. It needs to:
  - define what needs to be tackled (a crisis, a special opportunity) and offer a feasible concept for solution;
  - have scientific, 'technical', 'neutral' backing;
  - find (or help to create!) a window of opportunity;
  - fit to the overall norm of the European integration project and deliver added value;
  - simplify complexity and be marketable (e.g. label, key phrase) and thus leave enough room for interpretation.

b) **Interaction**: The diffusion and pushing through of ideas needs communication and interaction. As Europe does not have a common area of broad public communication on policy issues yet (e.g. Kielmansegg 1996), the direct interaction of stakeholders is both more difficult and more important than on the national level. Policy-specific European interaction is institutionalized on many different levels and arenas, and both the spontaneous and organized orchestration have to be taken into consideration, in order to understand the genesis of new interest definitions and finally policy change at European level.

c) **Central actor**: The European Commission as custodian of the European treaties must take action and functionally link ideas, experts and stakeholders in a way that not only lets ideas diffuse, but does so with a strong European impetus, i.e. the process management must create a broad perception of an added value potential in what is discussed at European level.

3. Last but not least, achieving sufficient consensus *takes time*. In the historic case of early EC programs, the process took almost ten years, from the first interaction of experts to discuss new R&D approaches and the institutionalization of new EC expert groups in the second half of the 1970s to the final decision on programs such as ESPRIT, RACE and BRITE and the Single Europe Act in 1986 that included R&D policy as a European policy area.

It goes without saying that history does not repeat itself and inter-temporal comparisons are risky. Above all, the shift towards a ERA has a different quality than the changes in the 1980s. The ERA does not add another area of policy competence to the European level, rather it changes the mode of operation within an established policy area. However, this change is the first serious attempt in 15 years and although it looks operational, it is strategic.

The ERA will in essence add a transnational program-like mode of research governance to the arena, complementing and – at a final stage – replacing the funding of a large number of short-term, small-scale and clearly specified projects. If the ERA is successful, the research landscape of Europe will change, the denationalization of research will accelerate, research institutions and companies alike will orient their networking activities more strategically on a European level and the self-organization of this process will speed up trans-border integration, and this will be realized largely without the interference of national policymakers. Although the aggregated national public R&D budgets will remain more important by far than the European ones, national policymakers will have to take into consideration that their national institutes and companies are involved in long-term research and networking activities that are beyond their reach. This change promises to be sweeping, and as any change, has already evoked fears and new uncertainties alongside new hopes and opportunities. Thus, a ERA will, at least in the short term, produce winners and losers, and the ERA debate is by its very nature a highly political process. Taking into account the historic lessons on R&D policy change in Europe and utilizing the framework developed above, how can we finally characterize this political process?

First of all, as regards the *consensus dilemma*, it is certainly true that the ERA discourse was framed in a way that heightened rather than reduced the perception of complexity and the necessity to reach consensus: only if European research organizations, companies, administrators and finally, political decision-makers, believe in the added value of long-term European networking and large-scale, largely self-organized projects, will the ERA materialize beyond the logic of extra money. However, compared to the 1980s, the heterogeneity in the European arena has become even bigger, as the ERA claims to be broader than the Framework Programmes (FPs) and to integrate or complement other European approaches, such as the European University Area,[29] COST or even EUREKA. In addition, in its original version it was geared towards the harmonization and deeper co-ordination of national programs, most importantly via Article 169, and toward the opening up of national programs, challenging national policymakers across the board.

Furthermore, if the existence of a *Leitidee* – as defined above – is a necessary condition for policy change, it is argued that this condition is met. The ERA indeed represents a European *Leitidee* which is based on a certain reading of the current crisis in Europe and a linkage of a new set of ideas. Similar to the key documents 20 years ago, the ERA documents present a *crisis definition* and an *ideational framework* and rationale that are fully in line with current mainstream thinking on innovation and growth. As for the *crisis definition*, only at first sight does the overall analysis from the European Commission, starting with the first ERA document (European

Commission 2000a), read very similar to older, traditional documents: Europe faces a research gap as compared mainly to the United States that endangers the long-term competitiveness of its economy. However, what is new beyond the analysis of under-investment in private and public R&D is the assessment that Europe suffers from *systemic failures*, mainly too little integration, networking, co-operation between European institutions, companies and administrations and compartmentalization of national and regional approaches. The danger and consequences of falling behind competing innovation systems as regards expenses for innovation and of actors towards networks of knowledge – in this framework – are extremely high. It is not only a loss of competitiveness, but it might very well cement the lack of the ability to *make the transition towards the 'knowledge economy'* (European Commission 2000a, p. 4).

It is obvious that this whole analysis of the European Commission, i.e. mainly DG Research, is framed within the *ideational context* of two recent major trends of economic thinking: it is about the *knowledge economy* and *innovation systems* – rather than about the technology community and R&D policies as was the case in the 1980s:

- In integrating the perspective of the *knowledge economy*, the ERA proposal has taken on a relatively recent concept. Again, as to the international diffusion of this concept, publications within and in connection with the OECD have pushed this new understanding most prominently (OECD 1996a; 1996b; 1997; David and Foray 1995; Smith 1995; Smith et al. 1995; Lundvall and Johnson 1994). In this concept, the meaning of knowledge becomes central for future economic growth, effective conditions and practices for the creation, diffusion and application of knowledge are therefore regarded as policy imperatives. With the major document 'The Knowledge-Based Economy' (OECD 1996a), the OECD put together the different strands of reasoning for the first time.
- Economic analyses of the 1990s not only stressed the importance of knowledge, they also called for a broad vertical and horizontal integration of all knowledge actors, not only for single, small-scale specific research projects, but more broadly, as a new structural feature of *innovation systems*. The innovation system approach was put forward and further developed by a number of scholars (see Nelson et al. 1993; Lundvall 1992; Edquist 1997) and meanwhile it is by far the most widely used framework for analysis, and has been pushed and streamlined by the OECD (1997). In this perspective, the compartmentalization and fragmentation of national public research structures and R&D policies was one of the most important obstacles to the necessary integration of knowledge-creating assets and actors.

The idea of integrating the conditions for knowledge creation and diffusion into innovation system-like approaches was, again, not born within the European Commission, and this is a major reason for its acceptance. As just seen above, the broad pertinent economic literature has again been summarized and pushed forward by the OECD, that had issued comparative work on national innovation systems and knowledge economies (OECD 1996a; 1996b; 1997). The OECD claimed that the 'understanding of these [innovation] systems can help policymakers develop approaches for enhancing innovative performance in the knowledge-based economies of today' (OECD 1997, p. 3). In framing the new approach in this context, the European Commission could claim to have theoretical backing and thus legitimization for its concept that was based on expertise.[30]

It was the achievement of the European Commission to capture and link these ideas and analyses to a rather traditional problem definition as regards research and technology in Europe, and postulate a new rationale: the effective, efficient and sustainable creation and distribution of knowledge is not only important for the R&D system, but for economic growth and welfare in general. Within this framework, the problem to be tackled at the European level is the effective generation and diffusion of knowledge in Europe, taking advantage of inter-institutional linkages.

In order to lift this causal concept up to the normative level – thus creating a *Leitidee* of the ERA – the European Commission found a window of opportunity at a very early stage. While in the 1980s convincing the highest national political decision-makers took place at the end of the process, the European Commission succeeded in introducing its ideas into the highest level of European decision-making right at the beginning of the whole debate. In March 2000, only two months after the ERA concept was first communicated, it was endorsed by the Lisbon European Council. Lisbon was a special European Council Meeting on 'employment, economic reform and social cohesion'. Here, not only did the European Commission fight for backing of its concept, but also a couple of high level experts discussed new approaches to foster innovation and growth throughout Europe with heads of state, organized by the Portuguese presidency.[31] The Presidency Conclusion interpreted the 'knowledge economy' as a quantum shift for the EU and declared the new strategic goal of the Union to 'become the most competitive and dynamic knowledge-based economy in the world ...' (European Council 2000, p. 2). This normative goal was linked to the establishment of a 'European Area of Research and Innovation', including the co-ordination of national programs (ibid., pp. 4–5). Thus the European Commission was given a mandate to go ahead, the ERA had its normative backing.[32]

These developments characterize the role played by the European Commission, the *central actor* of the institutionalization of a ERA. With Lisbon, the legitimization based on the integration of mainstream ideas was provided with a political will. If Caswill (in this volume) talks about the ERA as a *coup d'état* of the European Commission, he is right, as to the suddenness with which the policymaking community in the R&D field was hit by the new development. However, one should qualify this assessment that by winning over the heads of state, this was a revolution with green light from above. Next to the integration of current causal ideas into its concept, the second most important achievement by the central actor European Commission was convincing the Council in Lisbon. From the very beginning of the ERA debate, the European Commission acted as a political entrepreneur that was able to manage the ideational discourse in a functional, almost instrumental fashion.

In line with this very proactive strategy, the European Commission organized the activities to inform and mobilize stakeholders and build up a common understanding and consensus much more intensively than it did in the 1980s. In a very broad and concerted effort the European Commission tackled the different stakeholder groups – such as the national R&D policy administrations as well as the European institutions (most importantly the Parliament), interest groups (and individual big players) of the stakeholders, and finally the individual researchers, institutes and companies – at the same time. Most importantly, and in striking contrast to the developments 20 years before, all of this interaction now stood within the shadow of hierarchy, as the European Council had endorsed the ERA in principle at the very beginning of the mobilization.

The interaction that ensued should be thoroughly analyzed, which cannot be achieved within this paper. However, a very preliminary analysis based on Internet documentation of the communication and feedback process, as well as focussed journals[33] confirms the speed and the determination of the European Commission. The mobilization campaign included high level conferences, a series of targeted research and reference projects, the call for contributions and opinions from national ministries, industrial and scientific federations, companies and institutes. It was organized traditionally (issuing of documents, meetings etc.) and, in contrast to the 1980s, via the Internet.[34] The speed with which the European Commission issued several new Communications to clarify (e.g European Commission 2000a; 2002b) and to tackle complementary issues[35], and with which it reacted to the criticism contained in the hundreds of opinions it received, is impressive. Moreover, the European Commission interacted not only in conferences and through documents, but also in sending letters signed by European Commissioner Busquin directly to hundreds of stakeholders and by replying to contributions in three short reports launched in the Internet.[36] The peak of this mobilization campaign was the call for Expressions of Interest[37] as regards the usage of the two major new instruments geared towards the research community itself, *Networks of Excellence* and *Integrated Projects* (see Kuhlmann and Edler in this volume). Even if most of the expressions may not stand the test of time, more than 11 000 Expressions of Interest certainly indicate a mobilization success (European Commission 2002b).

In addition to this orchestration, the European Commission intensified its efforts to create a common ground for policymaking in Europe by moderating a process to define a common reference system for Science, Technology and Innovation and the related policies. This process integrated experts and administrators from the Member States and accession countries and materialized in a series of projects, workshops and conferences. Theses activities were at the heart of what Caracostas (in this volume) has labeled 'shared governance'.[38] This approach has the *explicit* backing of the Lisbon Council (Lisbon European Council 2000), that gave the European Commission the mandate to build up a common reference system for the European innovation system. Moreover, it continues a policy that had been started in similar fashion within the OECD (benchmarking of knowledge economies).[39] Therefore – and above all – this common definition of problems and indicators and the common benchmarking of policy practices has become a major means of consensus-building that may very well contribute to the convergence of the conceptual thinking about R&D and innovation in Europe.

To sum up, the main finding of this preliminary analysis of the ERA process in the light of the historic change process analyzed above is that the European Commission has successfully mastered the challenges of breaking up path dependency in European R&D policy by taking into account the meaning of interaction and, more importantly, underlying ideas. It has created, and to a large degree filled, a European area of policy discourse. In comparison to the developments leading to the first take-off in the 1980s, the relevant interaction and the exchange of ideas in the course of the ERA debate – this is the major conclusion of this inter-temporal comparison – were fully driven by the European Commission from the very beginning. While the inclusion of experts and mainstream theoretical rhetoric followed similar patterns as in the 1980s, the very early infusion of the ideas into the highest policy circles of the multi-level system led to a very different character of the discursive strategy.

From the perspective of the European Commission, this conclusion looks rather positive. However, the whole strategy of the European Commission surely has its pitfalls, and these began to show in the second half of 2002. *Firstly*, the momentum that was created was too big. The analysis of the call for Expressions of Interest has shown that many more actors applied than the system can include. Moreover, many of the proposals were not even eligible. Once the final call is launched and the first decisions taken, the resulting frustration for many stakeholders might backfire and endanger the legitimization of the whole endeavor.

Secondly, as the new instruments aim at large networks and projects, all stakeholders with sub-critical resources to play this game of size fear that they will be left behind. This fear has not been overcome by the explanations of the European Commission, as many contributions by research institutes, SME organizations and, most of all, administrations from small countries show.

Thirdly, the ERA project has evoked misunderstandings as it has never been made clear if it includes the 'innovation area' or not. While the Lisbon European Council in March 2000 and the Nice European Council in December 2000 endorsed an 'area of research and innovation', the European Commission, rather DG XII, has always stuck to a ERA rather than a EIRA (including innovation), although this has been asked for by various national governments and industrial federations. This friction points to an institutional problem within the European Commission, as DG XII and DG Enterprise – the latter being responsible for innovation activities – have different institutional rationales that seem to hinder integrative approaches. This is certainly not only a problem of the European administration and inhibits comprehensive innovation policy approaches in many countries as well. The problem, however, is aggravated as it potentially undermines the credibility of the ERA concept that is – implicitly – based on the innovation systems approach which above all demands the abolition of compartmentalization. A discursive strategy is endangered if the promoter does not comply to the norms of the underlying ideas of its own concept.

Fourthly, the national research ministries have started to apply the brakes. In a Council Resolution of 17 January 2002, the ministers endorse the concept in principle. However, they claim that the traditional instruments may further be applied and they want Art. 169 to be applied only in a 'limited number of pilot projects' on a case-by-case basis.[40] Commissioner Busquin objected in October 2002 that the administrations of R&D policymaking are still not in line:

> ... l'engagement des Etats membres et des administrations nationales est trop faible ou trop superficiel. Sur la base d'un bilan détaillé, la Commission va donc prochainement présenter des propositions pour donner un nouvel élan à l'entreprise de création de l'Espace Européen de la Recherche. Notamment en lui conférant des moyens plus puissants pour arriver à une véritable coordination des activités et des politiques nationales.

To be sure, the reluctance of national administrations has very diverse reasons, ranging from the fear of small countries of falling behind to the apprehension of big ones that the whole system might be too inflexible. As this analysis concentrates on the discursive conditions of the genesis of policy, it only wants to point to a possible strand of explanation that is very often neglected. One major reason might very well be that the administrators themselves were not a target group of the discursive strategy. While heads of state or national ministers have elaborated on the basic rationale of a ERA, and while stakeholders have been eager to be part of the game, national administrators have not been specifically addressed. However, for a smooth transition towards a ERA, it is the administrators who have to be convinced that what they seem to lose in supporting a ERA in fact can be a long-term advantage of the European, and hence national, innovation systems. While conceptually a ERA might link sensible causal ideas, and while normatively a ERA might have been labeled as a means to meet strategic goals of the EU, it still might not succeed if the persuasive strategy of the European Commission is not more inclusive towards the national administrations.

NOTES

[1] The terminology of the European Commission has long been 'RTD' policy, however, we follow the terminology 'R&D' which is more common internationally.

[2] The Sections 2 to 4, that explain the theoretical model and discuss the historical case needed for the comparative analysis, draw on Edler (2002).

[3] '*Konsenszwang*', translation by the author.

[4] For a detailed conceptualization see Edler (2000, pp. 46–64).

[5] This concept of a *Leitidee* is based on Göhler (1994) and is broadly elaborated in Edler (2000).

[6] DG XII is now labelled DG Research, however, this article deals with 'historic' developments and therefore will stick to the old numerical label.

[7] The few minor programs that had been implemented by the early 1980s had been decided upon under the general clause of article 235 of the EEC treaty.

[8] 1980. Moreover, this development fitted into the overall shift in economic (and political) paradigm towards supply-side economics, which replaced Keynesianism and concentrated on the build up of favorable conditions for growth (Edler 1993).

[9] There have been different labels for this recursive model of the innovation process, e.g. 'concomitance model' (EIRMA 1982b) '*Kopplungsmodell*', 'chain-linked model' (Kline and Rosenberg 1986).

[10] The literature produced at that time is abundant, see for example EIRMA (1982b); Keck (1986); Kline and Rosenberg (1986); OECD (1991); Nelson and Winter (1982); Freeman (1982); Nelson (1982).

[11] For the meaning of microelectronics, see OECD (1980); Perez (1983); Freeman and Soete (1985); Hohn et al. (1985).

[12] This of course only holds true within the limits set by rising transactions costs.

[13] The US experts were the main representatives of the systematic, evolutionary innovation theory Nelson (USA) and well-known analysts of the R&D process and its economic effects (Rosenberg, Fusfeld, Hirschmann, Gilpin, Rothschild), from Europe the group had nine renowned specialists, who had all published in the field, some of them were still active in industrial research management Caracciolo di Forino (I) Colombo (I), Delapalme (Fr), Freeman (GB), Gruson (Fr), Krupp (D), Lagermalm (S), Pavitt (GB), Rathenau (NL).

[14] By way of illustration see EIRMA (1978; 1983a; 1983b); Fusfeld and Haklisch (1979; 1982); OECD (1981); Giersch (1982). In addition, in the course of compiling the most relevant OECD report (OECD 1980) there were a couple of high level conferences organized in various countries.

[15] Columbo and Delapalme, for example, had been members of CERD (Comité Européen pour la Recherche et le Développement, a European scientific advisory body of the 1970s and 1980s) and of the EIRMA (European Industrial Research Management Association, see below).

[16] This information is based on various interviews with (former) members of the DG XII.

[17] These summits were later institutionalized in the G7 (soon G8) summits.

[18] This assessment is again based on several interviews with CORDI members from the Commission and from industry.

[19] Interviews with German representatives indicate that the link between CORDI and EIRMA was important for industrialists in order to learn at a very early stage what conceptual ideas were being processed and what their basic rationale was.

[20] Colombo had been a member of the expert group, of the European scientific committee CERD, president of EIRMA and contributed to the work in CORDI (Colombo and Lanzavecchia 1982). He is one important example of several high level experts linking the transnational and European academic and industrial discourse.

[21] In Germany, for example, the Commission chose the Federal Agency for Materials Research and Testing (BAM, *Bundesanstalt für Materialforschung und -prüfung*), which to a large extent is paid for by the federal government and is the focal point for materials research in Germany. Its final report (BAM 1982) can to a large extent be found in the first proposal for BRITE by the Commission (European Commission 1983).

[22] Based on analysis of various years of UNICE's 'Monthly Report' and other documents analyzed at the archive of UNICE, Brussels.

[23] Both ministries have meanwhile changed their names, BMFT now is BMBF and BMWi now is BMWA.

[24] Grewlich and Seitz both were senior members of Genscher's working staff in the foreign ministry.

[25] Grewlich gives a very concise and informed summary of the complex set of causal ideas making up BRITE (Grewlich 1984, pp. 255 ff.), and Genscher himself propounded this understanding (Genscher 1984; 1985).

[26] See among others: Richardson (1994); Nugent (1995); Bach (1995); Jourdain (1996).

[27] The right to file suit at court, mentioned by Lepsius (1991)), was not significant in research and technology policy up to now.

[28] Europe meaning the EU respectively EC countries.

[29] See *Kowi aktuell* **50**, 25 March 2002 and www.bologna-berlin2003.de.

[30] After all, representatives from the epistemic community were highly visible at the European level and even participated in relevant Community projects and networks (e.g. Lundval and Borras 1997; Cowan and van de Paal 2000). Cowan and van de Paal from MERIT summarise the major findings and conclusion of a project funded by the European Commission (DG Enterprise) on 'Innovation in a Knowledge Based Economy' which consisted of a number of different parts and publications all dealing with knowledge economy and the European dimension as for policy responses, see: http://www.cordis.lu/innovation-policy/studies/gen_study4.htm#download.

[31] Based on an informal report of a participating expert in the context of a scientific conference shortly after the Lisbon Council.

[32] Soon after the Lisbon Council, the Parliament, albeit criticising many details, endorsed the general idea of a ERA, too (European Parliament 2001).

[33] For the very specific ERA debate, the most relevant and thorough overview is provided by the Commission service CORDIS (Cordis NEWS: *R&D Beyond 2002: News and Events*, see also http://www.cordis.lu/R&D2002/era-debate/era.htm). Of several relevant journals, two were selected for screening, both delivering concise analysis and, above all, links to the ongoing discussions: *Research Europe* and *Kowi aktuell*.

[34] The Commission has set up two web-sites to promote the ERA: http://europa.eu.int/comm/research/ area.html and the one provided by CORDIS (see endnote above)

[35] For example: Co-ordination of national programs within the ERA (European Commission 2001a), ERA and internationalization (European Commission 2001b), ERA and regions (European Commission 2001c).

[36] http://europa.eu.int/comm/research/area/comments1.html (25 February 2001), followed by similar reports and comments on 4 April 2001 (...comments2.html) and 15 June 2001 (...comments3.html).

[37] Official Journal C 71/14 of 20 March 2002.

[38] For the common indicators see http://europa.eu.int/comm/research/era/sti_en.html. For the benchmarking process see http://europa.eu.int/comm/research/era/benchmarking2001_en. html.

[39] In doing so, the OECD continued its tradition of letting analytical frameworks and interpretations converge by working towards uniform indicators and reference systems, as had been done before for R&D (Frascati Manual) and Innovation (OSLO Manual).

[40] Common Position adopted by the Council with a view to the adoption of a Decision of the European Parliament and of the Council concerning the Sixth Framework Programme (FP6) contributing to the creation of a European Research Area, Interinstitutional File 2001/ 0053/COD), 15483/01, RECH 191 CODEC 1389, Brussels, 17 January 2002.

REFERENCES

Bach, M. (1995), 'Ist die Europäische Einigung irreversibel? Integrationspolitik als Institutionenbildung in der Europäischen Union', in Nedelmann, B. (ed.), *Politische Institutionen im Wandel*, Opladen, pp. 368–91.

BAM (1982), *Technische Materialforschung und -prüfung. Entwicklungstendenzen und Rahmenvorschläge für ein EG-Programm Basic Technological Research*. Berlin: Bundesanstalt für Materialforschung und -prüfung (BAM).

Bayne, N. (1987), 'Making sense of western economic policies: the role of the OECD', *The World Today*, **2**, 27–30.

Berger, P.L. and Th. Luckmann (1967), *The Social Construction of Reality. A Treatise in the Sociology of Knowledge*, New York.

Boyer, R. (1979), *Déterminants d'Evolution Probable de la Productivité et de l'Emploi*, Paris.

Braun, D. (1993), *Politische Steuerungsfähigkeit in intermediären Systemen am Beispiel der Förschungsförderung*, MPIFG Disscussion Paper, Cologne: MPIFG.

Colombo, U. and G. Lanzavecchia (1982), *Plan by Objective: R & D to Promote European Industry Competitiveness*, Rome: commissioned by the General Directorate for Research DG XII.

Colombo, U., W. Zegveld and E.J. Tuininga (1982), 'The European Community and Innovation Opportunities. Constraints and Recommendations', in European Commission (ed.), *1980–1990: a New Development on the European Scientific Policy*, proceedings on a conference held in Strasbourg 20–22 October 1982, Brussels and Luxemburg: European Commission, EUR 1721, pp. 271–386.

Cowan, R. and G. van de Paal (2000), *Innovation Policy in a Knowledge-Based Economy*, final report to the European Commission, June 2000, EUR 17023.

Cram, L. (1994), 'The European Commission as a multi-organization: social policy and IT policy in the EU', *Journal of European Public Policy*, **1** (2), 194–217.

Dahrendorf, R. (ed.) (1983), *Europas Wirtschaft in der Krise. Bestandsaufnahme und Analyse*, München: Wilhelm Goldmann.

David, P. and D. Foray (1995), 'Accessing and expanding the science and technology knowledge base', *STI Review*, **16**, Paris: OECD.

Delapalme, B. (1980), 'Letter of Transmittal', in OECD (ed.), *Technical Change and Economic Policy*, Paris, pp. 109–10.

Dooge-Committee (1985), 'Bericht des Ad-hoc-Ausschusses für institutionelle Fragen an den Europäischen Rat in Brüssel am 29. und 30. März 1985', in Weidenfeld, W. and W. Wessels (eds), *Wege zur Europäischen Union. Vom Vertrag zur Verfassung*, Bonn, pp. 130–45.

Edler, J. (1993), *Die Bedeutung von Ideen, Interessen und Institutionen bei der Herausbildung wirtschaftspolitischer Strategiewechsel*, Mannheim: University of Mannheim, dissertation.

Edler, J. (2000), *Institutionalisierung europäischer Politik. Die Genese des Forschungsprogramms BRITE als reflexiver sozialer Prozeß*, Baden-Baden.

Edler, J. (2002), 'How Do Economic Ideas Become Relevant in R&D Policy Making? Lessons From a European Case Study', in Biegelbauer, P. and S. Borras (eds), *Innovation Policies in Europe and the US: the New Agenda,* Ashgate, forthcoming.

Edquist, Ch. (1997), *Systems of Innovation. Technologies, Institutions and Organizations*, London and Washington: Pinter.

EIRMA (1978), *Workshop Technology 88, Paris, 15-17 March 1978,* Paris: EIRMA.

EIRMA (1982a), *Industry's Needs for Basic Research,* working group reports N° 23, Paris: EIRMA.

EIRMA (1982b), *The Role of R&D in the Innovation Process*, working group reports N° 27, Paris: EIRMA.

EIRMA (1983a), *Technological Challenges to European Industry Today*, special conference, Brussels, 22–23 September 1983, Paris: EIRMA, conference papers Vol. XXIX.

EIRMA (1983b), *The Role of Industrial R&D in the 80's*, proceedings of the EIRMA Annual Conference, Interlaken, 18–20 May 1983, Paris: EIRMA, conference papers Vol. XXVIII.

European Commission (1980), *Industrielle Entwicklung und Innovation*, Mitteilung der Kommission an den Europäischen Rat in Luxemburg am 1. und 2. Dezember 1980, Brussels: European Commission, 27 November 1980.

European Commission (1981a), *Basic Technological Research. Preliminary Ideas and Suggestions for Actions*, discussion paper, intern manuscript, Brussels: European Commission.

European Commission (1981b), *Zur Entwicklung der Industrie in Europa: eine Strategie der Gemeinschaft*, Brussels: European Commission, COM (81) 639 final, 12 November 1981.

European Commission (1982), *1980–1990: a New Development on the European Scientific Policy*, proceedings of the conference held at Straßbourg, 20–22 October 1982, Brussels and Luxembourg: European Commission, EUR 7121.

European Commission (1983), *Proposal for a Council Decision Adopting a Multiannual Programme of the European Community in the Field of Basic Technological Research*, Brussels: European Commission, COM (83) 350.

European Commission (1984), *The Research and Technology Policy of the EC: Developments Until 1984*, Brussels and Luxembourg: European Commission, Office for official publications.

European Commission (2000a), *Towards a European Research Area*, Brussels: European Commission, COM (2000) 6.

European Commission (2000b), *Making a Reality of the European Research Area: Guidelines for EU Research Activities (2002–2006)*, Brussels: European Commission.

European Commission (2001a), *The Framework Programme and the European*

Research Area: Application of Article 169 and the Networking of National Programmes, Brussels: European Commission, COM (2001) 0282, 30 May 2001.

European Commission (2001b), *The International Dimension of the European Research Area*, communication from the European Commission, Brussels: European Commission, COM (2001) 346, 25 June 2001.

European Commission (2001c), *The Regional Dimension of the European Research Area*, Brussels: European Commission, COM (2001) 549 final, 3 October 2001.

European Commission (2002a), *Introduction of the Instruments Available for Implementing the FP6 Priority Thematic Areas*, Brussels: European Commission, internal speaking notes, 2 April 2002.

European Commission (2002b), *Report on the Analysis of Expressions of Interest 2002*, Brussels: European Commission, September 2002, call identifier EII.FP6.2002.

European Council (1980), 'Schlußfolgerungen des Vorsitzes, 18. Tagung, Luxemburg, 1–2 December 1980', in Generalsekretariat des Rates (General Secretariat of the European Council) (1989) (ed.), *Europäischer Rat. März 1975 bis Dezember 1988 – 1. bis 40. Tagung – Schlußfolgerungen*, pp. 137–40.

European Council (1982), 'Schlußfolgerungen des Vorsitzes, 22. Tagung, Brüssel, 29–30 March 1982', in Generalsekretariat des Rates (General Secretariat of the European Council) (1989) (ed.), *Europäischer Rat. März 1975 bis Dezember 1988 – 1. bis 40. Tagung – Schlußfolgerungen*, pp. 150–53.

European Council (1983), 'Feierliche Deklaration zur Europäischen Union, verabschiedet am 19. Juni 1983 in Stuttgart', in Generalsekretariat des Rates (General Secretariat of the European Council) (1989) (ed.), *Europäischer Rat. März 1975 bis Dezember 1988 – 1. bis 40. Tagung – Schlußfolgerungen*, pp. 167–72.

European Council (1984), 'Texte, die den Beratungen des Europäischen Rats zugrunde lagen und dem Rat in seinen verschiedenen Zusammensetzungen zur Orientierung dienen könnten', in Generalsekretariat des Rates (General Secretariat of the European Council) (1989) (ed.), *Europäischer Rat. März 1975 bis Dezember 1988 – 1. bis 40. Tagung – Schlußfolgerungen*, pp. 175–86.

European Council (2000): *Presidency Conclusion of the European Council of Lisbon*, 23–24 March 2000.

European Parliament (2000), *Report on the Communication From the Commission 'Towards a European Research Area'*, Committee on Industry, External Trade, Research and Energy, final A5, 0131/2000, 9 May 2000.

European Parliament (2001), European Parliament Resolution on the Communication from the Commission: *Making a Reality of the European Research Area: Guidelines for the EU Research Activities (2002–2006)*, European Commission, COM (2000) 612, adopted February 2001.

Federal Ministry for Research and Technology [BMFT] (1984), *Bundesforschungsbericht 1984*, Bonn: BMFT.

Freeman, Ch. (1982), *The Economics of Industrial Innovation*, second edition, London.

Freeman, Ch., J. Clark and L. Soete (1982), *Unemployment and Technical Innovation. A Study of Long Waves and Economic Development*, London.

Freeman, Ch. and L. Soete (1985), *Informationstechnologie und Beschäftigung*, Sussex.

Fusfeld, H.I. and C. Haklisch (1979), *Science and Technology Policy: Perspectives for the 1980s*, New York: Academy of Science.

Fusfeld, H.I. and C. Haklisch (1982), *Industrial Productivity and International Technical Cooperation*, Fusfeld, H.I. (ed.), New York: Mimeo.

Genscher, H.-D. (1984), 'Die technologische Herausforderung', in Außenpolitik, *Zeitschrift für internationale Fragen*, **35** (1), 3–18.

Genscher, H.-D. (1985), 'Rede auf der ersten Eureka-Ministerkonferenz in Paris am 17. Juli 1985', *Europa-Archic*, **17**, D31–5.

Giersch, H. (1982), *Emerging Technologies: Consequences for Economic Growth, Structural Change and Employment*, Giersch, H. (ed.), Symposium 1981, Tübingen: Institut für Weltwirtschaft Kiel.

Göhler, G. (1994), 'Politische Institutionen und ihr Kontext. Begriffliche und konzeptionelle Überlegungen zur Theorie politischer Institutionen', in Göhler, Gerhard (ed.), *Die Eigenart der Institutionen. Zum Profil politischer Institutionentheorie*, Baden-Baden, pp. 19–46.

Grande, E. (1994), *Vom Nationalstaat zur Europäischen Politikverflechtung. Expansion und Transformation moderner Staatlichkeit – untersucht am Beispiel der Forschungs- und Technologiepolitik*, Konstanz: University of Konstanz, Habilitationsschrift.

Grewlich, K.W. (1981), 'Technologie – die Sicherheit Europas', *Außenpolitik*, **32** (3), 211–25.

Grewlich, K.W. (1984), 'EG-Forschungs- und Technologiepolitik – eine besondere Verantwortung für das wirtschaftlich-technologische "Flaggschiff?" ', in Wesels, W. and R. Hrbek (eds), *EG-Mitgliedschaft – ein vitales Interesse der Bundesrepublik Deutschland?*, Bonn, pp. 223–71.

Grewlich, K.W. (1985), 'Informationstechnologien – Europas Antwort', *Außenpolitik*, **36** (2), 127–35.

Guzzetti, L. (1995), *A Brief History of European Union Research*, Brüssel: European Commission, General Directorate XII.

Haas, P.M. (1993), 'Epistemic Communities and the Dynamics of International Environmental Co-operation', in Rittberger, V. (ed.), *Regime Theory and International Relations*, Oxford, pp. 168–201.

Henderson, D. (1993), 'International Economic Cooperation Revisited', *Government and Opposition*, pp. 11–35.

Hohn, E.J., H. Klodt and Ch. Saunders (1985), 'Advanced Machine Tools: Production, Diffusion and Trade', in Sharp, M. (ed.), *Europe and the New Technologies*, London, pp. 46–86.

Jachtenfuchs, M. and B. Kohler-Koch (1996), 'Regieren im dynamischen Mehrebenensystem', in Jachtenfuchs, M. and B. Kohler-Koch (eds), *Europäische Integration*, Opladen, pp. 15–44.

Jourdain, L. (1996), 'La Commission Européenne et la construction d'un nouveau modèle d'intervention publique. Le cas de la politique de recherche et de développement technologique', *Revue Francaise de Science Politique*, **46** (3), 496–520.

Kaiser, K. (1983), *EG vor der Entscheidung. Fortschritt oder Verfall*, Bonn.

Kalka, P. (1984), 'Die Genese einer gemeinsamen Forschungs- und Entwicklungspolitik in den Europäischen Gemeinschaften', *Polnische Weststudien*, **3** (2), 315–51.

Keck, O. (1986), 'Gesellschaftliche Steuerung der Technik – ein institutioneller Ansatz', in Bechmann, G. and F. Meyer-Krahmer (eds), *Technologiepolitik und Sozialwissenschaft*, Frankfurt am Main and New York, pp. 17–41.

Kielmansegg, P.G. (1996), 'Integration und Demokratie', in Jachtenfuchs, M. and B. Kohler-Koch (eds), *Europäische Integration*, Leverkusen, pp. 47–71.

Kingdon, J.W. (1984), *Agendas, Alternatives and Public Policies*, Michigan: University of Michigan.

Kline, S. and N. Rosenberg (1986), 'An Overview of Innovation', in Landau, R. and N. Rosenberg (eds), *The Positive Sum Strategy. Harnessing Technology for Economic Growth*, Washington DC, pp. 275–306.

Kohler-Koch, B. (1998), 'Bundeskanzler Kohl. Baumeister Europas? Randbemerkungen zu einem zentralen Thema', in Wewer, G. (ed.), Bilanz der Ära Kohl. Christlich-liberale Politik in Deutschland 1982–1998, *Zeitschrift für Gegenwartskunde*, Sonderheft **1998**, pp. 11–25.

Lepsius, R.M. (1991), 'Die Europäische Gemeinschaft: Rationalitätskriterien der Regimebildung', in Zapf, W. (ed.), *Die Modernisierung moderner Gesellschaften, Verhandlungen des 25. Soziologentages in Frankfurt/Main 1990*, Frankfurt/Main, pp. 309–17.

Lisbon European Council (2000): *Lisbon European Council 23–24 March 2000*, Presidency Conclusions.

Lundvall, B.Å. (1992), *National Systems of Innovation: Towards a Theory of Innovation and Interactive Learning*, Lundvall, B.Å. (ed.), London, UK: Pinter.

Lundvall, B.Å. and B. Johnson (1994), 'The learning economy', *Journal of Industrial Studies*, **1** (2).

Lundvall, B.Å. and S. Borras (1997), *The Globalising Learning Economy: Implications for Innovation Policy December 1997*, report based on contributions from seven projects under the TSER programme, DG Research, Brussels: European Commission.

March, J.G. and J.P. Olsen (1984), 'The New Institutionalism. Organizational Factors in Political Life', *American Political Science Review*, **78**, 734–49.

March, J.G. and J.P. Olsen (1989), *Rediscovering Institutions*, New York.

March, J.G. and J.P. Olsen (1994), 'Institutional Perspectives on Governance', in Derlien, H.U., U. Gerhardt and F.W. Scharpf (eds), *Systemrationalität und Partialinteresse. Festschrift für Renate Mayntz*, Baden-Baden, pp. 249–70.

Mayntz, R. and F.W. Scharpf (1995), 'Steuerung und Selbstorganisation in staatsnahen Sektoren', in Manytz, R. and F.W. Scharpf (eds), *Gesellschaftliche Selbstregulierung und politische Steuerung*, Frankfurt/Main and New York: Schriften des Max-Planck-Instituts für Gesellschaftsforschung, edition 23, Cologne, pp. 9–38.

Mazey, S. and J. Richardson (1996), 'La Commission Européenne. Une bourse pour les idées et les intérets', *Revue Francaise de Science Politique*, **46** (3), 409–30.

Meyer-Krahmer, F. and G.H. Walter (1982), *Barriers to International Cooperation Between Firms in the Field of Industrial Research and Development*, final report on behalf of the European Commission, Brussels: European Commission, Directorate General XII.

Moravcsick, A. (1991), 'Negotiating the Single European Act', in Keohane, R.O. and S. Hoffmann (eds), *The New European Community. Decision-Making and Institutional Change*, pp. 41–85.

Narula, R. (2000), 'Explaining the growth of strategic R&D alliances by European firms', *Journal of Common Market Studies*, **4** (37), 711–23.

Nelson, R.R. (1982), 'Public Policy and Technical Progress. A Cross-Industrial

Analysis', in Nelson, R.R. (ed.), *Government and Technical Progress. A Cross-industrial Analysis*, New York: Pergamon, pp. 1–8.

Nelson, R.R. (ed.) (1993), *National Innovation Systems: a Comparative Analysis*, Oxford and New York: Oxford University Press.

Nelson, R.R. and S.G. Winter (1982), *An Evolutionary Theory of Economic Change*, Cambridge and London: The Belknap Press.

Nugent, N. (1995), 'The Leadership Capacity of the European Commission', *Journal of European Public Policy*, **2** (4), 603–23.

OECD (1980), *Technical Change and Economic Policy*, Paris: OECD (Organisation for Economic Co-operation and Development).

OECD (1981), *Science and Technology Policy for the 1980s*, Paris: OECD (Organisation for Economic Co-operation and Development).

OECD (1991), *Background Report Concluding the Technology-Economy Programme (TEP)*, Paris: OECD (Organisation for Economic Co-operation and Development).

OECD (1996a), *The Knowledge-Based Economy*, Paris: OECD (Organisation for Economic Co-operation and Development), OCDE/GD(96)102.

OECD (1996b), *Transition to Learning Economies and Societies*, Paris: OECD (Organisation for Economic Co-operation and Development).

OECD (1997), *National Innovation Systems*, Paris: OECD (Organisation for Economic Co-operation and Development).

Perez, C. (1983), 'Structural change and assimilation of new technologies in the economic and social system', *Futures*, **14** (5), 357–75.

Peterson, J. (1995), 'EU Research Policy: the Politics of Expertise', in Rhodes, C. and S. Mazey (eds), *The State of the European Union: Building a European Polity*, Boulder, CO, pp. 391–412.

Richardson, J. (1994), 'EU Water Policy: uncertain agendas, shifting networks and complex coalitions', *Environmental Politics*, **4** (4), 140–68.

Sandholtz, W. (1992), *High Tech Europe. The Politics of International Co-operation*, Berkeley, Los Angeles and Oxford: University of California Press.

Scharpf, F.W. (1983), 'Interessenlagen der Adressaten und Spielräume der Implementation bei Anreizprogrammen', in Mayntz, R. (ed.), *Implementation politischer Programme II. Ansätze zur Theoriebildung*, Opladen, pp. 99–116.

Schneider, R. (1986), 'ESPRIT und EUREKA – Europas Antworten auf die pazifische Herausforderung? – Europäische Technologiepolitik zwischen Technologiegemeinschaft und High-Tech-Unternehmen', *WSI-Mitteilungen*, **39** (14), 679–88.

Schneider, R. and J. Welsch (1990), 'Europäische Forschungs- und Technologieförderung zwischen Industriepolitik und gesellschaftlicher Zukunftssicherung', in Weizmüller, R. (ed.), *Marktaufteilung und Standortpoler in Europa*, Köln: p. 272.

Science Council of Canada (1979), *Forging the Link. A Technology Policy for Canada*, Report 29, Ottawa.

Seitz, K. (1985), 'SDI – die technologische Herausforderung für Europa', *Europa-Archiv*, **13**, 381–90.

Smith, K. (1995), 'Interactions in knowledge systems: foundations, policy implications and empirical methods', *STI Review*, **16**, Paris.

Smith, K., E. Dietrichs and S.O. Nas (1995), *The Norwegian National Innovation System: a Pilot Study of Knowledge Creation, Distribution and Use*, Oslo, Norway: STEP Group.

von Hippel, E. (1978), 'A customer-active paradigm for industrial product idea generation', *Research Policy*, **7**, 240–66.

Wallace, H. (1983), 'Negotiation, Conflict, and Compromise: the Elusive Pursuit of Common Policy', in Wallace, H., W. Wallace and C. Webb (eds), *Policy-Making in the Europan Community*, Chichester, pp. 43–80.

Wendt, A. (1992), 'Anarchy is what states make of it: the social construction of power politics', *International Organization*, **46** (2), 391–427.

Working Party TGE (1983), *Technology, Economic Growth, Employment*, report of the Working Party 'Technology, Economic Growth, Employment', set up by a decision by the heads of states and governments at their summit in Versailles, 4–6 June 1982, Bonn: Federal Ministry for Research and Technology (BMFT).

Young, O.R. (1991), 'Political leadership and regime formation: on the development of institutions in international society', *International Organization*, **45** (3), 281–308.

PART II

Changing Governance:
the Sub-European Perspective

6 European Research Area: New Roles for National and European RTDI Funding Programs?

Michael Stampfer

Tous les événements sont enchaînés dans le meilleur des mondes possibles; car enfin, si vous n'aviez pas été chassé d'un beau château, à grands coups de pied dans le derrière, pour l'amour de mademoiselle Cunégonde, si vous n'aviez pas été mis à l'inquisition, si vous n'aviez pas couru l'Amérique à pied, si vous n'aviez pas donné un bon coup d'épée au baron, si vous n'aviez pas perdu tous vos moutons du bon pays d'Eldorado, vous ne mangeriez pas ici des cédrats confits et des pistaches. Cela est bien dit, répondit Candide, mais il faut cultiver notre jardin.

Voltaire

THE BEST OF ALL RESEARCH AREAS

If We Had Not Lost All Our Sheep in the Good Country of El Dorado ...

Complexity is the word coming to mind first when talking about the history, scenarios and settings of European Research, Technology, Development and Innovation (RTDI) policies and programs,[1] and there are a lot of them around: There are 15 national RTDI policies, soon 25. Most of the existing and future European Union (EU) Member States have a number of regions with their own RTDI policies and measures. Moreover, on the national level RTDI policies are not coherent or streamlined and in most cases, they are not dominated by top-down policy settings. Rather, they can each be described as a kind of arena (Kuhlmann 1999) with no single dominating actor, but with different and changing settings, raging bulls, a high number of open and vested public and private interests and, of course, an ever-turning, hopefully virtuous circle of negotiations between the different actors.

The European level of policymaking adds a further level of complexity, as those who have participated in the process of preparing a new Framework Programme (FP) know. The mere facts speak for themselves: Thousands of projects, a considerable number of languages, business and administration cultures, hundreds of mixed groups for administering, monitoring, evaluating and planning programs and other instruments of the European RTDI policy, from CREST (Committee for Scientific and Technical Research) to ad hoc groups and an ever growing number of instruments.

Moreover, the formal competencies for RTDI policy exist on different layers in the political landscape. The EU treaty regulates this policy field as a mixed one, giving some powers and responsibilities to the European institutions and allowing the Member States to plan and perform their own RTDI policies in a broad sense (see also Box 6.1). RTDI policy instruments, namely funding programs, are used on all policy levels.

The picture gets even more complex when taking a look at innovation (policy) theory: In the last two decades the concept of (national) innovation systems (Edquist 1997; Lundvall 1992; Nelson 1993) replaced the notion of a linear model. Good RTDI policymaking is therefore to concentrate on the different actors' ability to interact and also on the quality of links and bridges in a given system. Regarding funding programs, this means a shift towards more complex interventions, like science–industry co-operations or support for industrial clusters.

A final question regarding complexity: Can we even see what happens? There has been considerable progress in the field of RTDI policy and program evaluations. Nevertheless, many outcomes and impacts remain unclear, specifically the final socioeconomic impacts of RTDI funding programs (OECD 1997).

At least from the perspective of RTDI funding programs we have to acknowledge these complexities and the multi-actor, multi-level settings when we take a closer look at the new European policy venture called European Research Area (ERA) and it's implications on governance structures. We have to describe some of the settings. We have to see the role of RTDI funding programs as they sometimes enhance, sometimes reduce complexities and in many cases provide a kind of glue between different institutions and their interests. Finally we should not be too bold in our ambitions and, in the wake of a big ERA, should not forget to cultivate our own modest program gardens.

... We Would Not Be Here to Build a ERA

This contribution discusses three hypotheses regarding the role of programs in RTDI policy governance structures in a ERA context:

- Hypothesis 1: RTDI policy and program funding does with good reasons not easily allow a clear-cut classification as predominantly European or as predominantly national.

- Hypothesis 2: As in the past decades, the national actors will in the future probably still play the most important role in the European RTDI policy arena in our context though they will lose more ground to regional and namely European players and structures.
- Hypothesis 3: Changes and some Europeanization of governance structures will be rather slow than quick, will emerge rather in a soft cultural than in a hard legal form and will more often stem from needs and developments different than direct RTDI policymaking.

European semantics, be it in RTDI policy or other fields, is dominated by the wish to be something really big in the global arena: the most dynamic area, the strongest in the world in ten years, as stated by the European Council resolutions of 15 June and 16 November 2000. What is the (future) reality – also regarding RTDI policy as a tool for such visions? Europe, the thriving unified continent or just a set of rules for prospering Member States? On the other hand, and this can be illustrated by the installation of a European Convention, there is an need for clearer roles and definitions: what should be done on the European level and what on national level. But is RTDI policy the right field for such grand European designs?

Again when we talk about a ERA, we should ask what is feasible and possible, taking into account the pervasive nature of RTDI policies: They appear at European, national and regional level, they serve their intrinsic purposes and they should also serve a number of other policy interests, from fostering economic progress to providing solutions for ecological and social problems.

As mentioned, the first hypothesis of this contribution is that the nature of RTDI policy and programs do not allow a clear classification of this policy area as predominantly European, like foreign trade policy, or predominantly national, like cultural policy. We see the game being played on all levels, in different variations due to different interests, sometimes competing and sometimes co-operating, using programs as one main instrument. Is a 'Common European Policy' for RTDI imaginable (see Box 6.1 in this chapter)?

The second hypothesis of this contribution is that now and most probably in ten years from now, the national level is and still will be the strongest actor in RTDI policymaking. This point does not touch the question whether public actors will be policymakers at all in the context of multinational corporations in a globalized environment, but it is about the 'balance of powers' between national and European policymakers:[2]

- The national level still controls the majority of public institutions and funding instruments in our policy context. This is not likely to change.
- National policymakers know that RTDI policy is one of the last resorts of

active national economic policy for keeping business locations attractive and they will defend it. This is perhaps the most important argument in our discussion: RTDI policy is highly important for internal competition within the Union, without the harmful effects of other kinds of subsidies. Programs play an important role in this context.

Box 6.1　　*What is meant by the currently fictitious term 'Common Research Policy'?*

Like in other European policy areas it could be imaginable that in a future ERA there will not only be a policy toolbox (like FP funding, treaties with non-EU member countries) on the European level but also clear European governance, even legislative power over national policy settings. Contrary to RTDI policy, the European institutions have quite extensive legislative powers in a number of other European policy areas. Of course law-making in these 'European' policy areas lies in the hands of the executive, i.e. national government representatives assembled in the Council of the EU, with the European Council playing the role of a renaissance 'prince' (Puntscher-Riekmann 2001, p. 215). Nevertheless in these cases we talk about common policies: This means that directives and regulations shape national policies and leave to national parliaments only the detailed implementation. In areas like monetary policy or foreign trade policy the Member States are also heavily involved in decision-making via their roles and representatives in the European institutions, but national sovereignty is nevertheless limited in its power to act in different forms.

In RTDI policy this is not the case: The decisions can be taken at national level without the limitations of a common sector policy. National (and regional) policymakers are free to adopt laws, to set up and fund institutions, to design and run programs etc. Limitations rather come from other policy fields like the Single Market with the European state aid policy frameworks.

The ERA document (European Commission 2000, p. 10) nevertheless has a vague vision of proceeding in the direction of a 'Common Research Policy': 'The European market of supply and demand in knowledge and technology still remains largely to be created. For it to develop and function *a real European research policy* [sic! M.S.] needs to be defined.' This bold vision is toned down in the same chapter:

Decompartmentalisation and better integration of Europe's scientific and technological area is an indispensable condition for invigorating research in Europe. We need to go beyond the current static structure of '15 plus 1' towards a more dynamic configuration. This has to be based on a more coherent approach involving measures taken at different levels: by the member states at national level, by the European Union with the Framework Programme and other possible instruments, and by intergovernmental co-operation organisations.

- The existence of one single European voice or chorus is not so important in our context as it is in other policy fields like foreign trade policy, competition policy or the emerging Common Foreign and Security Policy.

Different orchestras could even be a source of strength and the enforce-ment of one overall tune to be played could prove impossible. Of course there are global challenges and globalization trends in RTDI policy (see Lundvall and Borrás 1997; Meyer-Krahmer 1999), but they influence both European and national policymaking.

- The issue of critical masses, as often used as argument for a stronger common European approach, is tricky in this respect: a) Some of the changes are driven more by globalization, while others are perhaps more technology-driven; b) Some changes stem from political fields other than RTDI policy; c) Some initiatives can only succeed on a global level while in other fields regional actors are more active than ever.[3]
- The instrument of programs finally allows a flexible approach to existing problems and shortcomings. Contrary to huge infrastructure investment projects like Mars missions or supercolliders there is a clear argument for subsidiarity – at least as long as criteria like the European Added Value remain rather vague.

Starting from here were first ask what the ERA concept is about, if we can see trends for stronger Europeanization in RTDI policies regarding the instrument of funding programs on national and European levels and finally revisit the first two hypotheses mentioned. While doing so, provide some arguments that possible changes of governance structures will be rather gradual and soft, as stated in the third hypothesis. Please note some of the arguments provided are derived from a practitioner's experience and therefore not solely on the basis of academic sources.

The ERA Concept

After nearly 20 years of 'cohabitation' between European Community (EC) RTDI policy and the respective, much stronger national policies, the consen-sus of separately running x plus one policies to have been replaced by a broad policy debate on establishing a more common rationale in this policy field. One of the main triggers of this discussion has been – as always, if we re-member the goals of Third and Fourth Framework Programme (FP3 and FP4) initiatives like ESPRIT – the comparison between Europe and the two other main economic powers, the United States and Japan.

This time the story goes like this: 'Well, the Americans still get most of the Nobel Prize winners' – 'But our science base is very good anyhow.' – 'So our real problem is our ability to effectively develop and provide new products, processes and services, that means to translate science into innovation.' – 'That means we have mainly output problems?' – 'That's true, but our input base is also weaker, just compare the GDP ratios for RTDI and the number of researchers per 1000 inhabitants' – 'And not to forget: What we really want is more societal relevance of science and technology.'

The main thrust of the current discussion seems to go in the direction of 'making the most out of the huge research potential in Europe ...' (Busquin in: European Commission 2000, p. 3) by better-co-ordinated RTDI policies and initiatives. It is accentuated by the growing importance of RTDI policies in the overall economic policy portfolio in Europe as shown in the 2000 Lisbon declaration of the European Council (European Council 2000).[4] Shortly before, in January 2000, the European Commission issued the ERA communication 'Towards a European Research Area', which set the guidelines for the following steps. A broad number of proposals on the level of instruments is to ensure that Europe can 'go beyond the current static structure of "15 + 1" towards a more dynamic configuration ...' (European Commission 2000, p. 10, see also Box 6.1 above). This is based on a still rather vague vision of a Common European Market for knowledge, so a free flow of all elements and a European framework would be necessary, the same as in the Common Market for goods, services, capital and persons.

The last two years have seen a lot of analytical activity and work, mainly on new instruments. Many of those activities, like 'benchmarking', 'mapping of excellence' or instruments like the new Sixth Framework Programme (FP6), would have probably happened anyway, but now they have been especially designed under ERA auspices. This means for some instruments a major reorientation and policy shift, highly visible in the FP6 design. Most of such visible changes are still on the level of European instruments and not on the national or regional level: It looks that it might be easier to design a new FP than to integrate European guiding principles into national policies. If we add the strong role of national authorities in the planning process of a new FP, we get a first impression of who is in the driving seat.

If the ERA is to succeed even in a very limited form, significant steps have to be made from two directions: In a top-down approach, EC instruments have to be utilized to link together and 'open up' different initiatives, institutions or frameworks, be it governmental RTDI programs, research infrastructures or legal provisions. Among the instruments, the forthcoming FP6 is of the greatest importance. This top-down approach needs complementary steps from the bottom up. Governments have to include European and transnational elements among their policy tools much more strongly than they have before. The cautious discussion about opening up national RTDI programs is just one first hint how difficult this process will be for policy institutions on the national and regional levels. Interest groups, both from the scientific community and from industry, will have to lobby for a ERA and for the better interplay of EC, national and regional instruments: If the RTDI performers do not press for a ERA, the bottom up side will remain very weak.

FUNDING PROGRAMS AS IMPORTANT RTDI POLICY INSTRUMENTS

What Are RTDI Funding Programs?

In the context of policy change and governance the issue of programs is especially interesting because of a number of features they show: They are highly visible, they are aimed at changing and influencing actors' behavior, they often bring together different players, they trigger other forms of financing, they are not made for eternity and therefore extremely open for learning and renewal, finally, they are a good mirror for the policymakers' way of thinking.

Funding programs are of course only one important part of the RTDI policy toolkit. Other instruments include the *legal framework* for people, activities, results, health and environmental protection, etc., *the regulatory environment*, the financial provisions for *RTDI infrastructures* of all kinds, the various institutions as movers and performers, and finally, the interface between RTDI and *Higher Education*. The term 'programs' is to be understood in a very broad sense (OECD 1995, pp. 25 ff.), ranging from non-specified programs to thematically focussed initiatives and missions to programs with very specific target groups or incentives, for example science–industry co-operation. RTDI funding programs are a form of public support for RTDI activities.[5] Such activities are performed by the private and/or the public sector. The term 'funding' is also to be understood very broadly in this context. While in most cases it will mean direct support for RTDI activities, particularly grants, the definition also includes programs that are funding networking activities, or providing other financial and managerial instruments for ensuring the co-operation of different actors.

RTDI funding programs provide a structural framework for funding or otherwise supporting a number of individual projects or initiatives. Within their structure a set of goals and rules define the activities supported by the respective program. Such specifications can be technology-oriented or defined in a more horizontal way aimed at functions within the innovation system. Within an RTDI funding program the activities supported should serve the common thematic or structural purpose of the program. The links between the activities supported under the program umbrella can be rather loose or strong.

Such programs generally have a limited lifetime. RTDI funding program itself is neither a legal entity nor an institution but an instrument accessible and of possible use to natural and/or legal persons. It is a set of activities run and governed by a responsible authority, like an agency, a ministry, or a research council.

The Role of Programs in a Systems Context

All Member States as well as the EU use the different kinds of programs as policy tools. As already stated, their mission is generally to change and influence the behavior of actors. In this respect programs play an important role in difficult institutional settings and in cases of considerable complexity. We have stated that in Europe – and elsewhere – RTDI policy settings are highly complex and we have mentioned the innovation systems paradigm as a guiding factor for policymaking in our field. So some roles for programs in our context can be described as follows:

- 'Free money' and 'short-/mid-term horizon': Contrary to many other legal and financial instruments, RTDI funding programs are of a flexible nature. An extra amount of money is dedicated to new activities. Programs can be changed rather easily – some say too easily[6] – without provoking intense institutional debates. On all levels there are old and big institutions with longstanding traditions. Changing missions, structures and rules is a grinding process. Programs can serve as toolboxes, as glue, as lubricants and/or as bypasses (see also below). This tendency to reshape actors and institutions with extra program-based financial incentives can be seen in nearly all Member States.[7]
- 'Clear goals': Programs at least should have a clear set of goals, so clear messages can be sent to the target groups and success can be evaluated according to the original set of goals. In the ERA context it has to be seen that major goals of most national programs explicitly address the enhancement of the (relative) competitiveness of the country or region that spends the public money for it.[8] Though societal and 'European' goals seem to be gaining ground, national and regional competition between numerous policy actors is obviously a main driving force and rationale for these actors. Nearly all RTDI funding programs in the Member States stress the importance of enhancing scientific and/or industrial competitiveness in the regional entity whose governing body provides the public funding. In the last few years the issue of societal relevance has also been gaining ground (see for example Caracostas and Muldur 1997, p. 158; PREST et al. 2002).
- 'Change agents': Programs provide incentives for actors to change their behavior. This means for example to co-operate more, to perform more long-term RTDI activities, to embrace market logics etc. In some cases programs have the – open or hidden – 'governance' agenda of changing the research culture[9] of whole parts of the relevant innovation system (see also Box 6.2).
- 'Glue': One specific change function is the role of programs in clustering

actors. More and more RTDI funding programs see it as their mission to bring together different actors with different rationales within an innovation system (see also Box 6.3 below). Therefore programs are perhaps the most powerful short-term instruments in the context of innovation system concepts. If the quality of such a system largely depends on the degree and quality of interaction between its different actors, programs act in this respect both as a 'solvent' within traditional institutional settings and as a 'glue' beyond such settings.

• 'Open windows': The internationalization of national or regional innovation system actors forms the main mission of a considerable number of programs. The goals range from the simple exchange of human resources to long-term co-operation.

So programs are designed in specific ways to serve specific goals, some of them touching systems issues. It should be mentioned that, of course, programs are strongly influenced by the institutional background of the respective policy system and also by their target groups, like the university system or industry. A number of issues matter, including size, traditions, culture, legal provisions and organizational arrangements.

Box 6.2   The case for evolving best practice approaches: The STRATA project MAP[10]

Multi-actor and multi-measure programs (MAPs) are complex RTDI funding programs addressing not a single company or research institution but whole (sub)systems of innovation like science–industry co-operation. The overall objective of the thematic network entitled 'MAP – Multi-actor and multi-measure programs in RTDI funding' within FP5 (IHP, STRATA) is the development of good practice regarding MAP (= program) management and its dissemination to agencies and policymakers all over Europe. The objective of this recently started network will be met by bringing together MAP managers, complementary organizations and related policymakers to exchange experiences and create common and codified knowledge. The background to the proposal is the growing complexity of both the innovation processes and the public RTDI funding programs, which involve an increasing number of actors and measures. The final aim is to advise EC and other policymakers and program managers on best practice of MAP development, implementation and evaluation which would lead to increased efficiency and comparability of the whole RTDI policy cycle. The network will draw on tacit and decentralized knowledge and develop this to improve the effectiveness and efficiency of public intervention in RTDI policy. The knowledge gained is to be codified in a 'roadmap' and discussed in a series of open events to ensure broader dissemination beyond the limits of the network itself. A number of governance-related questions will be touched in this network, namely the interface policy-program level or the role of programs as change agents.

Who 'Governs' RTDI Funding Programs?

Before we go into the national and European settings the question remains how and by whom programs are governed. Governance in our context includes the power to design, influence, direct and reshape a program, in a broader sense also to influence the behavior of those touched by the program, namely those funded by program means. Governance therefore is not so much about the activities of one single dominating actor, but about relationships between a number of actors. These relationships are shaped and expressed by a multitude of instruments also within a given program, from hard legislative or contractual measures to soft facts and measures like a common history, beliefs, advice, management and co-operation support, etc. As this paper is not intended as a contribution to the broad theoretical governance literature and as the number of governance definitions is vast, we want to present here only a hands-on but hopefully robust practitioner model of what happens between actors in program settings (for overviews of the current literature regarding governance see Kuhlmann and Edler 2002; Lossgott 2001, p. 180).

We can see in the context of RTDI funding programs at least *four levels* of governance. Within and between the different levels we find the recurrent negotiations mentioned above, as well as a number of actors in the RTDI policymaking arena:[11]

- *A first level of governance is constituted by very general (legal) frameworks, rules and cultural habits*, partly within the RTDI context, partly outside. Examples of context-specific framework governance are laws regulating the organization of public research institutions. An example of non-specific framework governance is corporate taxation, influencing the investment and research behavior of firms. A mixed example is European state aid policy, originating in Single Market policy but providing a strong and very detailed legal framework as to when, how and to what extent firms performing RTDI can be subsidized by public funds. This type of governance is abstract, far-reaching, long-lasting and, in many cases, not tailored to the specific needs of RTDI policy, therefore often giving unclear signals to the actors in this policy field.
- *A second level comprises legal and social regulations establishing and determining public RTDI funding programs.* Nearly all such programs are based both on specific traditions and legal acts, the latter, in the national context, mostly designed or issued by a responsible ministry. At European level the well-known legislative procedures determine the FPs as do the interaction patterns between the European Commission, national authorities and different pressure groups. On this level policymaking institutions like national ministries or the Council of Ministers together with European

Parliament, on the basis of a proposal from the European Commission, set the rules for the programs for a given period. Typical examples for second-level governance include funding guidelines for a given program. These rules are mostly formal, abstract, to a certain degree flexible and based on considerable knowledge about the relevant instruments and actors. Governance on this level is still abstract, but mid-term oriented and aimed at a specified group of actors. The rules themselves are primarily binding for public administration actors who then, on this basis, exercise operative governance on actors performing RTDI activities funded by a program.

- *A third level of governance concerns contracts between policymakers like ministries and operative funding units* like specialized agencies, and the culture of agencification. A considerable number of RTDI funding programs are run by actors other than those making the overall or specific (legal) rules. Here the most important instruments are contracts including the terms of reference, success criteria, procedures and other issues of a program. Further strong factors are trust, habits and the overall architecture of the system. Third-level governance is more detailed and still mid-term oriented. It is supposed to preshape the relation between an agency and its 'customers', namely the firms or research groups being supported under an RTDI funding program.

- The *relation between the agency and its 'customers'* (or in some cases the ministry/European Commission and its 'customers') *is regulated on a fourth level of governance*, which could be named operative governance. Both contractual and soft relations are designed and regulated in detail on this level. The culture of RTDI funding programs mainly derives from the activities of the agencies responsible. The rules are mostly concrete, partly for the whole program, partly on a case-by-case basis. The target group is clear and known. Governance is concrete and direct. The degree of freedom for the agency in it's relation to customers is sometimes higher and sometimes lower, depending on second- and third-level governance.

A question to finish with: Which level is strongest? It depends on the case, on the individual rules and regulations. While the FPs are embedded in a really strong second-level governance structure, national programs are often more strongly influenced by first-level governance, e.g. by European Commission state aid law and fourth-level governance, e.g. by highly autonomous funding agencies and research councils.[12] Of considerable importance is the influence of those who benefit from an RTDI funding program, be it by learning and feedback loops, be it by lobbying procedures. Which level in turn is most strongly affected? There is no general answer to this question, either, but we want to stress the great impact on the fourth level, i.e. on those who run the programs on a day-to-day basis. On this level the real, yet limited decisions are taken, on this level the real learning takes place, learning which is difficult to transfer back into the whole policy cycle.

The Role of Programs Envisaged in the ERA Document

The ERA document (European Commission 2000, see also '*The ERA Concept*') addresses a number of program issues. In the part 'Situation and objectives' the FPs are addressed as the main European policy instrument, lamenting that it makes up only about 5.4 per cent of the total public R&D financing effort (p. 10) and adding: 'However, the principal reference framework for research activities in Europe is national. Funding of the various initiatives of EC or intergovernmental scientific and technological co-operation does not exceed 17 per cent of the total public civilian expenditure on European research.' In the part 'A European Research Area' there are some issues where programs are seen as an appropriate answer: 'Networking of Centres of Excellence and Creation of Virtual Centres' (p. 13) is the subject of one of the most important instruments within the evolving FP6.

Under the heading 'More Coherent Use of Public Instruments and Resources' the issue of 'More Co-ordinated Implementation of National and European Research Programmes' (p. 15) is the most prominent instrument and includes initial steps towards 'the adoption of the principle of reciprocal opening-up of national programmes', starting with more information and comparable evaluation systems. 'Greater Mobility of Researchers in Europe' (p. 19), 'Greater Place and Role for Women in Research' (p. 20) and other kinds of mobility (pp. 22 f.) are the subject of a number of ongoing and planned programs on EC and national level. The Structural Funds, which increasingly include innovation issues, are programs in themselves (p. 21).

In other cases like 'Better Use of the Potential Offered by Electronic Networks' (p. 14), 'Encouragement of the Creation of Companies and Risk Capital Investment' (p. 17), 'Developing the Research Needed for Political Decisions' (p. 18), special programs will play an important role in the implementation process.

PROGRAMS WITHIN NATIONAL POLICY SETTINGS

Importance of Programs in Innovation Systems

The relative importance of funding programs in national RTDI policy agendas is quite high. This also holds true for the Member States of the EU. The reasons for this include difficulties and shortcomings of basic financing in the science sector, namely regarding general university funds, the concept of innovation systems with its focus on the relations between the different actors and the still growing demand for accountability, quality review and evaluations. Regarding the funding of research institutions, there is a long-standing discussion about the relationship between basic financing and different ways of program- and project-based funding in many countries (van der Meulen and Rip 1994, p. 56).

In many countries the relative importance of programs seems to be growing[13] *and* programs are getting more and more complex (Kuhlmann 2001; Stampfer 2003). As this contribution is not an empirical study but a discussion of trends and a presentation of stylized facts, no data on the changing relationship between basic financing and program financing can be presented here.

Governance in National Programs

Who is in the driving seat?
This question brings us back to the four layers of governance mentioned above. Here it is important to say that there is no clear prime mover, but in most cases an interplay of co-operating, competing, even conflicting actors on the national level. The arena model with its multitude of actors, the absence of one dominating party and its model of recurrent negotiations provides a good overall picture of the settings in which national RTDI funding programs are designed, managed and evaluated. Whoever the drivers are in a specific context, they are always to be found among the national actors. This means that a certain constellation of national ministries, agencies and research councils sets the agenda for program-based RTDI policies. In this respect we can observe a few typical structural features:

- Of course most innovation systems include structures for program management: One good and wide-spread example is the 'Generic RTD [Research, Technology and Development] Programme Management-model' (Arnold, Boekholt and Keen 1996, p. 9) with its division of labor between a) the ministry or other customer; b) the agency as program manager or other contractor; and c) those whose projects are funded. The relationship between ministry and agency concerns program matters, in our terms second- and third-level governance. The relationship between the agency and those funded concerns project matters, in our terms fourth-level governance. The model stretches over the whole policy cycle, from program design, implementation, selection procedures and reporting to project and program evaluation. At least in the model there is a clear division of labor between the strategic actor 'ministry', the operative actor 'agency', and those on the project level.[14]

- Governance of national RTDI programs is strongly determined by national laws, i.e. the first level of governance. One example is the existence of a kind of 'General R&D law' in some countries, setting the ground rules. Another example are strict general budgeting regulations like for instance the US GPRA , the third are the rules set by and for audit courts and other authorities monitoring the proper use of public money.
- A further point concerns second-, third- and fourth-level governance: As agencies are entrusted with RTDI funding programs, they generally enjoy a certain degree of autonomy.[15] In their role as operative actors and profiting from customer interaction they can learn and build up competencies. Streetwise as they are after some time, they have collected information nobody else has. This fact – and the existence of lobbies supporting the agencies feeding them – can give agencies considerable advantages over the (often distracted) strategic actors.

A postcard from Brussels
The second question concerns European governance – be it weak or strong, implicit or explicit – in national RTDI programs. There is a number of European influences on national program design and performance, but it always seems to be weaker than the governance exerted by national actors. European policymakers note that their national equivalents want to uphold their governance over most of the money and structures, keeping most of the resources for national programs or – if they have to go international – preferring intergovernmental initiatives to EC initiatives (Caracostas and Muldur 1997, p. 166).

There is a number of governance related issues here: Most of them are not based on hard facts and explicit legal settings, but on two parallel processes. National policy makers try to uphold their legal and financial autonomy *vis-à-vis* Brussels for their own national systems. In the same time they are deeply influenced in their activities and beliefs by being part of a perpetual series of games and activities on the European level. This continuous policy stream influences the actors involved and their behavior. Austria, for example, as a newcomer to the EU, developed within its innovation system over the 1990s an informal core group of policy makers, including public servants, representatives of specialized agencies and members of advisory groups. This rather loose core group of about 50 to 100 people on the one hand drew it's common beliefs, ideas and missions strongly from European sources, while on the other hand upholding their wish to remain autonomous as national policy makers. Their common characteristic was that they all, as Austrian representatives, were members of EU/FP decision-making or advisory bodies. In the second half of the 1990s we observed a number of conflicts between this group and the two traditional autonomous national funding bodies for scientific research and industrial research, whose representatives were rather reluctant to enter the European arena and rather relied on international inter-organizational mechanisms like European Science Foundation (ESF) or TAFTIE. While the latter group insisted on strictly national, project-based, bottom up funding mechanisms, the first group came forward with program- and systems-based approaches, more top down-oriented initiatives and calls. They advocated some opening up of national funding sources. Nevertheless they were eager not to give up the control and to remain in their driving seats. These conflicting positions started to blur in the end of the 1990s and were followed by a more integrated way of RTDI policymaking in Austria as regards funding.

This example shall show some of the impacts of Europeanization on RTDI programs and policymaking. As far as known to the author there is no systematic research on this issue. This is also the reason why only few and cautious and stylized first approaches can be brought forward on governance issues in this context:

- Highly implicit, but rather powerful, on all governance levels: National policymakers often tend to pay a lot of attention to the goals set by the on-going or planned FP. In some Member States, there is a lot of rhetoric to the effect that the choice and design of national RTDI funding programs should be influenced by the EU's RTDI priorities.[16] Programs should either reinforce FP priorities or they should complement them or they should, finally, set a deliberate contrast. However explicit this policy may be, recent national FP impact studies show with interesting results. There are examples of successful Member States without such a special policy (for Denmark, cf. Graversen and Siune 2000) and it can be shown that nearly all Member States are equally successful in nearly all subprograms of the FP4 in relation to their populations of researchers (Schibany et al. 2001, p. 45).
- Highly implicit, but rising, on the second governance level: A number of national RTDI programs have in their guidelines goals like the following: 'The funding should help those supported to succeed better in international RTDI programme competitions, specifically the Framework Programmes' (as example BMVIT 1998; 2001; see also Box 6.3 below).
- Implicit, on the second and third governance levels: The rationale for national RTDI funding programs changes from 'Those funded must have their location in the respective country' to 'What serves our nation/region best?' The latter approach allows funding agencies and other program managers to include foreign actors. This attitude has primarily something to do with the globalization of firms and possibly wider markets for knowledge. It also stems from a growing 'European' attitude towards

common markets and could be seen as one sign for the emergence of re-search areas different from national systems or borders. The notion of players like national funding agencies and ministries is very important in our context. If they fully embraced the idea of a 'European Knowledge Market', it could possibly be more powerful than any EC instrument.

- Highly explicit, on the first level of governance, but from another policy field: state aid policy and frameworks influencing all programs that fund market actors. For R&D there is a distinct EC state aid framework (Euro-pean Commission 1996) allowing or forbidding certain national funding activities. Most of the national programs undergo a formal Brussels notifi-cation procedure which has a tremendous governing effect on what is sup-ported and how programs are designed. Again it should be stated that this important hard governance does not come from European RTDI policy-making but from another field.[17]
- Implicit and slow, on all levels: Airplanes to and postcards from Brussels. Policymakers, researchers and other relevant actors meet all the time, chat, deplore the shortcomings of their RTDI cultures and even run common good practice projects (see Box 6.2, MAP as an example). Policy devel-opments in the national arena are often pushed forward via real or sup-posed 'Brussels' or 'European' standards, no bench remains unmarked. Ministry mandarins go to European meetings with their agendas in mind and come home with a kind of conviction that something must be changed in their country due to the 'standards' mentioned.[18] There are types of pro-grams and procedures more fashionable than others. It is difficult to judge whether all the talk about best practice will lead to a common European language where the same terms have the same meanings, given the still large differences in national legal frameworks, bureaucratic procedures, behavior of actors, language, perception and history in general.

So there are some signs of evolving common 'European' features in national RTDI policies. This is a slow process affecting the cultural and behavioral aspects of governance rather than any formal agreements. Therefore progress is difficult to measure. With the ERA venture an initial formalized discussion process has been started. One especially interesting strand concerns the opening up of national funding programs.

Opening Up of National Programs

As one instrument the ERA communication 'recommend(s) the adoption of the principle of reciprocal opening up of national programmes' (European Commission 2000, p. 15). This is reinforced by similar declarations in the Lisbon documents (European Council 2000).[19] This process is intended to

Box 6.3   The Austrian K plus program – example for an opening up

The Austrian K plus competence center program funds collaborative research facilities with a specified life time which were set up to carry out top-quality, long-term and internationally competitive Research and Technological Development (R&D) projects at a pre-competitive stage. The goal is to perform research that is highly relevant to both the academic world and industry and to develop human capital in areas that are either multi-disciplinary or relevant to a number of different sectors/companies. For information: *www.kplus.at.*

Up to now, 18 K plus competence centers have been set up. They are expected to play an important role in Austria's national innovation system and to establish firm international links in both research and human resource development. The program is internationally recognized as good practice (OECD 2001). Technologie Impulse Gesellschaft (TIG), a specializad agency of the Federal Ministry of Transport, Innovation and Technology (BMVIT), acts as program manager responsible for the selection, financing and development of the centers. The four levels of governance can be exemplified by this program: Regarding the first level, a number of European and Austrian legal documents are relevant and binding, from the University Organization Act to the R&D state aid framework. The second level is represented not by a law but by funding guidelines (BMVIT 1998 and 2001) issued by the Ministry and by an ex-ante policy document covering all relevant governance issues (Federal Ministry for Science and Transport [BMWV] 1997). On the third level, there are different contractual, other legal and also trust-based arrangements between TIG and the Ministry, while on the fourth level, TIG specifies the selection and funding of K plus centers via contracts, special guidelines and also management and support instruments.

The K plus program is a funding program with strong international links. Its design takes into account experience gained from foreign examples from Sweden, Canada, Australia and the United States. Six foreign peers evaluate each consortium applying for K plus status. There are international best practice comparisons and there is a constant inflow of foreign expertise. The centers are expected to co-operate with foreign partners, specifically within international programs.

One special aspect of the program is its openness to foreign scientific and industrial center partners: *Foreign firms* can fully take part in any center's funded work program; up to 25 per cent of the industrial share of the budget can be covered by non-Austrian firms. There is a number of examples where firms from Germany, the United States, Switzerland or Japan are treated as equal partners within the K plus center structure. Of currently about 250 industrial partners in 18 centers, about 10 per cent are foreign. Eligibility criteria include the respective company's usefulness for the center and strategic aspects, e.g. participation in multi-firm projects, specialized knowledge and usefulness for Austria. K plus funding goes to the center (for running a collaborative R&D program), and so do all company contributions. *Foreign research partners* can be core partners or partners co-operating more loosely, depending on coherence of the respective group of scientific proposers, special knowledge, etc. There are a number of K plus centers with, for example, German or Swiss scientific institutions as core partners. Apart from this, nearly all centers have their international PhD program, personnel exchange schemes and similar links.

dismantle somehow national funding schemes. As this is a very delicate field for national policymakers, the discussion process has been running under the heading of subsidiarity and has involved only a small circle of people. In 1998 and 1999 CREST already formed a new subcommittee on 'cross border co-operation within national RTD programmes'. A study (Technopolis Ltd. et al. 1999) was commissioned to compare the situations in the different Member States.

In principle most national programs are not open to foreign participation, though only a minority formally excludes foreign applicants (CREST 2000, p. 5; Technopolis Ltd. et al. 1999). This holds true for industrial and scientific programs and their respective target groups. While it is of course common practice that, for example firms with foreign ownership but with a production site in the country of the respective funding organization can apply for funding, real foreigners have problems in most cases. If they can apply at all, special requirements often have to be fulfilled. Some programs have changed their relevant evaluation criterion from 'Is the RTDI work to be funded being performed and commercially exploited in our country?' to 'Is the RTDI work to be funded useful for our country in a broader sense?' This change is not triggered by a ERA, but mostly driven by the internationalization of economic actors. In addition to this in many, especially smaller countries the majority of the best industrial RTDI performers are owned by foreign multinationals, so the question arises where the results of the research funded will be exploited. Exploitation within a given country can only be controlled to a limited extent. On the other hand co-operation programs are gaining ground – and interesting partnerships are often of a cross-border nature.

In the scientific funding community there is a tendency not to open schemes to scientists from foreign institutions but to co-ordinate the different national schemes. The ESF (European Science Foundation 2000, p. 6) started so called EUROCORES where ESF members, that is the national research councils and other science funding organizations, together define research programs. Proposal specification and parts of the reviewing processes will be organized jointly, but the funding decisions remain in the hands of the national funding bodies. This initiative is interesting but difficult from a bureaucratic point of view alone, given the different underlying organizational cultures.

The CREST working group itself did not recommend any real opening up measures. This was to be expected as all Member States are very cautious and fear a loss of influence – and governance. Effects of reciprocity are unclear, i.e. which countries would suffer a net loss.[20] So this CREST working group came up with a number of reasonable and cautious recommendations: More exchange of information between Member States on the level of program managers, evaluators from abroad as a common practice, comparable (ex-ante) evaluation procedures, explicit inclusion of foreign experiences in the design of new programs, common databases, soft standards and the like (CREST 2000).

Subsidiarity and no extra bureaucracy are the catchphrases. There is not supposed to be synchronized implementation or generalized cross-funding schemes. Some programs like the funding of RTDI consortia or mobility schemes are easier to handle in this respect than other schemes. All of this is to be seen under the heading of voluntary action. In the wake of the FP6 there is a good chance that the European Commission will co-fund such cross-border co-operation schemes between national program initiatives. Specifically, co-ordination initiatives and support measures could be eligible EC funding.[21] A lot is under discussion, like joint peer review procedures, joint calls or cross-border consortia.

As a preliminary result of this – ongoing – process it can be said that governance with regard to national programs will stay firmly in national hands in the next few years. There is a number of national programs open to foreign participation (for an example, see Box 6.3) but again this openness is more the consequence of changing framework conditions than of a political drive towards a common research area. We will see if the execution of the FP6 and the Lisbon/Barcelona process will bring any considerable changes.

EU PROGRAMS AND THEIR ROLE FOR A ERA

Past Achievements

R&D funding via FPs has been also the single biggest governance instrument at European level for the last two decades. Other – newer – instruments like Articles 165 and 169 have not really been used, major legal instruments to shape national policies have not been in place, national legislation has not been touched in a formal sense (see Box 6.1). Also note that in this context there is a real difference between national and European R&D policies. National policies are more about institutions, regulations, even people *and* programs while European R&D policy has been mostly about program funding in a strong governance framework. What has been said in regard to national programs and governance issues has to be repeated here: Most of the important questions are both of a complex and soft nature. There seems to be not much literature on governance issues regarding RTDI programs. The main point here is to provide some stylized facts about such governance-related policy developments.

Within the FPs, the *first* governance level has always been very strong, highly explicit and difficult to change. In Articles 163 ff. the EU Treaty determines a clear framework with a mission, goals, instruments and a strict, highly complex procedure including the major European institutions. This is highly specific as it directly addresses RTDI matters.

On the *second* level of governance we find highly explicit designs and settings, as well as a lot of informal, behind-closed-doors policymaking procedures. The explicit designs and settings include namely a) the co-decision procedure including Council, European Commission and European Parliament; b) the different preparatory stages and documents on different levels of the overall FP, the specific programs and on instruments/procedures; and c) a broad range of preparatory papers, working groups and conferences. Regarding the back stage procedures, one could at first be tempted to compare the making of a new FP to a Baroque opera or a Cecil B. de Mille film: lots of actors, tragedies, wooden but nicely painted settings, a highly formalized dramaturgy, a narrator, fate (a role often played by industry) and a very long narrative. If you take a second look, you will find that there is no big hero. No Cleopatra, no Orpheus, but a welcome to the arena with its multitude of actors. In both formal and informal procedures there are strong governing influences by European institutions like the European Commission or the Council – the latter in its role as a European lawmaker –, by national institutions like the national research administrations and 'voices' like the various national interests in the EC negotiation processes to be heard on the different levels of the Council: working groups, CREST, Council of Ministers and finally by interest groups like industrial and scientific lobby groups.

The *third* level of governance is not so visible because the European Commission has always been both co-designer and administrator of the FPs – but there are of course detailed EC documents determining it's role as manager of each FP. Just now some discussion regarding the issue of agencification, that is commissioning specialized agencies with parts of specific programs, is starting up. The elements of third-level governance are strong: There are highly explicit rules of procedure for the European Commission to run the programs and a vivid interplay between the European Commission as administrator and the accompanying program committees, the latter having the competence to steer programs and to influence funding decisions. In the program committees the different national interests are brought forward and there is room for multiple negotiations among the Member States *and* between Member States and the European Commission.

On the *fourth* level of governance perhaps the strongest impulses are generated. From project selection procedures via minimum requirements for consortia and procedural formalities to evaluation standards, effective governing signals are sent to the different European RTDI communities.[22]

Some final remarks: Governance in the FPs can be seen as a series of negotiations by a big number of different actors. There is a high degree of formality but also informal impacts on the EC-FP and vice versa are strong. From a procedural point of view this decade-long negotiation, application and funding cycle has brought together and influenced hundreds of thousands of researchers, industrialists and national and European officials. Tens of thousands of project consortia have been active. There is obviously some kind of European research culture evolving.[23]

The FP6: a Policy Shift?

Interplay FP6–ERA

The last FPs did not lead to a kind of common Europe-wide RTDI policy approach or something what is now called ERA. The national grip on European policy developments has been very strong, the logic of 15 plus 1 has not been questioned. While the goals of Article 163 of the Treaty and those of the individual FPs have always been ambitious, the immediate field of action has still been confined to the funding of collaborative projects.

Now a new, FP6 is about to start and it has been designed in the light of the ERA vision. First we can ask about it's impact on ERA-related steps and strategies. Regarding this question, there is one simple argument why the FP6 will be a very strong tool in the ERA kit: There are not many others. The FP still equals EC structures, money and real competencies. Other instruments like Article 169 will be limited to a small number of initiatives in the near future.

On the other hand we can ask about ERA impacts on the creation of the FP6. Here the first and most visible impact is the general design. There is money set aside for projects, studies, mobility, infrastructure co-ordination activities and specific support actions under two special headings, II and III, of the FP6. While the first heading covers the usual thematic priorities, heading two is called '*Structuring the European Research Area*', the third one '*Strengthening the Foundations of the European Research Area*'. These programmatic headings will, of course, include some activities which have always been funded within the FPs, but which also allow for the support of initiatives especially aimed at greater coherence of RTDI policies and structures in Europe (Council of the European Union 2002). For a second important design issue of the FP6, the new consortia-related instruments in heading I, see below.

New instruments: Networks of Excellence and Integrated Projects

There is currently a lot of discussion about the major new instruments within the FP6. Generally the range of instruments is to be broadened, from shared-cost projects in former FPs to 'Integrated Projects' (IP), 'Networks of Excellence' (NoE) and further instruments. The old shared-cost projects are now to be found under the headings of 'Stairway of Excellence' and 'Specific Support Actions' (see European Commission 2002).

NoE and IP are to help to create European critical mass, achieve ambitious objectives and reduce the European Commission's administrative workload. General guiding principles include simplification and streamlining, flexibility and adaptability, increased management autonomy and preserving public accountability. An IP is to 'generate the knowledge required to implement the [*thematic*, M.S.] priority themes by integrating the critical mass of activities and resources needed to achieve ambitious, clearly defined scientific and technological objectives'. The IP 'is therefore an instrument to support directly objective-driven research, where the primary deliverable is new knowledge'. (European Commission 2002, p. 5.) A NoE is:

> ... being designed to strengthen excellence on a particular research topic by networking together the critical mass of resources and expertise needed to be world force in that topic. This expertise will be networked around a joint programme of activity aimed primarily at creating a progressive and lasting integration of the research activities of the network partners ... .

The NoE 'is therefore an instrument designed primarily to address the fragmentation of European research on a particular research topic, where the main deliverable will be a restructuring and reshaping of the way that research is carried out on that topic'. (European Commission 2002, p. 9.) These instruments shall not be presented in detail, nevertheless three dimensions are interesting for our governance debate:

- Intentions: the instruments aim at the lasting integration of capacities and infrastructures (NoE), respectively at achieving critical mass (IP). The idea is to ensure higher visibility and to reinforce existing strengths – instead of funding thousands of European projects with little visible European impact.[24] This issue concerns second-level governance: RTDI (infra-)structures and playing fields are to be changed via the legal settings of a new FP, (national) actors are to be brought together in a form stronger than in the old FPs.
- Size: IP and NoE can be very large, up to several dozen million euro and including dozens of partners, that means hundreds of researchers. Note that questions of infrastructures are also tackled with this special program approach. It is not about creating new infrastructures but about the joint use of existing ones.
- Management issues: note that there will be a considerable change with FP6. A lot of management issues will be handed over to the consortia. There is to be a high degree of self-organization within these fewer and larger consortia. Note that the core members of these consortia are to be

allowed to arrange calls for proposals for further participants. Many questions are still open in this respect. Here we are talking about fourth-level governance and about an emerging fifth level: How is governance organized within consortia if they are allowed to distribute public money? How much of the original fourth-level governance is handed over to the consortia? How can fair access be guaranteed? In which forms shall subcalls take place? There are many such 'fifth level' questions under discussion now. A third-level governance question is also raised in this connection: 'Will there still be a role for Programme committees?'

As the first calls for expressions of interest are to be issued in spring 2002 and the first real calls in 2003, no relevant experience can be drawn on yet.

SUMMARY: OUR FRUIT-BEARING GARDENS

Funding programs are an increasingly important instrument of RTDI policies on different levels. They serve as change agents and cover a number of different governance issues. The discussion about a stronger European element in RTDI policies has had a considerable effect on programs, while, on the other hand, European FPs and most national programs have not remained unaffected by various kinds of 'cross-governance', i.e. formal and informal influences from the other side. Some of the main points underlying this contribution are listed here.

Past and Present

- In the past there has been a clear dominance of the national level: No formalized European governance within national programs, no need for openness and cross-border co-operation, weak regional actors, strong member state influence on FP planning and management procedures, most resources allocated via national budgets, mostly in the form of institutional funding like General University Fund (GUF) spending or other block funds.
- Currently we see a slow shift towards more European thinking and governance: Some national programs are beginning to cross borders, others are showing stronger European goals. National ministries are losing part of their power to govern to other actors in the national arenas. Programs are being used for broader policy goals. The regional level is becoming stronger, regional innovation networks and programs are increasingly being supported by the European level. The discussion about a ERA is strengthening the general awareness of common European RTDI

challenges and the preparation of the FP6 includes specific instruments to tackle structural questions. Beyond this, RTDI issues have gained higher priority on all policy agendas and there is greater pressure for the actors to come out of their corners.

Future, Possible Trends

In this contribution three hypotheses regarding the role of programs in RTDI policy governance structures in a ERA context were discussed. There are some preliminary answers, pointing in a certain direction. As the targets are moving and some issues here are based on stylized facts, such answers have to be brought forward with caution:

- A look at the conceptual, European and national levels clearly show the pervasive nature of RTDI policy, which does not allow a clear classification of this policy area as predominantly European, like foreign trade policy, or strictly national, like cultural policy. Innovation issues will be important on all levels, again being one of the last men standing in national (regional) economic policy portfolios (related to Hypothesis 1, see also below).
- There are indications that national policymaking will remain the strongest factor in the future, even though it will lose some ground to both the European and regional levels. RTDI policies and programs will remain a strong instrument of inner-European competition regarding the attractiveness of business locations – as other instruments like tariffs, investment aid, currency devaluations, etc. have been subject to strong 'European' restrictions more or less connected with the creation of the Single Market. This argument probably is of decisive character. How else shall Member States pursue an active economic policy in a Common Market? As this fact is clear every national policy maker, the RTDI policy domain will be strongly defended against Europeansiation. From today's perspective we also can neither see a big shift in budgets from national to European levels nor have ideas about European governance of national programs evolved into big and visible activities so far (related to Hypothesis 2).
- Some kind of ERA will most probably be evolving, also regarding programs, not in a very systematic way and not in the form of a 'Common Research Policy'. On the European level, bigger consortia and bigger projects will have a greater impact on underlying (national) RTDI structures. The management of the FP6 will bring us new, trans-European actors. On the national level, the pressure to include European goals, and perhaps even European money, will even increase. Budget constraints will influence not only questions of 'European' RTDI infrastructures, but perhaps

also of national programs (related to Hypotheses 1 and 3).

- From a ERA perspective it could be imaginable (if not very likely) that all major national and regional RTDI funding programs should include European goals and should, even in the future, be subject to a kind of widened European framework of approval: Do they fit into the ERA concept and what is their contribution to a ERA? This would imply a change of major legal provisions but there is a well-known example from the Single Market we already mentioned in this contribution: All national and regional programs now undergo a formal procedure regarding aspects of competition/state aid law. A similar procedure could be possible for ERA-related questions in a rather distant future – again this is not very likely to emerge (related to Hypothesis 2).

- Variety will increase – it is probable that we will see more mixed programs in the future, also programs promoting a number of different policy objectives. The different forms of role-sharing are still to follow the principle of subsidiarity (European Commission 2000, p. 25). Some voices (Amable, Barré and Boyer 1997; see Caracostas and Muldur 1997, p. 174) plead for 'a mutual recognition of the legitimacy and potential of the various configurations which are one of Europe's strengths'. Others (Caracostas and Muldur 1997, p. 174) fear a lack of overall European coherence in this respect (related to Hypotheses 1 and 3).

- Another issue in this context is the ability of public organizations to run highly complex programs. There is a great deal of experience on both the national and European levels regarding innovation networks and important factors like awareness of networking possibilities, searching for partners, building trust and a shared knowledge base, organizing a network, ensuring complementary resources and active co-operation (Polt 2001, p. 308). But in order to act strategically in difficult and complex systems a lot of 'intelligence' must be in place: Authors plead for an integrated use of tools for strategic intelligence, including participation, objectivation, mediation/alignment and decision support. There is no single best model but there are clear signs that this intelligence must be of a distributed nature: networking, active nodes, transparent access, public support and quality assurance are some core requirements (Kuhlmann 2001, pp. 22–31). It can be argued that the higher the number of actors and agendas, the more complicated the implementation of strategic intelligence as a prerequisite for good policy governance becomes. So if national systems including programs as key elements are not designed too foolishly, any European governance will be more difficult to construct and maintain than its smaller, more coherent national counterparts. We could ask: 'Could an ERA ever be governed ... even by distributed intelligence?' (related to Hypotheses 2 and 3).

- Finally, short-term ERA success will strongly rely on programs, as this kind of instrument is the fastest to apply. Long-term success is rather a question of institutional change (related to Hypothesis 3).

Where will we be in some years – back in our national gardens? Some kind of ERA will most probably be evolving, obviously not in a very systematic way, likely not in the form of a 'Common Research Policy'. The European level will be strong where common interests are strong. Regarding programs, national and regional instruments will be of high importance. The positive effects of competition within Europe should not be underestimated, nor the pervasive nature of innovation and related policy measures.

NOTES

[1] In this contribution the term 'RTDI' is used in most cases because of the growing notion of a broader definition including research, technological development and innovation. The term 'RTD' is often used in connection with formal EC documents like the EC Treaty, the Community state aid framework and most statistics, here we follow the terminology 'R&D' which is more common internationally.

[2] The text implies first that the national level is the strongest nowadays. The sheer numbers point in this direction. Of course we should also ask who really takes the decisions – and in this context discuss the power of organized industrial interest in the public R&D policy design processes. This point is left aside as it is not the question raised in the context of this book, but generally speaking we can be quite sure that the strong nation state will live for a long time. In this context, two recent examples from the United States are of interest: a) Privacy restrictions, for example in the financial sector after 11 September; b) The vulnerability of market globalization icons like Arthur Andersen in the wake of the Enron scandal and the role of public authorities in this case.

[3] Examples of a) WTO/TRIPS for globalization, software and internet standards for technology as a driving force; example of b) GALILEO; examples of c) the Global Space Station on the one hand, regional telematics initiatives on the other hand.

[4] 'The Union has today set itself a new strategic goal for the next decade: To become the most competitive and dynamic knowledge-based economy in the world, capable of sustainable economic growth with more and better jobs and greater social cohesion' (European Council 2000).

[5] There are few published definitions of RTDI funding programs around. This attempted definition draws from the STRATA 'MAP' project described in Box 6.2.

[6] There is a clear trade-off between the possibilities of quick reactions to changing environments on the one hand and the establishment of new rules, names and games every four years. Note that old, 'outdated' paradigms seldom leave the world but stay in the heads of those who have worked with them. RTDI policy – be it on a national or European level – can be seen in this context as a ragbag of fresh, five-year-old, ten-year-old and even older ideas, paradigms, approaches, structures, etc. Perhaps 'de-learning' some old routines will be the biggest of all ERA challenges.

[7] Note the spreading of competence center programs, of academic spin-off programs, of human resource exchange programs, and so on (see for example the long lists in the EU Innovation Trend Chart).

[8] See also the objectives set out in Art. 163 EC Treaty: '... objective of strengthening the scientific and technological bases of Community industry and encouraging it to become more competitive at international level, while promoting all the research activities deemed

necessary by virtue of other Chapters of this Treaty'.

9   The trademark 'CRC' of the Australian Cooperative Research Centre Programme (which funds competence centers) was unofficially renamed 'Changing Research Culture' – within and between institutions and through a program.

10   Project starts in January 2002. Partners are AT: TIG as co-ordinator, DE: Fraunhofer Institute for Systems and Innovation Research – ISI, ES: Association Unitec, UK: Technopolis, SE: VINNOVA, HU: Ministry of Education, SLO: University of Maribor, 'observers': EARMA – European Association for Research Managers and Administrators, Ireland: Irish Energy Agency, Flanders: IWT.

11   Of course habits, beliefs, bureaucratic routines and culture are strong forces on all of these levels, creating both bonds and differences between the respective actors.

12   Note, for example, the culture of lean ministries and strong agencies like VINNOVA, TEKES or RCN in the Scandinavian innovation systems.

13   It is difficult to get statistical material in digestible form on this point. In Austria there is an explicit policy to foster program-based funding and to freeze a number of basic funding lines, namely in the university sector. My rough personal guess is that program- and project-based funding in Austrian public RTDI budgets has grown from about 5 to 10 per cent ten years ago to about 15 to 20 per cent now (Federal Ministry for Education, Science and the Arts and Federal Ministry for Transport, Innovation and Technology [BMBWK and BMVIT] 2002). Within this portfolio the number and size of complex multi-actor–multi-measure programs is rising.

14   A simple example is reporting: The ministry stipulates in the funding guidelines that a reporting system should be set in place. The agency develops such a system and requires those who get funded to report a number of key data about the project. These reports only go to the agency. The agency reports to the ministry about the progress achieved and the state of the program.

15   The degree of autonomy varies wildly, but Research Councils generally have some formal autonomy regarding selection procedures and budget allocation to projects.

16   For example in Austria the FP6 preparation in 2001 once again provoked a lively discussion on how to put national actors in a better position for the big projects in the FP6 via national programs.

17   This European competence for national and regional schemes ends with European jurisdiction over state aid issues. As long as national or regional authorities design their programs within the state aid frameworks, there is no other kind of European governance on national programs.

18   What is meant by postcards from Brussels is that they are written at home. If you turn them, you will, like on the cent coins, find a national motif on the stamp.

19   '... develop appropriate mechanisms for networking national and joint research programmes ... take greater advantage of the concerted resources devoted to R&D in the Member States ...' (European Council 2000, p. 4).

20   In a real ERA there would be no net loss. But do we really want to have this best of all worlds with no strong RTDI instruments to explicitly foster regional and national economic growth?

21   We mainly talk about Art. 163 and 164 (FP activities), not about Art. 165 (co-ordination between Community and Member States) in this context. Within the proposals for the FP6 the third main avenue approaching ERA is called 'Strengthening the Foundations of ERA', with instruments aiming at co-ordination of research and innovation activities conducted in Europe at both National and European levels *and* through activities supporting the development of coherent research and innovation policies in Europe.

22   This is crucial: By 'educating' the different RTDI communities via Framework Programme rules it is made possible for national policymakers to raise governance standards in national programs. Evaluation standards, the use of foreign peers and open calls are only three examples of how (at least in Austria) European standards have helped and have been used as arguments in many national implementation procedures.

23   Not to forget the roles of COST, EUREKA, intergovernmental RTDI infrastructures, etc., in this process.

[24] The question could be: 'Building lighthouses or knitting a fabric?', see also Box 6.3 for a national example. Obviously there is the feeling that the fabric is already in place after five FPs.

REFERENCES

Amable, B., R. Barré and R. Boyer (1997), *Les Systèmes d'Innovation à l'Ere de la Globalisation*, Paris: Economica.

Arnold, E., P. Boekholt and P. Keen (1996), *Good Ideas in Programme Management for Research and Technical Development Programmes*, Brighton.

BMBWK and BMVIT (2001), *Research and Technology Report 2001*, report in accordance with §8 ROA on federally subsidised research, technology and innovation in Austria, Vienna: Federal Ministry for Education, Science and the Arts and Federal Ministry for Transport, Innovation and Technology (BMBWK and BMVIT).

Caracostas, P. and U. Muldur (1997), *Society, the Endless Frontier. A European Vision of Research and Innovation Policies for the 21st Century*, Brussels: European Commission, cit. Caracostas and Muldur.

Council of the European Union (2002), *Common Position Adopted by the Council on 28 January 2002 Concerning the Sixth Framework Programme*, Brussels: European Commission, 15483/3/01 REV 3.

CREST (2000), *Report on Cross-border Cooperation*, sub-committee of CREST, Brussels: CREST.

Edquist, C. (ed.) (1997), *Systems of Innovation. Technologies, Institutions and Organisations*, London, UK and Washington, USA: Pinter.

European Commission (1996), *Community Framework for State Aid for Research and Development*, Brussels: European Commission.

European Commission (2000), *Towards a European Research Area*, communication from the Commission to the Council, the European Parliament, the Economic and Social Committee and the Committee of the Regions, Brussels: European Commission.

European Commission (2002), *Introduction to the Instruments Available for Implementing the FP6 Priority Thematic Areas*, speaking notes, Brussels: mimeo.

European Council (2000), *Declaration of the Lisbon Summit*, http://ue.eu.int/en/info/eurocouncil/index.htm.

European Council (2002), *Geänderte Vorschläge für die Entscheidungen des Rates über die spezifischen Programme zur Durchführung des Sechsten Rahmenprogrammes*, Brussels: European Council, Doc. 5943/02.

European Science Foundation (2000), 'EUROCORES move ahead', *ESF Communications*, **41**, Strasbourg, p. 6.

Federal Ministry for Science and Transport (BMWV) (1997), *K-Plus, Forschungskompetenz plus Wirtschaftskompetenz*, Vorhabensbericht des BMWV zur Errichtung von Kompetenzzentren in Österreich, Vienna: BMWV.

Federal Ministry for Transport, Innovation and Technology (BMVIT) (1998), Richtlinien *für die Errichtung und Finanzierung von Kompetenzzentren K Plus*, Vienna.

Graversen, E.K. and K. Siune (2000), *Danish Research Cooperation in EU: Extent, Return and Participation. An Analysis of Cooperation in the 4th EU Framework Programme*, AFSK Report 2000/3.

Kuhlmann, S. (1999), 'Politisches System und Innovationssystem in "postnationalen" Arenen', in Grimmer, K., S. Kuhlmann and F. Meyer-Krahmer (eds), *Innovationspolitik in globalisierten Arenen. Neue Aufgaben für Forschung und Lehre: Forschungs- und Technologiepolitik im Wandel*, Opladen: Leske und Budrich, p. 11.

Kuhlmann, S. (2001), *Management of Innovation Systems. The Role of Distributed Intelligence*, Nijmegen.

Kuhlmann, S. and J. Edler (2002), *Governance of Technology and Innovation Policies in Europe: Investigating Future Scenarios*, forthcoming.

Lossgott, C. (2001), *Neue Wege der Technologiepolitik – Innovationsfähigkeit und Nachhaltigkeit*, Vienna: doctoral thesis.

Lundvall, B.Å. (ed.) (1992), *National Systems of Innovation: Towards a Theory of Innovation and Interactive Learning*, London: Pinter.

Lundvall, B.Å. and S. Borrás (1997), *The Globalising Learning Economy: Implications for Innovation Policy*, report based on contributions from seven projects under the TSER program, Brussels: DG XII G.

Meyer-Krahmer, F. (1999), 'Was bedeutet Globalisierung für Aufgaben und Handlungsspielräume nationaler Innovationspolitiken?', in Grimmer, K., S. Kuhlmann and F. Meyer-Krahmer (eds), *Innovationspolitik in globalisierten Arenen. Neue Aufgaben für Forschung und Lehre: Forschungs- und Technologiepolitik im Wandel*, Opladen: Leske und Budrich, p. 35.

Nelson, R. (1993), *National Innovation Systems: a Comparative Analysis*, Oxford and New York: Oxford University Press.

OECD (1995), *Impacts of National Technology Programmes*, Paris: OECD.

OECD (1997), *Policy Evaluation in Innovation and Technology. Towards Best Practices*, Paris: OECD.

OECD (2001), *The New Economy Beyond the Hype*, OECD Growth Project, Paris: OECD.

Polt, W. (2001), 'The Role of Governments in Networking', in OECD (ed.), *Innovative Networks. Co-operation in National Innovation Systems*, Paris: OECD, p. 307.

PREST, AUEB, BETA, ISI, Joanneum Research, IE HAS and Wise Guys (2002), *ASIF: Assessing the Socio-economic Impacts of the Framework Programme*, Manchester and Brussels: PREST.

Puntscher-Riekmann, S. (2001), 'Taming the European "Prince". Reflections Upon Current Debates About the Future of the European Union', in Markovits, A. and S. Rosenberger (eds), *Demokratie. Modus und Telos. Beiträge für Anton Pelinka*, Wien, Köln and Weimar: Böhlau, pp. 207–22.

Schartinger, D., A. Schibany and H. Gassler (2001), 'Interactive relations between universities and firms: empirical evidence for Austria', *Journal of Technology Transfer*, **26**, Amsterdam, 255ff.

Schibany, A., L. Jörg, H. Gassler, K. Warta, D. Sturn, W. Polt, G. Streicher, T. Luukkonen and E. Arnold (2001), *Evaluation of Austrian Participation in the 4th EU Framework Programme*, Final Report, Vienna.

Stampfer, M. (2003), 'Mehrebenenprogramme in Österreich – Konzeption, Rahmenbedingungen und Evaluierungsanforderungen anhand aktueller Beispiele aus der österreichischen Technologiepolitik', in Kuhlmann, S. (ed.), *Politische Steuerung von Innovationssystemen? Potenziale der Evaluierung von Mehrebenenprogrammen*, Heidelberg (forthcoming).

Technopolis Ltd., VDI/VDE-IT, IKEI and Logotech (1999), *Cross-border Coopera-tion Within National RTD Programmes*, Brighton.
van der Meulen, B. and A. Rip (1994), *Research Institutes in Transition*, Delft: Ebu-ron Publishers.

7   National but/and/or European: the Differentiation of EU-R&D Policy Subsystems in Three Countries

Which Lessons Can be Drawn for the ERA?

Peter Biegelbauer

INTRODUCTION

The lengthy negotiations on the Fourth Framework Programme for Research, Technological Development and Demonstration (FP4) had barely finished and the, by then, largest technology program had become active, when the discussions on the next FP were started by the European Commission. The logic of the European integration process called for a program even larger than the one before. In addition, the General Directorate XII (later: General Directorate Research), which was responsible for the co-ordination of the European Union's (EU) research and technology policy, had a new commissioner, Edith Cresson, the former French prime minister. Madame Cresson, as she was soon to be called in all the official EU languages, had set her mind to quickly establishing herself in the new position. And for a time, it actually seemed that she was to reach this goal.

Indeed, she was in a good position to start a successful second political career as the prime mover in the EU's political processes typically is the European Commission, which normally would suggest a program for political action. Only after the European Commission has set its mark, the proposal then is to be discussed on the national level, by the member state governments, and on the European level, in the framework of the Council of the EU as well as in the European Parliament. During the following legislative process the European Council and the European Parliament are to discuss the proposals of the European Commission, change them after their own preferences and, finally, reach a common decision. In the meantime, interest groups, associations, political parties and a variety of actors try to make themselves heard at supranational, national and regional levels.[1]

This process was to start, again, in 1995 with the initiative of the European Commission. The national research and technology policy communities in the 15 Member States knew they were to face quite a challenge during the years to come: they would have to react to the proposal on a FP with a new focus and with new management routines, larger and more complex than any before.

Whilst this situation was not so new to the policymakers in the 12 countries, who formed the EU up until 1994, it was completely new to the decision-makers of the Member States who had joined the EU in the beginning of 1995, namely Austria, Finland and Sweden. Of course, the politicians and civil servants of the three newcomers in theory had had the possibility to take part in the final negotiations on FP4 in 1994 – the year their countries had joined the European Economic Area, consisting of the EU Member States and the European Free Trade Agreement (EFTA) countries. But in reality the national governments in all three countries had been overwhelmed by the tasks they had to face and typically had been in the position of silent observers in the meetings preparing the documents, which were to form the basis for FP4.

And if one comes to think of it, it is not surprising that the civil servants and politicians of the three newcomer countries felt rather overwhelmed by the tasks they were facing. Only shortly before the Austrian, Finnish and Swedish governmental and administrative structures had been adapted to the complex EU policymaking processes, departments, agencies, commissions and other organizational solutions, which were to deal with European affairs, had been set up to fulfil these institutional functions which the other twelve Member States had long since become used to deal with. In addition, the three countries had to quickly educate civil servants, who were able to deal with the new requirements and become part of the newly set up institutions. And on top of that the rules of the political processes in Brussels were known to the vast majority of the new civil servants and the politicians alike only from papers and books, which can give only a meager reflection of the actual workings of the EU political machinery.

Whilst the actors in this situation are sure not to have always felt at ease with their new lives, the circumstances of decision-making in hindsight offer interesting information on the reactions of a given political system to a new demand. Indeed, an analysis of the processes leading to the establishment of the new EU-related institutions and procedural routines in the three new EU Member States has the potential to yield insights into the workings of political institutions of advanced industrialized countries.

The main focus of this chapter is the analysis of the national research and technology policy systems' reactions to the demands raised by the EU membership. Put into concrete research questions: How do national Research and Technological Development (R&D) systems differentiate into EU-R&D subsystems? What are the major determinants of this process? Why do these subsystems look as they look and work as they work?

The paper will set out to investigate the ways in which three small and neocorporatist EU Member States have dealt with the challenge of formulating national positions to the Fifth Framework Programme (FP5) of the EU. Thereby, Austria, the Netherlands and Sweden are to be compared with regards to the policy-finding processes, which, in the years from 1995–98, led to their respective positions.

As has been established before, Austria and Sweden entered the EU 1 January 1995. The Netherlands serve as a form of 'control case' insofar as they have been a founding member of the European Economic Community, the name under which the EU was founded in 1956.

The three countries otherwise are quite similar. All of them are small- to medium-sized countries, which in one or another way have been integrated into the EU for a number of years now. Most clearly this is the case for the Netherlands, but Sweden and Austria have also been close to the EU. With regards to the economic situation of the two latter countries, both have common borders with several EU Member States, the economically most important of which is Germany – which indeed has been dominating the trade structures of both Austria and Sweden. With the successive strengthening of the EU (then the European Economic Community [EEC]) in the 1970s, and much to the detriment of EFTA, the EU over time became also politically more important for both countries. By the mid-1980s many laws and norms had to be copied by Austria and Sweden, as the two countries had to stay compatible with the respective EU (then European Communities [EC]) regulations in order to minimize trade problems, as they may potentially result from different norms relating to, for example, food and consumer products. The process officially was seen as an autonomous duplication of laws, norms and regulations, but, due to the economic realities, was not a decision which could have been taken in any other way without endangering the export-led economic growth strategies of both Austria and Sweden.

Besides their size and closeness to the EU, there are still other similarities to note between Sweden, Austria and the Netherlands. Their political processes are all organized after a fashion, which might be broadly termed as 'neocorporatist' (Schmitter 1974; Lehmbruch 1974; for overviews see Czada 1994; Streeck 1994). In each of the three countries, associations have more or less exclusive rights of their clienteles interests' representation vis-à-vis the government. This is especially the case with regards to the organization of business–government relations, where either a single or only a few employers' and employees' associations dominate the scene. Of course, important differences are noticeable regarding the quality of this representation process, insofar as in Austria there exists a representation monopoly of one association for employers' and one for employees' interests. This is different from Sweden and the Netherlands, where several associations rival each other – although there are very few dominant actors in each case.

Moreover, the quality of the neocorporatist organization of politics varies not only over the factor geography, e.g. the three countries, but also over the factor time. In the post-Second World War history of each country there have been periods characterized by stronger or more strict variants of neocorporatism and others, in which the powers of the associations were smaller, governments were relatively more independent of associations. Then the co-operation between associations and government might be better characterized by slightly weaker forms of co-operation, such as in a 'concertation' of interests or forms of privileged, but not exclusive, access of associations to government – a form of co-operation which in fact is only a shadow of neocorporatism (Lehmbruch 1984; Talos and Kittel 2001).

A final characteristic shared by the Netherlands, Austria and Sweden is that their R&D systems are highly differentiated. Whilst this might be expected from highly advanced industrialized countries, again several differences apply in a comparison of the three nation states. The Netherlands have the richest and most diverse R&D system, displaying an unusually wide variation of types and forms of R&D institutions. In both Austria and Sweden the differentiation of the R&D system is smaller, with universities dominating the scene in both cases. This is still less the case in Sweden and more so in Austria, due to the missing large indigenous multinational companies in the latter case.[2]

Despite all of this, the similarities are overwhelmingly stronger than the differences when comparing the three countries of the sample with other highly advanced industrialized countries. Following from that one might expect that there should be also many parallels in the ways Austria, the Netherlands and Sweden have organized their processes of coming to a national position regarding FP5. This should apply all the more for Sweden and Austria, joining the EU together at the very beginning of the political process leading to FP5 in 1995.

As will be shown, this is less the case than one would believe. Quite a few differences are evident in the way the policy-finding processes of the three countries took place – with regards to the actors dominant in the process, the numbers and type of actors gaining access and the instruments utilized to come to a common decision on FP5.

As pertaining to the European Research Area (ERA), two questions shall be of interest here. First, what can we learn from the policy processes leading up to FP5 for the ERA initiative. Second, what can we learn from the way the three Member States in discussion reacted to the demands raised by the FPs for the reactions of the Member States to ERA.

Accordingly, the rest of the chapter will be organized as follows: First, the three countries are going to be introduced with an emphasis on the respective R&D structures and the business–government relations. Then the policy-finding processes leading to the national positions to FP5 will be introduced and compared. By way of conclusion an attempt to account for the differences in the processes will be made and the two ERA related questions shall be dealt with.

Most of the data for this paper have been gathered as part of the RP5-POL project, which has been carried out at the Department for Political Science of the Institute for Advanced Studies in Vienna from late 1999 until spring of 2002. The data basis for RP5-POL encompassed more than 100 structured interviews in Austria, the Netherlands, Sweden and in Brussels as well as a larger amount of background talks. Moreover, about 200 A4-files filled with protocols, position papers, non-papers, letters, mails and other documents have been analyzed, which were provided for the project team by the Austrian Ministry of Education, Science and the Arts, which has commissioned the research project.[3]

R&D SYSTEMS

In order to arrive at a comprehensive picture of the economic and political background of the discussed policy-finding processes, a short description of the three countries' R&D systems and an overview over the respective business–government relations will be attempted here.

As has been established, all three countries have highly differentiated R&D systems. Furthermore, all three countries have medium to high spending rates on R&D, with business coming up with at least one half of the total expenditures on R&D in each case. All three national economies are export-oriented and, similar to the respective R&D systems, highly competitive. Nevertheless, a number of interesting differences apply.

The economic structure of the three countries differs in some aspects, which are worth noticing. An important issue for R&D systems is the existence of large companies, insofar as these usually spend a higher percentage of their revenue on R&D than do small- and medium-sized enterprises (SMEs). Whilst the Swedish economy is dominated by a few highly successful multinational companies, there are no large Austrian multinational companies. Accordingly, a large part of Austrian R&D is conducted by foreign-based multinationals. The Netherlands hold a middle position in this respect, insofar as there are only a few Dutch multinationals, which moreover are less clearly

Dutch-based (take the example of the British-Dutch Shell).

The national expenditures for R&D mirror the three countries' economic structures. Figures on R&D expenditure are typically used as indicators for the respective R&D systems' level of development. Whilst this method might have shortcomings with respect to comparisons of countries with wildly differing backgrounds, it is useful in the case of broadly similar countries.[4] Table 7.1 compares the three countries' national expenditures on R&D after financiers.

Table 7.1   Comparison of R&D systems: R&D expenditure by financier

	Austria (1997)	**Sweden (1998)**	**Netherlands (1997)**
Total expenditure as percentage of GDP	1.8 %	3.8 %	2.0 %
Of which:			
Government	44.6 %	25.2 %	49.1 %
Business	51.2 %	67.7 %	45.6 %
Other	3.4 %	4.2 %	3.6 %

Source: European Commission (2000): 'Towards a European Research Area – Science, Technology and Innovation: Key Figures 2000', Brussels.

Clearly, Sweden outspends the other two countries. Mainly responsible for this is the high R&D spending level of Swedish industry, which is an effect of the economic dominance of a few large internationalized firms, concentrated in high-tech areas such as telecommunications, pharmaceuticals and aerospace. Indeed, ten Swedish companies are responsible for 50 per cent of the total national R&D expenditures (National Council for Industry and Technological Development [NUTEK] 1998). The structures of R&D expenditures are much more similar for the Netherlands and Austria, underlining the larger importance of SMEs and the smaller share of production in high-tech sectors for both countries in comparison to Sweden.[5]

Regarding the differentiation of the R&D systems, it has been noted before that the Netherlands display the richest choice of institutional solutions. This is the case with respect to the importance of extra-university research institutions, the differentiation of the tertiary education system, but also with regards to the intermediary R&D institutions. Whilst this is less the case for Sweden, where the universities are more dominant actors in the R&D system, aside from the commercial sector, the situation in Austria is more extreme.

Here the universities are clearly more dominant and the extra-university institutions are smaller and relatively weaker. Moreover, the relative deprivation of different institutional solutions does not stop with Austrian R&D performing institutions, but is also visible with the respective intermediary institutions. In the Netherlands and in Sweden these are more important in their functions of financing and planning of R&D, than they are in Austria. It should be mentioned, however, that the 1990s have seen the establishment of several Austrian intermediary organizations, most of all in the areas of technology and technology policy counseling and planning as well as in international R&D co-operation.

This trend goes hand in hand with another development in the governance of R&D – being however part of a much wider movement and encompassing other policy fields as well. Whilst the Austrian civil service traditionally has been always more centralized and hierarchically structured as Anglo-Saxon models, with the 1990s a trend has become visible to outsource some functions to newly set-up institutions, which sometimes are short-leashed, but at other times have more leeway in their work. This division of administrative functions has a much longer tradition in Sweden, where the central bureaucracy is smaller and less hierarchical and where the principle of 'arms-length government' leads to relatively more independent governmental agencies co-operating with the central ministries. The Netherlands are a rather mixed case, with both traditions being visible. This might be one reason why the country has such a diversity in R&D governance solutions.

BUSINESS–GOVERNMENT RELATIONS

Not only the centrality of private companies for modern capitalism, but also the importance of firms for research and, even more so, technological development, would suggest a look at the business–government relations in the three countries in discussion. It has already been established that all three countries display neocorporatist policy arrangements to a significant degree. In other words, by way of analysis one should easily identify a number of incidents, in which policymaking styles are dominant, which do resemble classic neocorporatist configurations. In these government, business and employees' associations form exclusive and stable relationships, as part of which they negotiate policies. There exist variations after policy fields, time and other factors. Nevertheless, neocorporatist policy arrangements have been found to be a significant factor for policymaking in all three countries (Schmitter and Grote 1997; Karlhofer and Talos 1999; Hemerijck et al. 2000; Talos and Kittel 2001).

In all three countries these policy arrangements have undergone a crisis in the last two decades, which changed some of the arrangements' defining variables. In the Netherlands, the crisis has been overcome in the first half of the 1980s, when government pressured the associations into a decentralization and flexibility of tariff negotiations, which normally are a central determinant of the neocorporatist arrangements. In the medium term, this led to a reduction of the dominance of neocorporatist policy-style in the Netherlands – in this case seemingly not to the detriment of economic prosperity, as the country turned from low growth and rising unemployment in the 1980s to a model case of economic development with moderate to high growth and low unemployment rates in the second half of the 1990s (Karlhofer and Sickinger 1999; Hemerijck et al. 2000; Reuter 2000).

In Sweden the crisis occurred in the early 1990s, when the largest business association pulled out of central tariff negotiations. Similar to the Netherlands, despite widespread predictions that this would be the end of neocorporatism in the country, policy arrangements were re-established a few years later – albeit in a more flexible form and without the centralized tariff negotiations. By the early 2000s, the organization density of both employers' and employees' associations has proved largely stable. The position of business representations has been strengthened, amongst other factors, by the merger of the two largest employers' associations in March 2001 (Karlhofer and Sickinger 1999; Benner and Vad 2000; Swedish Employers' Association [SAF] 2000).

In Austria a slow erosion of neocorporatist policy arrangements has begun with the mid-1980s with the gradual demise of Keynesian macro-economic policy management. Moreover, the conservative–nationalist coalition government, which came into government in 2000, was the first Austrian government in thirty years, to which the unions had practically no access. Presently this has led to a strengthening of the position of business, to temporary standstills in negotiations on tariffs and regulations and, more generally, to a marked decrease of influence of neocorporatist arrangements (Karlhofer and Talos 1996; 1999; Kittel 2000; Hemerijck et al. 2000; Talos and Kittel 2001).

POLICY-FINDING PROCESSES IN EU-R&D POLICY SUBSYSTEMS

After a few determinants of national (R&D) policymaking have been described, next will follow a short overview of the EU-R&D policy subsystems, which during the 1990s have differentiated from the established R&D policy systems in the three countries. First, the respective structures and their evolution will be depicted. Then, the policy-finding processes leading to the national positions to FP5 will be portrayed.

A first look at Table 7.2, displaying the structures of EU-R&D policy subsystems, clarifies that all essential functions of the respective systems are covered in Austria, Sweden and the Netherlands. In each case there is a co-ordinating actor at ministerial level, while other ministries are responsible for introducing their more specialized views into the policy process. The co-ordination of the central actors, which in all cases do not only include ministries, but other types of players, too, is institutionalized in all three countries through interdepartmental groups. In each country there exists a single non-ministerial institution, which gathers and processes information on EU-R&D for the national policy and R&D communities. So, at first glance (and perhaps even at a second) all of this seems to imply that the EU-R&D policy structures in the three countries are quite similar. Indeed, only further research can reveal that there exist several differences with regards to EU-R&D policy subsystems of the three countries.

Table 7.2   Structures of EU-R&D policy subsystems (1995–98)

	Austria	**Sweden**	**Netherlands**
Co-ordinating ministry	Ministry for Science, Transport and the Arts (BMWV/K)	Ministry of Education (Utbildnings-departementet)	Ministry for Economic Affairs (MinEZ)
Other important ministries	Ministry for Economic Affairs (BMWA), Federal Chancellery (BKA)	Ministry for Economic Affairs (Näringsdepartementet)	Ministry for Education, Culture and Science (MinOCW)
Institutionalized co-ordination EU-R&D	Programme Management Club (PMC)	Council Co-operation R&D-Policy	Interdepartmental Working Group Framework Programme (IWK)
Non-ministerial institutions specialized on EU-R&D	Bureau for International R&D Co-operation (BIT)	EU-R&D Council (EU-FoU Radet)	EG Liaison

A first difference of rather formal nature applies to the nature of involvement of the ministries. In all three cases it is essentially two types of ministries, which are most influential in the EU-R&D policymaking processes: the ministries for science/education and the ministries for economics. However, it is the ministries for science and education, which co-ordinate the policy processes in Austria and Sweden, while it is the economics ministry, which is responsible for this in the Netherlands. In all three countries, including federally organized Austria, regional governments play virtually no role in EU-R&D policymaking.

The influence of the different ministries varies otherwise: in Austria the chancellery is responsible for the EURATOM treaties. The economics ministry has not been very interested in EU-R&D policy during the political processes regarding FP5, so the lion's share of interest and influence was concentrated in the science ministry.

In Sweden, the economics ministry was, with regards to their resources and functions, an important actor, which has been rather active in the policy-finding processes, yet was not successful in getting its interests represented in Brussels. The main reason for this was the strong-willed education minister Carl Tham, who, by and large, had little interest in EU-R&D policy, yet had set his mind to prioritizing the inclusion of social science into the FP5 – a hotly debated topic during most of the negotiations around FP5. During this negotiation process Tham had given instructions to give up the other Swedish R&D priorities in order to include social science research into FP5. This had brought up the economics ministry and a large part of the business community against him, without, however, changing the minister's opinion on the issue.

In the Netherlands the economics ministry had not only an interest to represent its clientele in the field of EU-R&D policy, but also the means to do so as an effect of its co-ordination function. Nevertheless, the education ministry has been very active, too. Interestingly, the frictions between both ministries seem minimal despite the apparent interest both organizations have in the policy process.

An important reason for this consensual decision-taking lies in the way EU-R&D policy is co-ordinated in the Netherlands. There the 'Interdepartementale Werkgroep Kaderprogramma' (Interdepartmental Working Group Framework Programme [IWK]) is responsible for this informal co-ordination.[6] It was set up in 1992 and includes about 30 decision-makers from the central ministries and a few experts, who are all representing Dutch interests in one of the EU institutions. There is no representation of interest groups, non-governmental organizations or associations in the IWK.

The corresponding Swedish institution is the Council 'Cooperation R&D-Policy', which has been established in lieu of the Swedish EU accession. The institution was of about the same size as the Dutch IWK, but met on a more irregular basis. It consisted of civil servants from the relevant ministries and several experts from outside, including the 'Svensk Industriforbundet' (Swedish Industrial Association [SI]), the leading association representing large firms. The forum was largely used for information dispersal and for informal discussions. Most interview partners thought it non-influential.

The Austrian institution responsible for the co-ordination of EU-R&D was the Programme Management Club (PMC). Similar to the Swedish case, it had a predecessor in the group preparing the Austrian EU accession, which consisted of experts from the employers' and employees' associations and the ministries. As an effect, the social partners from the start had been included in EU-R&D policy processes. The PMC was larger than its Swedish and Dutch counterparts and, by 1998, with the final negotiations on FP5 approaching, had grown to up to 80 people. Its tasks consisted of information dispersal and, adhering to Austrian decision-making styles, informal background talks, in which more formal decision-making processes were embedded.

Besides the ministries and the co-ordinating committees, a third type of institution of importance was developed for EU-R&D policy systems: non-ministerial organizations specializing on EU-R&D, which serve primarily as means to gather and (pre)process information for central decision-makers. Despite the similarities these institutions display in all three cases, again there is some space for variety.

The Swedish EU-FoU Radet, with a staff of 13, was the smallest of the three organizations. Surprisingly, the size of the institutions does not prevent it from having the broadest array of functions when it comes to policy analysis. The institution gathered and analyzed the largest part of the input for the policy-finding process leading to the Swedish position on FP5. Nevertheless, the main business of the EU-FoU Radet, similar to its Dutch and Austrian partner organizations (the institutions do co-operate at the EU level), is the transfer of information from and to EU institutions, primarily the European Commission – to this purpose the institution has a small office in Brussels. The main clientele of the three institutions in this respect is, on the one hand, the national R&D community, firms as well as research institutions and, on the other hand, the ministries.

The Austrian BIT (Bureau for International R&D Cooperation) was the largest of the three national non-ministerial EU-R&D related organizations. By the end of the 1990s it consisted of close to 50 persons, which covered a wide range of programs, including the FPs. Similar to the Swedish EU-FoU Radet the BIT is quite independent: it receives funding from several sources and serves the national R&D community and the R&D-related ministries alike.

The situation for the Dutch EG Liaison is quite different. The organization has the longest history of the three organizations and was founded in 1983, almost a decade before the two other institutions were established. It was independent until 1996, when it was included into the Technology Agency, Senter. Senter belongs to the economics ministry and so EG Liaison has now more directly policy-related tasks to fulfil than it had when it was still independent. Regarding the size of the institution, by the end of the 1990s it consisted of about two dozen persons, placing it midway between the Austrian and Swedish partner organizations.

Reaching a Position on FP5: the Policy-finding Process

Generally speaking, the processes of arriving at national positions regarding FP5 were similar in all three countries. First the beginning of the process was trumpeted by the co-ordinating ministry in the framework of a large conference. After the European Commission had presented its first papers on FP5 (European Commission 1996; 1997), a process was set in motion, in each of the countries, which ended in national positions to be used as guidelines for the negotiations at European level. Again, the variety becomes visible only for those who look more closely at the procedures, which evolved in each case.

In Austria, an ambitious process was started utilizing a large number of instruments to reach the potential clientele of the FPs. These instruments included large national conferences and workshops, mailings of relevant EU-R&D related materials, in which respondents were asked to voice their opinions and needs as well as small-scale and personal meetings with key experts from the R&D community and business associations. Accordingly, the whole decision-finding process was complex, extensive and relatively slow. It kept several persons of the science ministry's EU Coordination Unit busy for the better part of three years. This unit was not only carrying out the administrative work involved, but, under direct supervision of the Head of Section,[7] who had made EU-R&D one of his top priorities, was also planning and managing the policy-finding process regarding the national position to FP5.

In Sweden, a similar effort was started, with the difference that a smaller number of national and a higher number of regional meetings were held. Moreover, not only the co-ordinating education ministry, but also the economics ministry (partially through the technology agency NUTEK) were engaged in the decision-finding process. However, the larger part of the administrative work was carried out by the EU-FoU Radet, which was responsible for the mailings, the processing of the incoming and outgoing information and the preparation of the majority of the national and regional meetings on FP5.

Upon closer inspection the whole process was quite different in the Netherlands. After the large start-up conference there was neither a nationwide, nor a regional gathering, in which the R&D community would be informed or asked for their opinions on the proposed policy stance of either European or national institutions. Instead, another informal instrument was used to gather information and responses – if on a rather infrequent basis. Sounding Boards ('Klankboard Groups') were small groups of experts in specific areas. They could be called by single civil servants, which were part of the IWK and so could base their own opinions on these feedback mechanism.

Table 7.3   EU-R&D policy-finding processes: Inclusion of interests (1995–98)

	Austria	**Sweden**	**Netherlands**
Institutionalized contacts, interest groups – Framework Programme delegates	Sounding Boards ('Fachkommissionen') diverse in function and composition	EU R&D Council (EU-FoU Radet), informal networks	Sounding Boards ('Klankboard Groups')
Co-ordination of inclusion of interest groups in the process of developing national positions	EU co-ordination unit of the BMWV/K	EU R&D Council (EU-FoU Radet)	IWK, partially 'Klankboard Groups'
Degree of inclusion of interest groups in the process of developing national positions	High, through intensive process (mailings, workshops, symposia)	High, yet in the end limited because of Minister Tham	Low, due to strict admission processes

Sounding boards were also used in Austria (under the name 'Fachkommissionen') in order to gain feedback. These commissions were introduced in Austria in 1995, while they had a longer history in the Netherlands. Although they had an important role in some R&D sub areas, they played a smaller role in Austria, due to the variety of other instruments utilized by Austrian civil servants. In Sweden the role of sounding boards were mostly taken by the informal networks of agencies such as EU-FoU Radet and NUTEK.

Not only was the form of inclusion of interests into the decision-finding process different in the three countries, but there was also significant variation as to the type of the organizations and groups invited to take part in the whole process. In Sweden and Austria the universities and extra-university research institutions were invited to voice their opinions – which they, by and large, did. In the Netherlands only a few experts were asked to take part in the sounding boards – the only way of incorporating opinions from outside the small policymaking circle.

Large firms were directly included into the process of decision-finding in Austria. Especially Siemens Austria and Böhler-Uddeholm, each of which soon delegated a manager to take care of the firm's interests in (EU-)R&D matters, were continuously involved and transmitted their opinions via several channels. In Sweden a few multinational companies were also directly invited to take part in the process of finding national positions – although they were soon quite disillusioned about their possibilities to influence the process – and a larger number of firms were put on the national mailing list regarding EU-R&D.

In the Netherlands most large firms went directly to Brussels in order to voice their opinion to the European institutions, most importantly the European Commission. A few of these companies were provided with the possibility to take part in the sounding boards on national level. Swedish and Dutch multinational firms were already present in Brussels years before FP4 started. A number of these chose to lobby the European Commission directly, either alone or via umbrella organizations such as EU-Car, which is an interest representation of most European automotive producers. Austrian firms were practically not present in Brussels during the time of the negotiations on FP5, a few highly specialized companies, such as the car engine producer AVL, taken aside.

The situation was even more diverse with employers' and employees' associations. In Austria both business and employees' associations from begin on were invited to take part in the decision-finding processes. Their position was exclusive in the sense that they were the only interests represented in all the activities of the ministries, e.g. the PMC, the national conferences and workshops, the mailings and the direct and personal contacts. Whilst the employees' association's activity engulfed mainly a few specialized written statements, business representatives invested larger amounts of time. Indeed, the two Austrian business associations, the Austrian Economic Chamber (ÖWK) and the Industrial Association (IV), both had established committees, which enabled them to gather opinions from their clientele. Mostly large firms and a few highly specialized SMEs took the opportunity to represent themselves in these groups.

In interviews Austrian business association representatives stated that they were nevertheless not satisfied with their possibilities to get their arguments across in the decision-finding processes. They pointed at the 1994 agreement between the two coalescing parties in the grand coalition government, in which the associations are granted the right to get information on all EU matters concerning their work and the privilege to be heard on these matters, if they were to give opinions on these.[8]

The situation regarding the representation of associations was quite different in Sweden. There the employees' organizations were not invited to take part in decision-finding processes. Whilst business associations were invited, this invitation was only realized in a systematic fashion by the SI. In the following the organization was regularly consulted by the EU-FoU Radet and the education ministry via different channels, in personal discussions, via the Council Cooperation R&D-Policy and mailings. Therefore, the business associations were granted a privileged right of access in comparison to other actors.

In the Netherlands the employees' associations were not invited to give their opinion. The main employers' associations were asked to come to sounding board meetings, which means that they were treated equally with company representatives and other interest groups. This came as no surprise, because the associations had not been treated differently before. The large associations, most importantly the business association Confederation of Netherlands Industry and Employers (VNO-NCW), have lobbying offices in Brussels and are used to represent their interest directly at the European institutions. This is similar to the situation of the large Swedish business associations, who opened their EU (then still EEC) representations in 1974. In comparison Austrian business associations were comparatively reluctant to deal with Brussels, opening a small office there only in 1989.

CONCLUSIONS

In the introduction the central aim of this chapter was defined as to find how national R&D systems differentiate into EU-R&D subsystems and what the major determinants of this process are. An important point was made about the similarities between Austria, Sweden and the Netherlands. If there would exist variations in this 'most similar countries' comparison, it would be easier to isolate the factors, which determine the differentiation of the EU-R&D subsystems.

And indeed differences appeared, which were identified by taking a closer look at the R&D systems, at the organization of business–government relations, the structures of EU-R&D policy subsystems as well as the processes and forms of inclusion of interest groups, associations and other actors into the policy-finding processes regarding the national positions towards FP5. Therefore a question remains to be answered: is there an explanation for the differences described in the last sections?

The following argument will consist of two levels. Firstly, the general structures and institutional set-up of the economy and the R&D systems and, secondly, the business–government relations shall be used to explain the differences in the EU-R&D policy subsystems' structures and processes.

Structures have always repercussions on processes (and vice versa). The structures of national R&D systems are a useful determinant for differences in EU-R&D related decision-finding processes. A good starting point is the economic structure of a country. The existence of large multinational companies in Sweden and the Netherlands with a tradition of R&D activities in the respective nation state had the effect that there was already a group of actors in existence on the national level, which by the mid-1990s was experienced in EU matters – perhaps more than the civil servants and politicians of the countries joining the EU in 1995. It meant also that the representatives of these companies used their resources to lobby a national government (or even several) in EU-R&D program matters, but that they were not dependent on the success of these efforts, because, in case of failure at the national level, they still could lobby the EU institutions directly.

In turn, the absence of large multinationals and dominance of SMEs and the existence of neocorporatist arrangements in Austria meant two things: first of all these companies were less experienced in lobbying affairs, since they were used to rely mostly on the respective associations for that and, secondly, that they were neither comfortable nor had experience with the political system of the EU.

Whilst in Sweden the disgruntled multinational companies chose to lobby the European Commission directly, the Austrian firms went to the business associations, with the associations lobbying primarily the Austrian government and to a much lesser degree the European institutions. The Netherlands worked differently, because the country features large firms with EU and lobbying experience, due to the longer Dutch EU membership and the geographical proximity of the country to Brussels. Moreover, the Dutch EU-R&D subsystem provided only scarce possibilities for business interests to get their opinion across, leaving only the way via Brussels open for those companies, which wanted to influence the negotiations on FP5.

Another structural factor related to the R&D systems of the three countries is the extent to which funding for R&D was available during the time of decision-finding towards FP5. The availability of resources indeed correlates (inversely) with the readiness to engage into EU-R&D and decision-finding on EU-R&D. Put differently, scarce funding raised the willingness to engage into the decision-finding processes on FP5. Indeed, it was these groups, which had the greatest need for funding, which most ardently engaged into the discussions about FP5. In Sweden, extra-university institutions rather than universities engaged into the FPs and also into the respective political discussions about FP5.

Similarly, in Austria the extra-university research institutions were, in comparison to their small size, over-represented in the deliberations on FP5. To be more precise, it was a special type of extra-university institutions, which invested more time than the other actors into the policy-finding processes: several small independent institutions had a more extensive (and often also more intensive) input than the larger extra-university research institutions. This correlates with the funding situation of the Austrian R&D system in the 1990s. The greatest need for EU-R&D funding was discernable from the side of the small independent research institutions. The large extra-university institutes had more chances to diversify their resource base, whilst the majority of the universities at that time were barely willing to engage into research funded by the EU and therefore had little interest in the political discussions on FP5.

Besides the structural argument, another explanatory factor for the differences of the decision-finding processes observed are the business–government relations, which are capable of accounting for the different roles associations played in the three countries. First, it should be called into mind that all three countries are regularly understood as typical cases of neocorporatism. Austria until the 2000s usually was listed as the classical case of a 'strong' neocorporatist system, with a strong government, strong business associations and a strong, albeit weakening union. Sweden since the 1990s counts as a model with decentralized structures, a relatively weak state, strong unions and strong business. The Netherlands are equally decentralized in the 1990s. They would be seen as a system with strong state, weak unions and relatively weak business interests (Katzenstein 1985; Schmitter and Grote 1997; Karlhofer and Sickinger 1999; Hemerijck et al. 2000).

By taking these factors into account, one would predict for the Austrian case an intensive inclusion of both social partners, for the Swedish case an inclusion of both social partners, and in the Dutch case an integration of social partners only at a low level – if at all. As we have seen, this picture would fit reality to quite a degree. It works for Austria and the Netherlands, yet it only partially works for Sweden, where employees' associations were not part of the deliberations on FP5. Here the historical evolution of the policy-field may help to account for this specificity: one has to take into account the large multinational firms, which have, for a longer period of time, in R&D policy-making dealt directly with government (Edquist and Lundvall 1993) and thereby established a tradition of co-operation with government long before the EU accession. Because of this, government had no necessity to include the social partners into R&D policymaking.

In lieu of this situation, it would seem interesting that this tradition was broken in Sweden by the EU accession. This seems to have been an effect of the need of the civil service to establish contacts with interest groups and associations in order to get actors to take part in the FPs, into which Swedish tax-payers' money was flowing (and which made it likely that the very tax payers one day would want to learn about the returns from the funds invested into EU-R&D programs). If that was the case in Sweden, would there be something similar observable in Austria?

Upon closer inspection it soon becomes clear that Austrian national R&D policymaking was influenced by the social partners for several decades, with the field of technology policy being dominated by them (Aichholzer et al. 1994). This began to change with the slow dismantling of the social partnership in the mid-1980s (Mayer 2003). Several interview partners have established that this dismantling was felt in Austrian R&D policymaking, when the social partners were pushed out, without getting other actors in. This trend was consistent – with two exceptions. One of these has proven short-lived: the steering board of the Innovations and Technology Fund (ITF) dominated in the first years of its establishment by high-ranking politicians and experts from the social partners, in which R&D policy discussions were transgressing the confines of the fund's tasks. The other exception pertained to the preparation committee of the Austrian EU accession in R&D-policy, which was the forerunner of the PMC, where the social partners have been involved from the start as preferentially treated partners. Whilst this may not qualify as the resurrection of neocorporatism in R&D policy, it certainly is a form of preferential treatment of the social partners in the framework of a policy network.

Altogether the EU accession brought, at first sight perhaps somewhat surprisingly, no loss of influence for associations in the policy field. In the case of Sweden, business associations were treated preferentially and in Austria both business and employees' associations could profit from the EU accession. Moreover, this trend has proven to be sustainable. During the negotiations on FP6 from 2000–02 in Sweden, the SI (and from March 2001 SI/SAF) has been included on a more regular basis and more exclusively than during the policy-finding processes on FP5. And, similarly, in Austria both social partners have been treated even more preferential than before. Since this goes against the grain of the general political developments in Austria – the dismantling of the social partnership and downgrading of the associations to just one type of political actor amongst many others – it is all the more worth noting that the EU integration process in the policy area has provided an impetus for closer co-operation between associations and the state, here represented less by politicians and more by the ministerial bureaucracy.

In fact, this observation is in line with research findings showing that, despite the adaptations a political system has to implement when joining the EU, at least in the short term the European integration is less likely to bring crucial changes to the policy styles of the new member countries. Rather, it is more likely to reinforce existing political arrangements deeply ingrained in the national systems (Karlhofer and Talos 1996; Falkner et al. 1999). Of course, the question remains open, if this trend proves substantial in the face of an ever closer Union.

Now only two questions posed in the introduction are left open. First, what can we learn from the policy processes leading up to FP5 for the ERA initiative. Second, what can we learn from the way the three Member States in discussion reacted to the demands raised by the FPs for the reactions of the Member States to the ERA.

As to the first question it has to be clarified if the two R&D initiatives are indeed comparable. In this respect two important issues are the framework in which FP5 and ERA are set and the challenge posed by FP5 and by ERA to the Member States. The framework remains largely the same: on a formal level (and in a rather narrow sense) it is in both instances the EU – an institution, which has not dramatically changed its character over the last few years. If understood in a somewhat wider sense the framework would include also the environment of the EU, encompassing factors such as the world economic situation and security-related questions, which have the potential to overshadow the relevance of innovation-related issues. Whilst the economic factors have changed over the second half of the 1990s to a degree, the impact of the changes should remain small enough to be neglected. With regards to security related questions, it seems clear that the incidents following 11 September 2001 in the United States have destabilized the geopolitical situation, thereby impacting (also) on all EU policy areas. However, their midterm effects are difficult to determine and will therefore not be included here.

More complicated is the question if FP5 and a ERA are comparable with regards to their impact on the EU Member States. From the outset it seems clear that a ERA is the larger and more encompassing initiative. The perhaps most important difference to the FPs as such is that the ERA aims at a co-ordination of Member States' R&D policies through ways extending the typical FPs, such as the internationalization and opening up of previously national research funds and a more general drive for harmonization of the Member States' systems of innovation.

Yet if one looks more closely into the question of how FP5 was perceived during the first two years of discussions about it and recalls the way the FP was heralded as a paradigmatic change of the EU-R&D policy, one might see FP5 as the effort of the construction of a similarly path-breaking initiative as the ERA.

FP5 from the outset was planned as a clear deviation from the earlier FPs due to its emphasis on societal problem solution. The perhaps most extreme version of this problem orientation were the 'task forces' as advanced by Commissioner Cresson in 1995 and 1996, i.e. before the hot phase of negotiations over FP5 actually had begun. The task forces were oriented towards industrially defined problem sets such as the development of an inter-modular European transport system. Therefore the first European Commission proposal on FP5 (European Commission 1996, p. 332) included a watered-down version of Cresson's original ideas on what EU-R&D policy should be about.

With the European Commission proposal from 1996 for the first time the disciplinary boundaries, which were dominating the earlier FPs, were to be completely dismantled and the programs were to be oriented on problem sets such as 'the aging population' or the 'city of tomorrow' or the 'culturally based identities' of Europe.[9] Nevertheless, with the first round of Member States' reactions on the initial European Commission paper on FP5 in late 1996, it had turned out that the Madame Cresson would not be able to carry this reorientation of the FPs out and that the disciplinary orientation of the program could indeed not be fully overcome. Indeed FP5 finally turned out to be a mixture of both forms of research, disciplinary and problem-related.

Because of all of this, it might be concluded that inferences drawn from the development of FP5 might have some relevance for the discussions around the ERA. If this is accepted, the argument would be that due to the vested interests in the FPs and the path dependencies of such institutions it is unlikely for the ERA to become established in only a few years after the inception of the concept in 2000 – just as it turned out to be impossible to radically change the nature of the FPs with FP5. A first proof seems to come from the structure of FP6, which showed that some elements of a ERA, such as an even stronger emphasis of EU-R&D policy on co-operation in international networks and the establishment of centers of excellency as nodal points of these networks, found their way into the program. Yet, it remains to be seen if other, more ambitious goals, such as a real co-ordination of national R&D policies shall be taking place during the lifetime of FP6 (or even FP7).

The second directly-ERA related question posed earlier on was on the issues to be learned from the way the Member States reacted to the demands raised by the FPs for the reactions of the Member States to the ERA. More concretely, the crucial question here addresses the way the ERA might impact on the EU Member States' innovation systems. This issue in turn is linked to the question of political reactions to the ERA from the sides of the Member States in the sense that those actors, which are likely to profit from the ERA are more likely to become part of the coalition pressing for the initiative, whilst those likely to have nothing to win from it might oppose it.

In a first step one might look into the question which of the innovation systems of the three countries in discussion might be more and which might be less compatible with the ERA. For such a discussion one would have to look at the level of the collective actors or group of actors in Austria, the Netherlands and Sweden. The data, which have been presented during earlier sections of this chapter, already sufficiently show that the Netherlands, and, especially, Sweden, have a number of large highly internationalized firms, which would have no difficulty to compete for funds in a deregulated R&D field such as the ERA. This is quite different from the situation in Austria, where most firms are SMEs with comparatively little research activities. Such actors have already a hard time to take part in the FPs despite all the existing efforts to foster SME participation. These SMEs certainly would have a much more difficult time with a deregulation of the R&D sector, diminishing the national niches, in which they could operate without having to compete with larger and more internationalized enterprises.

The situation is different with more academic institutions such as the universities. Modern European university systems, such as those featured by the three countries discussed here, are already internationalized. Yet their experiences with funding institutions varies to a large extent. One determinant, which has been highlighted before, is the need of the universities to seek external funding. This need depends again on a variety of factors such as the existence and nature of evaluation systems, the size and composition of state university funding and others. In Sweden and in Austria the need for universities to seek external funding is more limited in comparison to the Netherlands, which, as has been said, is an explanation for the comparatively low interest of large parts of the two national university systems in EU-R&D funding. As it is not likely that this factor is to change dramatically over the short term (despite ongoing university reforms in all three countries), the impact of the ERA – regardless how fast the concept is to be realized – on the universities in Sweden and Austria is to be limited, too.

It might even be worthwhile to think about the impact of the ERA on the different disciplines. If the logic of the FPs – which is a child of the EC and EU contracts upon which the EU-R&D policies are based – is directly taken into the ERA initiative (and it is difficult to see a way around this as long as the R&D related parts of the *acquis communautaire* are not changed), then the ERA will be as much industry-driven as the FPs have been until now. Whilst the economic logic of the FPs makes sense for a program directly and single-mindedly geared towards making the EU more competitive, it might not make sense to expose humanities and many social sciences, to name only two examples, to such a logic.

As has been pointed out earlier, extra-university institutions face not the same funding situations as universities and in general tend to be more internationalized in this regard. Austria has been put as an example of an innovation system offering little money for extra-university institutions. Following the streams of money by sheer necessity, Austrian extra-university institutions are likely to feel the impact of the ERA heavily – with the already internationalized part of these organizations profiting from the deregulation of the R&D market. However, these institutes, which were used by national policymakers for advice as a sort of low-key think tanks, often linked in some way with the social partners – are likely to increasingly face international competition most likely driving a number of these out of the market and others to reorganize.

The intermediate institutions of the three innovation systems are also likely to develop a variety of reactions to the ERA. Those, which are clearly geared towards a clientele, which is not likely to profit from the ERA, are highly likely to oppose the European initiative. In the Austrian case, the technology sponsoring Industry Research Promotion Fund ('Fonds zur Förderung der gewerblichen Forschung'), which mainly works through a bottom-up funding system, is opposing the ERA on grounds of the fear that the Austrian firms seeking funding with the institution will find it tough to deal with international competitors. Other intermediate institutions, which since a longer period of time have worked more internationally, are more likely to greet an initiative as the ERA on grounds of expected growth of importance and influence.

What therefore quickly becomes obvious is that there is no simple answer to the question of which countries are likely to profit from the ERA more than others, as the institutional set-up of the Member States' innovation systems is diverse enough so as to have winners and losers alike in each of the systems. When pulling all information together it seems more likely that the more internationalized parts of the innovation systems are to profit from the ERA – and therefore these are also more likely to greet the initiative – whereas the more nationally oriented parts are more likely to lose out when the regulated R&D markets are opened up – and therefore these are more likely to oppose the ERA.

Ultimately, the chances for the success of the ERA initiative then will depend on the ability of the European Commission to adapt the concept to the needs of the Member States and the Member States' governments to explain the merits of the idea to their policy communities. For this, it might become necessary to work on some of the rigid goals of EU-R&D policies, such as the narrow definition of competitiveness, which excludes large parts of European science and largely ignores problem sets of importance for the European integration process.

NOTES

[1] Introductory literature on the political processes of the EU is abundant (for example O'Neill 1996; Zbinden 1999; Borchardt 2000; Peterson and Bomberg 2000; Wessels and Weidenfeld 2000); the literature on EU-R&D policymaking has been growing in recent years, too (Krige and Guzzetti 1995; Grande 1996; 2000; Biegelbauer 1998; Sharp and Peterson 1998; Borrás 2000).

[2] A lively discussion on the issue of the importance of the geographic origin of multinational companies has been led for several years now. Evidence seems to grow that, for the time being, it indeed makes a difference for some business functions, if a company is investing

into its 'home base', where the likelihood of the establishment of, for example, R&D divisions is higher, or into another country (compare with Pavitt 1992; Dunning 1993; Patel and Vega, 1999; Biegelbauer et al. 2001b).

3 A number of people were crucial for our research project. First of all I should thank Raoul Kneucker and Ilse König, who both helped us with their expertise to see issues and find doors. Besides these two persons, a number of other staff at BMBWK and BMVIT helped us to gain information and funding. My gratitude extends also to the RP5-POL team, Alfred Gerstl, M. Feigl-Heihs and Susanne Pernicka; together we produced two research reports and a book (Pernicka et al. 2002).

4 Similar R&D expenditure levels are snapshots of longer-term developments; i.e. they can hide the fact that one country is investing little on R&D activities, but has reached a high level of development due to investments of the past, whereas another might spend relatively more, but might be in a process of catching up. Worse, the amount of spending does not necessarily say anything about the efficiency with which the funds are spent – the formerly state-socialist countries are a good example here.

5 For comparative literature on R&D systems, including the countries under discussion, see Nelson et al. (1993); Didieren and Stoneman et al. (1999); Biegelbauer and Borrás (2003).

6 The formal co-ordination in Austria, the Netherlands and Sweden alike is a task of the Foreign Service, which, however, practically never interferes with EU-R&D policies and simply represents the policy positions in the respective EU institutions such as COREPER (Comité des Représentants Permanents) and, in the case of the Netherlands, also the Council Working Group on R&D.

7 A position comparable to an under state secretary in the Anglo-Saxon system of civil service or a director in other continental European systems.

8 The original wording of the 'Europaabkommen' of the socialdemocratic SPÖ and the conservative ÖVP from 22 April 1994 is: '... in wichtigen sie [die Sozialpartner] berührenden Fachfragen die gleichberechtigte Teilnahme an der österreichischen Entscheidungsvorbereitung und Entscheidungsfindung im Rahmen der EU zugesichert. Zu diesem Zweck werden Vertreter der genannten Interessenorganisationen nicht nur an der innerösterreichischen Meinungsbildung umfassend beteiligt, sondern auch ihre offizielle Mitarbeit in den einschlägigen Gremien der EU (z.B.: Komitees, Ratsgruppen, Fonds, Stiftungen) sichergestellt'. In this passage (lit. 13a of the paper) the two parties then forming the Austrian federal government assure the social partners that they were to be included in the EU policy-related decision-finding processes regarding all matters important to them. To this end, goes the contract, the associations will be included in the national decision-making processes and in the negotiations at the EU level, for example in Council Working Groups. It has soon turned out that the original pledge of government to include associations directly into negotiations at the level of Council Working Groups and other committees was not compatible with EU regulations so that government had to step back of its original pledge (compare also with Falkner 2000; Müller 2000). Nevertheless, the right of information and consultation has been recognized by government.

9 Compare with the program names of, for example, the European Commission communications COM (1996) 332 and COM (1997) 142.

REFERENCES

Aichholzer, G., R. Martinsen and J. Melchior (1994), 'Österreichische Technologiepolitik auf dem Prüfstand', *Reihe Politikwissenschaft*, Forschungsbericht Nr. 13 des Institutes für Höhere Studien Wien, Wien.

Benner, M. and T.B. Vad (2000), 'Sweden and Denmark Defending the Welfare State', in Scharpf, F. and V. Schmidt (eds), *Welfare and Work in the Open Economy*, Oxford and New York: Oxford University Press.

Biegelbauer, P. (1998), 'Mission impossible: the governance of European science and technology', *Science Studies*, **11** (2), Helsinki, 20–39.

Biegelbauer, P. and S. Borrás (2003), *Innovation Policies in Europe and the US: The New Agenda*, Aldershot, UK: Ashgate.

Biegelbauer, P., A. Gerstl and S. Pernicka (2001a), *Politikvorbereitungsprozesse und Verhandlungsmechanismen im EU Politikfeld Forschung und Technologie*, Wien: RP5 POL Projekt, Projektbericht des Instituts für Höhere Studien.

Biegelbauer, P., E. Griessler and M. Leuthold (2001b), *The Impact of Foreign Direct Investment on the Knowledge Base of Central and Eastern European Countries*, Wien: FDI CEEC Project, Working Paper Nr. 77 of the Political Science Series 'Institut für Höhere Studien'.

Borchardt, K. (2000), *The ABC of Community Law*, Brussels: European Commission.

Borrás, S. (2000), 'Science, Technology and Innovation in European Politics', *Research Paper*, **50**.

Czada, R. (1994), 'Konjunkturen des Korporatismus: Zur Geschichte eines Paradigmenwechsels in der Verbändeforschung', *Politische Vierteljahresschrift*, Sonderheft **25**, 37–64.

Diederen, P. (1999), *Innovation and Research Policies: an International Comparative Analysis*, Cheltenham, UK and Northhampton, MA, USA: Edward Elgar.

Dunning, J. (1993), *Multinational Enterprises and the Global Economy*, Harlow, UK: Addison-Wesley.

Edquist, C. and B. Lundvall (1993), 'Comparing the Danish and Swedish Systems of Innovation', in Nelson, R. (ed.) , *National Innovation Systems*, Oxford and New York: Oxford University Press.

European Commission (1996), *Die Zukunft Gestalten*, Brussels: European Commission, COM (1996) 332.

European Commission (1997), Brussels: European Commission, COM (1997) 142.

European Commission (2000), *Towards a European Research Area – Science, Technology and Innovation: Key Figures 2000*, Brussels: European Commission.

Falkner, G. (2000), 'How pervasive are euro-politics? Effects of EU membership on a new member state', *Journal of Common Market Studies*, **38** (2), 223–50.

Falkner, G. and C. Müller (eds) (1998), *Österreich im europäischen Mehrebenensystem*, Wien: Signum.

Falkner, G., C. Müller, M. Eder, K. Hiller, G. Steiner and R. Trattnigg (1999), 'The impact of EU membership on policy networks in Austria: creeping change beneath the surface', *Journal of European Public Policy*, **6** (3), 496–516.

Goldthorpe, J. (1985), *Order and Conflict in Contemporary Capitalism*, Goldthorpe, J. (ed.), Oxford, UK: Clarendon Press.

Grande, E. (1996), 'The state and interest groups in a framework of multi-level decision making: the case of the European Union', *Journal of European Public Policy*, **3** (3), 318–38.

Grande, E. (2000), 'Von der Technologie zur Innovationspolitik Europäische Forschungs- und Technologiepolitik im Zeitalter der Globalisierung', in Simonis, G., R. Martinsen and T. Saretzki (eds), *Politik und Technik: Analysen zum Verhältnis von technologischem, politischem und staatlichem Wandel am Anfang des 21. Jahrhunderts*, pp. 368–87.

Hemerijck, A., B. Unger and J. Visser (2000), 'How Small Countries Negotiate Change Twenty-Five Years of Policy Adjustment in Austria, the Netherlands and Belgium', in Scharpf, F. and V. Schmidt (eds), *Welfare and Work in the Open Economy*, Oxford and New York: Oxford University Press.

Karlhofer, F. and E. Talos (1996), *Sozialpartnerschaft und EU*, Wien: ZAP.

Karlhofer, F. and E. Talos (1999), *Zukunft der Sozialpartnerschaft*, Karlhofer, F. and E. Talos (eds), Wien: ZAP.

Karlhofer, F. and H. Sickinger (1999), 'Korporatismus und Sozialpartnerschaft', in Karlhofer, F. and E. Talos (eds), *Zukunft der Sozialpartnerschaft*, Wien: ZAP.

Kassim, H., B.G. Peters and V. Wright (2000), *The National Coordination of EU Policy*, Basingstoke.

Katzenstein, P. (1985), *Small States in World Markets: Industrial Policy in Europe*, Cornell, New York: Cornell University Press.

Kittel, B. (2000), 'Deaustrification? The policy area specific evolution of Austrian social partnership', *West European Politics*, **23** (1), 108–29.

Krige, J. and L. Guzzetti (1995), *History of European Science and Technology Cooperation*, Brussels: European Commission.

Lehmbruch, G. (1974), 'Consociational Democracy. Class conflict and the New Corporatism', in Schmitter, Ph.C. and G. Lehmbruch (eds), *Trends Towards Corporatist Intermediation*, Beverly Hills: Sage Publications.

Lehmbruch, G. (1984), 'Concertation and the Structure of Corporatist Networks', in Goldthorpe, J. (ed.) , *Order and Conflict in Contemporary Capitalism*, Oxford: Clarendon Press.

Mayer, K. (2003), 'Running After the International Trend: Keynesian Power Balances and the Sustainable Repulsion of the Innovation Paradigm in Austria', in Biegelbauer, P. and S. Borrás (eds), *Innovation Policies in Europe and the US: The New Agenda*, Aldershot, UK: Ashgate.

Müller, W.C. (2000), 'EU Coordination in Austria: Challenges and Responses', in Kassim, H., B.G. Peters and V. Wright (eds), *The National Coordination of EU Policy*, Basingstoke: Oxford University Press.

National Council for Industry and Technological Development (NUTEK) (1998), *The Swedish National Innovation System*, Stockholm, Sweden.

O'Neill, M. (1996), *The Politics of European Integration*, London.

Patel, P. and M. Vega (1999), 'Patterns of internationalisation of corporate technology: location vs. home country advantages', *Research Policy*, **28** (2), 145–55.

Pavitt, K. (1992), 'Internationalisation of technological innovation', *Science and Public Policy*, **19** (2), 119–23.

Pernicka, S., M. Feigl-Heihs, A. Gerstl and P. Biegelbauer (2002), *Wie demokratisch ist die europäische Forschungs- und Technologiepolitik? Der politische Entscheidungsprozess zum fünften Forschungsrahmenprogramm aus österreichischer Perspektive*, Baden-Baden: Nomos.

Peterson, J. and E. Bomberg (2000), *Decision Making in the European Union*, The European Union Series.

Reuter, N. (2000), 'Das Modell Niederlande', *Wirtschaft und Gesellschaft*, **26** (3), 343–66.

Scharpf, F. and V. Schmidt (2000), *Welfare and Work in the Open Economy*, Oxford and New York: Oxford University Press.

Schmitter, Ph.C. (1974), 'Still the century of corporatism?', *Review of Politics*, **36**, 85–131.

Schmitter, Ph.C. and J. Grote (1997), 'Der korporatistische Sisyphus: Vergangenheit, Gegenwart und Zukunft', *Politische Vierteljahresschrift*, **1997**, 530–54.

Schmitter, Ph.C. and G. Lehmbruch (1979), *Trends Towards Corporatist Intermediation*, Beverly Hills.

Sharp, M. and J. Peterson (1998), *Technology Policy in the European Union*, New York: St. Martin's Press.

Streeck, W. (1994), 'Einleitung des Herausgebers: Staat und Verbände: Neue Fragen. Neue Antworten?', *Politische Vierteljahresschrift*, Sonderheft **25**, 7–34.

Swedish Employers' Association (SAF) (2000), *Labour Relations in Sweden*, Doc. No. G1.

Swedish Technology Foresight (2000), *The Foresighted Society*, Sweden.

Talos, E. and B. Kittel (2001), *Gesetzgebung in Österreich. Netzwerke, Akteure und Interaktionen in politischen Entscheidungsprozesse*, Wien: WUV.

Traxler, F., S. Blaschke and B. Kittel (2001), *National Labour Relations in Internationalized Markets*, Oxford and New York: Oxford University Press.

Van der Steen, M. (2003), 'Technology Policy Learning in the Netherlands 1979–1997', in Biegelbauer, P. and S. Borrás (eds), *Innovation Policies in Europe and the US: the New Agenda*, Aldershot, UK: Ashgate.

Visser, J. (2000), 'Zum Beschäftigungspakt am Beispiel der Niederlande (Polder-Modell)', in Piehl, E. and H. Timann (eds), *Der Europäische Beschäftigungspakt. Entstehungsprozeß und Perspektiven*, Baden-Baden: Nomos.

Wessels, W. and W. Weidenfeld (2000), *Europa von A bis Z. Taschenbuch der europäischen Integration*, Bundeszentrale für politische Bildung, Bonn: Europa Union Verlag.

Zbinden, M. (1999), *Die Institutionen und die Entscheidungsverfahren der Europäischen Union nach Amsterdam*, Bern.

8 Finnish Science and Technology Policy in the Context of Internationalization and Europeanization

Johanna Hakala

INTRODUCTION

After a fast recovery from the deep economic recession of the early 1990s, Finland has become one of the top countries in different comparisons on technological know-how and innovative performance (e.g. European Commission 2001). One explanation for this positive development can be found in an active science, technology and innovation policy and an increased R&D expenditure – both aimed at making Finland a 'knowledge-based society'. At the same time, it is clear that such development could not have been achieved without the success of the Finnish-based company Nokia, which has become the world leader in mobile communications and which accounts for more than 20 per cent of all expenditure on R&D in Finland (Ali-Yrkkö et al. 2000, p. 12).

During the 1990s Finland also became a member of the European Union (EU). In the field of science and technology, EU membership led to a fast extension of European networks and collaboration. However, it should also be noted that in Finnish science and technology policy, internationalization had been a top priority already since the mid-1980s. The rationale for this policy has remained the same: as a small country with a relatively small resource base in science and technology, the only way to succeed in international competition is to collaborate and utilize know-how produced elsewhere. This importing of knowledge applies to the design of Finnish science and technology policy: the basic policy doctrines, as well as the very government agencies responsible for them, have to a great extent been formulated according to the models developed in other countries and international organizations (Lemola 2002).

The focus of this article is on how Finnish science and technology policy[1] has been affected by membership in the EU and what kinds of changes can be expected as a result of the European Commission's 'European Research Area' (ERA) initiative – both in terms of the policymaking process as well as the content of policy. The empirical data consist of interviews with high-level civil servants responsible for Finnish science and technology policy.[2] The starting point for the analysis is that the significance of EU membership and the promises and challenges of the ERA initiative must be understood in the context of long-term attempts aimed at reforming the Finnish R&D system so that Finland survives in 'international competition' and 'conditions of global change' (e.g. Science and Technology Policy Council of Finland 2000).

It is also important to recall that the domestic response to pressures toward European integration in the field of science and technology depends not only on policymakers but on the willingness and capabilities of various R&D actors to accommodate to and benefit from, as well as resist changes induced by the EU R&D policy (Knill and Lehmkuhl 1999; van der Meulen and Shove 2001). In view of this, the article also provides a brief excursion into the university sector in Finland, examining the views of heads of departments and researchers on the impacts and significance of EU collaboration.

FINNISH SCIENCE AND TECHNOLOGY POLICY: KEEPING UP WITH INTERNATIONAL COMPETITION

The Main Policy Actors

At the level of science and technology policy, there are a fairly limited number of actors. Ultimately, Finnish S&T policy is decided by the Parliament and the Council of State. In practice, the most general guidelines for S&T policy are given by the Science and Technology Policy Council of Finland (previously Science Policy Council, founded in 1963), the members of which consist of ministers and representatives of funding agencies, research performing institutions as well as labor market organizations. The Council publishes a review of and strategy for Finnish science and technology policy every three years.

Other significant actors include the Ministry of Education, which acts as the general science ministry, and the Ministry of Trade and Industry, which is the main promoter of technology and industrial R&D. The Ministry of Education makes performance agreements with all universities[3] every three years and channels other (basic research) funding through the Academy of Finland. The main tool of the Ministry of Trade and Industry is the National Technology Agency (Tekes), which has an important role in financing applied research and development work. During the 1990s, the position of both the Academy and Tekes was reinforced significantly. In the government budget of 2001, circa 43 per cent of R&D funding was channeled through them, whereas circa 47 per cent of funding was given directly to research performing institutions (universities, sectoral research institutes and university hospitals) (Suomen Akatemia 2001). In the new situation, both organizations have assumed an active role in developing the goals and instruments of science and technology policy.

In addition, many other ministries[4] in Finland also play an important role in funding R&D, especially the Ministry of Social Affairs and Health and the Ministry of Agriculture and Forestry. Several ministries are responsible for one or more sectoral research institutes, with which they now make annual performance agreements. During the 1990s, the funding of these governmental research institutes became more varied, so that a significant part of their funding comes from other sources than the responsible ministry.[5] At the same time, however, the sectoral ministries have adopted a more active role in research policy through the so-called cluster programs, which are funded from several sources but administered by the sectoral ministries.

The National Innovation System Approach

The 1980s has been considered a crucial period for the development of Finnish science and technology policy into its current form. A national consensus was achieved on the necessity of increasing the level of technological know-how and to support new fields of technology, such as information technology. The new emphasis was visible in the decisions to found the National Technology Agency (designed after the Swedish Board for Technical development) and to expand the mandate of the Science Policy Council to include technology issues as well as in the development of national technology programs (Lemola forthcoming).

The economic recession of the early 1990s coincided with the adoption of the 'national innovation system' approach. The concept was introduced in the Finnish Science and Technology Policy Council's report in 1990 – only a few years after Christopher Freeman's pioneering book was published and before the OECD (Organisation for Economic Co-operation and Development) adopted it. The Finnish interpretation of the concept can be characterized as pragmatic. The basic idea is that innovations and technical progress result from a complex set of relationships among actors producing, distributing and applying knowledge. This means, for example, that universities are not regarded as separate entities but as an integral part of the national system of innovation. Through networking and collaboration within the system it is possible to increase the efficiency and relevance of R&D work, and thus ensure the attainment of societal goals, especially the international competitiveness of the economy (Kaukonen and Nieminen 1999; Miettinen 2002, pp. 60–87). In 1996 the Science and Technology Policy Council of Finland presented a complementary concept, the 'knowledge-based society', which underscores increased knowledge and expertise through education, training and R&D. This emphasis was backed by a decision to increase governmental R&D funding so that it would be 2.9 per cent of GDP by 1999 (Prihti et al. 2000). In 2001 the percentage was already 3.4 and the ratio between private and public funding was approximately 71:29 (Tilastokeskus 2003).

The instruments of policy have changed accordingly. Increased emphasis on competitiveness is particularly evident in the decision to channel the additional funds for R&D (1997–99) mainly through the two governmental funding bodies, the Academy of Finland and Tekes. Other examples of the increased emphasis on competitiveness are the Finnish centers of excellence policy of the Academy and the development of research and technology programs as well as the so-called cluster programs, which partly overlap with each other (see Tuomaala et al. 2001). The cluster programs were designed by the Science and Technology Policy Council in 1996 to foster the development of strategically important sectors of the Finnish innovation system, such as food industries, forestry, transport, welfare and the environment. In the 2000 strategy, 'key technologies' include information technologies, biotechnology and new materials, and process techniques. Accordingly, the various programs are not only directed at increasing quality through competition, but they direct research into certain areas and reinforce the application orientation of research.

At the same time, performance agreements have become a central way of steering the public actors within the Finnish innovation system. They are often linked to processes of defining organizational strategies. Also the number of research evaluations has grown constantly since the mid-1980s. The focus of evaluation has gradually shifted to cover not only 'quality' but also the relevance and impacts of research, as well as organizational dimensions (Oksanen 2000). Evaluations are typically done by international expert groups.[6] The consequences of evaluations for the allocation of money are seldom very radical, however, they constitute an important element in fostering competitiveness and efficiency in the research system.

Interviews with policymakers in the field of science and technology show that the innovation system perspective has been adopted widely. According to one interviewee, 'the concept of the innovation system, as it has been defined and understood in Finland, has been an absolute success throughout the 1990s – otherwise we would not operate with it'. Another interviewee says, in a more critical tone, 'the innovation [system] thinking, which is understood in terms of technology, now prevails over the whole field of science, technology and innovation policy'. Indeed, some interviewees – especially those responsible for the science side of S&T – think that innovation system thinking is too technology-driven. On the other hand, some of those interviewees who are responsible for technology policy emphasize that technology and technology policy are just tools: the real aim is to develop the 'innovation environment' which is the key to new kinds of economic activity.

As Eela (2001) points out, the adoption of the innovation system perspective has also signified a change in the perceived role of the state: it is depicted as one of the actors in the research and innovation system and as having a facilitating rather than a controlling role. According to this idea – which is essential in the so-called new public management approach – public governance is based 'more on concertation and negotiation than on hierarchy and imposition' (Kazancigil 1998, pp. 70–71). On the basis of the interviews, it seems that a change in the governance culture is real. All interviewees mention that networking among policymakers and their connections to other 'stake-holders' in matters concerning science and technology increased throughout the 1990s. Especially collaboration among the Academy, Tekes and the sectoral ministries has expanded, largely due to the establishment of research, technology and cluster programs. However, as one of the policymakers reminds, this development has taken place in a situation in which almost all actors within the system have more funds to spend than before (with the exception of universities) – in a more difficult economic situation things may change quickly.

To sum up, there seems to prevail a surprising consensus mentality in the Finnish science and technology policymaking community over the basic approach and how to implement it, as well as satisfaction with the current state of the innovation system.[7] One interviewee argues that this positive development can be at least partly explained by the existence of the Science and Technology Policy Council of Finland as a forum in which experts, political decision-makers and representatives of other interest groups can meet. Another interviewee says that the successful implementation of reforms is due to the small size of the country. The general feeling of satisfaction is, of course, also related to the good financial situation prevailing since the mid-1990s. The one ugly spot in the picture is the basic funding of universities, which has stagnated. It is feared that this has serious implications for the whole innovation system, for instance, in terms of a lack of competent employees for the needs of industrial R&D.

Internationalization of R&D as a Policy Goal

As a policy objective, internationalization of Finnish science and technology became a priority in the late 1980s. This shift was signified by membership in

EUREKA in 1985 and in ESA and CERN some years later.[8] Some Finnish researchers took part already in the Second and Third Framework Programmes (FP2 and FP3) of the EU (with national funding) but full participation became possible only in 1995 when Finland became a member of the EU.

The Science and Technology Policy Council of Finland emphasizes the importance of international collaboration from the perspective of scientific and economic competitiveness. It is believed that 'a major part of the knowledge needed in Finland is produced abroad – with the help of international research co-operation, results and knowledge can be obtained which are outside the possibilities of domestic research' (Science and Technology Policy Council of Finland 1996, p. 29). Earlier characterized as a peripheral country, which seeks contacts and collaboration in order to keep up with general developments, Finland is now seen as a country that chooses collaboration fields and partners according to a strategy and market needs (Eela 2001, p. 32).

Internationalization has been promoted actively by the Academy of Finland and Tekes. Both offer researchers different kinds of opportunities to travel abroad and to invite foreign researchers to Finland. Tekes also provides extensive support for those interested in participating, for instance, in EU, EUREKA or COST collaboration. As mentioned above, evaluations are typically done by international teams and international publications and other merits are considered an important criterion in applications for posts or project funding. Especially the Academy of Finland has invested a lot of resources in making internationality an integral part of all the research activities that it finances.

According to some critical voices, since Finland became a member of the EU, internationalization has become almost synonymous with Europeanization, which may not be a good thing in terms of the quality of research – after all, joining the EU was a decision in which science and technology issues had a marginal role. The recent co-operation schemes presented in the policy documents are based on collaboration between macro-regions of which the EU is self-evidently the most important. However, it is also stressed that internationalization should take place in a balanced way, so that the United States, Japan and other regions would not be forgotten either (Science and Technology Policy Council of Finland 2000; 2003; see also Eela 2001).

Not surprisingly, all interviewed policymakers regard the internationalization of Finnish research and development as a very positive thing. According to one interviewee:

> ... the internationalisation of science and technology really started across the whole science and technology field only during the 1990s and thanks to EU

collaboration. This is so because it has forced [Finns] to get involved in international collaboration and to create networks.

On the other hand, some interviewees also think that the EU dimension might have been emphasized a bit too much, at the expense of collaboration with the United States and other countries. An interviewee responsible for technology policy issues remarks:

> We don't be little European collaboration, it is very important to many companies and so on, but it is not something we could be content with. ... At the moment, more emphasis is put on utility – that the quality of participation and utility are more important than the quantity of participation ... the euphoria of the early stages of our membership is over.

Of course, attitudes toward EU collaboration depend to a large extent on the particular viewpoint: for example, interviewees in sectoral ministries tend to have somewhat more critical views and support more selective participation based on national needs, whereas Tekes is also interested in ensuring a high level of Finnish participation and thus the flow of money back from the EU. In general it seems that while the science and technology policy community continues to encourage Finnish participation in EU projects, more attention will now be directed to other countries and regions.

POLICY CO-ORDINATION WITH THE EU – AND WITHIN THE ERA?

The Impacts of EU Membership

As a small country Finland has always carefully monitored developments and policy directions in other countries. In the early stages of formulating Finnish science and technology policy – which took place in the 1960s, relatively late in comparison to other Western countries – the example of Sweden was especially important. However, very soon the OECD took its place as the main trendsetter (Lemola 2002). The interviews show that the OECD has also retained its importance, although membership in the EU has naturally marked a significant change in the international contacts of the policymaking community.

The main responsibility for the preparation of EU R&D matters in Finland belongs to the Ministry of Trade and Industry. Earlier the responsibility was shared with the Ministry of Education but it was centralized during preparation for the first Finnish EU presidency in 1999. According to the interviews, this arrangement has functioned satisfactorily, although some interviewees think the Ministry of Education has lost some of its influence in EU-related issues. Whether the ERA initiative will affect the balance between these two ministries is an open question, nevertheless it seems that the preparation of the Finnish position on ERA papers has proceeded without problems. Some interviewees also mention that the 'machinery' for gathering the opinions of various policy actors in matters concerning the EU R&D policy functions very well. This may compensate to some extent for the fact that Finns are not too well trained in 'lobbying' in the European Commission.

All interviewees recognize that the EU has also become an important player in Finnish science and technology policymaking. However, without exception they emphasize that there are no big conflicts of interest and therefore it would be wrong to say that the EU has influenced the direction of Finnish policies. Different EU and national emphases are not in conflict but complementary, and if problems exist, they typically concern the different styles of decision-making and administration in the EU and in Finland. Here again, the interviewees seem to speak with one voice: even if the EU has steered Finnish policies, it has been in directions that are acceptable from the Finnish perspective.

In fact, on the basis of the interviews it seems that the policymakers generally feel that, at the moment, Finland is doing so well that there are few models to be emulated. They need to monitor developments and policy reforms in other countries but to be very selective in emulating anyone else. The following three quotations illustrate the prevailing attitudes well:

In earlier days the recommendations of the OECD were regarded as God's words ... but now we perhaps know better the process in which they are formulated. And we also know that there is no superior wisdom anywhere to be found.

Well, let's say that we try to take into account other countries' experiences. But the situation now is ... it is difficult for us to take examples from anywhere else, because in many areas we are the ones that are considered an example. And people from all over the world come to ask us how we have carried out this technology policy, developed the innovation environment.

For example, when choosing priority fields or sectors, there aren't many countries to look at as examples. ... For example, considering research programmes, it is most often so that the themes on which the EU has the big programmes are such that we have had them already before. ... The fact that that we have started [such programmes] independently and before the EU is because in a small country decision-making is faster ... we do not need any complex political or administrative process [to start a programme].

In general, the interviewees are keen on emphasizing the role of Finland as a forerunner rather than as being at the receiving end of influence, as used to be the case not so long ago. The Finnish centers of excellence policy provide a good example of this new attitude: Finns are actively trying to influence the ERA debate so that a quality-based model reminiscent of the Finnish model would be adopted instead of the proposed model emphasizing relevance. More often, however, the channels of influence are more indirect: for example, it is believed that the foreign experts who are invited to evaluate applications for centers of excellence and to do other evaluations can mediate influences from Finnish policymaking to their own countries. It can also be mentioned that for several years the majority of Finnish science and technology policy documents have been translated into English and that almost all applications for research funding must be written in English. In this respect Finns are well prepared for more intense collaboration both at the level of research policy and funding and the level of actual research work.

Nonetheless, the interviewees admit that as a small country, the influence Finland can exert on others will never be very big, and to gain recognition for its approaches, the Finnish representatives have to be very active. In this respect, organizations such as the Scientific and Technical Research Committee (CREST), which functions as an advisory body of the European Commission and the Council of the EU, are important. As one interviewee underscores, they are significant not as such but because through them one can get to know the right people. However, in Finland lobbying is often regarded with some suspicion. According to another interviewee, attempts to influence, for instance, the process of designing the Sixth Framework Programme (FP6) should take place through the 'normal and official channels' and not through lobbying – otherwise attempts to export the Finnish administrative culture to the EU are doomed to fail (cf. Grande and Peschke 1999).

In general, being active is the keyword – ideas coming from a small country are seldom recognized without a lot of work, unlike in the case of the bigger countries. Furthermore, it is vital to utilize optimally the knowledge that is available from the OECD and the EU and to monitor developments in other countries, especially in emerging fields of research. For example, one policymaker believes that while technology foresights done in other EU member countries such as the UK and Germany can be very useful for Finland, the costs and benefits of investing in own foresight activities need to be considered carefully.

Many interviewees appreciate the fact that membership in the EU has made policy-level collaboration closer and more organized. In some respects, this has meant the decline of policy collaboration with the other Nordic countries. Special links to Nordic countries have been relatively few in the realm of technology policy and, as one interviewee remarks, in EU contexts it is often much easier to find common interests with Britain or Germany than with Sweden or Denmark.[9] In science policy, the tradition of Nordic collaboration is stronger and seems to continue even though with somewhat less significance.

Attitudes Towards the ERA Initiative

The ERA initiative has been a topic of discussion in Finnish science and technology policy circles since its announcement in January 2000. As the official Finnish comment paper from November 2000 shows, the general idea is regarded positively. In particular, the idea of a more co-ordinated implementation of national and European research programs as well as the establishment of 'networks of excellence' are welcomed. The Finnish comment paper emphasizes that centers of excellence can be also virtual and that they should be nominated on the basis of open competition and only for limited periods. In order to support innovative start-up firms, Finland considers direct support more appropriate than indirect measures. Furthermore, following its long-term policy guidelines, Finland opposes the creation of new EU organs or databases (Finland's Comments 2000).

The interviews reveal similar attitudes, which is not surprising as the interviewees are to a large extent the same persons who designed the official comments of Finland. As one interviewee states, from the Finnish perspective the ERA initiative has both alarming and promising aspects. According to her, 'the danger is that it will be a terribly bureaucratic system'. Instead of getting something done, there will be a host of reports concerning what is already being done, as in the case of mapping European centers of excellence. As regards the co-ordination of national policies and even division of labor, it is already being done to a great extent through the currently existing organizations. To do that from Brussels is a dangerous line of development. In a similar vein, another interviewee who is involved in technology policy emphasizes that co-ordination of R&D activities is possible and even desirable, but only if it takes place on the basis of market mechanisms:

> If by coordination is meant that some [countries or regions] concentrate more on certain kind of research in Europe ... it has to arise from the market pull, to be based on needs ... It is something that the public sector should not step into.

In general, the interviewees do not consider the measures suggested in the ERA initiative as something very radical, but rather as a (necessary) step in the direction that Finland has already for a long time considered beneficial to itself and to the EU as a whole – a step on the chosen path toward more competition and more efficiency. Most of the interviewees were somewhat reluctant to say much about the implications of the ERA for Finland, because they felt that it is wiser to wait for more detailed proposals.

By 2003, the situation had not changed very much. While there has been some concern about the possibilities for Finns to benefit from the so-called integrated projects in the FP6, the networking of national research and technology programs has been regarded very positively. In fact, the Academy of Finland has already established a few research programs with international partners (of which the Swedish Research Council is the most important) and the Academy and Tekes have together prepared a plan for further networking and the eventual opening up of research and technology programs to international participation (Suomen Akatemia and Tekes 2001). In other words, Finland has assumed a 'proactive' role regarding the networking of research programs, and thus it is no surprise that Finnish responses to the ERA-NET scheme by the European Commission in 2000 have been positive (Supporting 2002). However, the willingness to co-ordinate research activities should not be interpreted as willingness to forgo national autonomy in questions regarding science and technology policy.

EU R&D AND FINNISH UNIVERSITIES[10]

As the share of budget funding in university research has declined, universities have been forced to develop ways of attracting funding from other sources. For instance, they have started to create new kinds of research services and co-operation links with the private sector and public services, thus fostering more entrepreneurial cultures (cf. Clark 1998). In this situation, also EU funding has provided a welcome alternative.

EU funding to Finnish universities grew rapidly from 1995 to 1997 but then stabilized. In 1999, universities received €24 million from the EU, which accounted for 4 per cent of total university research funding and 7 per cent of external university research funding. The largest proportion of EU funding went to natural sciences and technology. Together their share comprised 50 per cent of total EU funding to Finnish universities in 1999. (Tilastokeskus 1997; 2001) Data provided by the Finnish EU R&D Secretariat indicate that participation by Finnish universities was still growing in the EU Fifth Framework Programme (FP5). The share of universities of all Finnish participation was approximately 30 per cent.

Statistics, however, tell little about the actual impacts of EU research collaboration on the universities and academics. Some insights into this can be provided on the basis of empirical data consisting of two surveys – Survey 1999 and 2000 – of the heads of departments and senior researchers in various disciplines. The survey data were supplemented with interviews.[11]

On the basis of these empirical data, it seems that EU collaboration has quickly become an important part of Finnish university units' activities.

According to Survey 1999, approximately 60 per cent of all units had taken part in EU collaboration.[12] Half of the respondents from these EU-active units considered EU collaboration more significant or equally significant in comparison to the other international collaboration of their units.

As to the benefits of EU collaboration, it seems that the advantages of EU collaboration exceed its disadvantages but many have doubts about the quality of EU-funded research. Money is important and often the primary reason for academics to join in EU collaboration, but not the only reason. From the perspective of departments and units, other important benefits include gaining experience in international collaboration and increasing the visibility of the unit, the training and mobility of researchers, and opportunities to disseminate research results. New knowledge is mentioned less often as an important benefit (see also Luukkonen and Niskanen 1998; Luukkonen and Hälikkä 2000). This fact can be related to opinions regarding the quality of EU funded research: in Survey 1999, 40 per cent of all respondents agreed with the statement 'EU research collaboration improves the quality of research' while 37 per cent disagreed. Furthermore, only 29 per cent of all respondents thought that 'EU research programmes have a positive impact on the development of [their] research field'. Expectedly, units with no experience of EU collaboration were more critical than those who had had EU projects. In general, respondents in medicine were the most critical.

The steering effects on research agendas have remained modest. In Survey 2000, approximately 60 per cent of all respondents thought that EU collaboration has not focused attention away from issues of national importance and only 6 per cent thought that it has done so. On this basis, it seems that EU-funded research does not conflict with national interests and that the fear that EU-funded research narrows down or distorts research agendas is exaggerated. In the interviews, especially heads of departments and units thought that EU collaboration has in many cases complemented and supported their units' research agendas.

Furthermore, Survey 1999 shows that while the significance of EU collaboration has grown, most respondents perceive the United States to be the most important country in view of their units' research activities. Here we encounter the question whether membership in the EU has directed academic collaboration in a way that contradicts the idea that Finns should collaborate only with the best partners (cf. Hakala 1998). However, although international collaboration always requires resources that might be put to better use elsewhere, it is not a zero-sum game. As the interviews show, many units are in a situation where collaboration expands to many directions at the same time.

In general, it seems that further participation in EU projects may be discouraged by excessive EU bureaucracy and factors relating to the basic resources of the units. Some researchers see their participation as significant for developing their own capabilities to establish and carry out research projects and for gaining more experience in EU collaboration, while others feel they already know the 'rules of the game' and have fairly stabilized European networks. The latter group is able and willing to pursue a more selective strategy in the future – both in terms of topics and partners. For both groups, especially in case there is not enough national funding available, EU collaboration is an important option.

ENSURING FUTURE SUCCESS IN THE CHANGING LANDSCAPE OF EUROPEAN R&D

The basic rationale for the Finnish national innovation system approach is to make Finland economically competitive in the international, or global, arena. Policy goals such as increasing the efficiency, accountability and relevance of research, and the accompanying policy measures such as competitive funding mechanisms and performance agreements – not to forget the emphasis on networking and negotiation – are essentially the same as those frequently recommended by the OECD and the EU. In this respect, the long tradition of carefully monitoring developments elsewhere continues. Attempts to make Finnish research more international are based on the same logic: as a small country Finland is dependent on knowledge produced elsewhere and the only way to develop the national innovation system is to make sure that Finland has access to this knowledge. Membership in the EU has signified new possibilities in this respect by enhancing not only cross-national but also cross-sectoral R&D collaboration.

It is possible to argue that Finland has made a virtue out of necessity: it has adapted to international requirements so well that it can function as an example to others. Jokes about Finland always being the best pupil in the EU classroom come to mind. However, as this article has tried to show, it would be wrong to describe the Finnish policy as passive adaptation. The early introduction in Finland of the concepts of the national innovation system and the knowledge-based society has proven successful. By providing a common language, these concepts have helped to create a dialogue among the different actors of the system (Lemola 2002). They have also served as a 'national ambition' and a positive vision (Jacobs 1998). The increased public funding for R&D has had an important role in supporting this vision. Also Nokia has promoted this vision, functioning as the driving force of the Finnish ICT cluster (Paija 2001).

Unlike many other countries, Finland has also paid attention to developing a relatively coherent policy of internationalization of science and technology (cf. Edler and Boekholt 2001). This has certainly contributed to the exceptionally high mobilization of Finns into EU research collaboration since 1995. However, although entering the EU has provided 'added value' to the research system, the interview data show that – at least in the minds of the science policymakers – the membership has not brought about any radical changes either in the content of the Finnish science and technology policy or in the policymaking process. Had the interviews focused more on 'innovation policy', the answers might have been somewhat different: as Lemola (1999) shows, the EU influenced significantly the decisions to reinforce the regional dimension of Finnish innovation policy.

It also seems that the Finnish policymakers have quickly learned to utilize the forums provided by the EU to improve their policy networks and to build bilateral relations with various policymaking organizations in the other member countries. This change has been parallel to the conscious development of a new governance culture based on networking and negotiation within the national system. Policy-level collaboration has also been facilitated by the fact that the policymakers do not see any major contradictions between EU priorities and national priorities but find them generally complementary. What they are more concerned about is how Finland could gain recognition for its own views within the EU, such as establishing a more transparent governance culture. Accordingly, they do not regard the ERA initiative as a very radical move, but rather as another step toward more collaboration, efficiency and competitiveness. There seems to be a firm belief that today Finns are able to collaborate and compete with other Europeans on an equal standing.

Data from the university sector show that academics regard EU collaboration positively but that they are also fairly critical of the quality of EU projects. As in the case of policymakers, few believe in any major steering effects. Changes suggested by the ERA initiative probably look different depending on disciplinary identity and previous experience of EU collaboration. In medicine and the natural sciences, where there are long traditions of competition and collaboration with Europeans and Americans as well as more 'critical mass', it is difficult to foresee any major problems. In contrast, academics in more nationally oriented fields are unlikely to benefit as much from the new opportunities provided by the ERA.

Understandably a lot depends on how the idea of the ERA will be interpreted, received and implemented by the various actors in European R&D. According to Kuhlmann and Edler (Kuhlmann 2001; introduction to this book) three scenarios are possible. In the first scenario, the ERA will become an increasingly centralized and dominating European innovation policy arena, resulting in the leveling out of 'national styles' in dealing with research, technology and innovation. In the second scenario, the direction will be opposite: there will be a loose integration of highly diverse systems (e.g. national and regional) that increasingly compete with each other. The third scenario presents a middle course between the other two. It entails a vision of a centrally mediated mixture of competition and co-operation. In this scenario, there are a multitude of regional, national and European actors. Cohesion remains a uniting target but the subsidiarity principle leaves space for strategic initiatives at various levels. Mediation takes place through arenas such as the Scientific and Technological Research Committee (CREST) of the EU.

From the perspective of the Finnish research system, the first scenario has little to offer. In fact, it has many alarming aspects. It is likely that in a more centralized system, small players like Finland would have little influence on the direction of R&D policies. Although currently no major contradictions exist between EU priorities and national priorities, such might appear in the future. In addition, Finland would lose one important advantage of its small size, namely the flexibility to change policies and instruments quickly according to needs. Last but not least, Finnish policymakers and researchers alike dislike the possibility that EU bureaucracy might increase.

The other two scenarios would probably have more positive implications from the Finnish perspective. A highly decentralized system, however, is unlikely to provide any major benefits for the Finnish actors: although regional R&D actors have become more powerful – partly due to support from the structural funds of the EU – they continue to rely on services and know-how provided at the national level also in the future. The same applies to the majority of firms interested in EU collaboration. In this Nokia is an exception: it is essentially a transnational company and a global player, although a major part of its R&D is still conducted in Finland (Ali-Yrkkö et al. 2000, p. 12).

Thus it is the third scenario that looks ideal from the perspective of most Finnish R&D actors. In comparison to the other two scenarios, it provides more opportunities to take advantage of the fact that Finland currently has a relatively strong consensus on its national science and technology agenda as well as well-developed networks within the national innovation system (cf. van der Meulen and Shove 2001). The third scenario offers not only the freedom to make one's own choices but also an overall framework and forums for the mediation of Finnish interests and for extending collaboration networks. In the case of Finland, such forums are particularly important also because human resources available for transnational policy networking and collaboration are fairly limited in comparison to the bigger countries and R&D actors within them. While the actual future form of the European Research Area remains an open question at this stage, the challenge for Finnish policymakers remains essentially the same: to recognize the fact that the EU continues to permeate the national innovation system at many levels and to seek ways in which the various interests can be balanced so that they can be pursued effectively in European policymaking arenas.

NOTES

1. However, it should be noted that distinguishing between science, technology and innovation policies has become increasingly difficult and often pointless as well (cf. discussion on the Finnish national innovation system below).
2. The interviewees represent the following organizations: the Science and Technology Policy Council, the Ministry of Education, the Ministry of Trade and Industry, the Academy of Finland, the National Technology Agency (Tekes) and three other ministries. The total number of interviews is 12, and they were conducted in spring 2000.
3. There are 20 universities in Finland: ten multi-faculty universities, three universities of technology, three schools of economics and business administration, and four art academies. A system of polytechnics was established at the end of the 1990s but at least so far the polytechnics have not undertaken research activities to any significant extent.
4. Here these are referred to as 'sectoral ministries' in contrast to the Ministry of Education and the Ministry of Trade and Industry, which function as the 'general ministries' for R&D.
5. Finland has 20 sectoral research institutes concentrating mainly on applied research. Unique among them is the Technical Research Centre (VTT), which has circa 3000 employees. Direct budget funding amounts for 28 per cent of VTT's research expenditure. In other sectoral research institutes the share of budget funding varies between 48 and 92 per cent (Suomen Akatemia 2001).
6. For example, 45 per cent of the members of the evaluation teams commissioned by Tekes and VTT were Finns and the rest came from countries such as the UK (12 per cent), United States (8 per cent), Sweden (8 per cent), Germany (5 per cent) and the Netherlands (4 per cent) (Oksanen 2000, p. 21).
7. This satisfaction is visible also in policy documents. As Eela points out, whereas in the 1970s and 1980s the reports of the Science and Technology Policy Council describe Finland as lagging behind other Western countries in science and technology, the tone changes in the 1990 strategy. In the guidelines of 2000, Finland is depicted as one of the top countries in information society development (Eela 2001, pp. 26–7).
8. Finland's cautious policy towards joining international organizations in the field of science and technology can be explained by political reasons as well as the late development of the research system in general (e.g. Hakala 1998).
9. He adds that finding a common viewpoint depends a lot on what the responsible ministry of the country is in a particular matter. Unlike in Finland, in Sweden EU R&D issues are the responsibility of the Ministry of Education.
10. This section is largely based on research done together with Pirjo Kutinlahti (whose surname was Niskanen until 2002) and Erkki Kaukonen (see Hakala, Kutinlahti and Kaukonen 2002).
11. Survey 1999 (conducted by Hakala and Kaukonen) was sent to all heads of departments and units in Finnish universities (N = 369); Survey 2000 (conducted by Pirjo Niskanen) was sent to senior researchers and heads of departments and units in nine universities (N = 189). The interviews (conducted by Niskanen) totaled 78 (see Niskanen 2001).
12. The number of projects reported varied from one to 25, and was most typically two. One-third of the departments and units had started EU collaboration already before 1995, that is, before Finland became a full member of the EU and participation was possible with national funding.

REFERENCES

Ali-Yrkkö, J., L. Paija, C. Reilly and P. Ylä-Anttila (2000), *NOKIA – a Big Company in a Small Country*, ETLA – Research Institute of the Finnish Economy, B162 Series, Helsinki: Taloustieto Oy.

Clark, B.R. (1998), *Creating Entrepreneurial Universities: Organizational Pathways of Transformation*, Guildford: Pergamon.

Edler, J. and P. Boekholt (2001), 'Benchmarking national public policies to exploit international science and industrial research', *Science and Public Policy*, **28** (4), 313–21.

Eela, R. (2001), *Tiede- ja teknologiapolitiikka valtion tiede- ja teknologianeuvoston katsausten valossa* (Science and technology policy in the light of the Science and Technology Policy Council's reviews), VTT, Teknologian tutkimuksen ryhmä, työpapereita nro 56 (01).

European Commission (2000), *Towards a European Research Area*, communication from the Commission to the Council, the European Parliament, the Economic and Social Committee and the Committee of the Regions, Brussels: European Commission, COM (2000) 6.

European Commission (2001), *2001 Innovation Scoreboard*, Brussels: European Commission, Commission Staff Working Paper SEC 2001.

Finland's Comments (2000), *Finland's Comments on the Commission's ERA Communication*, http://www.tekes.fi/eu/fin/eu_tutkimuspolitiikka/era/index.html, retrieved on 2 November 2000.

Grande, E. and A. Peschke (1999), 'Transnational cooperation and policy networks in European science policy-making', *Research Policy*, **28** (1), 43–61.

Hakala, J. (1998), 'Internationalisation of science. Views of the scientific elite in Finland', *Science Studies*, **11** (1), 52–54.

Hakala, J., P. Kutinlahti and E. Kaukonen (2002), 'Becoming international, becoming European: EU research collaboration at Finnish universities', *Innovation: the European Journal of Social Sciences*, **15** (4), 357–79.

Jacobs, D. (1998), 'Innovation policies within the framework of internationalization', *Research Policy*, **27** (7), 711–24.

Kaukonen, E. and M. Nieminen (1999), 'Modeling the triple helix from a small country perspective: the case of Finland', *Journal of Technology Transfer*, **24** (2), 173–83.

Kazancigil, A. (1998), 'Governance and science: market-like modes of managing society and producing knowledge', *International Social Science Journal*, **50** (155), 69–79.

Knill, C. and D. Lehmkuhl (1999), *How Europe Matters. Different Mechanisms of Europeanization*, European Integration online Papers (EIoP), 3 (7), http://eiop.or.at/eiop/texte/1999007a.htm.

Kuhlmann, S. (2001), 'Future governance of innovation policy in Europe – three scenarios', *Research Policy*, **30** (6), 953–76.

Lemola, T. (1999), 'Different Perspectives on the Problems and Challenges Facing the Finnish Innovation System', in Schienstock, G. and O. Kuusi (eds), *Transformation Towards a Learning Economy. The Challenge for the Finnish Innovation System*, Sitra 213, Helsinki: Hakapaino Oy, pp. 130–40.

Lemola, T. (2002), 'Convergence of national science and technology policies: the case of Finland', *Research Policy*, **31** (8), 1481–90.

Lemola, T. (forthcoming), 'The Finnish Science and Technology Policy', in Schienstock, G. (ed.), *Catching Up and Forging Ahead: the Finnish Success Story*, Cheltenham, UK, and Northhampton, MA, USA: Edward Elgar.

Luukkonen T. and P. Niskanen (1998), *Learning Through Collaboration: Finnish Participation in EU Framework Programmes*, VTT Group for Technology Studies, Helsinki: Helsinki University Printing House.

Luukkonen, T. and S. Hälikkä (2000), *Knowledge Creation and Knowledge Diffusion Networks. Impacts in Finland of the EU's Fourth Framework Programme for Research and Development*, Helsinki: Finnish Secretariat for EU R&D, January 2000.

Miettinen, R. (2002), *National Innovation System. Scientific Concept or Political Rhetoric*, Sitra Publications Series 252, Helsinki: Edita Prima Ltd.

Nieminen, M. and E. Kaukonen (2001), *Universities and R&D Networking in a Knowledge-based Economy. A Glance at Finnish Developments*, Sitra Reports Series 11, Helsinki: Hakapaino Oy.

Niskanen, P. (2001), *Finnish Universities and the EU Framework Programme – Towards a New Phase*, Espoo: VTT publications.

Oksanen, J. (2000), *Research Evaluation in Finland – Practices and Experiences, Past and Present*, Teknologian tutkimuksen ryhmä, Espoo: VTT.

Paija, L. (ed.) (2001), *Finnish ICT Cluster in the Digital Economy*, ETLA – Research Institute of the Finish Economy, B176 Series, Helsinki: Taloustieto Oy.

Prihti, A., L. Georghiou, J. Juusela, F. Meyer-Krahmer, B. Roslin, T. Santamäki-Vuori and M. Gröhn (2000), *Assessment of the Additional Appropriation for Research*, Sitra Reports Series 2, Helsinki: Sitra.

Science and Technology Policy Council of Finland (1996), *Finland: a Society of Knowledge and Skills*, Helsinki: Science and Technology Policy Council of Finland.

Science and Technology Policy Council (2000), *Review 2000: the Challenge of Knowledge and Know-how*, Helsinki: Science and Technology Policy Council.

Science and Technology Policy Council (2003), *Knowledge, Innovation and Internationalisation*, Helsinki: Science and Technology Policy Council.

Suomen Akatemia (2001), 'Tutkimus ja kehittämisrahoitus valtion talousarviossa vuonna 2001 (The Academy of Finland: research and development funding in the state budget of 2001)', *Suomen Akatemian julkaisuja*, **1** (01), Helsinki.

Suomen Akatemia and Tekes (2001), *Suomen Akatemian ja Tekesin näkemyksiä kansallisten tutkimus- ja teknologiaohjelmien kansainvälisestä verkottamisesta ja avaamisesta, muistio 25 October 2001* (The views of the academy of Finland and Tekes on the international networking and opening of national research and technology programs, memorandum), http://www.tekes.fi/eu/fin/eu_tutkimuspolitiikka/era/index.html, retrieved on 12 January 2002.

Supporting (2002), *Supporting the Cooperation and Coordination of Research Activities Carried Out at National or Regional Level. The 'ERA-NET' Scheme*, working paper prepared by Unit B.1, DG Research, European Commission, http://europa. eu.int/comm/research/fp6/eranet.html, retrieved on 19 June 2002.

Tilastokeskus (1997), *Tutkimus ja kehittämistoiminta Suomessa 1995* (Research and development in Finland 1995), Helsinki: Statistics Finland.

Tilastokeskus (1999), *Tutkimus ja kehittämistoiminta Suomessa 1997* (Research and development in Finland 1997), Helsinki: Statistics Finland.

Tilastokeskus (2001), *Tutkimus ja kehittämistoiminta Suomessa 1999* (Research and development in Finland 1999), Helsinki: Statistics Finland.

Tilastokeskus (2002), *T&k-menot sektoreittain vuosina 1999–2002* (Research expenditure by sector 1991–2002), Statistics Finland, http://tilastokeskus.fi /tk/yr/ttt_kta1.html, retrieved on 29 January 2003.

Tuomaala, E., S. Raak, E. Kaukonen, J. Laaksonen, M. Nieminen and P. Berg (2001), *Research and Technology Programme Activities in Finland*, Technology Review, 106 (2001), Helsinki: Tekes.

van der Meulen, B. and E. Shove (2001), 'National and European Dynamics of Social Environmental Research', in Dresner, S. and N. Gilbert (eds), *The Dynamics of European Science and Technology*, Aldershot: Ashgate, pp. 81–104.

9 Entering the Club

The European Research Area from the EU Candidates' Perspective

Peter Hilger

ENLARGEMENT AS A CHALLENGE TO FIFTH RESEARCH FRAMEWORK PROGRAMME (FP5)

European Union (EU) enlargement is on its way. For a number of years there has been no question whether there will an eastern enlargement but rather when it will take place. However the euphoria of the early 1990s is gone. The integration process was proceeding more slowly than originally expected. At the Nice summit in 2000 fundamental decisions for the functioning of the EU's decision-making framework were taken (voting power in the Council, number of Commissioners, expansion of majority rule) but the intergovernmental conference was marked by an astonishing revival of interest-driven national politics. Only at the end of the Swedish Presidency in 2001, the year 2004 was named for accessions to take place. With the agreements achieved at the Copenhagen summit in December 2002 the accession process entered into the final phase consisting of the ratification process and national referenda in the accession countries.

The preparations for accession began with a sophisticated screening of 31 policy areas. On this basis position papers of the European Commission and the Candidate Countries (CC) were presented and detailed negotiations were opened. Progress was documented in monitoring tables. Local delegations of the European Commission held permanent contact with the countries sending monthly reports to DG Enlargement in which changes and progress in implementation were being reported. Negotiations took place in committees of different levels, the more controversial issues were the higher the level of representatives involved. Once a year the European Commission summarizes the progress achieved in annual reports for each candidate country. With regard to the process of EU enlargement the question of governance got a specific outline: Some spoke of 'the EU governing the Candidate Countries', meaning that through the adoption requirement of the *acquis communautaire* the EU is steering the CC' s institution building.

At the same time the level of acceptance of enlargement was falling on both sides, within the Community and in the accession countries. Enlargement Commissioner Verheugen had to argue heavily in favor of enlargement wherever he went. It seemed that the more detailed the issues being discussed the more skeptical people were becoming. As a reaction Commissioner Verheugen kept bringing to attention the starting point of eastern enlargement, the common security in Europe and the stabilization of the young democracies which can best be consolidated through further steps of integration.

After having transformed into functioning democracies with open market societies in a rather short time, it is not easy to stand competition and put 23 000 community rules into work. More than one-fourth of today's Community population is going to join the EU, bringing with them only about 3 per cent of its GDP.[1] It will be the biggest enlargement so far and it demands for a change in quality. The countries involved in the southern enlargement of the 1980s have always been market economies whereas the Central and Eastern European Countries (CEEC) are still in a phase of transition. The income gap between EU members and the CC is high, they (with inclusion of Malta and Cyprus) reach only 38 per cent (1998) of the EU-15 level while the southern candidates met already two-thirds of the EU standard. In both waves of enlargement the agricultural sector was important, however productivity and yields are substantially lower in the present accession countries (Directorate General for Economics and Financial Affairs 2001, pp. 7–9). Beyond economic issues the sheer size of the community calls for a shift in the modes of decision-making. The European Convent recently presented a proposal for redefining the roles of the major Community institutions, the Council, the European Parliament and the European Commission.

Another area presently debated on is the general mode of governance in the EU. The European Commission has opened a debate on the rules, processes and behavior in policymaking with respect to openness, participation, accountability, effectiveness and coherence (European Commission 2001a). The process of enlargement is a unique challenge here because the evolving structure of the EU and the interests of future members have to be anticipated and integrated in the decision-making process. Therefore the CC were consulting members in the European Convent.

The area of research policy was one of the first were integration was brought on the track. Since 1999 the CC have been taking part in the Fifth Research Framework Programme (FP5) on an equal basis. In the accession negotiations, chapter 17 on R&D was one of the easiest to close provisionally as there were not many rules to adopt, even if some other chapters are affected by R&D as well (Ruente 2001), it is one of the easiest policies to reach agreement on. The CC also play a significant role in a major project of DG Research, the construction of a European Research Area (ERA). The question is how they contribute to the construction and the decision-making for a ERA.

This paper will address this topic by introducing an analysis of the structure of research co-operation between EU-15 and CEEC in the Fifth Framework Programme (FP5). This will lead back to look at the changes of the scientific landscape of Central and Eastern Europe (CEE). A third step will be made to inform about problems and experiences in collaborations of researchers from CEEC on the basis of case studies. This will prepare the ground for an evaluation of the ERA initiative from the CC' s perspective (in this context limited to the CEEC). Final remarks are devoted to integration and inequality in European R&D.

A MACRO-PERSPECTIVE: THE STRUCTURE OF RESEARCH CO-OPERATION BETWEEN EU MEMBERS AND ACCESSION COUNTRIES

Theoretical devotion, sophisticated competition and information exchange between laboratories belong to the ideal picture of a scientific community. Research consortia are formed for a number of reasons (Hasse 1996; Bergenwall 2000):

- access to know-how, methods, facilities and geographical, biological, physical, societal constellations and so on;
- the development of a critical mass to approach new fields of research as well as the wish to share the risks included;
- recruitment of skilled and talented co-workers;
- contact to application practice to learn about the relevance of results;
- strategic choice to get access to specific lines of financial support;
- and last but not least subjective aims and preferences of the persons included.

A common scientific goal is the fundamental frame for R&D collaboration but additional factors have to be taken into consideration, for example personal contacts are often transformed into institutional co-operations. In EU programs a co-ordinator and partners from three countries are obligatory to build a consortium, in practice this number is rarely sufficient. In order to enter such a consortium not only the level of expertise is important. Next to the research topic further criteria are European relevance of the project and its contribution to the EU's social aims, good prospects for economic exploitation as well as the management and partnership of the group. This requires experience and relations. Consequently out of four types of knowledge, knowledge about facts, about principles, abilities like skills and competencies and the social capability to co-operate, the latter, 'Know whom', is getting increasingly important (Lam 2001, p. 11). For CEE partners it is essential to enter or form new high-level consortia. Therefore the contact phase is extremely significant.

Researchers from CEE took part in a fairly high number of submitted proposals to the European Commission as contractors, members or even co-ordinators of research consortia. However the results were not as good as expected. A rather small number of contracts was signed in the first phase until March 2000. The performance of the CEEC was carefully monitored. An initial reaction was the advice of the European Commission to concentrate more on submitting proposals of high quality instead of trying to enter on a broad scale. In the following rounds the proposals were more concentrated and the success rates went up. However the performance is still not satisfactory. This raised concern in the CC.

In the year 2000, Poland, the Czech Republic and Hungary signed the highest number of contracts. Compared to the size of the countries first of all Slovenia and Estonia, but also the Czech Republic, Latvia and Hungary managed to participate on a larger scale. However compared to the average participation of the EU-15 only Slovenia was able to reach a similar level.

The performance in the early stage of FP5 did not only lead to disappointment, it has material consequences as well. The countries pay into the budget of the FP and they are receiving only a part of the money back. Only because PHARE[2] resources could be used to substitute a part of the spending during the first three years the balance remained slightly positive for some countries. The final year of FP5 participation will turn the balance into a negative saldo for many of them. The most prominent case is Poland with an estimated deficit of about €60 million. Facing these results the participation in the FP has been called in question by some. DG Research has understood this problem. It set up an internet base to create contact to existing consortia, organized and promoted conferences and brokerage events and introduced additional calls with an extra budget to integrate research facilities from CC into existing consortia. While the European Commission claims that the level of expertise is decisive for FP participation Peterson and Sharp observe a principle of '*juste retour*' working. The cabinet of Commissioners watches the distribution of the budget among participants of Member States (Peterson and Sharp 1998, p. 176) and eventually introduces additional actions to promote and include participants from certain countries. In the beginning of 2002 that has been the case with calls dedicated to CEEC participation. Also

national funding bodies like the German Ministry for Education and Research
started to pay more attention to their integration into the European R&D
landscape. It introduced additional measures to include CEEC partners into
research networks.[3]

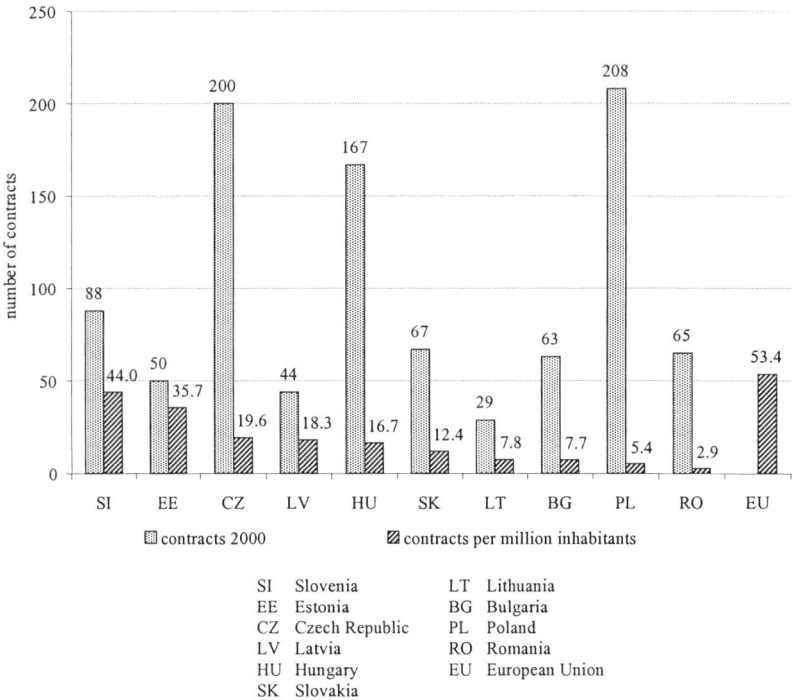

Source: European Commission 2001b: Research and Technological Development Activities
of the EU, Annual Report 2001; own calculations.

Figure 9.1   R&D contracts under FP5 signed by CEEC in the year 2000

The most important partners for the CEEC are located in the bigger EU
countries, especially Germany but also in the United Kingdom, France and
Italy. These countries have in general the highest total number of participants
and account for 50 per cent of all partners for CEEC. Remarkable is also the
importance of partners from the Netherlands for CEEC. Figure 9.2 shows the
share of partnership each EU-15 country represents for the group of CEEC.
Turning the perspective, for the EU-15 the CEEC play a minor role, research
groups from that region mostly account for between 4 and 6 per cent of their
partners. With the exception of Austria, where CEEC partners account for
7.9 per cent, border countries don't have significantly higher shares either.

One can separate three types of partner countries for CEEC: partners from EU-15, partners from other CEEC, and partners from other associated states and other third countries like Norway, Israel or developing countries for example. As FP5 is an EU-program partnership with R&D units from the EU play the biggest role. The relation towards other CEEC, the former 'brother countries', play a minor role today but they are not in any case weak. A stronger peer orientation can be observed in the case of Latvia, Lithuania and Romania where almost one-fourth of all partners come from the same region. However countries with more intensive peer co-operation have not necessarily little contact to EU Member States. The strongest orientation towards EU-15 can be found in the Czech Republic, Poland and Hungary. About 80 per cent of their partners are EU members. Figure 9.3 displays the percentage of partners from EU-15 and from other CCEC for each accession country.

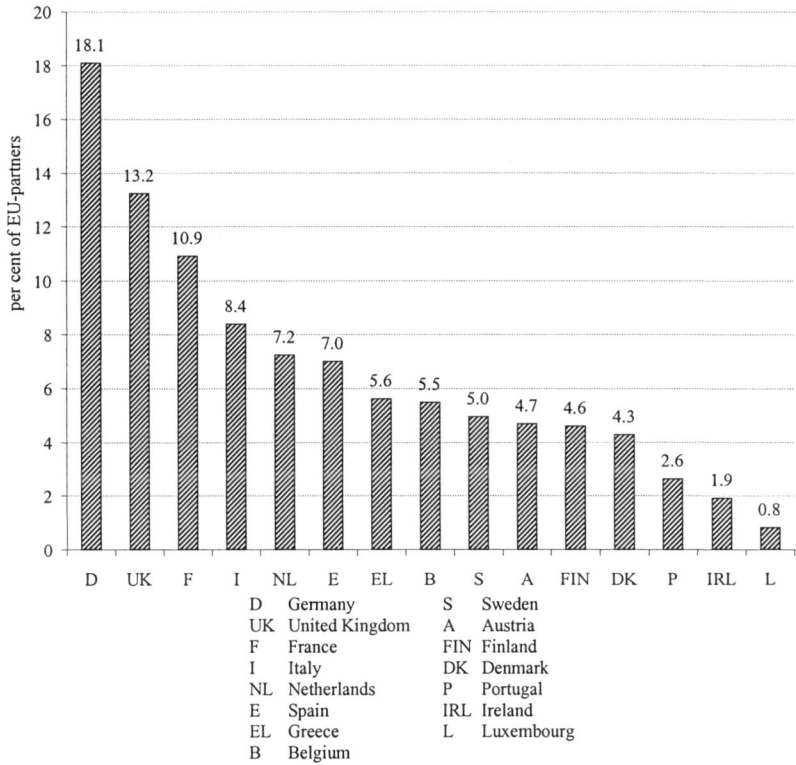

Source: European Commission 2001b: Research and Technological Development Activities of the EU, Annual Report 2001; own calculations.

Figure 9.2 Relevance of EU-15 countries for the group of CEEC

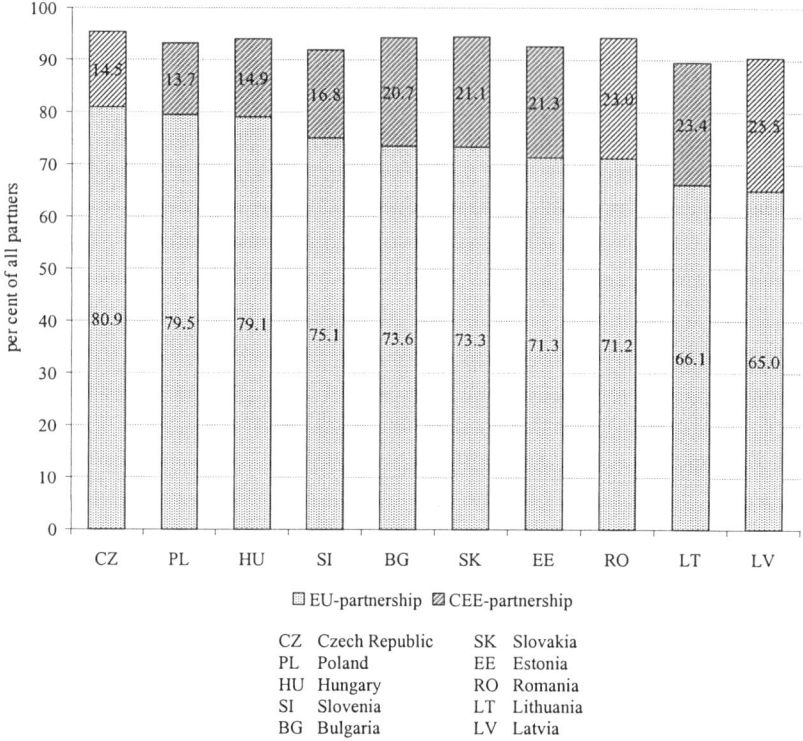

EU-partnership ☐   CEE-partnership ☒

CZ   Czech Republic   SK   Slovakia
PL   Poland   EE   Estonia
HU   Hungary   RO   Romania
SI   Slovenia   LT   Lithuania
BG   Bulgaria   LV   Latvia

Source: European Commission 2001b: Research and Technological Development Activities
of the EU, Annual Report 2001; own calculations.

*Figure 9.3   EU-15 and CC orientation of CEEC in EU-funded R&D
collaboration*

THE TRANSFORMATION OF THE SCIENCE SECTOR

Science and sports have always been fields of competition between the former western and eastern world. Utopias of affluent societies through scien-
tific-based technical progress have been influential on either side. But regarding the deficits in daily life in the former socialist countries they may
have even been more important there. The 'sputnik shock' had produced a
temporarily strong reputation for the scientific potential of the soviet type
societies which was lost again long before Czernobyl. In the planned economies science had, at the same time, a legitimating function and a real meaning
for improving the level of production. After the fall of the Berlin wall the

poverty of scientific production was discovered. However it included the chance to remember the strong academic tradition in the CEEC, where for example some of Europe's oldest universities are located.

For advanced societies, so called knowledge-based societies, the science sector is of growing importance. Not only scientific progress accelerates, it transforms technologies into daily life more and more rapidly and skilled workers are needed all around. The impact of research and technology is estimated to count for up to 50 per cent of economic growth (European Commission 2000). Within the EU, budget research policy is a sector on its own making up for more than 4 per cent. Therefore it is of crucial importance for the CEEC to use their cultural capital of an acknowledged high level of basic education for their development and transformation into knowledge-based societies.

Generally speaking, problems were substantial overmanning, old and ineffective infrastructure and equipment. Despite the high level of fundamental research there was a lack of new methodologies and application. The research system as a whole was highly segregated with ministerial branch institutes and academy institutes at the forefront. A reconstruction of the research landscape has taken place even if it is in some areas not yet completed. Central control and political guidance have diminished. In most accession countries the Academy of Sciences had been the main institution for research and the donor of scientific degrees whereas the role of the universities was restricted to the education of undergraduates. Now the role of the universities has been strengthened by reintroducing research as their general task as well as the right for dissertation, while the academies generally lost importance. Especially they gave up their science policy functions. However a number of its institutes gained strength. They have transformed into dynamic research centers orientated mostly towards basic research and act today more independently from the academy leadership. New private universities were founded but their quality often remains unclear. Scientific exchange has been pushed forward and competition for resources has been introduced on all levels. The infrastructure is eventually being renewed but major problems of financing investment and staff continue to exist. Despite the great number of achievements, compared to the countries of the EU problems are still visible in many areas.

Demand, both industrial and political, for R&D is low, prestige of science has diminished, brain drain, aging of R&D staff and the deterioration of research infrastructure do still cause problems. The working conditions are often not very good, with the exception of some recently established 'islands of excellence'. The gained freedom in research has been limited by scarce resources. Some institutes have started to increasingly engage in applied research in order to mobilize new financial resources. In the long run this includes the risk of neglecting basic research and loosing grip of the needs of the future (Füllsack 2001). The change has mainly been informed by the western model. But there is also criticism that the new priorities don't serve the needs of the transforming societies (Plesu 2001).

Mayntz has given a clear description of the different approaches of the Soviet demand pull model where science had to serve societal needs and was therefore centrally planned and organized, and the science push model in which basic research is the driving force of technological development (Mayntz 1998). Science was exercised under state control with high division of labor and a concentration of tasks in specialized organizations.

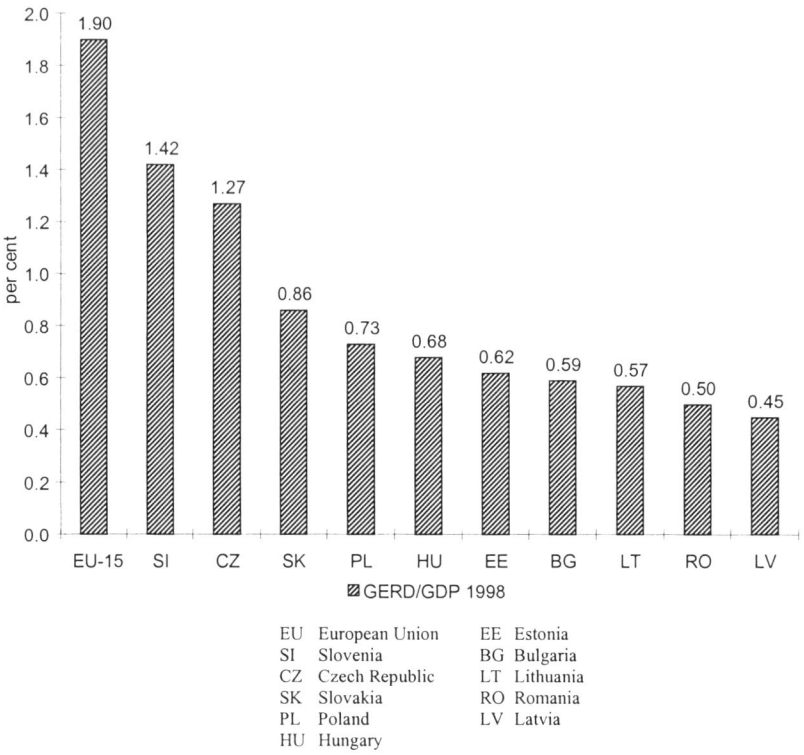

EU	European Union	EE	Estonia
SI	Slovenia	BG	Bulgaria
CZ	Czech Republic	LT	Lithuania
SK	Slovakia	RO	Romania
PL	Poland	LV	Latvia
HU	Hungary		

Source: Eurostat No 130/2000.

Figure 9.4   R&D expenditure in CEEC

As a result of the economic breakdown research in the business sector has almost collapsed and is only slowly recovering. R&D is mostly financed by the state budget. In Germany for example the private sector finances about 60 per cent of the R&D activities (BMBF 2000, p. 122), in the CEEC this ratio is equally high only in the Czech Republic, Slovakia and Romania. Therefore it is not surprising that the participation of CEE industry in European research is rather weak. But, and this is a second feature, also public expenditure on R&D is fairly low. Thus, as shown in Figure 9.4, in 1998 the overall R&D expenditure in no single country reached the average of the EU and most were far from catching up.

A MICRO-PERSPECTIVE ON R&D ENCOUNTERS

Interviews with Polish and Hungarian participants in the FP produced some insight into the micropolitics of R&D collaboration. For CEE researchers the most common way to enter R&D consortia is to be invited by well-established research units. Mostly the co-ordinator of a project takes the initiative to ask a partner from CEE.[4] Researchers from accession countries may be invited for a number of reasons. One of them is the level of expertise, but others are equally relevant. The wage level is lower and certain pieces of work can be done cheaper. With regard to the referee panel it can be interesting to include a partner from CEEC for strategic reasons. It is hard to enter a consortium by own efforts. To form a consortium by oneself is even harder – as the data from the first phase of FP5 shows: There was no co-ordinator from accession countries at all.

Conferences, workshops, publications (in English language) and visits are most important to make contacts. English is the lingua franca of the science world and a website in English is a necessity to open and present oneself to partners. Interviewees from CC pointed out clearly that the co-operation did result almost always from some kind of coincidence which provided for an initial personal contact. Once a contact was made it was fairly easy to keep it going, for example by e-mail. Because of the crucial role of encounters funds for travelling are very important. As travel expenses are high this has been a major difficulty for researchers from CEEC.

But for some reason researchers are also reluctant to take part in European consortia. As the funding tradition established in Poland by the Committee for Scientific Research (KBN) has been more familiar to researchers many felt that is was more promising to make an effort in the national programs. Being aware that success rates in European programs are not high they are becoming even more reluctant.

On the other hand participation in European projects offers new opportunities. Because of small budgets, the wage level (and the public recognition) is often not high and prospects to realize one's research ideas are limited by the state of the equipment. Some interviewees expect difficulties due to the fact that the most talented young graduates rather leave the universities than completing their doctoral degree. European projects open the opportunity to employ promising researchers and keep them inside the institution. To a certain extent the infrastructure can be improved by these projects as well. And even if there is a shortage of expensive experimental facilities and labs, membership in a consortium offers the possibility to get access to such facilities elsewhere and develop skills and knowledge.

Other problems remain. Weak infrastructure means also few secretaries, an university administration that lacks the experience to deal with the complicated rules of European projects, difficulties to finance delays in money transfer, the need to perform a second job besides scientific work to make a respectable living, old machinery and literature and so on. But altogether it is obvious that the situation of R&D is being improved substantially for those who participate in an international group equipped with extra resources.

The advantages go beyond financial aspects. Being a member of an European consortium meant for the interviewees to get access to scientific excellence. For some it was a new experience to co-operate beyond borders and discuss the results openly. It also meant recognition of their own scientific ideas and results and therefore had a very subjective function stabilizing the personal situation in times of disruption. It became more easy to face the change and cutbacks in R&D. Last but not least, it provides for reputation within the scientific community.

Yet these projects include certain risks. They may stabilize the situation of domestic scientific staff but they also offer the opportunity to use the contact to leave the country. Brain drain is still regarded as a problem in many CEEC. Measures have recently been introduced to keep researchers inside the countries by offering extra grants in case of staying or returning to the country of origin.

Due to the fairly small private R&D sector, applied sciences are in a difficult situation. There is not yet sufficient demand from industry. The potential for economic growth deriving from R&D activities can only be realized through exploitation in the industrial or service sector. The strength in theoretical areas is an excellent basis for the development of applied sciences but it is not sufficient by itself. In Hungary the Bay Zoltan Foundation has been founded and designed after the German Model of the Fraunhofer Society. However this doesn't improve the problem of financing R&D substantially as long as there is no vital industrial environment which demands – and pays for – scientific solutions.

Another aspect is related to the exploitation of results. European R&D projects develop high-level technologies which demand for application in high-tech industries. Scientists from CEEC have found themselves in a situation where they developed intelligent solutions which cannot be used in domestic industries because there is no market for highly sophisticated products. They fear know-how is given away for little money and the domestic industry gets even more into danger of loosing competitiveness.

Finally communication in European consortia is not a problem given that there is a substantial knowledge of English. Telephone, e-mail and internet make it easy to discuss questions of organization, the use of methods, exchange results and so on. However it was often reported that there was a certain amount of cultural differences between western and eastern partners which caused some irritation: Some expect letters to be answered immediately, others feel that they are not that urgent and prefer to solve questions orally when there is time to speak about them. Appointments may be interpreted as a precise point of time or rather as a period of time which can be brought in line with the schedule of the day. Some believe in what is arranged as a result of a discussion, others believe in written protocols to document arrangements. Almost every German researcher interviewed reported that he was delighted by the way he was welcome and accompanied throughout his stay abroad – and worried about how he could return this because he felt he was lacking time to do so. Collaboration always includes difficulties, they are easier to overcome if partners open themselves to unexpected styles of organization and behavior. Openness for intensive collaboration will surely be a requirement in an European Research Area.

THE ROLE OF THE CEEC WITHIN THE ERA

This chapter discusses the channels of influence for the CEEC in EU decision-making and their role inside the ERA. In addition to the common EU decision-making framework with its various levels (Marks, Hooge and Blank 1996) including corporations and interest organizations as informal third party actors (Grande 1996) the accession countries play a role as fourth parties. They are relevant actors but not formally included. However they exercise some influence. Firstly due to the considerable communication between the different DGs in workgroups and ad-hoc committees (Nugent 1995). DG Enlargement would introduce viewpoints with respect to CC in case it finds it necessary. Such has been the case with the initial paper concerning the European Research Area.[5] Because of the close connection between DG Enlargement and the national representatives throughout the screening and monitoring of the acquis implementation DG Enlargement can act to a certain extent as the 'voice' of the CC inside the European Commission.

Secondly the expert character of policymaking on the sub-systemic level (Peterson and Sharp 1998, p. 177) can be an advantage for the CC. Different from formal decision-making bodies like the Council they have the chance to speak in the various committees where a good argument has certain power on its own. Even without formal rights it is possible to contribute to debates, bring up points and create alliances and thus shape the outcome.[6]

Thirdly we can identify influence by negative co-ordination (Scharpf 1992; 1993). In order to concentrate negotiations on most crucial issues decisions which do not harm other actors are, for the sake of reduction of complexity, taken without discussion. Under this premise it is possible to assume that interests of CC are acknowledged even on the level of EUs' heads of states or ministers where bargaining is a major mode of policymaking. Thus the CC find their interests present at Council meetings even without being at the table,[7] at least when it is probable that neglecting them would cause problems in future.

These three channels of influence, DG Enlargement as a 'Trojan horse' inside the European Commission, expert representation in the 'comitology' and negative co-ordination in the Council have to compensate for the formal absence of future members in the ERA decision-making process. Under these condition it needs time and energy to raise awareness.[8]

The participation in the decision-making process is most urgent for the CC since most of them will be effected as new Member States by the program. But even as associated countries they enjoy the same rights as members in many areas. Beyond this the whole idea of the ERA calls for an integration at least on the level of joint action with Non-EU members. Therefore special measures are being introduced to strengthen their research systems (European Commission 2001c).

The ERA concept was developed in the light of worldwide R&D competition. One major objective is, as Achilleas Mitsos, Director General for Research puts it, 'that we succeed in identifying best teams in Europe ... and support the creation of networks between them' (Kowi 2000, p. 5).[9] However the major objective of the CC is to catch up with Member States, they want to integrate into the Community and participate in their programs. In the enlargement process many controversial issues are already connected with the adoption of the acquis. Therefore CC tend to exercise influence by consultation instead of also opening conflict in the field of R&D. They share the opinion that excellence is a requirement for R&D funding, being fully aware that domestic conditions are not always favorable in this respect.

Research ministers of accession countries participated for the first time in the Research Council of the EU on 12 July 2001 where every single country, Member States and accession countries equally, was offered five minutes for a position statement on the ERA. They took the chance to present their opinions (Cordis focus 2001, p. 4). Their bargaining power is weak, although there is some potential to exercise pressure due to the whole project of enlargement. But research policy is not crucial in this respect. However the CC have significant impact for the realization of an ERA, not only because they will be part of the EU, but also because they have significant scientific potential. One of the most significant obstacles remains the scientific infrastructure and equipment. High expectations are dangerous here because their improvement doesn't lay at the heart of the FP. Participation in framework programs helped catching up regions to improve skills and knowledge, the development of infrastructure however remains a task of structural funds and domestic politics (Sharp 1998).

Not all CEEC have presented a position paper on the ERA but shared positions can be identified.[10] The CC formally welcome the approach. Their position papers usually consist of statements referring to the countries' own efforts to contribute to the making of an ERA and a number of papers try to point at matters of specific concern with regard to their position in the evolving entity. The main points are:

- The CEEC call for support with regard to the development of the domestic R&D infrastructure. This is a major point of concern because recent experience with FP5 has made it clear that integration can only be achieved if the conditions for scientific work in CEEC improve. This calls for European solidarity as well as for domestic politics providing for a higher share of the GDP devoted to R&D.
- Two measures of the Sixth Framework Programme (FP6), the Integrated Projects and the Networks of Excellence, are perceived as a threat to CEEC chances unless special support for smaller R&D units is offered. There is a fear of being dominated in these projects by core groups of active and recognized R&D teams, which are expected to come mostly from active Member States. There is fear of loosing grip on the development and application of high-level technologies as they integrate easier into the market situation of advanced economies.
- Specific emphasis is given to mobility and returning grants for scientists as they are the key to internationalization and the prevention of a brain drain.
- The CC call for additional thematic priorities with reference to the ongoing effects connected with the economic transformation, for example pollution, water management, industry restructuring and the social situation.
- Assistance in preparation and administration of R&D proposals is called for as they are a key to better participation in European projects. The network of National Contact Points plays a key role here and the experience with R&D support measures in CC is not yet satisfactory.
- Special help for the establishment of small- and medium-sized enterprises is important to improve the transfer of knowledge into the business sector – a crucial matter as private R&D is weak in CC.

- Regional and bilateral co-operation among CEEC is proposed as a strengthening strategy.
- Finally there is a call for better integration into the decision-making process, involvement in the forming process and the formulation of rules connected with the FP outline.

From the candidates' perspective the present situation is still marked by a lack of relevant information of EU members on promising R&D within the CC. Visits of institutes are very useful, but mobility is to the present state too often a one way track into the EU. The domestic industry doesn't have sufficient financial resources, courage and imagination to invest into research. Advisors propose that attitudes of researchers should become more creative, flexible – and commercial – to disseminate ideas into the world of business. Also the management of R&D should improve (Illnerova 2001). Being present on the EU level with proposals and being evaluated is important as it raises awareness. In personal contacts people realize that researchers from CEEC 'also have two hands and a brain, that they are normal and that it is possible to work with them' as one representative from Latvia puts it.

Small states can exercise power if they manage to create alliances. As candidates the accession countries naturally form a group with shared interests. The Visegrad States (Czech Republic, Hungary, Poland, Slovakia) and the Baltic States have closer links, but the CEEC as a whole hardly appear as one actor. Due to the regatta model of the enlargement process they found themselves in a competition among each other. The ranking within the annual status reports is only a symbolic expression for this 'race'. As soon as accessions take place, the objectives for the new members change – thus the foundations to find common positions will easily get weaker.

CONCLUSION

The Challenge of Enlargement and the Need to Participate in European R&D

The EU and the CC easily reached agreement on chapter 17 (R&D) in the enlargement negotiations. The legal framework is set but as shown above the difficulties lay beyond it. Due to the importance of R&D with regard to the economy, education and the cultural development the objective has to be a position of an equal partner on the European level. To achieve a competitive position in European R&D in the CC' public expenditure for R&D is crucial. However raising public spending for research will hardly be sufficient. As long as the business sector remains small serious problems in developing and applying high-level technologies remain. The success story of Ireland in the EU provides for an example – but cannot be a model for all. Entering the EU means the need to transform into knowledge-based societies where R&D has a great impact. The risks of a brain drain and loss of know-how as well as the researchers' reserve to move beyond the domestic funding system are other factors to be addressed. International exchange and co-operation will gain significance, therefore it is important to succeed in using the possibilities offered by the European institutions in order to participate in common projects and develop the R&D system.

The EU might face integration problems if the current performance of the CEEC inside the Research FP doesn't improve. Countries which have to make efforts to built up more efficient and competitive R&D systems shouldn't transfer budget resources into European research from where they are allocated to already powerful actors. If the accession countries remain net-payers, acceptance of FP membership will hardly rise. This will also impede the making of an European Research Area.

Consortia as Key Opportunities

Interaction between the scientific worlds is rising but is still not balanced. It mainly works in an east–west direction. Personal relationships play a significant role in forming consortia. For entering high-level groups of scientists, it is most effective to be present at conferences or workshops and build up a personal contact. Therefore mobility of students and researchers from CEEC should be supported. This refers first of all to travel expanses, but also residence regulations, social insurance, family relations or career patterns may cause difficulties.

Participation in international consortia raises awareness for cultural differences and provides for experiences with other nationalities. It has an impact on constructing one's identity as a 'European professional' rather than as a citizen of one nation (Krige 1997). Scientists and high school teachers are multipliers in the dissemination of knowledge about other nations and peoples.[11] This is an important cultural factor of European integration.

Institutional learning is another significant aspect of European consortia. European projects provide for an administrative contact to institutions of Member States and the European Commission. R&D systems work in different traditions and environments, and knowledge about the institutional and practical framework of institutes, faculties and other facilities elsewhere can be transferred through contact within consortia. They also offer the chance to exchange experience with European regulations and promote integration on this level.

The Political Role of the CC

The role of CC as actors in EU policymaking is limited. The objective of CEEC is to participate not only in the ERA itself but also in the decision-making process. The bargaining power of CEEC in front of the door can only be strong when they manage to act as one group. Formulating common positions towards EU policy is not very common, the regatta model for accession separated them. Tensions are visible between countries that went further in the negotiations by giving up positions, like Hungary and Estonia, and those who did negotiate hard, like Poland for example. As long as their positions remain similar they can easily be connected in an informal way. Once the first accessions have taken place it will be more difficult to address common problems.[12]

At the present stage the CC have to rely on the indirect channels of influence described above. The European Commission has significant impact on the development of the European Research Area but the situation is far from evolving into one single R&D policy. The national R&D budgets are by large higher than the European share and the co-ordination of research activities has to prove in practice first. Competition on various levels will remain within the evolving ERA. Decision-making power under the conditions of network governance (Eising and Kohler-Koch 1999) has many faces. This includes the chance for the CEEC to use appropriate channels of influence wherever they find them, even if participation in Council meetings may be regarded as a more substantial way of exercising influence.

Facing an Excellence Dilemma?

Human resources are crucial for many CEEC. The ERA involves great chances for improved mobility of researchers. But the infrastructure remains a risk, the conditions for outstanding R&D are only partly existing. The initiative for a European Research Area aims at increased establishment of first-rate R&D and improved competition with the United States and Japan. At the same time it aims at the integration of European R&D. The double objective of competing on the global scale and promoting cohesion inside the Community may lead to tensions. Unequal chances to get access to R&D funding will raise inequality between R&D units inside Europe and cause integration problems.

Science should by nature be excellent. But a possible dilemma may result from the current situation. FP6 with its strong emphasis on excellence has provoked criticism because it is assumed that it offers too little space for smaller players. This applies to CEEC in particular. A Matthew-effect as described by Merton (1985) may arise: The chances to improve the scientific position of poorly equipped facilities are generally low already. Due to the rationale of the ERA the chances to improve them through European grants are not very high either. Therefore the orientation towards excellence and large consortia may result in an accumulation of advantages and disadvantages on either side. In the best case it helps to develop 'islands of excellence' in CEEC, in the worst case it will lead to a colonization or destruction of R&D activity in that region. That however does not open the door to the European club of knowledge-based societies. An at least to a certain extent homogeneous and integrated European Research Area requires not only the legal preconditions but also the effective participation in European research.

NOTES

[1] This article refers to the group of ten central and eastern European Candidate Countries, of which Bulgaria and Romania meanwhile declared that they intend to join the EU only as early as 2007.

[2] The PHARE-Programme (Pologne, Hongrie: Assistance à la Restructuration Economique) was set up in the early 1990s to assist Poland and Hungary in the transition phase. Later it was extended to all CEEC. It is one of the major means of the EU to allocate financial and knowledge resources to the accession countries.

[3] See for example: Bekanntmachung der Förderinitiative des BMBF 'Netze Erneuerbare Energieforschung' from 20 December 2001, http: www.bmf.de/677_3821.html, 22 March 2003.

[4] In a survey done by the author about 50 per cent of the scientists from Lower Saxony reported that the coordinator's invitation was decisive for the integration of CEEC partners, only in 16 per cent of the cases the CEEC partner himself took the initiative (Hilger 2002, p. 67).

[5] I take this information from interviewing done in the European Commission.

[6] It is therefore surprising that the chance to take part in informal meetings is only used with restraint. A European Commissions' director complained that evaluators from 'CC don't show up in panels' although it would be an important field to acquire tacit knowledge and experience.

[7] One could also refer to the 'shaming mechanism' analyzed by Schimmelpfennig (2001). He argues that moral pressure forces Member States to regard CC interests even if their preferences are different.

[8] A Hungarian representative said one has to 'say things 200 times in parallel channels and meetings before they are taken up'.

[9] It is not self-evident that 'best teams' are willing to cooperate. Research policy is marked on various levels by competition. One may start by looking at the German federal states (Deutinger 1999). This applies for competition among Member States as well.

[10] Position papers can be found on: www.cordis.lu/rtd2002/era-debate/associated.htm, retrieved on 22 March 2003.

[11] As scientific communication is highly codified, it is also easier for scientists to overcome common problems of intercultural communication. There is less chance for misunderstanding.

[12] Already now some accession countries are in a better position than some EU members and pursue specific objectives.

References

Bergenwall, M. (2000), 'Impact of Tekes' grants for applied technical research', *VTT working papers*, **49**/00, Espoo: VTT Group for technology studies.

BMBF (2000), *Bundesbericht Forschung 2000*, Bonn: Bundesministerium für Bildung und Forschung (BMBF).

Cordis focus (2001), *Community Research & Development Information Service*, **178**, Brussels: European Commission, 30 June 2001.

Deutinger, S. (1999), 'Stile regionaler Forschungspolitik. Die Bundesländer zwischen Kooperation und Konkurrenz', in Ritter, G.A., M. Szöllösi-Janze and H. Trischler (eds), *Antworten auf die amerikanische Herausforderung*, Frankfurt/Main: Campus, pp. 266–85.

Directorate General for Economics and Financial Affairs (2001), 'The economic impact of enlargement', *Enlargement papers*, **4**, June 2001, II/419/01EN, Brussels: European Commission.

Eising, R. and B. Kohler-Koch (1999), 'Governance in the European Union', in Kohler-Koch, B. and R. Eising (eds), *The Transformation of Governance in the European Union*, London: Routledge, pp. 267–85.

European Commission (2000), *Towards a European Research Area*, Brussels: European Commission, COM (2000) 6.

European Commission (2001a), *European Governance. A White Paper*, Brussels: European Commission, COM (2001) 428, final.

European Commission (2001b), *Research and Technological Development Activities of the European Union. 2001 Annual Report*, Brussels: European Commission, COM (2001) 756.

European Commission (2001c), *The International Dimension of the European Research Area*, Brussels: European Commission, COM (2001) 346 final.

Eurostat (2000): *Release No. 130/2000*, 20 November 2000, Brussels: European Commission, http://europa.eu.int/comm/eurostat/, retrieved on 22 March 2003.

Füllsack, M. (2001), 'Gesundung oder Zerfall? Zum Schicksal der rußländischen Wissenschaft', *Osteuropa*, **51** (1), 3–15.

Grande, E. (1996), 'Das Paradox der Schwäche: Forschungspolitik und die Einflusslogik europäischer Politikverflechtung', in Jachtenfuchs, M. and B. Kohler-Koch (eds), *Europäische Integration*, Opladen: Leske + Budrich, pp. 373–99.

Hasse, R. (1996), *Organisierte Forschung. Arbeitsteilung, Wettbewerb und Networking in Wissenschaft und Technik*, Berlin: edition sigma.

Hilger, P. (2002), *Forschungseinrichtungen vor der Herausforderung der EU-Osterweiterung: Niedersächsische Erfahrungen. Die Beteiligung niedersächsischer Akteure an EU-geförderten Forschungs- und Bildungsprojekten (1987–2000) und ihre Zusammenarbeit mit Einrichtungen aus Mittel- und Osteuropa*, Hannover: EU-Hochschulbüro, http://www.eu.uni-hannover.de/eu_buero/index.htm, retrieved on 22 March 2003.

Illnerova, H. (2001), 'Conference Statement', in *An Enlarged Europe for Researchers*, proceedings of the conference held in Brussels on 27 and 28 June 2001, Brussels: European Commission, pp. 13–15.

Kowi (2000), 'Interview mit Achilleas Mitsos, neuer Generaldirektor Forschung: ERA und das 6. FRP', *Kowi aktuell*, **45**, Bonn and Brussels, 31 July 2000, 3–6.

Krige, J. (1997), 'The Politics of European Scientific Collaboration', in Krige, J. and

D. Pestre (eds), *Science in the Twentieth Century*, Amsterdam: Harwood Academic Publishers, pp. 897–918.

Lam, A. (2001), 'Changing R&D Organisation and Innovation: Developing the New Generation of R&D Knowledge Workers', revised version of a paper presented at the conference: *The Contribution of European Socioeconomic Research to the Benchmarking of RTD Policies in Europe*, 14 March 2001, Brussels: European Commission, http://www.cordis.lu/improving/socioeconomics/conf_bench.htm, retrieved on 22 March 2003.

Marks, G., L. Hooge and K. Blank (1996), 'European Integration from the 1980s: State-centric vs. Multi-level Governance', in Nelsen, B. and A. Stubb (eds), *The European Union: Readings on the Theory and Practise of European Integration*, Boulder: Lynne Rienner Publishers, pp. 273–94.

Mayntz, R. (1998), 'The Impact of Radical Regime Change on the East European Academies of Sciences', in Mayntz., R., U. Schimank and P. Weingart (eds), *East European Academies in Transition*, Dordrecht: Kluwer Academic, pp. 1–12.

Merton, R. K. (1985), *Entwicklung und Wandel von Forschungsinteressen: Aufsätze zur Wissenschaftssoziologie*, Frankfurt/Main: Suhrkamp.

Nugent, N. (1995), *The Government and Politics of the European Union*, Houndsmills, London: Macmillan, 3rd edition.

Peterson, J. and M. Sharp (1998), *Technology Policy in the European Union*, Houndsmills, London: Macmillan.

Plesu, A. (2001), 'Probleme der Forschung. Zum Beispiel Rumänien', *Merkur*, **55** (623), 255–60.

Ruente, M. (2001), 'Conference Statement', in European Commission (ed.), *An Enlarged Europe for Researchers*, proceedings of the conference held in Brussels on 27 and 28 June 2001, Brussels: European Commission, pp. 17–19.

Scharpf, F.W. (1992), 'Die Handlungsfähigkeit des Staates am Ende des Zwanzigsten Jahrhunderts', in Kohler-Koch, B. (ed.), *Staat und Demokratie in Europa. 18. Wissenschaftlicher Kongreß der Deutschen Vereinigung für Politische Wissenschaft*, Opladen: Leske + Budrich, pp. 165–85.

Scharpf, F.W. (1993), 'Coordination in Hierarchies and Networks', in *Games in Hierarchies and Networks. Analytical and Empirical Approaches to the Study of Governance Institutions*, Frankfurt/Main and Boulder, CO: Campus, Westview, pp. 125–65.

Schimmelpfennig, F. (2001), 'The Community trap: liberal norms, rhetorical action and the Eastern enlargement of the European Union', *International Organization*, **55** (1), 47–80.

Sharp, M. (1998), 'Competitiveness and cohesion are the two compatible?', *Research Policy*, **27** (6), 569–88.

10 Introducing Regions and Innovation-related Needs in the Multi-layer Logic of the European Research Area

A Typology Proposal

Emmanuel Muller, Andrea Zenker and Jean-Alain Héraud

INTRODUCTION

In the new framework of the European Research Area (ERA), fundamental questions must be re-examined: a) what regional dynamics are to be encouraged? (balanced spreading, specialization, concentration, networking); b) what organizational/spatial grid should be favored? (architecture around the European Science and Technology (S&T) backbone vs. array of co-ordinated local production systems); and c) in their present forms, aren't the policy goals rather contradictory? (technological catching up and competitiveness in a globalized world, equitable development and intra-European convergence, forming European identity and solidarity). Most of the countries and regions have developed policies and institutions for supporting innovation, technology transfer, economic valorization of scientific research, etc. Such institutional sets constitute the regional context that must be kept in mind when designing any new policy device at supraregional level. Nevertheless, across such a variety of situations, some broad tendencies can be observed.

Starting from policies devoted to strengthening innovation behavior directly, the new priorities now seem to focus on indirect measures: improving absorptive capacities, systematizing co-operation between firms and public research, supporting innovative business services in the proximity of the firms, regrouping firms in strategic networks, etc. Within this general policy framework we address here the issue of international and interregional coherence. What is the optimal level of territorial competition? The European goal of coming back to the forefront of the research and innovation scene implies reformulating the regulation schemes, the latter being presently mostly national in certain countries and both at national and regional level in others. Fundamentally, the perspective of developing the new European science and technology policy raises the problem of interfacing two types of territory-related actions. It is clear that ERA policies will precisely rely on networks of the major science and technology poles, using present leading territories (regions or urban areas) as building blocks. At the same time, traditional tools of regional development will certainly be implemented by local actors, and the EU itself will go on helping weaker territories to improve their innovation capacities. At European level, the question is: 'What can the (leading) regions do to improve European competitiveness in the new knowledge-based world economy?', whereas at local level, the question is: 'What can Europe do to help our (ordinary) regions to keep pace with all these new challenges and reduce economic and social disparities?'

The possible coincidence of the two rationales – European competitiveness by networking science and technology excellence, and intrinsic regional development – cannot be achieved without taking into account the regional context. Since we are addressing the innovation context, let us remember the basics of innovation economics: the creative process is fundamentally non-linear and results from the networking of many actors. For a given territory, it means that: a) scientific infrastructure and exclusive access to codified knowledge is not necessarily the engine of local innovation; and b) the existence of various partners and facilities in firms' environment often prove to be crucial. We can summarize the policy issue in two questions: what is needed for innovation, and to what extent is it necessary to supply it regionally? Let us consider some typical examples:

- Innovators need science, but it is neither essential in all cases as a direct input, nor needs to be supplied in firms' close environment.
- They need knowledge and human competence to understand how to use science: this is certainly a more relevant issue for smaller firms and policy-setting in regional contexts.
- They need well-educated and skilled employees: on that point, for instance, the impact of a good university established within the territory is certainly a precious asset.
- They need firms supplying specific and sometimes tailor-made business services in a large variety of functional activities like strategic counseling, management of knowledge and intellectual property rights, marketing of innovative products, specialized financing, etc.

Obviously, the nature of regional firms and the structure of local fabrics (in-cluding services), which vary from one region to another, lead to important differences of innovation contexts and therefore of 'innovation needs'. The possible meaning and the actual impact of ERA within such complex and diversified settings will strongly differ as well.

The core assumption in this paper, following the preceding remarks, is that science and innovation policy at regional level must be considered in a quite different way in the case of leading regions (exhibiting a real innovation sys-tem or benefiting from some industrial clusters in advanced technological fields) and in the case of the 'average region', not to speak of those trying to catch up with the rest of the EU. Due to the variety of regional contexts, the notion of 'innovation-related needs' does not necessarily have the same meaning everywhere, any more than policies responding to such needs can be analyzed within the same conceptual framework. The paper aims at discuss-ing this issue on the basis of an empirical enquiry in ten European regions concerning an intermediary range of science and technological levels. Even limited to a relatively homogeneous subset of territories, i.e. eliminating ma-jor poles (like urban regions of London, Paris or Munich) as well as rural zones, a variety of situations can be observed, suggesting a typology of both the 'needs' and the policy settings of regions.

INNOVATION-RELATED NEEDS: THE POLICY CONTEXT

The issue of research and innovation policies for regions is not really new, but the specific problem raised by the ERA perspective is the *targeted intri-cacy of research policy and innovation policy*.

As Chabbal (1995) pointed out in an OECD publication, national *research policy* concerns public organizations and large firms, whereas *innovation policy* aims mostly at firms of limited economic and geographical scope. A consistent fact of innovation policies is that they are still to be implemented at the level of local industrial fabric and must typically focus on traditional SMEs.

Considering more precisely the issue from a regional perspective, it ap-pears that the European regional policy is now at a crossroads. It is clear that important changes in the underlying philosophy have occurred, leading to new relationships with innovation policy. In this respect, at least two main axes can be distinguished: a) one focuses on a European macroeconomic policy supporting the objective of social and economic cohesion; b) the other redefines the objectives and means of regional policy in putting stress on educational infrastructures, improvement of human capabilities, harnessing innovation for the sake of regional development, putting Regional Innovation

Strategies (RIS) at the core of the regional development policy. Taking firms' innovation-related needs as a starting point, the issue is clearly to support firms in the improvement of their innovativeness or at least to favor their absorptive and adaptive capacities. In this respect, the institutional supply is generally abundant and diversified, but not necessarily optimized: it is even sometimes described by firms as an over-dimensioned system with overlapping instruments. Answering firms' needs is obviously the declared aim of all policies, but one cannot be convinced that policies have been based on real analytical knowledge of the demand. The first reason is that firms' do not express an innovation 'demand'. It is sound reasoning to stress the interest of starting from the demand, instead of imposing top-down procedures regardless of the field, but then the question to ask is who expresses or reveals the demand. Isn't the 'need' for new knowledge, for strategic advice, etc. largely a constructed notion? If yes, what is the implicit rationale behind the notion? Another way to consider the problem is to address the ambiguity of the policies. There is often a real lag between the image regions want to build and the real needs of the local economic fabric. Shouldn't policy action focus more on other aspects or externalities of knowledge-based economies, such as local benefits in terms of general education, quality of life, long-term sustainability of socioeconomic development, etc.?

The aims of regional policies can be summarized as follows: a) growth; b) equity; and c) stability. The growth aim postulates that an efficient distribution of production factors in the territories of a nation state leads to overall growth within the national economy, whereas the equity aim focuses on a decrease in unequal living conditions within a state. The last aim – stability – is based on the assumption that there are not only sectoral, but also regional business cycles leading especially to unemployment in regions with declining industries (cf. van Suntum 1981, pp. 30 ff.). Considering the aims of regional policy in detail, it becomes obvious that they cannot all be achieved with one type of policy. Goal conflicts are the consequence, especially between growth and equity. Consequently, following the growth aim leads to the distribution of production factors in locations that promise the highest marginal revenues, whereas pursuing the equity aim would favor an equal distribution of production factors within the territory. Pursuing the first goal thus would result in a 'picking the winner' strategy, the second in a 'supporting the less favored' policy. Regional policy generally focuses on the equity aim, i.e. the support of equivalent circumstances and living conditions in all parts of the territory. The 'regional policy approach' of the European Union (EU) also takes equal conditions as its main goal, assuming that convergence between European regions will lead to more competitiveness for the Union as a whole:

'Socioeconomic disparities between regions can, however, be harmful to the whole

Union. Underperformance in weaker regions leads to a fall in consumer demand for European products, hinders economic development, distorts competition in the single market and ultimately reduces the EU's competitiveness world-wide.' (European Commission and DG Regional Policy 2001).

Besides regional policy, several sectoral policy types have spatial impacts, without being conceived as spatially oriented policies. Infrastructure policies, education policies (locations of universities, etc.) or technology policies have primarily different aims, but support of these aims very often has regional implications. Without having regionally oriented goals, certain policies like technology policy might even increase regional disparities.[1]

Considering research and technology development (R&D) policies as practiced in Europe, it appears clear that the main focus consists in strengthening the science and technology base of the different actors constituting the innovation system and in bolstering their international competitiveness. Nevertheless, additional aims are considered also, such as the stimulation of training and researchers' mobility, co-operation between firms and academic institutions in and between Member States as well as with non-EU member countries. In this respect, the articulation between R&D policies and regional development policies raises at least three important issues:

- the issue of (intra- and interregional) networking, i.e. how do actors involved in innovation processes co-ordinate their, efforts depending on the territories in which they are located;
- the issue of territorial equity (rather than 'equality', since regions benefit from different initial allocations): investment decisions related to scientific and technological activities may for instance significantly affect regional development paths, especially in regions lagging behind;
- the issue of overall efficiency: since the results of innovation efforts appear as (at least partially) dependent on the spatial environment in which they are performed, it seems necessary to ensure that innovation investment and activities are adapted to their location.

In particular, focusing on the situation of regions in Europe, two facts must be noted (cf. Clarysse and Muldur 2001): a) discrepancies between European regions, notably in terms of economic indicators, are not decreasing as clearly as between Member States; and b) regional discrepancies related to innovation capacities and results are more important than economic discrepancies. Figure 10.1 provides an overview of the structures of regional innovation systems. Basically, two contradictory forces may profoundly affect the evolution (and even the existence) of such regional innovation systems. On the one hand, investments flow towards the 'poorer locations' where production factors are cheaper, which supports convergence. On the other hand, due to the effects of scale and scope economies, the 'rich locations' get richer, strengthening divergence. For usual economic variables there is no systematic dominance of one of the forces in the long run (model regions of the industrialization era have become 'has beens' – and then sometimes returned recently to successful development; rural areas of the early 20th century now belong to the core of the European technological backbone; etc.). Nevertheless, in a knowledge-driven economy, the tendency towards interregional divergence may be stronger than the convergence forces, since:

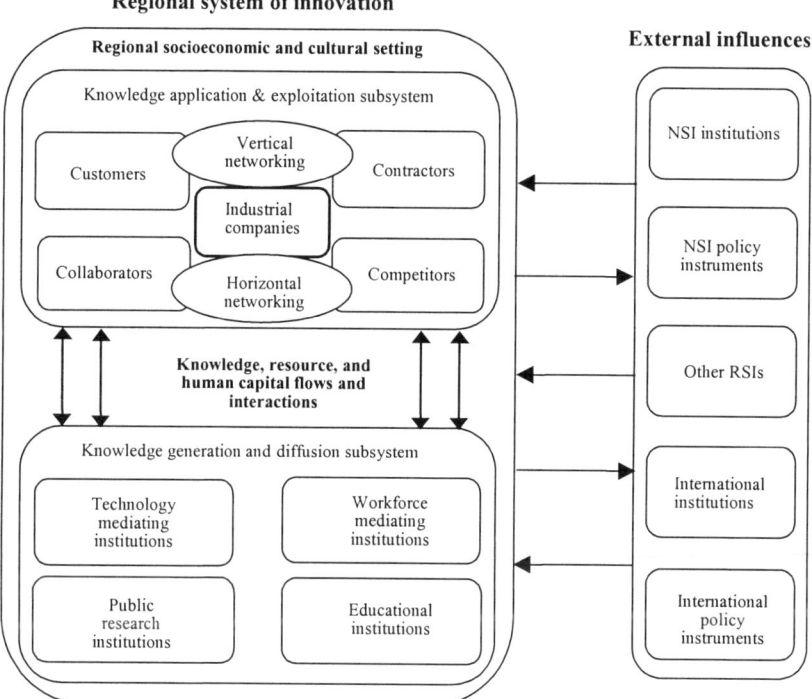

Source: Autio (1998, p. 134).

Figure 10.1 Schematic illustration of the structuring of regional systems of innovation

- knowledge production proceeds generally through combinations of existing knowledge;
- although highly codified in their formal contents, big science and high technology need a lot of tacit knowledge to be processed, then proximity and agglomeration is favored;

- knowledge-intensive flows between actors of the innovation process (notably private firms) suggest the existence of a dominant spatial hierarchy in terms of knowledge exchanges, diffusion and use (cf. Wood 1998) considering the case of knowledge-intensive business services).

Turning to firms' needs related to innovation, a whole range of potential or explicit requirements can be listed while trying to explore the corresponding 'grey literature'.[2] A part of these requirements explicitly concerns the links firms want to establish with institutions supporting innovation. These links shape the *context* of demand. In some cases the regional setting forms a simple contextual aspect of demand (a regional specificity in the process of transformation of 'needs' into 'demand'). In other cases, demand is really 'formatted' by firms' partners. The three following categories of explicit demands can for instance be taken into account:

- demand for personalized services, uniqueness of contact, close relationship with experts that can be trusted: understanding firms' specific problems, respecting confidentiality, etc.;
- demand for assessment of strategic options, strategic watch, analysis of potential markets (all these needs appear in many studies as more urgent than pure technological counseling);
- demand for adapted 'partnership processes', a continuing assistance often required, under various forms: simple or complex, individual or collective, local or remote.

Beyond the context and nature of innovation-related needs, the *consistency* of demand should be analyzed: Is manifested demand consistent with the means and absorptive capacities of the firm? The quality of the support policy can be typically tested here. And it reveals also an implicit meta-demand of the firms. What is the real value of the requested information or required knowledge for the firm? Generally, the value of information is known only when it has been consumed. One can even consider that in certain circumstances information is a negative good (a noise). This remark is to be linked to the fact that total cost of innovation sometimes surpasses to a large extent the classical R&D expenses and other learning efforts. As stated in the Oslo Manual on the measurement of scientific and technological activities (OECD 1997, p. 60), 'R&D expenditure ... is only one part of the financial input' and 'Expenditure on technological products and processes includes all expenditures related to those scientific, technological, commercial, financial and organizational steps which are intended to lead, or actually lead, to the implementation of technologically new or improved products and processes.' Therefore, explicit demand is not necessarily the expression of well-assessed needs. Information about a priori value of information is difficult, but very useful. Prior to making a typology of 'needs', it is necessary to characterize their functional relationship with 'innovation'. In this respect, the following cases can be considered:

- needs for innovation (for instance needs for innovative products): Innovating is a goal for the firm and the needs are precisely expressed requirements to meet the goal (for instance, designing a new material or new equipment necessary for the industrial production of a product already designed).
- needs for innovative solutions (for instance in terms of process innovations): The new ways of producing do not lead automatically to innovative products, they are just adopted for increased productivity or quality. They are imported and not designed specifically. Here, the process is closer to a diffusion process of a new technological standard than to breakthrough innovation.
- ordinary needs leading to innovation: Innovation is a final consequence. It is not planned by the firm. It is then impossible to express and classify such needs as 'innovative needs'. They nevertheless lead to innovation in the long run.

The policies corresponding to each of the preceding categories of 'innovation needs' are clearly different and as one may observe, variations in how innovation is defined play an important role. In this respect, it appears relevant to try to investigate how far categories of needs can be aggregated at regional level. In particular, the establishment of different 'regional profiles' in terms of innovation-related needs would highlight the potential influence of the introduction of the ERA on European regions.

A REGIONAL TYPOLOGY PROPOSAL

Adopting a vision of European regional evolution corresponding for instance to a polycentric spatial development model, a significant contribution of the ERA could be to promote the development of networks of regional competencies through balanced and sustainable regional innovation policies. Policy tools developed in the frame of the ERA will not be spontaneously consistent with regional (and national) expectations and needs in terms of innovation capacities and economic development. In this respect, the RETINE (Regional Typology of Innovation Needs) project, performed on behalf of the European Commission (DG Research) by Fraunhofer Institute for Systems and Innovation Research ISI (Karlsruhe) and BETA (Université Louis Pasteur,

Strasbourg) may provide a useful tool. In particular, such a typology may establish a basis for negotiations between regions, Member States and EU. The statistical work performed in the frame of RETINE was based on the ERIS (European Regional Innovation Survey) database. ERIS investigates innovation and networking behaviors and conditions of different types of actors in different regional contexts. In order to get an exhaustive and comparable picture, the ERIS database is based on postal inquiries, in some regions complemented by additional interviews. This survey was performed between 1995 and 1997, covering innovation and co-operation characteristics of manufacturing and service firms as well as research institutions.[3] ERIS covers a variety of European regions: the metropolitan regions of Barcelona, Stockholm and Vienna, regions with medium-sized cities or regional capitals (research triangle of Lower Saxony, Gironde, South Holland), transformation and/or peripheral regions (Saxony, South Wales) and two border regions (Alsace, Baden). The structure of the ERIS database aimed at reflecting the diversity of regional innovation systems in Europe excluding nevertheless the 'extremes of the spectrum', i.e. core metropolitan agglomerations and regions lagging behind.[4]

The French region of *Alsace* borders Germany at the Rhine river. The region consists of the 'départements' Haut-Rhin and Bas-Rhin with the urban centers of Strasbourg, Mulhouse and Colmar. The industrial fabric is mainly composed of small- and medium-sized firms, but Alsace simultaneously has a considerable number of large production units, often branches of national companies or multinational groups. For decades, Alsace has been among the leading French regions in terms of direct foreign investment (a model of exogenous regional development strategy). The most important sectors are the metal, vehicle and food industries.

Baden, the western part of Baden-Württemberg, is located on the German side of the Rhine river. With the universities of Karlsruhe and Freiburg, numerous further research organizations and technical colleges and a high share of high-tech firms, Baden hosts the highest density of researchers in Europe. The focus of industrial activities are electronics, data processing, mechanics, vehicle construction, mechanical engineering, paper/printing and the chemical industry. Baden is considered a very innovative and wealthy region in Germany.

Barcelona, the capital of Catalonia, is one of the industrial R&D centers in Spain with a high share of public R&D. The tertiary sector is very important and covers tourism, health care, knowledge infrastructure and financial services. One innovation obstacle is the still lacking co-operations between universities and industry.

Gironde is part of the region Aquitaine in the southwest of France. The regional capital Bordeaux is the economic center of Gironde. More than 50 per cent of the industrial employees work here. Besides agriculture and viticulture, the oil, automotive, chemical and pharmaceutical industries, Gironde hosts high-tech industries such as aerospace. To that extent it belongs (more than Alsace) to the French national system of innovation, based on strategic industries. The economic structure is dominated by small- and medium-sized enterprises and the region has a considerable share of foreign direct investments, although less than Alsace.

The research triangle *Lower Saxony* (Hanover–Brunswick–Göttingen) is the economic core of the German 'Land' (federal state) Lower Saxony, it has also the highest population density of the whole 'Land'. Economic activities are concentrated on automotive industries. The headquarter of Volkswagen is located within this region. Various research organizations are located here and the size structure of regional firms is dominated by large businesses. However, industrial R&D is below the German average.

Saxony is one of the new German 'Länder'. Due to its transformation and restructuring processes, Saxony has a high rate of unemployment and a low purchasing power. Most firms are small ones while large enterprises and industrial R&D are widely lacking.

The province of *South Holland* is one of the largest and most populous regions in the Netherlands. Eighty per cent of the workforce are employed in the tertiary sector. South Holland is the home region of Rotterdam with the world's largest harbor and The Hague, the seat of government. Regional industries and services are to a large extent related to the harbor. Thus, transport, logistics and distribution play important roles. South Holland has rather mature industries and few high-tech sectors.

South Wales which covers Gwent, Mid, South and West Glamorgan, restructured its mining, iron and steel and shipbuilding sectors during the last decades, but also attracted foreign firms from the electrical engineering and automotive industries, especially from Japan and the United States. Regional R&D is rather modest, but intraregional networking is highly supported by the regional development strategy.

The metropolitan region of *Stockholm* has a high share of industrial R&D. The secondary sector is dominated by paper/wood/printing, vehicle construction and mechanical engineering. Firms are mainly small ones, but Stockholm is also home region for large Swedish multinationals that partly transferred their R&D activities abroad.

Like Stockholm, *Vienna* – the third metropolitan region of the sample – also represents a capital region. The tertiary sector is highly represented, and the region has high R&D intensities, accompanied by a favorable education and research infrastructure. The firm structure is dominated by SMEs that are often not innovative. Due to its proximity to eastern European countries, Vienna is a preferred location for firms that wish to capture these markets.

Table 10.1   Samples and response rates in the case study areas
(number of distributed questionnaires, valid sample,
response rate)

Region	Manufacturing Firms (including SMEs)	Service Firms (KIBS)
Alsace (France)	1 753 263 15.0 %	955 147 15.4 %
Baden (Germany)	2 715 430 15.8 %	1 198 279 23.3 %
Barcelona (Spain)	2 650 405 15.3 %	684 118 17.3 %
Gironde (France)	797 101 12.7 %	947 157 16.6 %
Lower Saxony (Germany)	1 807 372 20.6 %	1 351 240 17.8 %
Saxony (Germany)	3 767 1.004 26.7 %	1 472 365 24.8 %
South Holland (The Netherlands)	1 894 260 13.7 %	1 882 267 14.3 %
South Wales (United Kingdom)	1 593 280 17.6 %	850 161 18.9 %
Stockholm (Sweden)	1 902 456 24.0 %	1 301 334 25.7 %
Vienna (Austria)	985 196 19.9 %	651 189 29.0 %
Total	**19 863 3,767 18.9 %**	**11 291 2,257 19.9 %**

Source: European Regional Innovation Survey (ERIS). Data collected by the Fraunhofer Institute for Systems and Innovation Research Karlsruhe, the University of Hanover, the University of Cologne and the Technical University Bergakademie Freiberg.

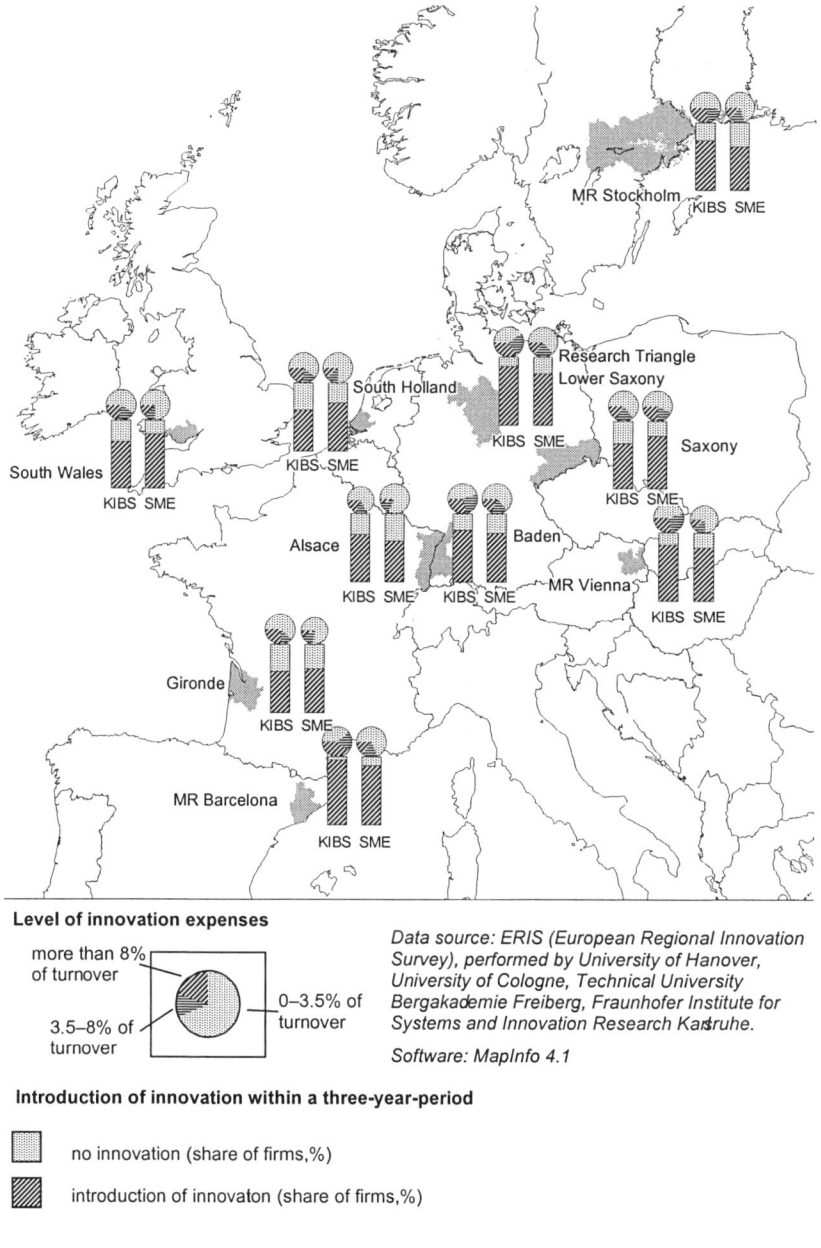

Figure 10.2 Innovation activities and innovation expenses of manufacturing SMEs and KIBS in the surveyed regions

Table 10.1 shows the samples and response rates in the different case study areas. Response rates differed between 13 per cent and 29 per cent with an average of nearly 20 per cent. This set of data allows us to draw conclusions and interregional comparisons concerning innovation and co-operation be-havior as well as perceived needs for innovation support.[5] Some comparative data depicting innovation activities and expenses of the surveyed firms are displayed in Figure 10.2.

Table 10.2   Needs proxy-variables

Variable	Variable description	Knowledge-intensive business services (KIBS)	Manufacturing small- and medium-sized enterprises (SMEs)
		Variable labels	Variable labels
VC_AVAIL	Regional availability of venture capital	1: Negative perception 2: Neutral/ positive perception/ no answer	1: Negative perception 2: Neutral/ positive perception/ no answer
RES_CAP	Perception of the regional research capacities	1: Negative perception 2: Neutral/ positive perception/ no answer	1: Negative perception 2: Neutral/ positive perception/ no answer
COOPFIRM	Lack of co-operation opportunities with firms	1: Lacking co-operation opportunities with firms 2: Satisfactory co-operation opportunities with firms/ no innovation/ no answer	1: Lacking co-operation opportunities with firms/obstacles 2: Satisfactory co-operation opportunities with firms/ no answer
COOPRES	Lack of co-operation opportunities with research organizations	1: Lacking co-operation opportunities with research organizations 2: Satisfactory co-operation opportunities with research organizations/ no innovation/ no answer	1: Lacking co-operation opportunities with research organizations/obstacles 2: Satisfactory co-operation opportunities with research organizations/ no answer

WORKFORC	Perception of the regional workforce	1: Negative perception 2: Neutral/ positive perception/ no answer	1: Negative perception 2: Neutral/ positive perception/ no answer
PERC_CLI	Perception of regional clients	1: Negative perception 2: Neutral/ positive perception/ no answer	1: Negative perception 2: Neutral/ positive perception/ no answer
LACK_CAP	Lack of capital	1: Lacking capital 2: Satisfactory capital/ no innovation/ no answer	1: Lacking capital 2: Satisfactory capital/ no answer
INNOCLIM	Perception of regional innovation climate	1: Negative perception 2: Neutral/ positive perception/ no answer	1: Negative perception 2: Neutral/ positive perception/ no answer
COOPREAD	Perception of co-operation readiness within the region	1: Negative perception 2: Neutral/ positive perception/ no answer	-
CONSULT	Perception of regional consultancy supply	-	1: Negative perception 2: Neutral/ positive perception/ no answer

Besides their innovation and co-operation characteristics, firms have also been asked to assess their respective regional framework conditions with respect to innovation support. The data collection methodology followed the OECD innovation survey standards.[6]

The variables extracted from the ERIS database are in particular relevant for an analysis of firms' innovation-related needs since they contain information dealing specifically with: a) firms' perception in terms of framework conditions for innovation; b) innovation obstacles; and c) innovation-related co-operation willingness and opportunities. Generally, these characteristics have been assessed on a three-point or a five-point scale, but for the purpose of the RETINE project, especially the negative assessments were emphasized and treated in a comparative manner.[7] In order to get further information about innovation characteristics and behavior, as well as different types of innovation-related needs, the following set of variables was constituted for this analysis:

- variables characterizing firms' structure;
- innovation-related indicators;
- different types of needs (proxy-variables).

Table 10.2 gives an overview of the third variables set. The regional location of the firms as well as their fields of activity and their size belong to the variables that characterize the samples. Innovation behavior of manufacturing SMEs and KIBS is for instance shown by their patenting and export activities, the share of turnover spent for research and development, their innovation performance and their information sources for innovations. Besides capital availability, co-operation opportunities and research capabilities, firms' assessment concerning the regional workforce, the regional innovation climate, the perception of regional clients and firms' assessment of regional framework conditions (consultancy, infrastructure, economic and technology policies) are proxy variables for firms' innovation needs. Thus, the chosen variables give first indications concerning so-called latent innovation needs of manufacturing and business service firms. Variables were coded in a dichotomous way, opposing needs-proxy assessments to neutral or positive ones (and missing values). The aim was to sharply depict indications for innovation needs, represented by negative assessments or expression of obstacles respectively.

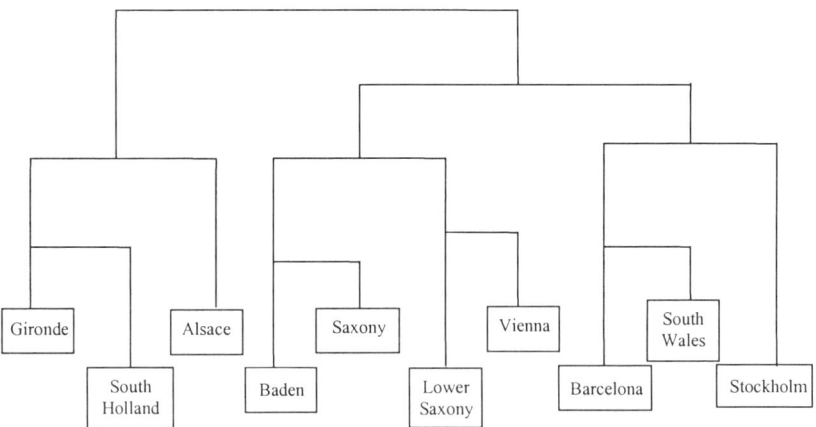

Figure 10.3 Dendrogram of regional innovation needs profile (all firms)

In the frame of the RETINE project, different types of statistical data treatments were performed in order to get a comprehensive insight into innovation-related needs of manufacturing SMEs and KIBS in the ten regions (cf. Muller et al. 2001). In order to establish distinct regional profiles in terms of firms' innovation-related needs, one procedure is of particular interest: the so-called 'hierarchical cluster analysis'. Hierarchical cluster analysis is a multivariate exploratory technique that aims at forming homogeneous groups of variables according to their characteristics. This is based on similarities or distances between variable features. For the clustering of regions according to the innovation needs of their firms, the distances have been recorded by Euclidean distance and 'linkage between groups' has been chosen as the merging method.[8] The clustering process leads to a typology of the ten sample regions and to a characterization according to their innovation needs (cf. Table 10.3 and Figure 10.3).

RESULTS AND IMPLICATIONS FOR POLICIES IN THE CONTEXT OF THE ERA

At regional level, and from a pragmatic point of view, the issue of public intervention is to be considered in the light of the degree of proactivity or reactivity of policies devoted to innovation support. As such, the question of the identification of (and response to) firms' needs is of crucial importance. In this respect, proactive regional policies may be defined as policies based on the innovation-related needs expressed or identified and strongly oriented towards their satisfaction, whereas reactive policies consist rather of an accompaniment of firms' existing innovation activities. It seems meaningful to make the link with local firms' attitude towards innovation (i.e. voluntarism vs. reactivity) in order to better appreciate how far firms' innovation related needs should determine the orientation of regional policy.[9] In fact, in regions where firms display strong capacities in terms of strategic initiative (as is the case for instance in Baden), a rather reactive policy intervention is appropriate whereas proactive policy support is strongly requested when firms are not characterized by a comprehensive innovation culture (like for instance in Alsace). As a further dimension to be considered, clear divergences in terms of regional policy priorities can be observed, notably concerning the importance attached to endogenous and exogenous development (as for instance is the case in Baden and in Alsace respectively).

In other words, the issue of identification of firms' needs must be considered in the light of coherence between policy objectives and practices in order to ensure (economic) sustainability. Consequently, to orient policy action on innovation-related needs of firms located in a region may be strategically

Table 10.3 Matrix of frequencies extracted from SMEs and KIBS samples (percentage of firms with negative assessments)

SMEs Regions Variables	Alsace	Baden	Barcelona	Gironde	Lower Saxony	Saxony	South Holland	South Wales	Stockholm	Vienna
CONSULT	15.04	14.32	11.59	5.10	17.58	10.16	6.85	12.59	28.01	13.68
COOPFIRM	19.51	28.64	14.82	7.14	31.21	22.18	15.32	11.48	26.16	30.53
COOPRES	19.92	22.82	13.48	6.12	28.18	16.22	7.26	11.11	27.78	21.58
INNOCLIM	15.85	21.60	14.29	10.20	34.85	16.53	8.06	13.70	21.53	32.11
LACK_CAP	17.07	25.24	18.60	10.20	33.03	38.30	11.69	18.52	10.65	16.84
PERC_CLI	11.38	27.43	9.97	11.22	26.36	24.54	10.08	29.63	22.22	16.84
RES_CAP	11.79	13.83	11.86	5.10	16.97	10.88	10.89	22.59	23.15	19.47
VC_AVAIL	14.63	28.16	20.75	11.22	33.03	33.26	14.52	21.85	23.38	37.89
WORKFORC	13.82	22.33	16.71	11.22	19.39	16.53	31.85	34.07	31.71	20.53

KIBS Regions Variables	Alsace	Baden	Barcelona	Gironde	Lower Saxony	Saxony	South Holland	South Wales	Stockholm	Vienna
COOP?FIRM	20.41	24.73	37.29	22.29	36.94	19.17	18.87	32.72	35.83	38.42
COOPREAD	6.80	27.96	23.73	19.75	28.38	18.29	26.04	25.31	37.92	34.21
COOPRES	17.01	20.43	28.81	15.92	23.42	12.09	12.08	24.07	26.25	26.84
INNOCLIM	8.84	26.16	11.02	22.29	45.05	23.60	16.60	20.37	29.17	37.37
LACK_CAP	39.46	44.80	65.25	36.94	59.46	50.44	29.06	49.38	46.25	57.89
PERC_CLI	8.16	22.22	15.25	10.83	36.49	32.45	17.36	24.07	13.33	19.47
RES_CAP	4.76	23.66	11.02	5.73	24.32	10.32	15.85	14.81	18.75	16.84
VC_AVAIL	12.93	42.65	30.51	18.47	48.65	38.35	18.87	35.80	23.33	40.00
WORKFORC	3.40	24.01	20.34	15.29	23.87	16.22	19.25	21.60	28.33	17.89

misleading, depending on the regional context. It is important to keep in mind that regional political actions derived from the identification of firms' needs consist in general of rather 'modest' policies (which however may be particularly efficient). This corresponds to a logic of incremental improvement of the regional system, favored through 'trial and error' processes. At the opposite end, big project-oriented policies which do not correspond to identified needs of existing local firms (i.e. so-called 'cathedrals in the desert') may give an impetus to a whole regional economy. This of course is true as long as such big projects are successful, keeping in mind that such policies obey a 'one-shot' logic (a second trial – in the case of an obvious failure – would necessitate numerous years, if not decades). Each big project of this kind aiming at the generation of numerous new opportunities (without considering local existing firms' needs) is somehow 'unique' and cannot be easily compared with other public initiatives.

The three clusters resulting from the proposed typology display divergent regional profiles in terms of innovation-related needs (corresponding at the same time to distinct innovation features). These divergent profiles lead to dissimilar 'regional positions' towards the introduction of ERA. The observation of the clusters reveals that these positions may be critical for different reasons.

The first cluster associates the two French regions (Alsace and Gironde) and South Holland. Cluster 1 regions appear as relatively 'satisfied' in the sense that financial and cognitive factors are assessed as sufficiently provided. On the one hand, the fact that most firms located in these regions do not appear as particularly innovation-intensive may indicate prudent innovation behavior rather than satisfaction. On the other hand, the role of (adequate) public support should not be underestimated. One possible conclusion related to the introduction of the ERA would be that the establishment of an 'innovation culture' could foster innovations and surpass existing activities over incremental innovations. The question to be asked is how far will such regions be able to clearly establish themselves within the ERA in order to benefit from it?

The second cluster relates to the three German regions (Baden, Lower Saxony, Saxony) and the metropolitan region of Vienna. In this case, especially capital is expressed as innovation need. KIBS rather than SMEs assess an existing lack of capital for innovation activities. This indicates that in regions of this cluster, capital is provided for innovative manufacturing SMEs to a higher extent than for innovative KIBS. Thus, the acceptance of KIBS as innovators and therefore the provision of innovation input for them seems to be necessary in these regions. Firms located in those regions can be viewed as rather 'pragmatic' in the sense that they seem to rely more on classical business development than adventurous science-pushed schemes. At the same time, they are clearly more concerned about the search for capital than firms located in Cluster 1 regions. To a certain extent, and due to a stronger orientation in terms of innovation activities, Cluster 2 regions appear as better positioned towards ERA than Cluster 1 regions.

The third cluster contains the metropolitan region of Barcelona, South Wales and the metropolitan region of Stockholm. If firms' demand for cognitive assets is interpreted as a proof of motivation and spirit of innovation more than as a lack of adequate knowledge supply in the regional environment, then Cluster 3 regions would correspond to a model of innovation which may be seen as 'knowledge-oriented'. At least for the metropolitan regions of Barcelona and Stockholm, it seems difficult to analyze the negative perception in the latter way, as these urban areas are far from a science and technology desert. In so far, regions corresponding to this profile can be seen as displaying a high potential, in terms of benefits to be gained from the introduction of the ERA. Nevertheless, this potential is strongly dependent on the intensity of relations between industrial activity (i.e. both manufacturing and service firms) and regional research infrastructure.

To conclude in the light of these explorative results, the main question is to which extent are ERA's objectives compatible with the issue of firms' innovation-related needs? The ERA will be implemented in order to be efficient on a European scale, but not necessarily on a regional scale. ERA does not aim principally at regional convergence within the EU, but at increasing EU competitiveness in science and research. Examining the potential impacts of ERA's realization on European firms and regions, it appears clear that large (R&D-intensive) firms and specific (leading) regions will be affected primarily. Nevertheless, as a corollary, this implies that: a) most European regions; b) most manufacturing SMEs; and c) most service firms will not benefit directly from the establishment of the ERA. These firms and regions must base their development on competencies not directly linked to the science–industry interface. Therefore, one suggestion would be to supplement the realization of the ERA with complementary policies, targeting: a) non-leading regions; b) non-R&D-intensive firms; and c) non-manufacturing firms.

Adopting a vision of European regional evolution corresponding for instance to a polycentric spatial development model,[10] a significant contribution of the ERA could be to promote the development of networks of regional competencies through balanced and sustainable regional innovation policies. Policy tools developed in the frame of the ERA will not be spontaneously consistent with regional (and national) expectations and needs in terms of innovation capacities and economic development. As a consequence, regional typologies expressed in terms of firms' innovation needs may provide a useful tool, establishing for instance a basis for negotiations between regions, Member States and EU.

On the one hand, it can be argued that a ERA – even though not aiming at regional development and regional convergence – can give incentives for non-participating regions to increase their absorptive capacities and to qualify themselves for further development. In other words, a ERA does not only strengthen competition for organizations that want to participate in the Research Area, but also creates incentives for non-participants to profit from the ERA. On the other hand, the establishment of a ERA not only potentially endangers regional convergence in Europe, but may even favor increased divergence. The realization of a ERA constitutes for European regions a danger and an opportunity at the same time. In the frame of the ERA, the priority given to big projects in terms of financial volume (in order to reach a critical mass) will make a regional and interregional co-ordination crucial. In this respect, the real challenge for most European regions will consist in improving their absorptive capacities. Consequently, a significant point is the motivation of regional actors, for instance: creating opportunities instead of complaining about weaknesses, thus to concentrate on endogenous potentials.

Referring to the different scenarios presented by Kuhlmann and Edler in the introduction of this book, depicting potential futures in European innovation policy, some observations can be expressed with regard to the relevance of clustering innovation needs at regional level. In scenario I, the reinforcement of pan-European institutions would establish a strong transnational structure and as a consequence, would probably reduce the diversity of the European landscape in terms of regional innovation systems. Such a perspective would possibly be more favorable for 'Cluster 3 regions' (comparatively to regions belonging to the two others clusters). Moreover, in the logic of such a scenario, to consider firms' innovation-related needs at regional level could constitute a strategic variable in the perspective of a pan-European allocation of resources. *A contrario*, the second scenario corresponds to a situation in which the expression of too many contradictory regional and national interests leads to a reinforced competition and to a growing gap between economically powerful and weaker regions. In such a perspective as well, the analysis of firms' innovation needs may be of strategic importance, but rather at local level (in order to reinforce regional competitive advantages). In such conditions, even if some regions may take advantage of the development of their own innovation capacity, it seems difficult to expect a beneficial evolution for the whole system. The third option described by Kuhlmann and Edler, i.e. the development of a multi-level and multi-actor system (reinforcing the principle susbsidiarity) may favor some targeted grouping at regional level. As a consequence, the possibility of some '*géométrie variable* regional alliances' – based for instance on common needs and expectations related to innovation activities – should be considered. The question remains open to what extent such a development would endanger or favor European cohesion.

Finally, and from a more general point of view, a ERA might be an opportunity for European regions since its realization faces the challenge of so-called 'regional intelligence'. As Nauwelaers (2000) indicates, a lack of intelligence on the regional level – e.g. the lack of flexibly adapting policy instruments to changing conditions – often hampers the setting up of an efficient and 'systemic' regional innovation system. Regional intelligence thus comprises the ability and competence for a deep and holistic understanding of the regional socioeconomic context when identifying firms' needs. In order to create and maintain a successful regional innovation system, regional intelligence has to be combined with policy learning. Policy learning implies that the evolution of the regional system is supported by adequate policy aims and tools. At present, policy answers to firms' innovation-related needs are often hindered by fragmented regional governance: public and semi-public actors appear as compartmentalized and as competing within the same region. As a result, for most firms regional public action is perceived as opaque. In this respect, the development of a ERA may constitute a chance to introduce more transparency. Transparency can be supported by the development of a regional 'policy evaluation culture' which favors policy learning. Furthermore, if a ERA succeeds in associating the different levels of governance (regional, national and supranational), then it may contribute to promote capacities of regional authorities to negotiate in the frame of networks. Besides the direct effect of a ERA – the creation of a competitive research area in Europe – the implementation of a multi-level negotiation and learning mechanism could be generated. A real involvement of regional actors in the implementation process of a ERA can only take place if negotiation mechanisms are set up which allow the simultaneous and multi-lateral confrontation of innovation-related objectives and means at regional, national and European levels.

CONCLUSIONS

Are the policy aims of the ERA and the expectations of European regions necessarily in contradiction? In fact, from an overall perspective and for each scientific field which is a priority for the European Community, efficiency should lead to focusing R&D action on the (few) specialized regions with critical mass, instead of spreading support everywhere. At the same time and from a regional perspective, it is clear that in most European regions, actors tend to develop parallel initiatives (and individually request support), because their vision of the regional entity is that of a system living *per se*. As a consequence, there is real need for a reasonable vision, leading to a balanced position between global competition and European cohesion. This implies compromises among regional, national and European governance.

European research policy setting must take into account the fact that there is no unique or 'one best way' of innovation-related development at regional level. On the one hand, only a few regions will massively evolve following the science-based model of development and it is not necessary to have all the components of the chain-linked innovation process in every region. On the other hand, the existing variety of regional innovation systems must be stressed. This implies a diversity (in terms of local dominant type of competence to innovate) which, in turn, favors a multiplicity of mode of organization of the innovation activities at regional level. Moreover, it must be kept in mind that regional innovation systems are not closed systems, and that every actor located in a region defines its own relevant cognitive networks, which are seldom limited to the region (Héraud 2000). One question to be addressed is under which conditions will the ERA – relying on networks of centers of excellence – be compatible with cohesion objectives. One possible answer is that such networks constitute mid-term assets for global competition, whereas regional convergence may ensure European competitiveness in the long run.

Taking firms' innovation-related needs as a starting point, the issue is clearly to support firms in the improvement of their innovativeness or at least to favor their absorptive and adaptive capacities. For that sake, the institutional supply is generally abundant and diversified (it is even sometimes described by firms as an overdimensioned system with overlapping instruments). Answering firms' needs is obviously the declared aim of all policies, but one cannot be convinced that policies are always based on real analytical knowledge of the demand. Such an evolution would constitute a collateral (and beneficial) effect of the introduction of a ERA for European regions.

NOTES

[1] There are examples of 'spatially oriented technology policies' though, e.g. the BioRegio competition organized by the German Federal Ministry for Education and Research. The aim of this competition was to identify and support so-called 'Bio Regions', i.e. regions that already possessed pre-requisites for a successful development of biotechnology. This was supposed to contribute to the overall goal of decreasing the 'biotechnology lag' of Germany in comparison with other nations (see for instance Dohse 2000).

[2] For an overview, cf. Muller et al. (2001, pp. 17–21).

[3] This database has been conceived and developed by the University of Hanover, the University of Cologne, the Technical University Bergakademie Freiberg and the Fraunhofer Institute for Systems and Innovation Research Karlsruhe on behalf of the German Research Foundation. The data collection in France benefited from the support of the department of economics (BETA) of the Louis Pasteur University of Strasbourg and from the department of regional economics (IERSO) of the Montesquieu University of Bordeaux. The research in South Holland, South Wales, Stockholm, Vienna and Barcelona was performed by the

Erasmus University of Rotterdam, the University of Wales, the Royal Institute of Technology Stockholm, the Business University of Vienna and the University of Catalonia, Barcelona.

4   Further information concerning the regional samples are given by Sternberg (2000, pp. 397 ff.) and Rink (2000, pp. 59 ff.). The regions that have been selected do not systematically correspond to the NUTS classification, whereas it is possible to introduce comparisons by using the NUTS levels 2 and 3 (cf. Muller et al. 2001, pp. 63–5).

5   The special issues of European Planning Studies, No. 4 (2000) as well as of *Raumordnung und Raumforschung* (No. 4, 1998) detail the ERIS samples and contain numerous papers on innovation and co-operation patterns in the investigated regions.

6   In particular, the recommendations expressed in the Frascati and Oslo manuals (OECD 1994; 1997).

7   In this respect, 'needs' are defined by proxy variables, i.e. on the base of firms' (negative) assessment concerning innovation conditions in their region.

8   The analysis was performed with SPSS, version 8.0.

9   The targets and orientation of regional policy actions were the object of field studies conduced in the frame of the RETINE project with the help of interviews in Alsace (France) and in Baden-Württemberg (Germany) (cf. Muller et al. 2001, pp. 67–91).

10 Cf. European Commission (1999, pp. 19–34).

REFERENCES

Autio, E. (1998), 'Evaluation of RTD in regional systems of innovation', *European Planning Studies*, **6** (2), 131–40.

Chabbal, R. (1995), 'Characteristics of innovation policies, namely for SMEs', *STI Review*, **16**, Paris: OECD: 103–40.

Clarysse, B. and U. Muldur (2001), 'Regional cohesion in Europe? An analysis of how EU public RTD support influences the techno-economic regional landscape', *Research Policy*, **30** (2), 275–96.

Dohse, D. (2000), 'Technology policy and the regions – the case of the BioRegio contest', *Research Policy*, **29**, 1111-33.

European Commission (1999), *European Spatial Development Perspective – Towards Balanced and Sustainable Development of the Territory of the European Union*, Luxembourg: Office for Official Publications of the European Communities.

European Commission and DG Regional Policy (2001): *Mission of the DG Regional Policy*, http://europa.eu.int/comm/dgs/regional_policy/mission/missi_en.htm, January 2001.

Héraud, J.A. (2000), *Regional Innovation Systems and European Research Policy: Convergence or Misunderstanding?*, paper presented at the Fifth Regional Science and Technology Policy Research Symposium (RESTPOR), Kashikojima, Japan, 5–7 September 1999.

Muller, E., R. de la Paix, K. Koschatzky, J.A. Héraud, F. Munier, I. Hugo, P. Shapira, R. Kahn and A. Zenker (2001), *RETINE (Regional Typology of Innovation Needs)*, report to the European Commission DG Research, Directorate C – Competitive and Sustainable Growth, Karlsruhe: Fraunhofer Institute for Systems and Innovation Research, ISI.

Nauwelaers, C. (2000), *Policy Learning for Innovation in European Regions*, paper presented at the Fifth Regional Science and Technology Policy Research

Symposium (RESTPOR), Kashikojima, Japan, 5–7 September 1999.

OECD (1994), *Proposed Standard Practice for Surveys of Research and Experimental Development*, Frascati Manual, fifth edition, Paris: OECD.

OECD (1997), *Proposed Guidelines for Collecting and Interpreting Technological Innovation Data*, Oslo Manual, second edition, Paris: OECD.

Rink, D. (2000), *Forschungskooperationen von Forschungseinrichtungen im Europäischen Vergleich*, Diploma thesis (unpublished), Marburg: Philipps-Universität Marburg.

Sternberg, R. (2000), 'Innovation networks and regional development – evidence from the European Regional Innovation Survey (ERIS): theoretical concepts, methodological approach, empirical basis and introduction to the theme issue', *European Planning Studies*, **8** (4), 389–407.

van Suntum, U. (1981), *Regionalpolitik in der Marktwirtschaft. Kritische Bestandsaufnahme und Entwurf eines alternativen Ansatzes am Beispiel der Bundesrepublik Deutschland*, Monographien der List Gesellschaft e.V, Volume 5, Baden-Baden: Nomos.

Wood, P. (1998), *The Rise of Consultancy and the Prospect for Regions*, paper presented at the 38th Congress of the European Regional Science Association, Vienna, 28–31 August 1998.

11 German Corporatism in Industrial R&D: Its National Structure and European Challenge

Hans-Willy Hohn and Jürgen Lautwein

INTRODUCTION

In most industrial societies, small- and medium-sized firms are more important for production and employment than the big companies. One of the reasons for this is that small- and medium-sized enterprises (SMEs) have a higher innovation potential than big, vertically integrated firms. However, unlike big companies, SMEs cannot create the preconditions for innovation internally. Their competitiveness and economic success depends largely on external support structures including, for example, access to public research organizations, information on technical components and complementary knowledge, and co-ordination services provided by private or public actors to facilitate collaborative research.

After the Second World War special institutional arrangements evolved in all national innovation systems that aimed to improve the export competitiveness of SMEs. As the research has shown these institutional regimes at the national level are quite diverse and differ strongly in their structure and performance. Nonetheless there are two basic types of national innovation systems and public funding of industrial research: the market-oriented Anglo-Saxon type that is mainly based on competition and the co-ordinated German model of innovation system that is mainly based on negotiations and co-operation. As a result, the German landscape of research and development is often viewed as a stable and organized system that favors incremental innovations in applied technologies. By contrast, the Anglo-Saxon system is seen as comparatively heterogeneous and unco-ordinated but, correspondingly more flexible and responsive and, therefore more likely to produce radical innovations (Soskice 1997).

Under the present conditions of economic globalization and European integration, however, these systems are getting more and more under the influence of, and into interaction with, transnational and supranational arrangements that are not necessarily compatible with the national structures. Up to now and at least with regard to SMEs European research policy corresponded more or less to the Anglo-Saxon model that does not easily fit with special governance forms of the German regime. This, of course, raises the question of how the structures of the national and supranational support systems for small and medium-sized firms interact and what institutional changes are emerging from their interaction.

This article gives a rather tentative answer to this question for the German case that is confined to a special research organization, the so called 'Arbeitsgemeinschaft industrieller Forschungsvereinigungen' (AiF) or 'German Federation of Industrial Cooperative Research Associations'.[1] The AiF represents a corporatist model of industrial research and development. The purpose of the AiF is *'Gemeinschaftsforschung'* or 'collective research' that is organized by the German economic associations.[2] It conducts and facilitates collaborative industrial research and development as a 'collective good' of whole industrial sectors and has its main focus on helping small- and medium-sized firms to innovate. This model of industrial R&D is very typical for the coordinated and co-operative structure of the German innovation system and in fact it is unique to this system.

The AiF is a relatively small research organization in terms of its financial budget and has even lost significance in the past decades compared to other organizations such as the Fraunhofer Society (FhG). Yet it meets crucial requirements and fulfils important functions for the existence and competitiveness of a broad and qualified '*Mittelstand*' which is an integral part of the German innovation system. *Gemeinschaftsforschung* contributes to a high degree to a 'diversified quality production' (Streeck 1991) of the German industry. But at the same time its capacity to innovate is largely limited to improvements of existing products. This corporatist model of industrial research seems well suited to facilitating incremental innovations in established technologies of the 'old' economy, but tends to be detrimental to the development of radical innovations and new technologies. Its co-operative and 'dense' institutional structure creates rigidities and favors innovations that conserve competencies and qualifications rather than destroying them. Hence, the organizational structure of *Gemeinschaftsforschung* seems hardly appropriate for the creation of new products and new markets.

Despite these weaknesses its organizational structure has remained stable for many decades. Hitherto there have been no endogenous attempts to reform this model and to experiment on alternative forms of research organization. However, the process of European integration is about to change the structure of the AiF and has already led to new forms of research organization within the associations. Facing growing pressures to adapt to the European research policy the associations however initially failed to extend the model of *Gemeinschaftsforschung* to the supranational level. Up to now at the European level there are no corporatist structures, and for a long time it seemed unlikely that the European Community would establish them since this appeared to be in conflict with the central guidelines of its research policy. As a result, the AiF developed a 'hybrid' structure and turned partly to the Anglo-Saxon model and its market-oriented instruments of research funding. The associations were forced to adapt to new forms of research organization oriented not only towards the production of collective goods, but towards private club goods of individual firms too.

This first phase of one-sided adaptation of the AiF to the conditions of European research policy now appears to be followed by a second phase of mutual adjustment. Surprisingly for most of the political and scientific observers, the European Commission recently has changed its strategy. Although it seemed for long time that *Gemeinschaftsforschung* remained limited to the German innovation system, European research policy now has established this corporatist model of research organization within the Sixth Framework Programme (FP6). This new attitude towards the model of *Gemeinschaftsforschung* is part of a general paradigmatic and strategic change of the European research policy. The FP6 is in fact a turning point in the European research policy as it recognizes for the first time the different structures of the national innovation systems and the different interests of the national research organizations.

As Chris Caswill points out in this volume, the new program can be seen as a reaction of the European Commission to increasing difficulties to cope with the institutional heterogeneity of the European research landscape and growing criticism by the Member States on the efficiency of its research management. As a result, European research policy has now turned towards a strategy of externalizing management tasks. This strategy aims at shifting the instruments and management of funding from the level of the European Union (EU) to the national innovations systems and national institutions. Accordingly, the research policy of the EU seems to change from a supranational regime to a heterogeneous and complex multi-level system. The outcomes of this change are highly uncertain and not predictable.

However, as the FP6 opens for corporatist actors it seems possible that at least in the case of research for SMEs it may lead now to a 'hybrid' structure of the European research system too. As a result of the new program a new structure may evolve that comprises elements of the Anglo-Saxon and German type of support systems for SMEs and even combines the advantages of the different regimes. The following Section 2 gives a coarse picture of the operative principles that constitute the institutional logic of the model of

Gemeinschaftsforschung and its typical strengths and weaknesses. Section 3 then sketches out the institutional changes that have taken place both at the national and European level.

NATIONAL INNOVATION SYSTEMS AND THE STRUCTURE OF *GEMEINSCHAFTSFORSCHUNG*

The institutional and organizational framework of production and application of scientific and technological knowledge in industrialized countries has a profound influence not only on economic performance but also on the rate and characteristics of innovation. The organizational structures of these 'national systems of innovation' (Freeman 1988; Nelson et al. 1993) obviously differ between countries. These national differences are frequently classified into two distinct groups: Anglo-American market-based structures and continental European corporatist structures, the United States representing the principle features of the former and Germany those of the latter (Porter 1990).

By way of illustration, public support of research in the United States is limited to basic research in 'core', often targeted, areas – such as health and defense – while research over and above this is usually left to the market. In contrast, support of industrial research and development and the provision of an appropriate organizational infrastructure is regarded as a responsibility of the state in Germany (Abramson et al. 1997). Accordingly, the German landscape of research and development is a stable and organized system that favors incremental innovations in established technologies and a 'diversified quality production' (Streeck 1991) while the US-system is heterogeneous and unco-ordinated but, correspondingly, more flexible and responsive and, therefore more likely to facilitate radical innovations and new technologies (Hollingsworth and Boyer 1997; Whitley 2000).

One of the undisputed advantages of the German innovation system lies in its ability to co-ordinate and organize industrial research and development on a co-operative basis. Since the Second World War, a polycentric and carefully delineated division of labor has developed that is specialized in particular technologies (Hohn and Schimank 1990). This system is highly oriented to the diffusion and transfer of technological knowledge and designed to facilitate co-operation between public research organizations and German industry (Jansen 1996). It is made up of corporatist actors that are specialized for specific types of investigation and divided into firmly defined organizational domains such as basic and applied research. This structure is guided by the idea that innovation processes correspond to a serial model of knowledge transfer from academic research to industrial development. Accordingly, the organizational architecture of the German innovation system is supposed to replicate a flow of knowledge that follows the different steps of this model (Hohn 1999).

In the realm of non-higher education the Max Planck Society (MPG) commits itself to 'pure' basic research while about twenty big science centers conduct applied basic research, for example in the fields of nuclear energy, biotechnology, and computer science. The FhG is designed to undertake industrial contract research and the AiF operates applied research and development partly financed by the German economic associations that represent whole industry sectors. At the same time, these corporatist actors are closely co-ordinated, integrated and networked into business. Innovation processes follow priorities set by German research policy and are, simultaneously, organized as a horizontal and largely self-co-ordinating transfer process. This structure facilitates enduring collaborative research between both the producers and the users of new knowledge.

These features of the German innovation system embody both its strengths and its weaknesses – one major weakness being that the potential for rapid reallocation of financial and organizational resources is significantly reduced. This reinforces specialization, segmentation, and fragmentation between the research organizations. It prevents the development of overlapping fields with multiple, heterogeneous, and competing research programs, restricts the free flow of new ideas and makes the evolution of new combinations of heterogeneous knowledge unlikely (Whitley 2000).

A similar effect can be attributed to the long-term, co-operative relationships obtaining between producers and users. These relations constitute 'ties' that cannot be severed easily and favor strategies of research and development that fall within established parameters and are oriented towards the incremental improvement of existing products. These are two sides of the same coin, which enable the German innovation system to produce high quality, if hardly radical, innovations (Sturgeon 1997). Radical innovations produce discontinuities and are, therefore, more likely to evolve in an uncoordinated and competitive system where agents act independently, as they do in the United States, than in a co-ordinated and co-operative system like Germany's (Casper 2000).

The typical strengths and weaknesses of the German innovation system are clearly visible in the case of the *Arbeitsgemeinschaft industrieller Forschungsvereinigungen* (AiF). The purpose of the AiF is *Gemeinschaftsforschung*. It conducts and facilitates collaborative research and development as a 'collective good' of whole industrial sectors and has its main focus on helping small- and medium-sized firms to innovate in incremental steps. This model of industrial R&D as a 'collective good' is unique to the German innovation system and does not occur in a similar form anywhere else in the world. Under the general umbrella of the AiF there are 107 research associations with approximately 50 000 SMEs. The associations run some 57 research institutes and also contract with other agents within the German innovation system (for example, the FhG and the German universities).

According to the logic of collective action (Olsen 1965) such an organization of collaborative industrial research and development is extremely difficult to achieve. It is facilitated by economic associations which play a predominant role in the German economy. The aim of the AiF, which was set up in the early 1950s, is to stimulate industrial R&D without distorting competition through subsidies or grants to individual businesses. The economic associations, with their own research institutes whose 'products' have the nature of club goods, offer a largely neutral form of state support for R&D. This type of support for industrial research and development in Germany appears simultaneously to have solved the problem of collective action and to have put forward innovation strategies across a whole range of industrial sectors. One of the main principles of the model of *Gemeinschaftsforschung* rests in the fact that the state does not directly intervene but rather provides funds to match the research funds (money and valued internal performances) raised by the associations. These so-called 'global' funds are allocated internally and without external intervention through a complex and multi-leveled process in which the associations compress the heterogeneous interests of the SMEs into research plans and decide on the industrial relevance of the different approvals. A multitude of different groups are party to the process. Around 50 per cent of the group members are from higher educational establishments and the other 50 or so per cent are from industry. The approval committee's vote is the basis for receiving the project budget from the AiF's global fund.

The AiF enjoyed a monopoly in the area of publicly funded industrial research and development in Germany until the late seventies when the FhG was added to the organizational landscape of the German innovation system in order to complement *Gemeinschaftsforschung* with industrial contract research. The FhG is also funded 'globally' and receives public funding as a percentage of the research funds its institutes raise through industrial contract research. However, the growth rates for contract research are much larger than those for the AiF's research. Today the budget of the FhG by far exceeds that of the AiF. In 1999 e.g. the FhG's budget approximately came to €610 million and was about twice the size of the budget of *Gemeinschaftsforschung* (AiF 1999; FhG 1999). This already indicates that the model of *Gemeinschaftsforschung* seems to be appropriate only to a specific type of innovation.

The AiF type of collective research allows small- and medium-sized firms which otherwise would hardly be able to afford such activities to participate in research and development. It also contributes to a dissemination of research resources and knowledge such that small firms benefit from the accumulated know-how of other members and of large companies in their sectors. At the same time, the results of this type of collective research have far-reaching consequences since they do not represent private or exclusive goods, as in contract-based research, but are instead available to every company, in reality predominantly the membership firms involved in the research association.

Apart from that, the AiF also has an unofficial function. It provides a platform for the informal exchange of information between the engineers and technical specialists of individual companies, who at this level are relatively free of the control of their employers. Their interaction facilitates a rapid diffusion of knowledge within firmly institutionalized interfirm networks. In sum, *Gemeinschaftsforschung* favors innovation policy that is permanently self-renewing in that research activities are embodied institutionally over the long term. As a result of these embodied cumulative competencies, the associations can strategically focus on research priorities which are regarded as furthering the competitiveness of the members.

It must hardly be mentioned that these operative principles of the model of *Gemeinschaftsforschung* require stable relationships of trust between the member firms of the associations. Stable relationships of trust are a *conditio sine qua non* of *Gemeinschaftsforschung* and play a more significant role than in short-term joint ventures and strategic alliances. As companies frequently have to provide as much information as possible on their strategic goals – simply in order to define collective projects – *Gemeinschaftsforschung* can only function properly on the basis of a normative integration that protects individual members from opportunistic competitive behavior.

It is here, however, that the competitive disadvantages of this model appear. In general the speed of innovation within the framework of *Gemeinschaftsforschung* often is determined by the least innovative and technologically most conservative companies. Moreover, *Gemeinschaftsforschung* depends predominantly on what Sturgeon calls 'thickly relational interactions between firms' (Sturgeon 1997), which are closely associated with structural rigidities. The operative principles of *Gemeinschaftsforschung* create 'strong bonds' and captive networks among the firms. While norms of trust and reciprocity prevent deviations from generally accepted behavior and reduce the threat of opportunism, they also tend to produce 'lock-in' among the actors. Accordingly, one of the main principles of *Gemeinschaftsforschung* is that the projects have to be for the benefit of all participants and must not provide any firm with an individual advantage.

As a consequence of these 'strong bonds' the model of *Gemeinschaftsforschung* often seems to show little more 'porosity' than vertical integration. While *Gemeinschaftsforschung* may ease and speed the information flow within the confines of networks, it creates substantial barriers to the free exchange of information with actors outside these networks. This is analogous to the effect of the boundary of the large, integrated firms. In fact, collective research in Germany in many cases boils down to a mere functional equivalent of vertical integration, as the strategic research objectives of the associations are, to a large extent, determined by big companies which have a vested interest in improving the productivity of their suppliers.

According to its operative logic, the model of *Gemeinschaftsforschung* performs very differently in different sectors and technological fields. It shows typical strengths in those sectors in which prevailing technologies allow continuous and incremental improvements in products and procedures. *Gemeinschaftsforschung* works well in the realm of machine-drive engineering where research is focused on the internal combustion engine, which can only be incrementally improved. The same appears to be true for the pump manufacture industry and research on fluid dynamics. Also in industrial adhesives, where there is a common need of chemical expertise to improve products incrementally, the model of *Gemeinschaftsforschung* seems to be beneficial (Lütz 1993).

In contrast, however the model of *Gemeinschaftsforschung* is ill equipped to develop radical innovations and to adapt to disruptive technological change. An area such as machine tools is illustrative of the problems this model encounters where technological change is discontinuous. Since the early eighties microelectronics and software engineering have increasingly replaced mechanical engineering in this sector and transformed it into a rapidly changing technological field. However, the AiF's research associations have not been able to cope with this transformation. Only through massive intervention by the federal government and through special aid programs have the small- and medium-sized firms been able to adapt to the new technologies in the machine tool industry. The microelectronic revolution gave rise to similar problems for the associations in the field of electromechanics. Within such technologically dynamic environments, collective research appears to be inappropriate. It is paralyzed by conflicting interests and disputes about research objectives and research strategies.

Despite its weaknesses the organizational structure of *Gemeinschaftsforschung* has remained stable for many decades. Hitherto there have been no endogenous attempts to reform this model of research organization, at least, not in those sectors and technological fields where its rigidities have led to serious competitive disadvantages for the member firms. However, the exogenous processes of European integration has challenged the endogenous stability of *Gemeinschaftsforschung*. As it appeared for a long time impossible to extend this model to the European level the associations were forced to adapt to new forms of research organization. This has led already to changes that seem non-reversible although European research policy itself recently has changed its strategy and now provides the possibility of *Gemeinschaftsforschung* at the European level.

FAILED ATTEMPTS TO CREATE A STRUCTURE FOR *GEMEINSCHAFTSFORSCHUNG* AT THE EUROPEAN LEVEL AND THE FP6

As the German model of *Gemeinschaftsforschung* does not occur in this form in any other European country the AiF and its associations have tried for a long time to create such a structure at the European level, but these attempts failed in the past. In the absence of corporatist actors in other countries and institutional arrangements that support this model at the supranational level, there was hardly a solution to the problem of collective action within the European context similar to the German one. This did not exclude that structures similar to the model of *Gemeinschaftsforschung* evolved at the European level in some sectors. However, this was restricted to special circumstances and special cases. In general *Gemeinschaftsforschung* seems the less attractive for the firms, the more the industries are subject to radical and discontinuous technological changes and the more the firms within sectors display heterogeneous and competing research interests. This has lead to a functional shift of the model of *Gemeinschaftsforschung*. Rather than conducting and facilitating collective research, the associations have develop into service organizations that provide support for interfirm collaboration at the European level.

The attempts of the AiF and its associations to create a corporatist structure at the level of the European research policy date back to the early seventies and led to the establishment of the 'Federation of European Industrial Cooperative Research Organisations' (FEICRO) in 1974. From the perspective of the AiF, FEICRO seemed to provide an opportunity to extend the German model of *Gemeinschaftsforschung* to the European level. It was supposed to serve as an umbrella organization for national research associations that acted according to the German model on behalf of the European Commission. As the AiF and its associations, however, had no organizational counterparts within the member countries of the EU, very heterogeneous members including individual firms make up FEICRO. Because of its heterogeneous structure, the federation was hardly able to pursue collective action. Moreover, the European Commission has not awarded FEICRO legal status as a negotiation partner.

In the past decades and Framework Programmes (FPs), the central guidelines of the European research policy differed strongly from the principles underlying *Gemeinschaftsforschung* as they were not oriented towards the production of collective, but private, club goods. In the past European research policy attempted to create transnational innovation networks mainly by funding bilateral or multilateral research collaboration between individual firms. The European Commission has established for this purpose the legal form of the European Economic Interest Grouping (EEIG), which should be of special benefit to small- and medium-sized firms. Two or more European partner organizations can found an EEIG and apply for project funds from the European Commission. This legal form has been used increasingly by other European research organizations to enter transnational collaborations, but has hitherto largely prevented the AiF and its associations from doing so. In principle, the AiF may also use the legal form of EEIG to extend its activities to the European level, but the organization would then have to co-operate with individual firms or other European partners whose interests might not square with the guidelines of *Gemeinschaftsforschung*.

Furthermore, the conditions of research funding put in practice by the European Commission conflict with the principles of self-regulation and self-government of *Gemeinschaftsforschung*. Extending its activities to the European level would put the autonomy of the AiF at risk and jeopardize the bottom-up processes of reaching consensus on research objectives and research strategies. Up to now European funds have been earmarked and not at the internal disposal of the AiF and its associations. 'The AiF has no control over this money', as a representative of the organization put it. The European Commission, on the other hand, argues that affording 'global' funds to the AiF to be allocated internally by the associations would be an unjustifiable privilege. Therefore, the European Commission refuses to finance the research activities of the AiF according to the German model through 'global' funds.

For a long time the German research associations hesitated to develop a strategy of internationalization. Many associations only recently opened their doors to the affiliation of foreign companies since they feared 'leakage' of know-how to foreign competitors and were worried about the solidarity of the German enterprises. Since the process of European integration confronts each single association with the same structural problem the AiF is facing, no strategy was developed to target the supranational level. In the late nineties, however, some of the big associations dropped their wait-and-see policy and took the initiative for another attempt at extending the model of *Gemeinschaftsforschung* to the European level. Arguing that they could not wait until the AiF implemented a corporatist structure at the European level, they used the legal form of EEIG to create institutions that are functionally equivalent to the model of *Gemeinschaftsforschung*. In order to gain leverage at the level of the European research policy they attempted to bring together in transnational associations the highest possible number of firms from the respective sectors.

However, after initial success this strategy came to a standstill. In the late nineties the German Engineering Federation (Verband deutscher Maschinen- und Anlagenbau e.V., VDMA) succeeded in forming the European Association of Pump Manufacturers (Europump). This association includes most European pump producers and, in fact, seems to come close to the model of *Gemeinschaftsforschung*. Accordingly, Europump was first taken as an example of how to extend this model to the supranational level. However, Europump appears to be an exception to the rule and cannot be generalized. The German associations did not manage to extend this model to other sectors furthermore. Arguably the most important reason, that allowed Europump to be successfully established as a transnational association, lies in the fact that pumps are standardized to a high degree and all manufacturers face similar basic technological problems. As a consequence, consensus on research and development projects usually aiming at incremental technological improvements can be easily reached. By contrast, in technologically more dynamic and discontinuous sectors it is less attractive for European firms to converge on the model of *Gemeinschaftsforschung* and the building of consensus is much more difficult and depends on contingent conditions.

Given the shift from national to supranational research and development activities and the obstacles to extending the model of *Gemeinschaftsforschung* to the European level, the German associations have increasingly been concerned about losing their *'raison d'être'*. In order to secure their structural stability and survival they have started to build up new infrastructures that are designed to support bilateral and multilateral research projects at the European level and enable small- and medium-sized firms to enter EEIGs. As a result, the associations already have transformed themselves to a certain degree from producers of collective goods at the German level into service organizations intermediating between the national and the European level. They provide support to German firms for research collaborations and strategic alliances with individual firms in other European countries and they help with the acquisition of European research funds. Apparently the traditional model of *Gemeinschaftsforschung* has lost significance in Germany. Yet with the intermediary services provided by some of the member associations of the AiF an opportunity for small and medium-sized German firms has emerged to engage in collaborative European research and development projects rather than being stuck in national containment and paralyzed by the need to achieve consensus in the AiF.

Accordingly, it came as a great surprise to most of the observers of the European research policy that the European Commission has changed its attitude towards the model of *Gemeinschaftsforschung* recently. Within the

FP6 for the period 2002–06 the European Commission now has established 'collective research' as a new instrument of research funding, and the AiF and its associations will be allowed to apply for funds at the European level.

This revised attitude towards *Gemeinschaftsforschung* is part of a new strategy of the European Commission that recognizes for the first time the national innovation systems and national research organizations as a bases for the implementation of its own policy. This radical strategic change has met considerable opposition within European research policy and is seen as a '*coup d'état*' of Research Commissioner, Philippe Busquin, who avoided successfully the conventional process of program formulation. In a social science perspective, however, the reform just as well appears as an attempt to solve the problems of 'bounded rationality' of hierarchical co-ordination by externalizing the management of the programs and projects.

In last years European research policy has been confronted with growing criticism by Member States, industry, and internal actors on the efficiency of its research management (see Edler in this volume). Especially the instruments of research funding for SMEs have been increasingly criticized as bureaucratic, ineffective, and costly. In face of these problems European research policy strives, as it seems, to delegate the tasks of program and project management to organizations like the AiF. This strategy of externalizing management tasks comes down to a loss of power of European research policy, but at the same time it reduces its transactions costs. It serves as reasonable solution to the external problems and internal conflicts of the Union or, as Chris Caswill puts it in his contribution to this volume, as a path through 'minefields'.

So it looks as if European research policy is on its way to a 'hybrid' system too. A system that shows a 'rich' institutional structure and comprises both market-oriented and collectively co-ordinated structures of research funding à la Great Britain and à la Germany. It does not appear impossible any longer that corporatist structures at the supranational level and even in other European countries may evolve. The new FP seems to facilitate a solution to the problem of collective action and to provide, therefore, a real chance for the AiF to extend the corporatist model to the level of the Union and other Member States.

Accordingly, the AiF already considers seriously the possibility of reviving FEICRO. Also projects on collective research issues have already started within a first program involving about 500 firms. As it shows, however, the different associations use the new possibilities of European research funding differently. Some participate in collective research projects, others prefer to engage in research collaborations. This would suggest that a diversified structure of research organization is evolving on the European level, which may provide the freedom to choose between different options according to the research requirements of the firms.

But nothing definite is known. The European Commission's new strategy of externalizing management tasks to the national level also may create a heterogeneous and complex multi-level system that leads to new imbalances and new conflicts. It may favor Member States that are provided with powerful organizational infrastructures and put nations at a disadvantage that are not equipped with such structures. However, at present it is not possible to predict the structural and institutional consequences of the European Commission's strategic change for European research policy and the national innovation systems. European research policy seems to be far away from institutional stability and still may lead to many a surprise.

NOTES

[1] This article is based on an ongoing project at the Research Institute for Public Administration Speyer on the transformation of the German research system outside the universities. As it is a report from the workshop, it presents preliminary empirical evidence and remains to a great extent speculative. More research is needed to identify the emerging patterns of structural and institutional change.

[2] Very broadly, *Gemeinschaftsforschung* can be translated as 'collective research'. However, it is better left in its original form in this paper as this term is associated with a specific collaborative and collective mode of research, which becomes lost in translation.

REFERENCES

Abramson, H.N., J. Encarmacao, U. Reid and U. Schmoch (1997), *Technology Transfer Systems in the United States and Germany*, Washington DC: National Academy Press.

AiF (1999), *Geschäftsbericht Arbeitsgemeinschaft Industrieller Forschungsvereinigungen*, Köln: AiF.

Casper, S. (2000), 'Institutional adaptiveness, technology policy and the diffusion of new business models: the case of German biotechnology', *Organization Studies*, **21**, 887–914.

Doremus, P.N., W.W. Keller, L. Pauly and S. Reich (1998), *The Myth of the Global Corporation*, Princeton, New Jersey: Princeton University Press.

FhG (1999), *Jahresbericht Fraunhofer-Gesellschaft*, München: FhG (Fraunhofer Society).

Freeman, C. (1988), *Technology Policy and Economic Performance. Lessons from Japan*, London: Pinter Publishers.

Hohn, H. (1999), 'Big Science als angewandte Grundlagenforschung. Probleme der informationstechnischen Großforschung im Innovationssystem der "langen" siebziger Jahre', in Ritter, G., M. Szöllösi-Janze and H. Trischler (eds), *Antworten auf die amerikanische Herausforderung. Forschung in der Bundesrepublik und der DDR in den 'langen' siebziger Jahren*, Frankfurt/Main and New York: Campus, pp. 50–80.

Hohn, H. and U. Schimank (1990), *Konflikte und Gleichgewichte im Forschungs-system. Akteurkonstellationen und Entwicklungspfade in der staatlich finanzierten außeruniversitären Forschung*, Frankfurt/Main and New York: Campus.

Hollingsworth, R. and R. Boyer (1997), 'Coordination of Economic Actors and Social Systems of Production', in Hollingsworth, R. and R. Boyer (eds), *Contemporary Capitalism: the Embeddedness of Institutions*, Cambrigde: Cambrigde University Press, pp. 1–48.

Jansen, D. (1996), 'Nationale Innovationssysteme, soziales Kapital und Innovatonsstrategien von Unternehmen', *Soziale Welt*, **45**, 411–34.

Kitschelt, H. (1991), 'Industrial governance, innovation strategies and the case of Japan. Sectoral governance or cross-national comparative analysis', *International Organization*, **45**, 453–93.

Lütz, S. (1993), *Die Steuerung industrieller Forschungskooperation. Funktionsweise und Erfolgsbedingungen des staatlichen Förderinstruments Verbundforschung*, Frankfurt/Main and New York: Campus.

Nelson, R.R. (ed.) (1993), *National Innovation Systems. A Comparative Analysis*, New York and Oxford: Oxford University Press.

Olsen, M. (1965), *The Logic of Collective Action*, Cambridge: Harvard University Press.

Porter, M. (1990), *The Competitive Advantage of Nations*, New York: Free Press.

Soskice, D. (1997), 'Technologiepolitik, Innovation und nationale Institutionengefüge Deutschland', in Naschold, F., D. Soskice, B. Hancké and U. Jürgens (eds), *Ökonomische Leistungsfähigkeit und institutionelle Innovation. Das Produktions- und Politikregime im globalen Wettbewerb*, Berlin: Edition Sigma, pp. 319–48.

Streeck, W. (1991), 'On the Institutional Conditions of Diversified Quality Production', in Matzner, E. and W. Streeck (eds), *Beyond Keynesianism. The Socioeconomics of Production and Full Employment*, London and Newbury Park: Sage, pp. 21–61.

Sturgeon, T.J. (1997), 'Turnkey Production Networks: a New American Model of Industrial Organization?', *BRIE-Working Paper*, **92A**.

Whitley, R. (2000), 'The institutional structuring of innovations strategies: business systems, firm types and patterns of technical change in different market economies', *Organization Studies*, **21**, 855–86.

PART III

Changing Governance: a Sectoral Perspective –
the Case of Biotechnology

12 International Innovative Activities, National Technology Competition and European Integration Efforts

Ulrich Dolata

INTRODUCTION: THE CASE OF BIOTECHNOLOGY

Biotechnology is a dizzy new field of scientific research and industrial innovation activities extending far beyond national institutional frameworks and policies. Firstly, the generation of new knowledge takes place in research institutions that are linked up by international scientific discussions, co-operations and research races with foreign counterparts. Secondly, the economic commercialization of biotechnology is determined by the activities of both established multinational enterprises and new technology-based start-up firms which invest, compete and co-operate principally at international level (Kuemmerle 1999; Dolata 1999; 2003).

Moreover, biotechnology policies too have been subdivided into a multi-level governance structure in the past two decades. Besides national innovation and technology policies regional biotechnology clusters and sub-national innovation policies have emerged and have constituted specific modes of local interaction between firms, banks and venture capital organizations, federations of industries, universities and technology transfer institutions (Center of Technology Assessment in Baden-Württemberg 2000). On the other hand the European Community has not only set a legal framework for biotechnological research and production, field trials, genetic food and plant protection but has also installed specific biotechnology research programs and – most recently – has developed a concept to link up the technology policies of the Member States and strengthen European integration in this policy field (European Commission 2000; 2001b).

Against this background I will take a look at the architectures of biotechnology policy and discuss the following questions: How are the different levels of policymaking intertwined? Is there a significant shift of policy efforts from the national to the sub-national and especially to the European level? And also: What remains of specific national systems of (biotechnological) innovation and especially of distinct national innovation and technology policies? Are the competencies and capacities of national policies being eroded under these circumstances?

THE EMERGENCE AND POLITICAL SUPPORT REGIONAL BIOTECHNOLOGY CLUSTERS

I will first take a brief look at the sub-national level – and the role that innovation policy activities play in the emergence of regional biotechnology clusters.

In the United States earlier and in Western Europe since the 1990s, one can observe an increasing concentration of biotechnological research and commercialization activities in a few regions or districts[1] of excellence – a phenomenon that is of growing importance for the competitive advantage of the leading nations in biotechnology. Typical characteristics of regional biotechnology clusters are a critical mass of scientific knowledge, embodied in excellent research institutions and qualified scientists, a high density of start-up firms, the existence of venture capital, of technology-transfer institutions and of local science parks as well as close (and often informal) collaboration structures between scientists, firms, banks, the local government etc. (Prevezer 1997; Center of Technology Assessment in Baden-Württemberg 2000; Braczyk et al. 1998).

These typical characteristics of biotechnology clusters are based on the traditional excellence of biotechnological research and education and the concentration of scientific institutions in the region that have encouraged the evolution of biotechnology start-ups as well as local investments of large-scale industry (Kenney 1986). To some extent since the 1980s and particularly during the 1990s, such evolutionary, bottom-up clustering dynamics were given strong support especially by specific national initiatives and programs – in the form of small business innovation research programs (in the United States or Great Britain) or inter-regional contests (like the BioRegio contest in Germany). Such national initiatives, especially the German contest, turned out to be major impulses in bundling up the formerly scattered regional resources and competencies and were crucial forces in connecting the regional actors (Dohse 1998; Audretsch 2001; Cooke 2001).

Until now the political support of regional clustering has been driven forward mainly by national authorities and policies. Regional innovation policy initiatives have become part of the national technology policies and reflect the increasing role that regional centers of scientific, technological and economic excellence play in the transnational innovation competition: The competitive advantage of the leading nations in biotechnology not only depends today on a strong science base and industrial performance in general, on the political support of large-scale domestic industry or on the provision of the general political-economic and legal conditions that stimulate investment and innovation. It depends, too, on the existence of a few areas where industrial and scientific activities are clustered and which are attractive for investments from wherever they come from.

Against this background my *first argument* is that in the leading countries biotechnology regions must be considered first of all as parts of their national systems of innovation and governance. The competitive advantage of the leading nations in biotechnology depends increasingly on the existence and efficiency of such regional centers of excellence. The national technology policies have reacted (sometimes very successfully, as in Germany) to this challenge: National programs, initiatives or contests have played (and still play) an important catalytic role in the evolution of regional biotechnology clusters. Regionalization has therefore not led to a loss of influence of national policies. Instead it seems that this is a guided regionalization, stimulated and co-ordinated first of all by national policies – and, of course, underpinned by additional efforts of regional authorities and actors.

NATIONAL INNOVATION SYSTEMS AND COMPETING BIOTECHNOLOGY POLICIES

The leading countries have increasingly developed a broad spectrum of instruments to influence technological development, the environments for scientific research and industrial innovation or the public perception of new technologies since the 1980's. Regional innovation policies are only a part of the corresponding national activities which range from financing the public research institutions, funding research projects and establishing specific technology programs through to initiatives designed to stimulate the networking between and the technology transfer from academia to industry and to economic incentives that aim at supporting the emergence of new technology firms (Meyer-Krahmer 1999; Kuhlmann 2001). This is also the position in biotechnology. On the other hand the national policies are confronted with highly internationalized innovation and commercialization dynamics in this technology field. In contrast to the assumption of a 'continuing domestication of large firms' 'innovative activities' (Pavitt and Patel 1996, p. 146; Patel 1995) the major European pharmaceutical and agrochemical groups in particular are highly internationalized corporations. They have located their biotechnological R&D activities, production facilities and inter-firm co-operation projects at various sites in Western Europe, North America and partly in Japan and have become ever more independent of national policies since the 1980's (Schwartz and Dibner 1992; Dolata 1996; OECD 1996; Kuemmerle 1999; Hagedoorn et al. 2000).

Against the background of such highly internationalized innovation environments a very obvious question to pose is, what remains of distinct national innovation systems and technology policies? Are the national systems converging to uniformity under these circumstances? And are the competencies and capacities of national policies being eroded against the background of the indisputable strong internationalization of markets, firms and technologies (Grande 2001a)?

I will make two points concerning these questions:

1. There is strong empirical evidence that international knowledge production, technology races and commercialization efforts have not led to a uniformity of the national innovation systems and technology policy initiatives in biotechnology until now. Of course, the leading countries clearly copy each other. In biotechnology they try to learn especially from the outstanding US model. Especially with initiatives that aim to intensify the competition between research institutions, to stimulate the technology transfer from academia to industry, to support the development of start-up firms or to promote the emergence of regional biotechnology clusters the Western European countries try to imitate and adapt successful elements of the US American biotechnology innovation system. But they do it their own special way, with different priorities and emphasis and against the background of very different national innovation cultures, institutional contexts and political systems. Recent research has shown that there are still great differences in biotechnological innovation patterns not only between Western Europe as a whole and the United States but also between the European countries. These differences range from the distinct national research and education systems and unique structures of the biotechnology-related industry and inter-firm collaborations through to the financial systems, the demand and market structures or the public perception and social management of biotechnology. And they are also based on a considerable capacity gradient between the leading countries (Germany, Great Britain and France) and the weaker nations (such as Italy or Greece) (Senker and van Zwanenberg 2001; Henderson et al. 1999; Gottweis 1998; Bartholomew 1997). All in all there is little evidence so far of advanced tendencies towards uniformity or the emergence of a coherent European biotechnology innovation system. The European biotechnology space is characterized to a great extent instead by distinct as well as fragmented national innovation systems of different sizes and capacities, market and

demand structures, public discussions and policy activities.

2. These fragmented national systems of innovation and the national policies are first of all intertwined by patterns of competition and rivalry. The leading European countries clearly compete for the pole position in European biotechnology – and they do so with distinct national policy efforts (Ernst & Young 2001, pp. 66–74; for Germany see BMBF 2000b, pp. 14–23; 2001).[2] The international performance of the corporations involved sets the tone of this rivalry – in two respects: On the one hand the multinational corporations have emancipated themselves from their national innovation systems and the territorially-based scope of national policies and today are able to choose the best locations for their investments globally. This forces the national policies to compete for the most excellent and attractive innovation-oriented infrastructures as major prerequisites for their competitive advantage in biotechnology. On the other hand, since the links between national policies and domestic corporations have been loosened, the main emphasis of national technology policy activities in Europe has changed significantly. It has shifted from the direct public support of the leading home-based companies to more indirect strategies concerning the promotion of innovative landscapes that are attractive for both further scientific development and economic commercialization – a strategic turn that is, incidentally, widely accepted by the major enterprises involved which are more interested in reliable legal frameworks or in excellent research institutions and start-up firms which are open for co-operation than in the direct public subsidy of their traditionally self-organized and self-financed corporate activities.

A remarkable strategic change of this kind in Germany may be observed as an example. In the 1980s national activities were still concentrated on the support of the big industrial players such as Hoechst, Bayer or BASF and the political authorities 'seemed to accept the view that German competitiveness in biotechnology could be achieved without creating new forms of corporate enterprise, such as the American start-up firms, or more systematic university–industry linkages' (Jasanoff 1985, p. 30; Dolata 1996). This traditional strategy changed significantly during the 1990s. Increasingly from the mid-1990s onwards, the German biotechnology policy was renewed by a bundle of initiatives and contests to stimulate the emergence of regional biotechnology clusters (the BioRegio- and BioProfile contests), to concentrate the research in a few lead projects and world-class research centers (so-called 'Leitprojekte' and 'Kompetenzzentren'), to strengthen national networks between public research institutions and industry and to support new start-up firms. In terms of effectiveness one can hardly say that this strategic reorientation was not successful: Although Germany made a relatively late start in the commercial development of this technology and lagged behind other comparable nations up until the first half of the 1990s it is today the leading country in European biotechnology together with the United Kingdom. The recent national biotechnology policy initiatives made a considerable contribution to this outcome (Barnett et al. 1998; Ernst & Young 2000; BMBF 2000a; 2001).

All these things considered, my *second argument* is that despite all prophecies of doom, national innovation and technology policies do matter even in such highly internationalized environments as those in biotechnology. Of course, the state's capacity is limited. Technology policies are not able to influence the directions of scientific research and economic commercialization significantly (but, in all honesty, this is something they have never been able to do). The latter are first of all determined by the autonomous and self-organized dynamics that take place mainly within the scientific and the economic system itself, particularly in such fast-paced, small-sized and decentralized technology fields as biotechnology. Moreover, the formative influence of an internationalized economy on national policies has undoubtedly increased – and has led to the omnipresent struggles for competitive technological and economic advantage that dominate national policies today.

But these structural limitations of and external influences on national technology policies have not led to a far-reaching erosion of state capacity in biotechnology policy, as, for instance, Edgar Grande (2001a) suggests. When it is accepted that the biotechnology innovation systems are still nationally based and internationally intertwined first of all by patterns of rivalry, coherent national innovation and technology policies are of crucial importance for their modernization, advancement and competitiveness. They can play an active part in the shaping and supporting of innovation-oriented biotechnological infrastructures that range from internationally acknowledged research establishments and efficient technology transfer mechanisms to regional clusters of scientific and economic activities through to a strong sector of start-up firms as well as important domestic facilities of multinational corporations. Furthermore it should not be forgotten that national authorities also remain indispensable for the mediation and the social management of the public controversies surrounding this technology. Taken together this amounts to a great deal.

EUROPEAN STATE OF THE ART: LEGAL ACTIVITIES AND TECHNOLOGY POLICIES WITHIN THE EU

In fairness it should be stated that this is not the whole picture. In Europe national biotechnology policies and innovation systems are not only intertwined by patterns of competition and rivalry but at the same time linked up by systems of transnational negotiations, which take place mainly within the European Union. Over the past twenty years the European Community has reached a new level of governance in biotechnology – mainly in two areas: in the implementation of a legal framework for biotechnological research, production and commercialization, and in the institutionalization of specific biotechnology research programs (Cantley 1995).

European Governance I: Legal Activities

Responsibilities for the set up of a *legal framework* have shifted heavily from the national to the European level since the late 1980s. Meanwhile, the responsibilities concerning legal aspects take place mainly at the European level (Schenek 1995) – and are reflected in a whole string of relevant directives that have been enacted by the European Union ranging from regulations for biotechnological research, production and marketing over rules for the deliberate release and the commercial planting of genetically modified crops through to regulations concerning novel food and patent protection (European Commission 2001b, pp. 17–22). In addition to the directives that have to be transferred into national law new regulatory authorities have emerged within the European Union. The European Medicines Evaluation Agency (EMEA) is a prominent example here. Since its inauguration in 1995 it has co-ordinated the drug approval system within Europe and has installed centralized approval procedures for biotechnology medicines (Senker and van Zwanenberg 2001, pp. 54 f.).

As a result the negotiations and decisions dealing with legal aspects of biotechnology have also shifted from the national to the European Governance level – with the European Commission and the European Parliament, the governments and responsible ministries of the Member States and the relevant pressure groups of the European lobbying process – attention should be drawn in particular in this context to the industrial federation EuropeBio established in 1996 – as influential negotiation parties (Cantley 1995, pp. 633–5; Bandelow 1997; 1999).

But even this significant Europeanization of the legal activities and regulations concerning biotechnology has not led to a dramatic loss of influence of national authorities, actors and controversies until now. National actors and interests are closely involved in the European negotiations and are often able to set the tone in the decision-making processes.

Under the influence of industrial and scientific demands as well as national controversies and a persistent low public acceptance of the technology, the governments (or the responsible ministries) of the Member States have intervened time after time with own initiatives in the European decision-making process. Moreover, they have several times slowed down the transformation of existing directives into national law or blocked the executive process. We can observe this by taking a brief look at the discussions and negotiations concerning re- or deregulation of the existing European directives since the mid-1990s. The first initiative to amend the existing directives was developed by the German government in the mid 1990s and aimed at a deregulation. During the following years, food crisis, the BSE scandal and the persistent skepticism of the public against genetically modified products set the governments of the Member States under heavy pressure and altered their political outlook significantly. Towards the end of the decade the Member States agreed on a moratorium for the commercial planting of genetically modified crops, and some of them also agreed to block any new licenses until the European Union had developed a more restrictive legal framework. Moreover, some Member States have decided to stop the import of genetically modified crops on their own authority. These vehement interventions of the Member States, together with controversial domestic debates of the issues frequently conducted in a highly emotional tone, have led to revised rules on the deliberate release of genetically modified organisms into the environment and on food safety that differ significantly from the existing ones (Dreyer and Gill 2000; Hodgson 2000; Bauer and Gaskell 2002, pp. 21–94; European Commission 2001b, pp. 17–22). In summary, it was the national governments that turned out to be the proactive authorities (not only) in this debate and the negotiations that followed, while the European Commission remained reactive and had to be pushed forward by the political pressure of the Member States and the national controversies on the risks and regulations of biotechnology.

Moreover, the European lobbying and pressure groups involved, including the well-organized ones, remain highly dependent on the resources and expertise of their national members. Even the most influential industrial federation EuropeBio has only a small staff in Brussels. The bulk of legal and political expertise still comes from the national federations that are members of EuropeBio – in Germany this is the so-called *Deutsche Industrievereinigung Biotechnologie (DIB)*, a subdivision of the *Verband der Chemischen Industrie (VCI)* – and is provided mainly by the large-scale enterprises as the most influential members of the national pressure groups. The latter do not only try to influence the European Commission's policy directly through the activities of EuropeBio but at the same time collaborate closely with their national governments and also aim to influence their initiatives in the European negotiations (Grant 1993; Greenwood 1997; Ronit 1997; Bongert 2000, pp. 137–41). The advanced Europeanization of legal policies in biotechnology has not led to a clear-cut shift of lobbying activities from the national arenas to the European level but has constituted patterns of coexistence: Because the

European policy arena is of increasing importance for lobbying activities especially in the field discussed, the activities of the European pressure groups have increased as well. But they remain influenced by the power and dependent on capacities of their national counterparts. Besides, the national interest groups often pursue their own activities to influence the European decision-making process by collaborating with their national governments.

Finally, while the legal responsibilities have shifted to the European governance level, the public controversies around the technology mainly take place in very distinct national settings. The 1990s have shown that the peak, the priorities and the fierceness of controversial discussions differed significantly between the Member States and have enforced specific national modes of conflict management and the organization of public debates that range from establishing issue-specific advisory groups, commissions and hearings to round tables and mediation projects (Behrens 2000; Dreyer and Gill 2000; Bauer and Gaskell 2002). Of course, the European Commission had to react to the growing public concern over the social impact of biotechnology in the Member States and has established its own bioethics advisory group as well as an advisory panel of prominent biologists to consider such controversies (European Commission 2001b, pp. 14 f.). But this doesn't alter the fact that the main arenas of the social debates concerning novel food, deliberate release or the cloning of human cells and animals remain the national ones. European debate on biotechnology has until now not been much more than the sum of the national debates that the national authorities have to moderate and struggle with.

My *third argument* is therefore, that of course there has been a significant shift of legal responsibilities from the national to the European Governance level in the 1990s. During the past decade the European Union became a major player in the regulation of biotechnology and has developed and enacted a body of directives that are binding for the Member States. But this cannot be interpreted as the emergence of a new hierarchical structure with the European Commission as the new leading actor on the top and the European arena of policymaking as the most important one today. The European Union's legal activities are embedded in a multi-level governance system instead. Even in the case discussed national authorities, actors and debates still play a key role and are able to initiate and to speed up as well as to protract or to block the European negotiation and decision-making process.

European Governance II: Innovation and Technology Policies

In the second field of European biotechnology activities, *technology policy*, such a comprehensive shift is scarcely to be identified through to the present.

It is true that the European Union has become a serious player in technology policy too. Since the early 1980s the EU has established ever increasing Framework Programmes (FPs) for research and technological development that are targeted at a number of advanced technologies, particularly including sectoral programs to support the research in information and communication technologies and in biotechnology. The sum of the European Union's spending on biotechnological research has increased substantially through to the present, has caught up with the corresponding resources of the leading Member States and is of considerable importance in supporting the biotechnology related research and infrastructure in the weaker countries (Bongert 2000; European Commission 2001a).

But European biotechnology policy has not yet been able to integrate the fragmented national research infrastructures of the Member States and to stimulate the scientific co-operation within Europe effectively, to strengthen the transnational networking between academia and industry or to co-ordinate the national innovation and technology policies of the Member States. The European Commission itself stresses this negative record in its 'Communication Towards a European Research Area' by stating that 'it cannot be said that there is today a European policy on research. National research policies and Union policy overlap without forming a coherent whole'. Furthermore: 'Above the European research effort as it stands today is no more than the simple addition of the efforts of the 15 Member States and the Union' (European Commission 2000, p. 7). All this is also applicable to biotechnology – with the exception of the Human Genome Program, which was established as a joint European reaction to the US American counterpart (Abels 2000).

What are the reasons for this 'fragmentation, isolation and compartmentalization of national research efforts and systems', to use the European Commission's own words again?

The first reason for the lack of coherence and co-ordination in European technology policy has already been mentioned: All leading nations are heavily involved in international technology races and fierce struggles over competitive economic and technological advantages around this technology. These struggles do not only take place between economic blocs – the United States and Western Europe, for instance – but also between the leading Member States of the EU. To become No. 1 in European biotechnology is, for instance, the official goal of German policy since the mid-1990s. In this competitive environment the capacities of the national innovation systems in biotechnology remain of high strategic importance and support the persistence of national selfishness as well as the fragmentation of national innovation and technology policies within Europe (Kuhlmann 2001; Dolata 2001).

Another reason can be derived from the typical characteristics of the technology itself. Biotechnology is not a large technical system or a network technology, its development and application are small-sized and decentralized. For the most part there is no technology-based need for large-scale projects which can only be financed and implemented through a few internationally organized networks or consortia. On the contrary scientific research as well as the emergence of technological applications in biotechnology are driven forward by countless (academic and industrial) projects and numerous co-operations, which are mainly organized by the scientific and economic actors involved themselves. Apart from a few exceptions (such as the Human Genome Project mentioned, which can be characterized as small big science where decentralized activities have to be co-ordinated efficiently) there is no political necessity to organize and co-ordinate big projects and large research facilities – neither on the national nor on the European level (Dolata 2000).

Finally, the remarkable lack of industrial interest in European technology policy and especially in biotechnological research programs is worth mentioning (Bongert 2000; Abels 2000). The industrial actors involved here, especially the big players, are interested in reliable legal frameworks that support their activities, in excellent academic research establishments and efficient technology transfer systems, in a strong sector of new start-up firms with which they can collaborate or in tax incentives. But they are not much interested in participating in public research programs. In contrast to the information technology industry, the research and development of the pharmaceuticals and chemicals industry is traditionally self-organized and self-financed. The industrial actors involved here, especially the big players, do not only organize their research and development activities for themselves, they also prefer to collaborate and co-operate with academic institutions and other firms directly, without the medium of public programs. And they prefer to go shopping whenever and wherever they like – and pay the bills. They do so not only because of their philosophy, they can do so because of the specifics of this technology as described above: In contrast to large technical systems and big science, it is small-sized, very specialized and applicable in decentralized surroundings. This supports fluid and self-organized collaborations within the industry and between industry and academia – without state aid (Dolata 2002).

My *fourth argument* is therefore, that even though the European Union has become a relevant player in biotechnology policy too and has increased its spending on biotechnology related research programs substantially, Europe has until now failed to develop a consistent and coherent research and technology policy. This failure is rooted firstly in the fact that the national policies are of high strategic importance for obtaining competitive advantages, secondly in the typical characteristics of the technology discussed and finally in the fact that the European Commission has until now not been able to depend on powerful industrial counterparts that want or need a strong European technology policy in this field.

ARCHITECTURES OF THE INNOVATION AND GOVERNANCE SYSTEM IN BIOTECHNOLOGY

Let us pause to take stock of the political and innovation system structures in biotechnology (see Figure 12.1). What is worth mentioning?

First of all, the Europeanization of biotechnology policy and regulation has developed differently. A significant shift towards the European governance level and – not discussed in this paper – towards international organizations and regimes too[3] can be observed in the implementation of legal frameworks for this technology. The main reason for the advanced Europeanization and internationalization in this case is that the international harmonization of reliable legal frameworks is – like norms or standards in other technologies – a major prerequisite for research, production, commercialization and trade in this area. In contrast to this, the strategies and policies that aim at getting competitive advantages are still the domain of national technology policies, programs, negotiations and decisions. Over and above this, the national settings are also the main levels where the public controversy around this technology takes place.

Secondly, biotechnology policies (and not only these) are today embedded in a multi-level governance system (Grande 2001b). But this is not a hierarchically structured system, where the policies of the Member States are becoming subordinate to the European policymaking level. The various policymaking levels exist side by side instead. In relevant fields of governance national arenas, authorities and actors remain of substantial importance. But even where a significant Europeanization of policies is to be seen national authorities, actors and interests are able to bring a strong influence to bear. They are systematically included in the European negotiations and decision-making procedures. And especially the leading countries have the power to stimulate and speed up as well as protract or block European integration and harmonization efforts.

And *finally*, the European system is not only a system of negotiations (it is that of course, too) but at the same time an area of fierce competitive struggles, technology races and strategies to win economic and technological advantages. It is true that negotiations have become an essential mode of political interaction within the EU. But at the same time biotechnology policies are embedded in and influenced by an international system of competition. The leading nations and economic blocs do not interact at all exclusively by patterns of co-operation and negotiation but also by patterns of (economic)

Figure 12.1 The innovation and governance system in biotechnology

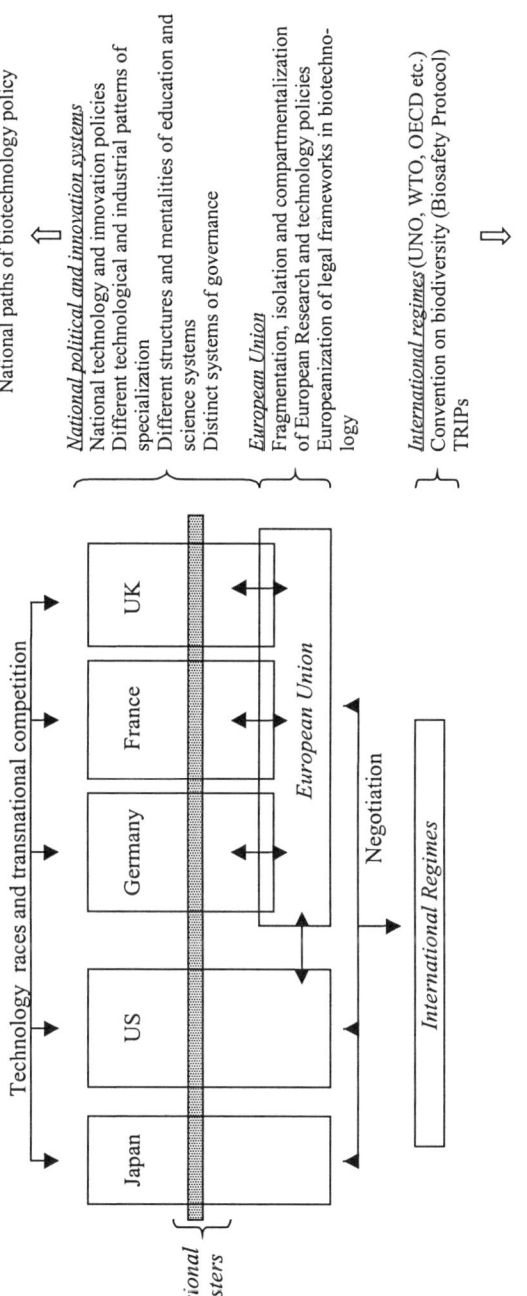

rivalry. One can hardly explain the lack of coherence and co-ordination in European technology policy when one loses touch with this competitive level of political interaction.

TOWARDS AN EUROPEAN RESEARCH AREA?

During the past two years the European Commission has developed a new concept that aims at integrating research and co-ordinating technology programs and policies within the EU in a more efficient and coherent manner. Against the background of the discussed case I will finally make a few more or less speculative remarks on the idea and the perspectives of a 'European Research Area' as outlined by the European Commission (European Commission 2000; 2001a; 2001b; see also Caracostas, Banchoff and Caswill in this volume).

The *first remark* concerns the *problem of disintegrated science and research* in Europe. It is an obvious fact (and an old problem) that the European research space is populated by a lot of smaller institutes that are struggling to achieve critical mass instead of by a few European centers of excellence. So it is not surprising that the European Commission has made suggestions to strengthen and intensify the European *networking* of existing national research centers as well as public/private partnerships. They range from opening up the national research programs for transnational access through to the support of European centers of excellence and the networking of specialist research centers and industrial research facilities throughout the countries of the Union. Even though this is not a new goal of the European Commission's policy, the featured instruments could well be so: The European Commission seems to have recognized that networking cannot be ordered from the top down, but depends to a great extent on the autonomous and self-co-ordinated initiatives and activities of the research establishments themselves – especially in such fast-paced, decentralized and fragmented technology fields as biotechnology. Accordingly, the Community seems to prefer a soft and indirect strategy of stimulating networks. It is based on benchmarking activities, which aim at comparing the quality of public, and, where possible, private research as well as identifying centers of excellence that are able to carry out common programs of activities. Schemes to finance such centers are to be developed on the basis of periodical evaluations and competition. Networking in general should be stimulated first of all by calls for proposals and contests.

All this may lead to stimulating effects on the integration of science and the European networking of research establishments. But especially against the background of biotechnology we have to bear in mind that the quality and intensity of co-operations and networking is first of all dependent on the self-organized and self-co-ordinated activities of the research institutions and corporations involved themselves – national and particularly European initiatives are only of additional importance. And besides this we have to consider that the envisaged concentration of science and research in a few centers of excellence may not be the ideal way to support such a small-scale and specialized technology as biotechnology. There are almost endless frenetically paced and decentralized activities in myriads of small-scale establishments and start-up firms, which have a considerable impact on the development of the technology too. Small can be beautiful.

My *second remark* concerns the *lack of coherence and co-ordination of national and European technology policies*. Although the European Commission is aware of this problem, the only suggestions made are to develop a benchmarking system of national research policies and to improve science and technology foresight, statistics and indicators. In contrast to the past, the European Commission doesn't claim new competencies in technology policy but instead emphasizes its role as a catalyst and co-ordinator of activities, which take place mainly on the national and sub-national level. This is an admirable restraint which recognizes the persistent dominance of national technology policies within the EU as well as the fact that even though the industrial innovative activities are highly internationalized the national and sub-national innovation infrastructures remain the most important ones concerning the production of new knowledge and technologies.

The future role of the European Union as a player in technology policy will be confined to the forecasting of technological developments and the benchmarking of national policies as well as to the co-ordination of the national activities and the stimulation of European networking. Paradoxically, concentrating on this restrained scope of duties may turn out to be a successful strategy for further European integration – not only because it takes into account national selfishness but particularly because it acknowledges the necessity of distinct and autonomous national and sub-national policies. Therefore one can hardly expect the emergence of a European technology policy which could replace or compete with the national policies. So far as I can see the recent initiatives undertaken will not remove the existing balance between the European and national responsibilities and competencies in technology policy.

NOTES

[1] California (San Francisco, Los Angeles, San Diego) and the Northeast (Massachusetts, New York) in the United States, London and 'Oxbridge' in Great Britain, Munich, Berlin and North Rhine Westphalia in Germany and the Paris area in France are among the most important regional biotechnology clusters (European Commission 2001b, p. 11).

2   See, for instance, the general outline of the Federal Research Report of the German Ministry of Education and Research: 'The innovative strength of business and science will determine Germany's sustainable success in the future. The framework conditions for education and research and for dynamically evolving markets must be improved in order to cope with the process of globalization and the changeover from an industrial to a knowledge society. Germany has both highly skilled people and an excellent scientific-technological foundation for the technologies of the 21ˢᵗ century. But it will be the rapid implementation of new technologies on the world markets that will decide whether our country will be able to keep pace with ever shorter innovation and product cycles. The Federal Government focuses on the innovation process as a whole. The results of research and development, both those obtained in Germany and those available worldwide, must be converted into new products, processes and services faster than ever before, so as to enable Germany to hold its own against the competition of other leading technology regions of the world. This requires above all internationally competitive framework conditions.' (BMBF 2000b, pp. 14 f. [translated by the author]).

3   Worth mentioning are firstly the 'Agreement on Trade Related Aspects of Intellectual Property Rights' (TRIPS) which was negotiated within the 'General Agreement on Tariffs and Trade' (GATT) and regulates besides other things intellectual property rights concerning biotechnological inventions. And secondly, the 'Convention on Biological Diversity' (CBD) and the 'Biosafety Protocol' included which regulate the protection and the (industrial) use of biological diversity as well as safety precautions concerning the use of and trade with genetically modified organisms (Barben 2001).

REFERENCES

Abels, G. (2000), *Strategische Forschung in den Biowissenschaften. Der Politikprozeß zum europäischen Humangenomprogramm*, Berlin: edition sigma.

Audretsch, D.B. (2001), *Die Rolle kleiner Unternehmen in der Entwicklung US-amerikanischer Biotech-Cluster*, Stuttgart: Akademie für Technikfolgenabschätzung in Baden-Württemberg, Arbeitsbericht Nr. 107.

Bandelow, N. (1997), 'Ausweitung politischer Strategien im Mehrebenensystem. Schutz vor Risiken der Gentechnologie als Aushandlungsmaterie zwischen Bundesländern, Bund und EU', in Martinsen, R. (ed.), *Politik und Biotechnologie. Die Zumutung der Zukunft*, Baden-Baden: Nomos, pp. 153–68.

Bandelow, N. (1999), *Lernende Politik. Advocacy-Koalitionen und politischer Wandel am Beispiel der Gentechnologiepolitik*, Berlin: edition sigma.

Barben, D. (2001), 'The Global Configuration of the Biotechnology Regime in Comparative Perspective', in Bammé, A., G. Getzinger and B. Wieser (eds), *Yearbook 2001 of the Institute for Advanced Studies on Science, Technology and Society*, München and Wien: Profil, pp. 41–86.

Barnett, R., G.J. Clements, J.N. Grindley, N.M. MacKenzie, U. Roos and D. Yarrow (1998), *Biotechnology in Germany,* Report of an ITS Expert Mission, Bonn.

Bartholomew, S. (1997), 'National systems of biotechnology innovation: complex interdependence in the global system', *Journal of International Business Studies*, **2** (4), 241–66.

Bauer, M.W. and G. Gaskell (2002), *Biotechnology – the Making of a Global Controversy*, Cambridge: Cambridge University Press.

Behrens, M. (2000), 'Nationale Innovationssysteme im Gentechnikkonflikt: Ein Vergleich zwischen Deutschland, Großbritannien und den Niederlanden', in Barben, D. and G. Abels (eds), *Biotechnologie – Globalisierung – Demokratie.*

Politische Gestaltung transnationaler Technologieentwicklung, Berlin: edition sigma, pp. 205–27.

BMBF (2000a), *Bericht des Fachdialogs 'Beschäftigungspotenziale im Bereich Bio- und Gentechnologie' im Rahmen des Bündnisses für Arbeit, Ausbildung und Wettbewerbsfähigkeit*, Bonn: BMBF (Federal Ministry for Education and Research).

BMBF (2000b), *Bundesbericht Forschung 2000*, Bonn: BMBF (Federal Ministry for Education and Research).

BMBF (2001), *Rahmenprogramm Biotechnologie – Chancen nutzen und gestalten*, Bonn: BMBF (Federal Ministry for Education and Research).

Bongert, E. (2000), *Demokratie und Technologieentwicklung. Die EG-Kommission in der europäischen Biotechnologiepolitik 1975–1995*, Opladen: Leske + Budrich.

Braczyk, H.J., P. Cooke and M. Heidenreich (1998), *Regional Innovation Systems*, London: UCL.

Cantley, M.F. (1995), 'The Regulation of Modern Biotechnology: a Historical and European Perspective', in Brauer, D. (ed.), *Biotechnology: Legal, Economic and Ethical Dimensions*, vol. 12, Weinheim: VCH, pp. 505–681.

Center of Technology Assessment in Baden-Württemberg (2000), International Workshop on Comparing the Development of Biotechnology Clusters, Stuttgart (presented papers).

Cooke, P. (2001), *Biotechnology-Cluster in Großbritannien*, working paper N° 107, Stuttgart: Akademie für Technikfolgenabschätzung in Baden-Württemberg.

Dohse, D. (1998), *The BioRegio-Contest – a New Approach to Technology Policy and Its Regional Consequences*, Kiel Working Paper N° 880, Kiel: The Kiel Institute of World Economics.

Dolata, U. (1996), *Politische Ökonomie der Gentechnik. Konzernstrategien, Forschungsprogramme, Technologiewettläufe*, Berlin: edition sigma.

Dolata, U. (1999), 'Innovationsnetzwerke in der Biotechnologie?', *WSI-Mitteilungen*, **2**, 132–41.

Dolata, U. (2000), 'Hot House – Konkurrenz, Kooperation und Netzwerke in der Biotechnologie', in Barben, D. and G. Abels (eds), *Biotechnologie – Globalisierung – Demokratie. Politische Gestaltung transnationaler Technologieentwicklung*, Berlin: pp. 181–204.

Dolata, U. (2001), 'Weltmarktorientierte Modernisierung. Eine Inventur rot-grüner Forschungs- und Technologiepolitik', *Blätter für deutsche und internationale Poltik*, **4**, 464–73.

Dolata, U. (2002), 'Strategische Netzwerke oder fluide Figurationen? Reichweiten und Architekturen formalisierter Kooperationsbeziehungen in der Biotechnologie', in Herstatt, C. and Ch. Müller (eds), *Management-Handbuch Biotechnologie*, Stuttgart: Schäffer-Poeschel, pp. 159–72.

Dolata, U. (2003), *Unternehmen Technik. Akteure, Interaktionsmuster und strukturelle Kontexte der Technikentwicklung: Ein Theorierahmen*, Berlin: edition sigma.

Dreyer, M. and B. Gill (2000), 'Die Vermarktung transgener Lebensmittel in der EU – die Wiederkehr der Politik aufgrund regulativer und ökonomischer Blockaden', in Spök, A. (ed.), *GENug gestritten?! Gentechnik zwischen Risikodiskussion und gesellschaftlicher Herausforderung*, Graz: Leykam, pp. 125–48.

Ernst & Young (2000), *Gründerzeit. Ernst & Youngs zweiter Deutscher*

Biotechnologie Report 2000, Stuttgart.

Ernst & Young (2001), *Integration. Ernst & Young's Eighth Annual European Life Sciences Report*, London.

European Commission (2000), *Towards a European Research Area*, Brussels: European Commission, COM (2000) 6.

European Commission (2001a), *Proposal for a Decision of the European Parliament and of the Council Concerning the Multiannual Framework Programme 2002–2006 of the European Community for Research, Technological Development and Demonstration Activities Aimed at Contributing Towards the Creation of the European Research Area*, Brussels: European Commission, COM (2001) 94 final.

European Commission (2001b), *Towards a Strategic Vision of Life Sciences and Biotechnology: Consultation Document*, Brussels: European Commission, COM (2001) 454 final.

Gottweis, H. (1998), *Governing Molecules. The Discursive Politics of Genetic Engineering in Europe and the United States*, Cambridge, US and London: MIT Press.

Grande, E. (2001a), 'The erosion of state capacity and the European innovation policy dilemma. A comparison of German and EU information technology policies', *Research Policy*, **30**, 905–21.

Grande, E. (2001b), 'Von der Technologie- zur Innovationspolitik – Europäische Forschungs- und Technologiepolitik im Zeitalter der Globalisierung', in Simonis, G., R. Martinsen and T. Saretzki (eds), *Politik und Technik. Analysen zum Verhältnis von technologischem und staatlichem Wandel am Anfang des 21. Jahrhunderts*, Politische Vierteljahresschrift, Sonderheft 31/2000, Wiesbaden: Westdeutscher Verlag, pp. 368–87.

Grant, W. (1993), 'Pressure Groups and the European Community: An Overview', in Mazey, S. and J. Richardson (eds), *Lobbying in the European Community*, Oxford: Oxford University Press, pp. 27–46.

Greenwood, J. (1997), *Representing Interests in the European Union*, Basingstoke and Hampshire: Macmillan.

Hagedoorn, J., A.N. Link and N.S. Vonortas (2000), 'Research partnerships', *Research Policy*, **29**, 567–86.

Henderson, R., L. Orsenigo and G.P. Pisano (1999), 'The Pharmaceutical Industry and the Revolution in Molecular Biology: Interactions Among Scientific, Institutional and Organizational Change', in Mowery, D.C. and R.R. Nelson (eds), *Sources of Industrial Leadership. Studies of Seven Industries*, Cambridge, UK: Cambridge University Press, pp. 267–311.

Hodgson, J. (2000), 'EC struggles to unravel regulations', *Nature Biotechnology*, **7**, 705–6.

Jasanoff, S. (1985), 'Technological innovation in a corporatist state: the case of biotechnology in the Federal Republic of Germany', *Research Policy*, **14**, 23–38.

Kenney, M. (1986), *Biotechnology: The University-Industrial Complex*, New Haven and London: Yale University Press.

Kuemmerle, W. (1999), 'Foreign direct investment in industrial research in the pharmaceutical and electronics industries – results from a survey of multi-national firms', *Research Policy*, **28**, 179–93.

Kuhlmann, S. (2001), 'Future governance of innovation policy in Europe – three scenarios', *Research Policy*, **20**, 953–76.

Meyer-Krahmer, F. (1999), 'Was bedeutet Globalisierung für Aufgaben und Handlungsspielräume nationaler Innovationspolitiken?', in Grimmer, K., S. Kuhlmann and F. Meyer-Krahmer (eds), *Innovationspolitik in globalisierten Arenen. Neue Aufgaben für Forschung und Lehre: Forschungs- und Technologiepolitik im Wandel*, Opladen: Leske + Budrich, pp. 35–65.

OECD (1996), *Globalization of Industry. Overview and Sector Reports*, Paris: OECD (Organisation for Economic Co-operation and Development).

Patel, P. (1995), 'Localised production of technology for global markets', *Cambridge Journal of Economics*, **1**, 141–53.

Pavitt, K. and P. Patel (1996), 'What Makes High Technology Competition Different From Conventional Competition? The Central Importance of National Innovation Systems', in Koopmann, G. and H.E. Scharrer (eds), *The Economics of High-Technology Competition and Cooperation in Global Markets*, Baden-Baden: Nomos, pp. 143–71.

Prevezer, M. (1997), 'The dynamics of industrial clustering in biotechnology', *Small Business Economics*, **9**, 255–71.

Ronit, K. (1997), 'Wirtschaftsverbände in den Bioindustrien. Stabilität und Dynamik deutscher und europäischer Interessenvermittlung', in Martinsen, R. (ed.), *Politik und Biotechnologie. Die Zumutung der Zukunft*, Baden-Baden: Nomos, pp. 81–97.

Schenek, M. (1995), *Das Gentechnikrecht der Europäischen Gemeinschaft. Gemeinschaftliche Biotechnologiepolitik und Gentechnikregulierung*, Berlin: Duncker & Humblot.

Schwartz, R.A. and M.D. Dibner (1992), 'International strategic alliances', *Bio/Technology*, **5**, 528–33.

Senker, J. and P. van Zwanenberg (2001), *European Biotechnology Innovation Systems*, Final Report, TSER Project No. SOE1-CT98-117, October 2001.

13 Innovation Policy in a Multi-level Governance System

The Changing Institutional Environment for the Establishment of Science-based Industries[1]

Robert Kaiser

INTRODUCTION: INNOVATION POLICY IN A MULTI-LEVEL
GOVERNANCE SYSTEM

Although the European Union (EU) has in recent years considerably increased its efforts to support Research and Development (R&D) in high-
technology industries, the EU Member States are still in danger of falling
behind their major competitors, especially Japan and the United States, in
view of their innovation performance. This development has been related to a
'European paradox' (European Commission 1995, p. 7), which claims that
the limited capacity to convert scientific progress into marketable products
and services is not due to a lack of resources devoted to R&D. From a European perspective, this innovation deficit originates primarily from a limited
coherence of R&D and innovation policies conducted at the regional, national
and European levels. Consequently, the creation of a 'European Research
Area' (ERA) aims at strengthening the co-ordination of public policies at the
different levels, which affect Europe's innovation capacity.[2]

However, there are remarkable examples of success in the establishment of
highly innovative, science-based industries at least in some of the EU Member States. This holds true especially for the pharmaceutical biotechnology
sector, which has emerged in Great Britain, France and Germany since the
late 1980s. In Germany, for example, the successful commercialization of
scientific knowledge in pharmaceutical biotechnology can be traced back to
various changes in the institutional embeddedness of the biotech industry.
The existence of successful solutions to the 'European paradox', however,
raises some critical questions: Firstly, to what extent are the EU Member
States and their sub-national entities still able to act widely autonomous in

their innovation policies; secondly, to what extent has the European level contributed to these successful solutions, and thirdly, in which areas do public policy actors from different levels act together as a result of shared competencies in a multi-level governance system. By answering these questions, this paper will try to contribute to the discussion of how a stronger co-ordination of Member States' innovation policies within a ERA will affect these highly innovative clusters and thereby the ability of EU Member States to promote the establishment of science-based industries under the conditions of competition of 'National Innovation Systems'. Such an evaluation certainly requires cross-national and cross-sectoral analyses in order to assess specific peculiarities that exist in certain countries and/or industries. Under that precondition, this paper provides only limited insights, because it is concentrated on only a single sector, i.e. pharmaceutical biotechnology, as it refers – in its empirical part – to a specific case in only one EU member state that is Germany (see also Kaiser, forthcoming).

The paper is organized into five sections. The first section summarizes the basic aspects of the innovation system approach, which provides the analytical framework for this study. The second section gives some information about the empirical case of the Munich cluster for pharmaceutical biotechnology, which has emerged since the mid-1990s. The subsequent section is concerned with the institutional changes, which were of enormous importance for the creation and dynamic development of this cluster. Based on the analysis of the role of the various public policy actors and their contributions to the successful commercialization of pharmaceutical biotechnology in the Munich area, section four will discuss how a more intensified innovation policy co-ordination within ERA might affect such a regionally clustered science-based industry. Section five will summarize the major findings.

THE ANALYTICAL FRAMEWORK: THE INNOVATION SYSTEM APPROACH

The paper is based on the assumption that the successful commercialization of pharmaceutical biotechnology research in Germany mainly occurred due to reforms of the institutional environment in which the industry is embedded. In order to analyze these institutional changes, the following five indicators will be applied which are considered crucial for the innovation process: the regulatory framework, public R&D and innovation policies, the financial system, the research and education system and the mode of knowledge production. For each of these indicators, the role of different institutions at the regional, national and European level will be evaluated. These indicators stem from systemic analyses of technological development and innovation and especially from the analytical concept of the national innovation system (Dosi et al. 1988; Edquist 1997; Freeman 1987; 1995; Lundval 1992; Nelson 1987; 1993; OECD 1999a; 1999b; 2001; Porter 1991). Analyzing innovation processes under a systemic approach has the advantage that differentiation in institutional, infrastructural or cultural conditions for innovation, which exist among countries and sectors, become visible. These conditions determine the relationships among private industrial actors, public administration and the science and education system, as well as the forms and intensity of their interactions.

More recently, systemic analyses of innovation have also been related to studies on the development of political systems, since 'both systems' are exposed to processes of reconfiguration and differentiation over various territorial levels (Grande 1999; Kaiser and Prange 2001; Kuhlmann 1999; 2001). Whereas in view of political systems the discussion is very much focused on new forms of governance in a multi-level European policy or in international relations, the driving forces behind the re-configuration of innovation systems are both the internationalization of markets, technologies and firms as well as the localization and clustering of innovation capacity and the development of competitive advantages at the regional level.

Because of the dynamics, systems characteristics and interdependencies that are similar to those existing in national innovation systems, regional clusters can be considered as reduced-scale national innovation systems (Roelandt and den Hertog 1999, pp. 413–14). They can be described as groups of innovative enterprises, academic and research institutions, local development agencies and other supporting institutions. Thus they combine industry, government and non-governmental organizations, together with a number of knowledge specific players, such as universities, research institutes, management consultancies, patent lawyers, etc. (European Commission 2001b). Clusters usually exist as cross-sectoral networks, which contain dissimilar and complementary firms specialized around a knowledge base in the value chain. Depending on the technology concerned, such value chains can differ considerably in view of their length. Value chains in biotechnology, for example, tend to be relatively short as they rely almost exclusively on laboratory-based research. In mature clusters with relatively stable technologies, the value chain can be expected to be longer and actors rely more heavily on exogenous sources of knowledge (Bergman et al. 2001, p. 10). As a consequence, cluster-oriented public policies have to be co-ordinated vertically, involving policy actors at different levels of governance, and horizontally, including various innovation and non-innovation policies. Cluster-oriented public policy is therefore not a new or separate type of policy, but an integrated and general approach, which requires interdepartmental co-ordination.

THE EMPIRICAL BASE: THE MUNICH BIOTECH CLUSTER

With about 120 biotech and pharmaceutical companies, the Munich area has the highest density of corporate actors in the life sciences industry in Germany and is ranked second (behind London) in Europe. Five of the twenty largest pharmaceutical companies in the world are represented in Munich, whereas the number of small- and medium-sized biotech companies has increased dynamically between 1996 and 2000 from 36 to 101. Within the same period of time, only three biotech start-ups have failed. In 2000, the Munich-based life-sciences industry employed about 12 200 people.

Biotechnology in the Munich area is clustered at two different locations. Pharmaceutical biotechnology is concentrated in Martinsried/Grosshadern in the Southwest of Munich, where more than 50 biotech companies, several research institutes – especially the Max Planck Institutes for Biochemistry and Neurobiology – and the clinical center of the University of Munich (LMU) are located. Moreover, the LMU is presently establishing a life-sciences campus in Grosshadern, which will bring together about 6000 scientists from the departments of chemistry, pharmacy, and biology. Agricultural biotechnology activities are concentrated in Freising/Weihenstephan in the north-east of Munich. Apart from the Technical University of Munich, which has established a Center for Life Sciences in Weihenstephan, there are other publicly-funded research organizations such as the University of Munich, the University of Applied Sciences Weihenstephan, the Bavarian Institute for Soil and Plant Production, and the Fraunhofer Institute for Process Engineering and Packaging, which all focus on animal and plant breeding, food and nutrition, and the discovery of new materials in the non-food sector. In view of the commercialization of scientific knowledge in agro-biotechnology, the cluster Freising/Weihenstephan follows the example of Martinsried, although corporate activities are clearly less developed than in the pharmaceutical sector. This development can be partially traced back to the fact that until today most public policy activities as well as resources provided by private actors, such as finance and consultancy, are focused on pharmaceutical biotechnology. For this reason, only the institutional changes concerning the establishment of the Martinsried cluster for pharmaceutical biotechnology will be taken into consideration.

INSTITUTIONAL REFORMS FOR THE ESTABLISHMENT OF A SCIENCE-BASED INDUSTRY

As mentioned before, this paper applies five indicators in order to assess how institutional changes laid the foundation for the establishment of a pharmaceutical biotechnology industry in Germany, and more specifically in the Munich area. Four of these indicators, the regulatory framework of the sector, public R&D and innovation policies, the financial system, and the research and education system directly refer to public policy actions, whereas the fifth indicator, the mode of knowledge production, is related to organizational behavior as knowledge production takes place primarily in an organization that is immediately concerned with the innovation process. However, the institutional environment strongly influences the ways and means of organizational knowledge production. This holds true especially if co-operation with external knowledge providers plays a significant role in this process.

The Development of a Regulatory Regime for Pharmaceutical Biotechnology in Germany

Prior to 1990, no regulatory framework for genetical engineering was enacted in Germany. The approval of respective research laboratories or production facilities fell under the authority of regional regulation bodies. The decisions of these bodies differed considerably depending on the political majorities in each individual federal state. At the federal level, a first attempt to initiate national 'regulation' for the biotechnology sector was made in 1978 when the Federal Ministry of Research and Technology (BMFT) issued a guideline on genetical research, which was obligatory for publicly-funded research organizations, whereas private actors committed themselves to these guidelines on a voluntary basis.

However, given the broad public skepticism toward genetical engineering in Germany, both companies and opponents called for a federal law, the former ones because they had predictable legal standards as a precondition for their activities in mind, the latter ones because they assumed a federal law could be used to impose tight restrictions. There is at least one well-documented case which shows that the establishment of a genetic engineering production facility failed due to the non-existence of a respective regulation. In 1989, the Administrative Court of Hesse decided against an authorization, which would have allowed the pharmaceutical company Hoechst to establish a genetical engineering based production facility for human insulin. The Court argued that as long as no legislative act explicitly permitted the application of genetical engineering, no research or production facility could be established regardless of the assessment of the potential risk of an individual facility (Aretz 1999, pp. 245 f.). This judgment, along with the decision of Hoechst to build the facility in France, increased the pressure on the federal government to initiate legislation on genetic engineering.

Federal legislation was finally introduced in 1990 by enacting the 'Embryonenschutzgesetz' (Embryo Protection Law) which prohibited researchers from using embryo for genetic experiments and the 'Gentechnikgesetz' (Genetic Engineering Law) which set legal standards for the authorization of genetic engineering laboratories and production facilities and regulated field trials with genetically modified organisms. Both laws were considered by the German government to be a compromise between commercial interest in biotechnology and the disapproval of genetic engineering by various groups in German society.

Compared to US standards, however, the law was certainly more restrictive especially in view of its obligations for public participation in administrative authorization procedures. Nevertheless, the law provoked sharp criticism from opponents of genetic engineering, whereas big pharmaceutical companies, especially Bayer and Hoechst, moved most of their genetic-related research and production activities primarily to the United States under the pretext of unacceptable regulations at their home base.

Regardless of whether the federal genetic engineering law actually forced traditional pharmaceutical companies to conduct biotechnological R&D and production outside Germany, it certainly imposed barriers to the commercialization of scientific knowledge, which existed mostly in non-university research institutes. As a result, the political debate over the country's competitiveness in this sector was intensified only a short time after the enactment of the law. In 1993, the genetic engineering law was revised in order to reduce administrative hurdles for the authorization of biotechnological research and production. This holds true especially for R&D facilities, which normally fall under the lower risk categories. For those facilities, summary proceedings were introduced which do no longer require either public participation or special authorization by a federal commission for biological safety.

Whereas the 1993 revision of the Genetic Engineering Law was mainly motivated by the fear that the national industry was in danger of loosing ground in an innovative high-technology area, further amendments clearly occurred because of regulatory activities taken at the European level. The EU introduced biotechnology-related legislation for the first time in 1990, through Directive 90/219/EEC on activities related with genetically modified microorganisms in closed systems and the Directive 90/220/EEC on the handling of genetically modified microorganisms in field trials and open production systems. These directives have since been amended twice, in 1996 and 1998. In Germany, only the 1996 amendment has as yet been implemented. A further regulatory measure agreed on at the European level, which is important for the biotechnology industry, concerns the marketing authorization for pharmaceutical products. In 1995, new centralized procedures went into force, which allowed community-wide authorization for medical products granted by the European Commission on the basis of a scientific evaluation by a newly established European Agency for the Evaluation of Medicinal

Products (EMEA).[3] Such procedures are mandatory for certain pharmaceutical products, which have been developed by means of biotechnological processes. Since such procedures are widely compatible with the authorization procedure employed by the US Federal Drug Administration (FDA), the regulatory standards, which guide the drug development process on the pharmaceutical lead markets in Europe and North America, are now more or less identical.

Even though the EU has grown into a central role in regulating pharmaceutical biotechnology, the overall regulatory regime also has a strong regional dimension, at least in federal organized countries, such as Germany. Since the authority to enforce biotechnology-related regulations is rested with the states ('Länder'), the degree to which the enforcement agencies are supportive of the industry differs considerably among the states depending on the political attitude of the respective government. State government action is not only relevant at the regional, but also at the federal level, since amendments to the national regulatory framework for biotechnology require the consent of the 'Länder' governments in the 'Bundesrat', even if the amendments implement European legislation. Moreover, due to their right to participate in federal legislation through the 'Bundesrat', state governments are also entitled to introduce bills implementing European laws. The state government of Bavaria, for example, introduced a legislative proposal to amend the federal genetic engineering law in November 2000 in order to speed up the implementation of the Directive 98/81/EC (former directive 90/220/EEC).[4] This directive further deregulates the biotechnology sector, especially through the simplification and shortening of administrative procedures for the notification or approval of research and production facilities.

New Public Policy Initiatives for the Commercialization of Biotechnological Research

Germany's position as a latecomer in the commercialization of biotechnology does not indicate that public policy was not engaged early enough in this field. On the contrary, Germany was the first country at all that implemented a publicly-funded research program in biotechnology in 1972. However, early public investment in biotechnological R&D did not prevent a country known as the 'pharmacy of the world' losing ground in an emerging technology. During the 1980s, Germany fell significantly behind other industrialized nations in terms of the existence of small- or medium-sized biotechnology companies. Whereas 245 such companies existed in the United States in 1984 and 157 in Japan, Germany had only 15. Even five years later the situation had not improved. The number of biotechnology SMEs in the United States had further increased to 388 in 1989 while only 17 were active in Germany.

One reason for this development was certainly the chemistry-driven research tradition of big pharmaceutical companies. This tradition was not only reflected by strategic decisions of corporate actors concerning their own R&D programs, but also influenced public R&D policies since the Research Ministry invited the leading industry association, the DECHEMA (German Society for Chemical Engineering), to define the policy goals. DECHEMA, along with their corporate members, proposed to support traditional second-generation bioprocessing, but not third-generation post-DNA recombination which was already on the research agenda in other countries (Adelsberger 2000, pp. 107 f.). The second reason was that public policies did support R&D efforts of the industry, but was not active in providing incentives for the commercialization of scientific knowledge, which consequently did not step out of its traditional places, universities and non-university research organizations. Nevertheless, the federal government did invest in the academic infrastructure and established four national centers for genetic research in Berlin, Cologne, Heidelberg and Munich. The selection of these locations was not accidental, but aimed at strengthening those regions in which the scientific infrastructure (i.e. universities and Max Planck Institutes) was already strong.

The situation changed significantly when the federal government initiated the BioRegio program in 1995 and simultaneously proclaimed a pretty ambitious goal: to become the leading biotechnology nation in Europe by the year 2000. Indeed, the BioRegio program itself was an innovative policy tool, which had no model at that time, but was copied by many countries thereafter. The BioRegio program actually was a contest aimed at stimulating the creation of biotechnology clusters, and thereby the commercialization of scientific knowledge.

A total number of 17 regions entered the contest and had to demonstrate that they were able to set up a working and interacting infrastructure for the commercialization of biotechnology. The Federal Ministry for Education and Research ('Bundesministerium für Bildung und Forschung', BMBF), which was responsible for the program, designed the contest in a way, which clearly favored locations where the infrastructure was already developed. The political intention behind this strategy was to further strengthen already strong and established locations. As a result, the three winners of the competition – the bioregions around Cologne ('BioRegio Rheinland'), Heidelberg ('BioRegio Rhein–Neckar–Dreieck') and Munich – have already been favored in the 1980s through the establishment of the national centers for genetic research. A special award was given to the bioregion Jena, the leading location in the new federal states. The BMBF supported 57 R&D projects within the four regions between 1996 and 2000 and invested a total of €72 million.

In fact, the BioRegio program was able to initiate the commercialization of biotechnological research not primarily by the provision of funds. The more important factor was clearly the establishment of a network structure in the different local clusters involving all relevant private and public actors. In Munich, for example, networking activities depend largely on one central actor, the Bio-M AG, which was founded in 1997 and originated from the publicly-funded initiative committee which prepared Munich's application for the BioRegio contest.[5] In contrast to that, the Berlin biotechnology cluster was the only location where a National Gene Center had been established, which did not succeed in the BioRegio contest, especially due to the lack of public financial support for a central networking actor.

In many respects, regional policy initiatives taken by the Government of the state of Bavaria positively influenced the development of the Munich biotechnology cluster. Firstly, the Bavarian government participated – earlier than other states – in federal-state consultations, which took place in order to prepare the BioRegio contest. These consultations led to the agreement to strengthen already well-developed locations and to invest only a 'symbolic' amount of public money. The basic idea of the program had been to make clear that public policy was ready to support biotechnological research and to improve the conditions for biotechnology companies. At the same time, the Bavarian government started initiatives that were aimed at upgrading the research infrastructure and the provision of risk capital at the regional level. It invested a considerable amount of money gained from the privatization of its share in the former utility and energy company VIAG AG in venture capital funds, provided by the newly established state agency Bayern Kapital, as well as in the expansion of the university infrastructure. Since the federal government was not ready to provide its share for this investment – which was mandatory since the establishment of the university infrastructure is a common responsibility of the federal government and the states – Bavaria decided to pre-finance the federal share.

The EU has been increasingly engaged in the promotion of R&D in biotechnology since the 1990s. In contrast to the EU's actions in other technology fields, such as information technology, companies from the chemical and pharmaceutical sector were not overly interested in European programs such as ESPRIT for the IT sector, because of their engagement in their own transnational research programs, which were mostly concerned with competitive rather than pre-competitive research as proposed by the European Commission. From the industry's perspective, the dialogue with the European Commission was aimed at liberalizing national regulation, which the private sector considered to be too restrictive. As a result, within the context of the first three Framework Programmes (FPs), the EU financed R&D in biotechnology with a relatively limited budget. This situation changed, however, with the Fourth Framework Programme (FP4), which made it easier for the participants to co-operate with non-European research groups especially in the United States and Japan. Moreover, since the FP4 the European Commission began to consider biotechnology as one of the key technologies along with information technology, material sciences and telecommunications (Nollert 2000, pp. 210–18).

The Fifth Framework Programme (FP5, 1998–2002) placed more emphasis on the efficient interaction between research organizations and industry. In this sense, the EU explicitly encourages applicants to cluster their projects involving core centers and associated laboratories in order to create a critical mass and in view of promoting interaction between fundamental and applied research as well as between academic research and industry (European Union 1999). Between 1998 and 2002, the EU financed the above-mentioned activities with a total of €483 million. Additionally, the quality of life program provides money for a key action called 'The Cell Factory' which is addressed to companies in the life sciences sector, which are engaged either in health, environment or agriculture. This action was financed by about €400 million.[6]

New Patterns of Financing Science-based Industries: the Emergence of a Venture Capital Market in Germany

The biotechnology sector, in which most of the start-up companies are established as spin-offs from academic research and in which – at least when the company is engaged in drug development – enormous R&D investments are necessary in order to bring a product to the market, is certainly the most capital intensive high-technology industry. Therefore, the development of a biotechnology sector depends heavily on the availability of capital, regardless whether it is provided by public or private institutions.

Traditionally, Germany has had a bank-centered financial system in which economic activities are primarily funded by firms that finance expansion through profits or by banks which grant loans to such companies which proved their credit-worthiness through their corporate performance in the past (Adelsberger 2000, p. 113). Either way, bank-centered financial systems are regarded to be disadvantaged to produce radical innovations or to promote a start-up industry over a system, which is based on the availability of venture capital and the existence of high-tech specialized stock exchanges, which are important as an exit-option for risk capital providers.

The dynamic development of the German biotechnology sector underlines how important venture capital is for the expansion of high-technology industries, and thus verifies that the times of a bank-centered financial system in Germany are (long) over. However, that does not mean that the dynamic development of the biotechnology sector in Germany is largely the result of the existence of private risk capital. On the contrary, since the mid-1990s, it has been the goal of state intervention not only to establish the framework conditions for the provision of private venture capital, but also to act itself as a venture capital provider. In Germany, the relation of private and public risk capital within the biotechnology industry is 1 to 0.8. This figure, which is by far higher than in the United States or Great Britain, demonstrates the importance of the public sector for the provision of venture capital (Ernst & Young 2000, p. 126).

Actually, the state does not act as a venture capital provider in a common sense, but allows for refinancing of private risk capital through public financial institutions such as the 'Kreditanstalt für Wiederaufbau' or the 'Deutsche Ausgleichsbank'. Both institutions jointly created the 'Technologiebeteili-gungsgesellschaft' (tbg), which has issued a number of equity capital programs since 1989. Between 1989 and 2000, the tbg has offered more than €250 million to private venture capital companies (Adelsberger 2000, p. 115).

The importance of public risk finance activities in the development of an innovation biotechnology industry can be seen even at the regional level. In the early phase of commercialization, when private venture capital firms were not very engaged in Bavaria, the public VC-agency Bayern Kapital, a company in which the State of Bavaria holds 100 per cent of the shares, provided early stage seed capital to biotechnology start-ups in the Munich area. In the meantime, more than 20 private venture capital firms and investment banks which invest in the biotechnology sector, have been established in Munich, whereas Bayern Kapital has been able to reduce its efforts for pharmaceutical companies in Martinsried and now concentrates more on commercialization of biotechnology scientific knowledge at other locations in Bavaria. Many start-up biotechnology companies in the Munich area were initially funded by a co-investment of a private VC company, an investment by the 'Technolo-giebeteiligungsgesellschaft', an investment by Bayern Kapital and project-based funds provided by the BMBF or the Bavarian Ministry of Finance.

Germany's venture capital market has increased significantly since the mid-1990s. In 1998/99 a total sum of €1.2 billion was invested into the biotechnology sector, in the year 2000 the total amount of venture capital in Germany reached €6.4 billion with a share of more than 30 per cent reserved for the biotechnology industry. All in all, since 1998 about ten out of at least 37 venture capital funds have spent at least half of their capital for biotechnology investments.

The EU's contribution to the emergence of a venture capital market in Germany is relatively small. Looking at the European level, one can state, that the venture capital market is still highly fragmented. The amount of risk capital, which is available in the various Member States, differs significantly. A European stock market for high-technology firms could not be established with the concurrence of the leading European stock markets in Frankfurt, Paris or London. As a consequence, the Stockholm European Council set up a risk capital action plan[7] in 1998, which is aimed at establishing an integrated European risk capital market by 2003. However, the action plan proposed some structural reforms, which are likely to meet resistance at least from some Member States, such as the removal of tax burdens. In Germany, for example, tax regulations are still disadvantageous for employee stock-option plans.

Reforms in the German Research and Education Systems

Universities and non-university research organizations were of special importance for the commercialization of biotechnological research since most of Germany's small- and medium-sized biotechnology companies were established out of publicly-funded research organizations. In the Munich pharmaceutical biotechnology cluster, for example, about 30 of the total 54 biotechnology start-ups originate from one of the three leading research organizations in the area: the Max Planck Institute for Biochemistry, the GSF Research Center, and the Gene Center of the Munich University. Researchers from at least two of these institutions founded three of them.

Traditionally, universities are important actors in basic research in various academic disciplines. Since most of the universities, which have departments of biology, chemistry, medical sciences etc., are active in any field of biotechnology it is hardly possible to determine the number of chairs or research groups and their specific research interests. However, according to the German Statistical Office, 450 university institutions were involved in biotechnological research in 1995 (European Commission 2000b, p. DE-24). About 48 universities offer academic programs in biotechnology, of which 20 are more oriented towards technical aspects, the other 28 more towards studies in biology, microbiology or biochemistry. In addition to that, 16 universities of applied sciences (polytechnics) initiated programs in biotechnology in recent years.

The 'Deutsche Forschungsgemeinschaft' (DFG, German Research Foundation), the major funding organization for academic research in Germany, has increased its budget for medical and biological research considerably. Since 1997, total expenditures in these areas have surged by more than 25 per cent to €431 million in the year 2000 (Deutsche Forschungsgemeinschaft 2001, p. 56). Out of its 278 collaborative research centers ('Sonderforschungsbereiche') a total of 110 are engaged in the field of biotechnology.[8]

According to the nature of biotechnological research, the most important non-university research organization in the field is the Max Planck Society (MPG). In January 2001, the MPG maintained 79 research institutes, which employed roughly 9500 scientists. In the wider area of biological and medical research, the MPG possesses 34 institutes or independent research groups which usually work outside the departmental structure of the respective host institute. In recent years, the MPG has placed special emphasis on biological research and concentrated about one-third of its total expenditures on this sector. In 1999, biological research was financed with a total of €325.9 million. Other research organizations, such as the Fraunhofer Society, the Helmholtz Society or the so-called 'Blue-List Institutes' are considerably less involved in biotechnological research, either because of their focus on applied research or because of their concentration on research areas, which require an extensive technical infrastructure.

As an interdisciplinary and science-based industry, modern biotechnology requires the existence of qualified personnel not only from various disciplines, but also with different levels of education and different fields of knowledge. This holds especially true for a highly dynamic market environment in which the lack of certain competencies both in quality and quantity can hinder the development of an industry. Looking at the German biotechnology industry, one can identify some areas in which qualified personnel are not available as needed. One area concerns the discipline of bioinformatics. Since bioinformatics is a relatively new discipline, the German university system – comparable to the situation in other countries – has not been able to offer specialized programs in this field. Only recently have many universities and polytechnics started programs in bioinformatics, however, it will take time until students will be available to the industry. Other countries, especially the United States, reacted in a different way. In order to bring qualified personnel early into the industry, they simply combined existing programs for informatics and biology or biochemistry and thus reduced the time in which students qualify for a degree in bioinformatics. Concerning the number of students who enter the universities for studies in natural sciences it is predictable that the German biotechnology industry will be confronted with a lack of qualified personnel at least in the field of chemistry. However, this could be compensated by an increasing number of graduates in the fields of biology and medical sciences (BMBF 2000a, p. 19).

From the corporate side, the German university system is further criticized because of its relatively low international orientation. Since only few universities offer courses in English language, it is difficult for foreign students to study natural sciences in Germany. Consequently, the lack of qualified scientists in the German biotechnology industry can not be compensated with foreign students or scientists. Moreover, scientists who decide to commercialize a certain discovery originate primarily from non-university research organizations, but not from universities. The main reason for this development is that post-doctoral graduates employed by universities largely depend on the research areas and interest of their academic chair and are not able to apply for their own research funds. Non-university research organizations, however, have changed their respective policies in recent years (especially the Max Planck Institutes) and offer young scientists the opportunity to join independent research groups.

A lack of qualified personnel has also been experienced at the level of technical assistants ('MTA' and 'PTA'), who are increasingly required to work in biotechnology laboratories. Traditionally, technical assistants were educated within the vocational training system and have later been employed mostly within the medical system (i.e. hospitals and pharmacies). As a result of the dynamic development in the biotechnology sector, most companies are not able to employ technical personnel according to their needs. Moreover, since demand is still growing, mobility of technical personnel is increasing because of the opportunity to realize a higher salary in a new job.

Given Germany's institutionalized joint decision procedures ('Politikverflechtung'), which requires horizontal policy co-ordination for the university and research system, as well as vertical policy co-ordination for the education system, reforms are unlikely to happen early enough to react to immediate needs. On the contrary, such reactions occur, if at all, at the regional level. In order to provide a solution for the shortage of human resources, the Bavarian Ministry of Culture and Education initiated a working group comprising all concerned parties, which will prepare a concept for the establishment of a new vocational training institute for technical employees. European student exchange programs do not significantly contribute to a better provision of scientific personnel in the Munich biotechnology cluster. This is, however, due to sector specific reasons. Because of the fact that the US biotechnology industry is years ahead of the German one, many organizations in the Munich biotechnology cluster, especially publicly-funded research institutes, consider a postgraduate training in the United States the most important qualification of new employees.

Modes of Knowledge Production: Local Innovation Milieus and International Alliances

In an innovative organization, the production of knowledge takes place either internally or on the basis of external relations mainly with suppliers and customers, but also in horizontal co-operations with other actors, for example, through collaboration in research projects. This part concentrates on external relations as an increasingly important mode of knowledge production. In the German pharmaceutical biotechnology industry, as it is the case in most other ones, external relations largely exist as formal and informal contacts with other actors within the same cluster, as R&D co-operations with other biotechnology firms or as strategic R&D alliances with traditional big pharma companies. In the Munich pharmaceutical biotechnology cluster, the dominant areas of co-operation are the local innovation milieu and strategic alliances with national or international pharma companies. Co-operation in research projects or formal R&D agreements with biotechnology companies in the same geographical area is rarely seen.

In terms of co-operative R&D, the focus of Munich-based biotechnology companies is clearly an international one. This holds true especially for the three leading biotechnology firms in Martinsried: Medigene, GPC Biotech and Morphosys. In view of alliances with big pharmaceutical companies, the intensity of co-operation is growing, showing that from the perspective of traditional pharma companies the firms have reached a competitive position. Not only that partnership agreements have been signed with all major pharmaceutical companies, but in more and more cases the reason for co-operation are drug development programs, in which biotechnology firms are either able to reach milestone payments or in which they are participating in revenues originating from marketing a pharmaceutical product which has been commonly developed.

The international orientation becomes even more evident in view of intra-biotech alliances, which have also increased considerably since the year 2000. Especially Morphosys and GPC Biotech made use of such partnerships and they both have chosen primarily US-based biotechnology firms. Apart from the R&D co-operation between GPC Biotech and Morphosys, there is no strategic partnership between private actors in the Martinsried cluster. The reason for this is that biotechnology companies use those partnerships to compensate for knowledge that does not exist in-house or in order to optimize their product or service portfolio. By doing so, geographical proximity does not play a decisive role.

Even in publicly-funded research projects, most actors in the Munich biotechnology region have chosen regional partners only in a limited number of cases. The analysis of biotechnology-related projects funded by European R&D programs shows that the projects with more than one actor from the Munich biotechnology cluster are clearly outnumbered by projects with only a single regional actor. This applies especially to the local universities and non-university research organizations, which participate in a large number of projects. The European key action on 'The Cell Factory', for example, funded 18 projects in which Munich based universities or non-university research institutes participated. However, in only one single case, two of them are working together within one of these projects.

Moreover, participation of Munich-based biotechnology firms in EU-funded programs, and thus the contribution of the European level to the production of knowledge with private actors in the cluster, is very low. Until

2001, only five out of more than 50 pharmaceutical biotechnology firms in Munich were involved in only eight EU-funded research projects. The reason for this is twofold. First, given the administrative efforts related with EU-funded research programs, these projects are considered to be less attractive than projects funded by the federal or the state government. Second, in view of financial resources there is still an oversupply at least in the Munich biotechnology cluster for firms, which depend on venture capital. For companies, which have already managed an Initial Public Offering (IPO), engagement in publicly funded R&D projects is hardly attractive as such engagements generally provoke negative comments from stock market analysts who are used to consider such programs not as part of the core business.

REGIONAL CLUSTERS IN THE ERA

As shown above, the EU contributed to the development of a pharmaceutical biotechnology industry in the Munich area mostly by deregulating the sector through which regulations in Europe have become more or less compatible to those on the US-American lead market. Moreover, European R&D programs still play only a minor role at least for private sector actors who tend to focus either on local or international – and primarily US-based partners – for co-operation in R&D. One reason for the limited role of the European level for the establishment of a regionally clustered biotechnology industry in Germany certainly is that the EU has only tardily considered a regional and innovation-related perspective as crucial for the European R&D policy. 'Regional Innovation Strategies' (RIS) as well as 'Regional Innovation and Technology Transfer Strategies' (RITTS) have been implemented first in 1994 under the European Regional Development Fund and the Community R&D FP4, respectively. A European innovation policy emerged only in consequence of the 1995 green paper on innovation and the subsequent implementation of the first action plan for innovation in Europe in 1996.

In view of the creation of the ERA, there is much evidence that the regional perspective will become even more important. In a communication on the 'Regional Dimension of the European Research Area' the European Commission has argued that 'upgrading "knowledge" and increasing technology diffusion at regional level may prove one of the most efficient routes for economic growth'. Accordingly, the communication stresses the importance of high-technology clusters as the main drivers of regional development. Within an emerging ERA, in which the 'open method of co-ordination' is the most important instrument, public policy actors at the European, the national, the regional and even the local level will be increasingly involved in order to ensure that measures taken at the different levels will be mutually consistent

(European Commission 2001b). Under this premise, innovation policies implemented at various levels in Europe will be considerably more integrated in a multi-level governance structure as they will be characterized both by a bottom-up process of co-ordination as well as a centralized process of continuous benchmarking of these policies under the responsibility of the European Commission. This benchmarking process has already been initiated through the creation of a European Innovation Scoreboard that measures innovation performance of the Member States on the basis of 17 indicators.[9]

Especially for two reasons, multi-level innovation policy in Europe will be based primarily on these new 'soft instruments'. First, in a EU of 25 or 30 Member States, heterogeneity of national science and innovation systems will increase, even if a Europeanization of the candidates' science and technology policies has already taken place in the 'pre-accession phase' (Prange 2001). Second, a European innovation policy is confronted with a double co-ordination problem as it requires a high degree of policy co-ordination both horizontally (that is in view of the integration of various sectoral policies) and vertically over different political levels. As many authors have argued, European science and technology policy so far has hardly been able to manage these co-ordination problems. Within the ERA, co-ordination costs are, on the one hand, likely to increase with each additional territorial level participating voluntarily in negotiations that are designed in a non-hierarchical and non-majoritarian way. On the other hand, the European Commission might be able to reduce co-ordination costs by focussing on existing centers of excellence and integrated projects instead of financing and managing a large number of research projects at the micro-level. Outside R&D funding, however, open co-ordination of innovation policies across territorial levels extensively expands the number of jurisdictions involved. In a situation in which co-ordination takes place without a 'shadow of hierarchy' (Scharpf 1997) efficient solutions can only be expected if the scope of measures remains limited and if implementation is not obligatory. (Peterson and Sharp 1998; Grande 2001; Kaiser and Prange 2002).

In view of the leading science-based industry clusters in Europe it seems to be likely that they will be able to benefit from the new instruments of the ERA and the Sixth European R&D Framework Programme (FP6). This holds true especially for the proposed 'networks of excellence' which are aimed at a durable integration of research and innovation actors both in a regional as well as in a transregional perspective. Further instruments, such as the networking of national R&D programs as well as the participation of the EU in those national programs, could reduce barriers for research and innovation actors who still rely mostly on national or regional public research funds. Empirical data suggest that even under earlier community research framework programs, the industrial leader regions on the one side and the less developed regions on the other side profited most from European public R&D funds (Clarysse and Muldur 2001). As long as European technology policy is oriented towards a competitive selection process based on excellence as well as it intends to foster regional cohesion, this trend will certainly go on. However, with respect to very much internationalized science-based industries, such as the pharmaceutical biotechnology industry, it is increasingly important that European research programs are open for participation of research organizations from third countries. For that reason, the ERA concept includes a new strategy of international co-operation which is aimed at paving the way for further development of relations between the EU and non-EU member countries (European Commission 2001a).

CONCLUSIONS

Since the end of the 1980s, the commercialization of biotechnological research in Germany has occurred only after considerable institutional reforms of the regulatory framework and the financial system, whereas innovative public policy instruments have been initiated especially at the national and the regional level. Reforms of the German research and education system have taken place only with regard to certain elements and could hardly be influenced by European policy because of the prerequisites for horizontal and vertical policy co-ordination in Germany. A significant contribution from the European level can be stated especially in view of the establishment of a new regulatory framework for biotechnological R&D.

With respect to the empirical case that has been presented in this paper, the most important public policy initiatives have been undertaken under a high degree of autonomy of the relevant actors at the regional and federal level. Even in cases in which co-operative action within the German federal system would have been required (especially in view of the co-financing of the university research infrastructure) the respective regional government was able to guarantee the required investments even without federal participation.

In conclusion, it is fair to say that a multi-level governance system in innovation policies might emerge with the implementation of the ERA. As for now, the case of the establishment of the Munich cluster for pharmaceutical biotechnology clearly verifies two important aspects, which have motivated the European Commission to stress the regional dimension of the ERA concept. Firstly, many European regions are largely autonomous in developing their own research, technological development and innovation policies, and they do that, secondly, especially in collaboration with their national counterparts (European Commission 2001b).

NOTES

1   This paper grows out of research done within the project 'National Systems of Innovation and Networks in the Idea–Innovation Chain in Science-based Industries', funded by the European Community under the TSER program (Contract No. SOE1-CT-98-1102). The German project team was directed by Prof. Edgar Grande at the Technical University Munich.

2   Apart from the co-ordination of public policies, the ERA concept also includes various measures like the networking of Europe's scientific centers of excellence, a common approach towards financing large-scale research infrastructure and the promotion of mobility of scientists within Europe. However, this paper is mainly focused on the aspect of co-ordination.

3   Council Regulation (EEC) No. 2309/93 of 22 July 1993 laying down Community procedures for the authorization and supervision of medicinal products for human and veterinary use and establishing a 'European Agency for the Evaluation of Medicinal Products' (OJ L 214, 24 August 1993, p. 1).

4   *Gesetzesantrag des Freistaates Bayern zum Entwurf eines Gesetzes zur Änderung des Gentechnikgesetzes*, BR-Drs. 781/00, 28 November 2000.

5   Today, the shareholders of the Bio-M AG are banks and venture capital firms (initial investment: DEM4.7 million), pharmaceutical companies (DEM4.45 million), the state of Bavaria (DEM3.75 million) and private investors (DEM1.3 million). The Bio-M AG has two business activities: the provision of venture capital and the establishment of a network for consultancy and information. In view of the first business activity, Bio-M is working profit-oriented, the second business activity is still supported by public funds from the federal and state level. This business activity makes Bio-M the center of the Munich biotechnology network.

REFERENCES

Adelsberger, K.E. (2000), 'Semi-sovereign leadership? The state's role in German biotechnology and venture capital growth', *German Politics*, **9** (1), 103–22.

Aretz, H. (1999), *Kommunikation ohne Verständigung. Das Scheitern des öffentlichen Diskurses über die Gentechnik und die Krise des Technokorporatismus in der Bundesrepublik Deutschland*, Frankfurt/Main: Peter Lang.

Bergman, E.M., D. Charles and P. den Hertog (2001), 'In Pursuit of Innovative Clusters', in OECD (ed.), *Innovative Clusters. Drivers of National Innovation Systems. Enterprise, Industry and Services*, Paris: OECD, pp. 7–15.

BioM AG (2001), *BioTech-Region München, Geschäftsbericht 2000*, München: BioM AG.

BMBF (2000a), *Beschäftigungspotenziale im Bereich Bio- und Gentechnologie*, Bonn: BMBF (Federal Ministry for Education and Research).

BMBF (2000b), *Biotechnologie – Basis für Innovationen*, Bonn: BMBF (Federal Ministry for Education and Research).

BMBF and Ständige Konferenz der Kultusminister der Länder in der Bundesrepublik Deutschland (2001), *Bildung auf einen Blick*, essential statements of the OECD to the edition 2001, Berlin: OECD (Organisation for Economic Co-operation and Development).

Caspar, S. and H. Kettler (2000), 'National Institutional Frameworks and the Hybridization of Entrepreneurial Business Models Within the German and UK Biotechnology Sectors', *European Pharmaceutical Regulation and Innovation Systems*, working paper, http://www.unisi.it/ricerca/prog/epris/3.htm.

Clarysse, B. and U. Muldur (2001), 'Regional cohesion in Europe? An analysis of how EU public RTD support influences the techno-economic regional landscape', *Research Policy*, **30**, 275–96.

Deutsche Forschungsgemeinschaft (2001), *Jahresbericht 2000. Aufgaben und Ergebnisse*, Bonn: Deutsche Forschungsgemeinschaft.

Deutscher Bundestag (2000), 'Zur Situation der Biotechnologie in Deutschland, Antwort der Bundesregierung auf die Kleine Anfrage der Abgeordneten Annette Widmann-Mauz, Wolfgang Lohmann (Lüdenscheid), Dr. Wolf Bauer, weiterer Abgeordneter und der Fraktion der CDU/CSU', *BT-Drs.* **14/3969**, 2 August 2000.

Dosi, G., C. Freeman, R. Nelson, G. Silverberg and L. Soete (eds) (1988), *Technical Change and Economic Theory*, London: Pinter.

Edquist, C. (ed.) (1997), *Systems of Innovation. Technologies, Institutions and Organizations*, London: Pinter.

Ernst & Young (2000), *Gründerzeit. Zweiter Deutscher Biotechnologie-Report 2000*, Stuttgart.

European Commission (1995), *Green Paper on Innovation*, Brussels: European Commission.

European Commission (2000a), *Innovation in einer wissensbestimmten Wirtschaft*, communication from the Commission to the Council and the European Parliament, Brussels: European Commission, COM (2000) 567 final, 20 September 2000.

European Commission (2000b), *Inventory of Public Biotechnology R&D Programmes in Europe: National Reports*, Luxembourg: European Commission.

European Commission (2001a), *The International Dimension of the European Research Area*, communication from the Commission, Brussels: European Commission, COM (2001) 346 final, 25 June 2001.

European Commission (2001b), *The Regional Dimension of the European Research Area*, communication from the Commission, Brussels: European Commission, COM (2001) 549 final, 3 October 2001.

European Union (1999), *Council decision of 25 January 1999 adopting a specific programme for research, technological development and demonstration on quality of life and management of living resources (1998–2002)*, 1999/167/EC.

Freeman, C. (1987), *Technology Policy and Economic Performance: Lessons from Japan*, London: Pinter.

Freeman, C. (1995), 'The "National System of Innovation" in historical perspective', *Cambridge Journal of Economics*, **19**, 4–24.

Giesecke, S. (2000), 'The contrasting roles of government in the development of biotechnology industry in the US and Germany', *Research Policy*, **29**, 205–23.

Grande, E. (1999), 'Innovationspolitik im europäischen Mehrebenensystem. Zur neuen Architektur des Staatlichen', in Grimmer, K. et al. (eds), *Innovationspolitik in globalisierten Arenen. Neue Aufgaben für Forschung und Lehre: Forschungs-, Technologie- und Innovationspolitik im Wandel*, Opladen: Leske + Budrich, pp. 87–103.

Grande, E. (2001), 'Von der Technologie- zur Innovationspolitik – Europäische Forschungs- und Technologiepolitik im Zeitalter der Globalisierung', in Simonis, G. et al. (eds), *Politik und Technik*, PVS-Sonderheft **31**/2000: pp. 368–87.

Kaiser, R. (forthcoming), 'Technological Paradigm Shifts and New Modes of Coordination in Science-based Industries', in Hemlin, S. (ed.), *Creative Knowledge Environments*, Cheltenham, UK and Northampton, MA, USA: Edward Elgar.

Kaiser, R. and H. Prange (2001), 'Die Ausdifferenzierung nationaler Innovationssysteme. Deutschland und Österreich im Vergleich', *Österreichische Zeitschrift für Politikwissenschaft*, **30** (3), 313–30.

Kaiser, R. and H. Prange (2002), 'A new concept of deepening European integration? The European Research Area and the emerging role of policy coordination in a multi-level governance system', *European Integration online Papers (EIoP)*, **6** (18).

Krauss, G. and T. Stahlecker (2000), *Die BioRegion Rhein-Neckar-Dreieck. Von der Grundlagenforschung zur wirtschaftlichen Verwertung*, Stuttgart: Akademie für Technikfolgenabschätzung in Baden-Württemberg.

Kuhlmann, S. (1999), 'Politisches System und Innovationssystem in "postnationalen" Arenen', in Grimmer, K. (ed.), *Innovationspolitik in globalisierten Arenen. Neue Aufgaben für Forschung und Lehre: Forschungs-, Technologie- und Innovationspolitik im Wandel*, Opladen: Leske+Budrich, pp. 11–39.

Kuhlmann, S. (2001), 'Future governance of innovation policy in Europe– three scenarios', *Research Policy*, **30**, 953–76.

Lundval, B.Å. (1992), *National Systems of Innovation: Towards a Theory of Innovation and Interactive Learning*, London: Pinter.

Marschall, L. (2000), *Im Schatten der chemischen Synthese. Industrielle Biotechnologie in Deutschland 1900–1970*, Frankfurt/Main and New York: Campus.

Momma, S. and M. Sharp (1999), 'Developments in new biotechnology firms in Germany', *Technovation*, **19** (5), 267–282.

Nelson, R. (1987), *Understanding Technical Change as an Evolutionary Process*, Amsterdam: North-Holland.

Nelson, R. (ed.) (1993), *National Systems of Innovation: a Comparative Analysis*, New York, USA and Oxford, UK: Oxford University Press.

Nollert, M. (2000), 'Biotechnology in the European Union: a Case Study of Political Entrepreneurship', in Bornschier, V. (ed.), *State-Building in Europe. The Revitalization of Western European Integration*, Cambridge, UK: Cambridge University Press, pp. 210–43.

OECD (1999a), *Boosting Innovation. The Cluster Approach*, Paris: OECD (Organisation for Economic Co-operation and Development).

OECD (1999b), *Managing National Innovation Systems*, Paris: OECD (Organisation for Economic Co-operation and Development).

OECD (2001), *Innovative Clusters. Drivers of National Innovation Systems*, Paris: OECD (Organisation for Economic Co-operation and Development).

Peterson, J. and M. Sharp (1998), *Technology Policy in the European Union*, Basingstoke: Macmillan.

Porter, M. (1991), *The Competitive Advantage of Nations*, London: Macmillan.

Prange, H. (2001), 'Europeanization of science and technology policy', *Current Politics and Economics of Europe*, **10** (4), 419–38.

Roelandt, T. and P. den Hertog (1999), 'Cluster Analysis and Cluster-based Policy Making: the State of the Art', in OECD (ed.), *Boosting Innovation. The Cluster Approach*, Paris: OECD (Organisation for Economic Co-operation and Development), pp. 413–27.

Scharpf, F. W. (1997), *Games Real Actors Play: Actor-centred Institutionalism in Policy Research*, Boulder: Westview Press.

The Boston Consulting Group (2001), *Positionierung deutscher Biotechnologie-Cluster im internationalen Vergleich. Strategien für den internationalen Erfolg*.

14 The European Research Area and the Social Contextualization of Technological Innovations

The Case of Biotechnology[1]

Gabriele Abels

INTRODUCTION

Technological innovations are not successful until they are deeply embedded in social practices. The social contextualization of technologies in social subsystems – ranging from the legal, political and economic subsystems to the cultural system and the individual – is a very demanding process. It is the result of social interaction among numerous and heterogeneous actors, including industrialists, scientists and politicians, civil society actors and individual consumers. Furthermore, the difficulties encountered in the contextualization process are specific to the technology under debate and to its particular characteristics. For example, nuclear energy does not raise the same questions regarding our cultural understanding of life as biotechnology, yet artificial intelligence may do. The modes of governing this contextualization also depend on the sector and, in addition, on particular applications. Corporatist bargaining may work for biotechnology relating to work safety issues (such as genetic diagnosis at the workplace), but it may be of limited value when target populations are large and heterogeneous, as is the case with consumers regarding food safety or prospective parents as regards prenatal diagnosis. Public policies that aim at supporting the contextualization of technological innovations and theories that try to explain why some nations are more innovative than others ('National Systems of Innovation' approaches) have to consider carefully the relation between technological and social innovations (for biotechnology cf. Behrens 2001; Giesecke 2000). A focus on legal regulation, on university–industry relations, on economic incentives or public policies is only part of the game; what is too often neglected is the social contextualization at the micro-level, that is, people's attitudes, public acceptance of new technologies and consumer behavior.

Biotechnology provides a paradigmatic case for understanding the social difficulties technological innovations may face on their way from the research laboratory to the market and 'from the farm to the fork'. In the 1990s, biotechnology – encompassing food and agricultural as well as medical biotechnology – has become the most contested technology in all European Union (EU) Member States, as well as at the supranational (and international) level. After some 15 years of intense debate over public policies promoting and regulating biotechnology as well as over industrial research and development, there are still hardly any biotech products to be found on the common market or in the pipeline, especially agricultural products such as plants which are considered as one of the largest biotech applications. Until now, the EU is lagging behind the United States as key economic data demonstrate (cf. OECD 2001): for example, the total of public R&D expenditure is way higher in the United States than in the EU Member States and the same is true for venture capital investments on biotechnology; the United States is still a leader for biotechnology products on the international market.

The social conflicts over biotechnology have led to rhetorical as well as real changes in the governance of research policy at the supranational level. One examples includes an intense debate over research priorities and funding (for example, the inclusion of technology assessment, research on 'Citizen's and governance in the knowledge society' and on 'Science and Society'); others center on recent attempts for broader public participation in biotechnology policymaking (and regulatory decision-making), organizational restructuring of the European Commission services as well as the establishment of advisory committees on bioethics and biotechnology. These changes are part of a broader transformation from an industrial policy orientation to an innovation-based approach in research policy promoted by the European Commission since the 1990s (Grande 2001). The European Commission communication 'Towards a European Research Area' – along with a number of more specific policy papers published by the European Commission since 2000 – is the latest conceptual outcome of this development. These papers address some key aspects that are important for the social contextualization of biotechnology. They respond to a political need by inducing changes in the governance of the science–society relationship and the effects on research policymaking.

My contribution focuses on the ways in which the social contextualization of biotechnological innovations is taken up in the concept of the European Research Area (ERA) and related documents. I concentrate on the following questions: What is the situation for biotechnology in the EU? What challenges for successful innovations does the European Commission address in its policy papers? What changes in governance and policy are suggested and what factors and key actors trigger these changes? Finally, what lessons can be learned for the ERA?

BIOTECHNOLOGY – A CONTESTED TECHNOLOGY IN THE EU

In the 1990s, biotechnology has served as a hot issue, first, with regard to public opinion at the level of the Member States as well as at the national policymaking level and, secondly, at the supranational level, especially among the EU institutions. While in some countries such as Germany the political debate goes back to the 1980s, biotechnology became an object of public scrutiny in other Member States often facing strong public opposition – and sometimes even radical actions such as destruction of field trials – but not until the mid-1990s. Gaskell and Bauer (2001) call the time span between 1996 and 2000 'the years of controversy': Dolly, the sheep and the trade controversy between the United States and EU over the import of genetically modified organisms (GMO) like soybeans and maize into the common market have promoted a massive politicization of biotechnology in Member States such as France and Great Britain where there had so far been less resistance. All of these tensions are further exacerbated by the European food crisis over mad cow disease (BSE) and foot-and-mouth disease and its mismanagement.

Several public opinion polls on people's attitudes towards biotechnology have been conducted as part of the Eurobarometer surveys since the early 1990s. The data allow us to draw some conclusions about development of public attitudes over time. The most recent survey, Eurobarometer 58.0 conducted in 2002, clearly illustrates that there is no generalized distrust against science and technological developments among the European publics (Gaskell et al. 2003, pp. 8 f.). However there are strong resentments against certain technologies: Almost 80 per cent of the Europeans believe that information technologies and telecommunication will improve their lives, followed by more than 70 per cent who support solar energy for the same reason; but only 43 per cent believe that biotechnology or nuclear energy (27 per cent) will do so.

This general judgment requires further elaboration. Skepticism towards biotechnology is not directed against the technology as such but against particular applications of it. While there is, on average, high acceptance of so-called 'red' (health-related) biotechnology, there is a far greater skepticism toward 'green' (agricultural) biotechnology (Durant, Bauer and Gaskell 1998; Gaskell and Bauer 2001). Genetic diagnosis, for example, receives more support than genetically engineered plants, animals or novel food, because it is considered a less risky, more useful and morally acceptable application.

Nevertheless, some 'red' applications in research policy are also regarded as morally difficult, especially human cloning or embryonic stem cell research, which has recently been a salient issue in most Member States as well as at the supranational level in connection with the Sixth Framework Programme (FP6) for research (cf. Abels et al. 2003). Finally skepticism has grown between 1996 and 1999: The number of people who think that applications of biotechnology are morally acceptable and that they should be encouraged has decreased considerably (averaging 11–16 per cent, depending on specific application).

Simultaneously, we observe a change in the framing of the biotechnology controversy in the Member States as well as at the supranational level. While risk has provided the dominant frame in the 1970s and 1980s, ethics has gained prominence in strategic decision-making and public policy since the 1990s. As of 1997, ethics has moved to center stage in public policy and media discourse (Lindsey et al. 2001). In a liberal society, with its characteristic normative pluralism, ethical issues require different modes of conflict resolution than conflicts over competing interests or the status of scientific knowledge. All three conflict dimensions – ethical values, interests and knowledge – are intermingled in the debate over biotechnology (Abels 2002, pp. 2 f.).

One prominent response to the controversy in many Member States has been a proceduralization strategy. Established mechanisms and institutions for policy advising have been modified in ways that adhere to a 'mood for dialogue' (Irwin 2001). National advisory boards on bioethics have been established in many Member States, normally encompassing a plurality of scientific disciplines (Fuchs 2001). Policymakers have experimented with participatory modes of technology assessment such as consensus conferences to allow more participation by stakeholders and the general public particularly in relation to biotechnology (Joss and Bellucci 2002; Joly and Assouline 2001). Sometimes they have also introduced more radical changes in the relationship between governments and organized interests so as to manage the controversy in many Member States (Behrens 2000).

Public controversy at the national level has had major effects at the supranational level – both with regard to research policy and regulation. From an innovation-theoretical perspective, these aspects are closely related. A legal and regulatory framework affords the foundation upon which research strategies can build, in order to develop new products for the market.

The struggle over biotechnology has affected research policy, a controversy starting with the human genome analysis program in the late 1980s. Proposed by the European Commission in 1988 as part of the international Human Genome Project, the research program stirred a debate among the institutions and in some Member States as to how EU research policy should take social outcomes of technologies into consideration. The pragmatic and ad hoc solution finally found was to include an accompanying program for technology assessment (Abels 1998; 2000). The program for assessing the ethical, legal and social aspects (ELSA) served as a catalyst for the development of supranational technology assessment (TA). In the follow-up Framework Programmes for R&D, ELSA studies covered the whole field of biotechnology. In 1991, the presidents of the European Commission, the Council and the European Parliament all decided that bioethics should become an integral part of research policy and corresponding institutional changes were introduced.[2] The European Commission's 1991 report on 'Promoting the Competitive Environment for the Industrial Activities Based on Biotechnology within the Community' states:

> At the same time, biotechnology suffers from a bad image amongst policy-makers and the general public ... . Although some of the expressed fears seem exaggerated they are, nonetheless, of great political influence. It is imperative therefore that problems of public acceptability, and ethical questions raised, be recognised and dealt with. It is suggested that there should be advice available to the Commission in the area of ethics in biotechnology (European Commission 1991, p. 41).

From now on ethics and the economic component were no longer seen as opposing but rather as interdependent factors. Kohler-Koch and Edler speak of a 'new paradigmatic view abut the relationship between research, technological innovation, and economic growth' (Kohler-Koch and Edler 1998, p. 199 [my translation]) in the 1980s. They characterize this emphasis as a 'guiding regulatory idea [my translation]'. With regard to biotechnology policy in the 1990s, this triangle has evolved into a quadrangle: now ethics has joined research, innovation and economic growth. It has become an essential part of the guiding regulatory idea for the EU's biotechnology policy. The emphasis on ethical issues is part of a more general openness dating back to the days of Commissioner Cresson, serving to take the social prerequisites of technological innovations into account, as Peterson and Sharp point out:

> The diffusion of innovations involves constant change and a reciprocal moulding process between technologies on the one hand and societies on the other. Yet, technology policy is a uniquely technocratic area of policy in which experts are powerful and the general public is not. Efforts by the Commission under Cresson to make EU-funded research more socially relevant and sensitive to the 'needs of society' reflect a new and general enthusiasm for open debates about how technology policy can serve broad social needs (Peterson and Sharp 1998, p. 20).

In addition, the controversy has affected the EU regulatory policy towards biotechnology. The EU had started regulating the field even before many Member States. Since the 1990s, a number of product- and process-oriented regulations have been introduced, so that the EU today is the dominant regulatory actor limiting the policies of Member States.[3] All these regulations have been very controversial and hotly contested. Since the mid-1990s, one can even speak of a regulatory crisis surrounding biotechnology that has led to a severe institutional crisis. For example, it took ten years to decide on the patenting directive. After the European Parliament and the Council reached a compromise on the first proposal in the conciliation committee under the co-decision procedure, it was turned down by the European Parliament in 1995. The final directive from 1997 has not yet been implemented in all Member States due to the ongoing struggle at the national level. Since 1998, there has been a *de facto* moratorium on the market release of GMOs. Approval for placing GMOs on the market has always been controversial among members of the Article 21-committee (that is the implementation committee in charge). The European Commission's approval of the so-called bt-maize – against the outspoken will of 14 Member States in the committee – triggered a new institutional crisis. This incident led to a reform of the comitology system (Bradley 1998; Toeller and Hofmann 2000) and, moreover, underscored the urgent need for a revision of the deliberate release directive. For the first time the new directive 2001/18/EC, decided on in early 2001, introduces the option allowing for an ethical evaluation of agricultural GM products in addition to implementation measures for the precautionary principle (such as monitoring). The directive had to be implemented in the Member States by October 2002 – and it was again a contested subject. Finally, there is the long-lasting controversy over the novel food directive and the technical maximum values required for labeling of GMOs. The European Commission pushed for a 'one door–one key' solution for GM food and feed; it proposed two regulations on traceability and labeling as well as on GM food and feed. Following the adoption of both regulations in July 2003, the moratorium was finally lifted by the Council.

All in all, in response to the political crisis over biotechnology, EU policymakers in the 1990s opened themselves to the fact that technological innovations need to be 'socially robust' to be successful. They introduced new instruments and institutions into research policy and regulation, such as integrating broader forms of expertise, multiple programs for TA, ethical and special biotechnology advisory committees and an enforced precautionary principle. These mechanisms aim at managing the problem of social re-contextualization of technological innovations in order to adjust them to strategies for competitiveness. While the European Parliament has been a strong and sometimes influential advocate of these changes, the European Commission has remained in the driver's seat in coming up with and implementing changes – partly due to its strong position in the EU policymaking process and partly due to its strong commitment to the technological-market imperative.

BIOTECHNOLOGY AND THE EUROPEAN RESEARCH AREA

My reading of the ERA paper is that it offers a radical change for the common research policy in many ways; but with regard to the problems addressed here the question remains whether or not it is, in fact, a further step in the direction described. The ERA concept takes up the problem of social contextualization of technologies. The aim of the next section is to identify those aspects in the concept relating to controversies over biotechnology. My analysis also considers some policy documents by the European Commission related to the ERA paper and presents some in-depth debate on central issues mentioned in the paper.

The Status and Meaning of Expertise and Ethics in the ERA

The ERA paper (European Commission 2000c) starts off with a description of the current situation for research in Europe. According to the European Commission, the EU risks losing the race for growth and competitiveness in a global economy, insofar as 'Europe might not successfully achieve the transition to a knowledge-based economy' (ibid., p. 4). Science and technology – particularly biotechnology – are vital for such transition. The European Commission notes that the negative situation is partly due to a lack of public and private investment and partly due to the fact that 'the image that Europeans have of science is also less positive than it was. Scientific progress seems to inspire as much anguish as hope, and the gap between the scientific world and the people at large is growing' (ibid., p. 5). The European Commission concludes that 'it is time therefore for an in-depth debate to define a policy approach in order to reinvigorate research in Europe' (ibid.).

The European Commission identifies a number of important aspects for the development of the ERA. Scientific expertise and ethics are regarded as two key factors for embedding biotechnology research and development into society. But how does the European Commission frame and conceptualize the issues at stake? What strategic conclusions does it draw?

According to the European Commission, the development of a common system of scientific and technical reference shall help to build up research actually needed by political decision-makers (European Commission 2000c, pp. 14 f). The aim is to improve the implementation of public policies, for example, safety regulations in the field of food and the environment. There is a need for 'a reliable and recognized system of validating knowledge and methods of analysis, control and certification also needs to be put in place' (ibid.). Furthermore, the European Commission criticizes the different ways in which expertise 'is provided for decision-makers according to country and subject matter' as well as the fact that 'experts are also forced to leave the ground of solely scientific consideration'. In order to tackle the diversity issue, the European Commission recommends the establishment of a common system of reference at the EU level that 'would be built up on the basis of national reference centers, European agencies, the various scientific commit-tees and the organizations established at European levels, such as the Food Safety Authority, free of industrial and political interests and open to public enquiry and scientifically recognised' (ibid.).

The issue of expertise relates the ERA to the more general White Paper on European governance (European Commission 2001b). Here the European Commission links the issue of a scientific reference system to the need for democratizing expertise (ibid., p. 19). This aspect was identified as a matter of great importance for strengthening coherence and effectiveness of EU policies, especially in the field of biotechnology (European Commission 2001a). While policymaking and regulation rely heavily on expert advice, biotechnology has illustrated that advice beyond 'pure' scientific facts is necessary; there is lack of public confidence in expert-based policymaking, the European Commission declares. By establishing a European scientific reference system, the European Commission hope to handle the 'challenges, risks and ethical questions thrown up by science and technology' (European Commission 2001a, p. 33).

The second dimension of particular relevance to biotechnology is the de-velopment of an area of shared values (European Commission 2000c, pp. 20 f.). This dimension has two aspects: the questions of science and society in their European context and the development of a shared vision concerning the ethical issues of science and technology. The European Commission states that science–society questions are increasingly evident at the EU level (for instance, in relation to environment and health). A key instrument suggested here is to encourage 'new and sustained forms of dialogue between research-ers and other social operators' (ibid., p.20). There is need for the exchange of experiences regarding new types of dialogue as well as a need for experi-ments at the European level. The European Commission refers, for example, to consensus conferences 'organized at European level on issues emerging at that level' as a means for 'ordinary citizens' to express their opinions and concern over issues of science and technology.[4]

The ethical dimension is especially prominent in the domain of biotech-nology. While differences with respect to 'culture and moral sensitivity' shall be respected, too great a difference may pose problems in areas of common policy. Hence, it is 'important to foster convergent and coherent approaches' (ibid., p. 20) for instance by establishing stronger links between ethics committees at the national and EU levels. With regard to national and EU research programs, 'the rules in force and the criteria on ethics ... should be compared with a view to alignment around shared principles and respect for differences in sensitivities and opinions' (ibid., p. 21). The recent debate over FP6 was a first test for the possibilities of shared values. One of the controversial issues was the question as to whether ethically controversial research such as embryo research should be funded, given that Member States have differing national regulations based on ethical and legal concerns (cf. in detail section *The Status of Ethical Concerns*).

Biotechnology and the Science–Society Issue

In addition to its general outline for the ERA, the European Commission has published several policy papers in which key issues for biotechnology are further developed. These papers include the working document 'Science, Society and the Citizen in Europe' (European Commission 2000b) and the accompanying action plan (European Commission 2001c) as well as the consultation document 'Towards a strategic vision of life sciences and biotechnology' (European Commission 2001d) and the follow-up strategy paper (European Commission 2002).

In the science–society papers, biotechnology is a dominant issue (of action), because, as declared by the European Commission, 'GMOs, and more specifically transgenic plants, have come to symbolise all that is wrong in the relationship between science and society' (European Commission 2001e). The European Commission repeatedly confirms the need for a 'new partnership' (European Commission 2001c, p. 4) by promoting open dialogue between researchers, industrialists, policymakers, interest groups and the public (European Commission 2000b, pp. 6, 16). Such dialogue is deemed necessary especially at the European level, but also at the national, regional and local levels (European Commission 2001c, pp. 12 f.).

The European Commission denounces a simplistic and linear model of technological innovation, namely from scientific invention to useful products; technological innovations are recognized as outcomes of social networks that incorporate a wide range of social actors, including users (ibid., p. 8). People should be involved 'particularly in defining the priorities of publicly-funded research' via consultative and advisory bodies (ibid., pp. 8 f.) in order to 'bring science policy closer to the citizens' (ibid., pp. 5, 14). The experiences with participatory research policymaking 'now need to be widened and deepened to systematically include other sectors of civil society at all stages' (ibid., p. 14).

The European Commission has, in fact, already put some of these new instruments to the test – again with regard to biotechnology. In autumn 2001, it initiated a public consultation process by releasing the Consultation Document 'Towards a strategic vision of life sciences and biotechnology' (European Commission 2001d); it organized a Stakeholder Conference as part of this process. The overall aim of the consultation process is to invite 'comments from citizens, consumers, as well as organized civil society, scientists, public authorities and operators with economic interests in industry, agriculture of services to contribute to the European Commission's reflections' (ibid., p. 5). The document presupposes that the life sciences hold a vast potential for ensuring the competitiveness of the EU (ibid., p. 3 f.). The challenge is to transform research into new products and services. The successful transformation requires a society fully committed to technological innovation:

> Most importantly, this potential can only be realised if there is broad public support. Consequently, there is increasingly a need for awareness and enlightened policy decisions on the societal priorities, and in particular on the societal framework and the ethical basis for development and applications of the new sciences and technologies ... . It is fundamental that these questions, of key importance to public perception, be properly addressed (ibid., p. 4).

The European Commission seeks public advice on basic problems related to the social contextualization of biotechnology, ranging from its ethical implications, regulation and public involvement to trade, international collaboration and development policy.

It proclaims: 'The key to success lies with all stakeholders in Europe – public authorities, science, economic operators and consumers as well as the general public.' (European Commission 2001d, p. 4) In short, the nexus between science and society is thought to have a direct effect on Europe's economic future. The European Commission concludes that the life sciences are of 'strategic importance for Europe's quest to become a leading knowledge-based economy', an opportunity Europe 'cannot afford to miss' (ibid., p. 27). The broad public debate has demonstrated the need to find 'socially acceptable solutions'.

The outcome of the consultation process is the paper 'Life sciences and biotechnology – A strategy for Europe' (European Commission 2002). In this strategy paper, the European Commission ascribes the fact that Europe has 'only slowly and with difficulty addressed the challenges and opportunities' of biotechnology to 'the absence of a shared vision of what is at stake' as well as to a lack of 'common objectives and effective co-ordination' (ibid., p. 3). It then presents a rather deterministic vision for biopolitics: the choices for Europe are either to assume 'a passive and reactive role, and bear the implications of the development of these technologies elsewhere, or develop proactive policies' (ibid.). It holds that:

... uncertainty about societal acceptance has contributed to detract attention in Europe for the factors that determine our capacity for innovation and technology development and uptake. This has stifled our competitive position, weakened our research capability and could limit our policy options in the longer term (ibid., p. 4).

The basic question is: 'How can Europe deliver effective, credible and responsible policies which enjoy the confidence and support of its citizens?' Ethical and societal implications are important to consider. Yet, the choice for the EU is 'not whether, but how to deal with the challenges posed' (ibid., p. 3).

The science–society relationship is addressed in chapter 4 of the strategy paper and in the annexed action plan (European Commission 2001c). Governance of biotechnology, that is 'the way public authorities prepare, decide, implement and explain policies and actions' (ibid., p. 11), is designated a 'key element for responsible policy'. For the EU, five lines of action are important:

- fostering societal dialogue;
- advocating development in harmony with ethical values and societal good;
- pursuing demand-driven applications;
- enhancing public confidence through science-based regulation; and
- increasing respect for Community and international regulatory principles and legal obligations.

The European Commission stresses the need for 'constructive' and 'meaningful' dialogue open to all stakeholders, which has to be 'balanced and rational' (ibid., p. 12). It distinguishes between 'real issues' and 'false claims' – without explaining how to draw the line or indicating who decides it. The key significance of the dialogue is 'to help the public and stakeholders better understand and appreciate' (ibid., p. 13) the complex issues raised by biotechnology. Yet, the EU should actively pursue the science–society dialogue; it should be ongoing and not restricted merely to product regulation only.

In the action plan, the European Commission announces its intention to take the initiative for establishing a 'broadly based Stakeholders' Forum' and encouraging public debates (Action 13). Furthermore, it wants to strengthen research into socioeconomic and ethical issues (Action 14) and to help identify areas for possible consensus on ethical principles, above all in relation to biomedical applications such as stem cell research or genetic testing. It proposes, where appropriate, to set up self-regulatory guidelines for scientists and industry (Action 16).

CRITICAL EVALUATION OF THE FRAMING AND THE STRATEGY

The questions I attend to in this section are as follows: Is the way in which the European Commission frames the problems and the strategic conclusions it draws for political structures, processes and policies appropriate and sufficient? Do they actually meliorate the controversy over biotechnology? I will focus on three dimensions: trust, expertise and ethics.

Does the 'Trust Model' Overturn the 'Deficit Model'?

In their critique of the papers analyzed above, Levidow and Marris welcome the European Commission's initiative, but they are most critical about the way in which the issues are framed. They claim that these papers indicate a change 'from public ignorance to loss of trust' (Levidow and Marris 2001, p. 348) in the European Commission's view. So far, the European Commission has attributed societal opposition and resistance to biotechnology to a lack of public understanding, to ignorance and people's fear ('deficit model'); now trust is the new catchword. Trust in technologies and the accompanying social order cannot be forced by compulsory education ('we teach you the advantages you don't yet or don't want to know about') nor by paternalistic politics ('we know what's good for you'). Trust requires a reciprocal relationship and, therefore, new policy tools: The European Commission puts much emphasis on new relationships and better communication between researchers, industry, policymakers and citizens as well as on the broader participation of stakeholders and the general public.[5] The issue of trust is related to legitimacy. Political institutions can help to foster trust and legitimacy not only by having citizen's participate in policymaking (input legitimacy), but also by delivering policies that actually respond to social need and adequately solve political problems (output legitimacy) – in this case promoting the benefits of the technologies society wants and effectively managing their risks.

According to Levidow and Marris, the new rhetoric is double-edged and contradictory, because participatory talk often just covers the former 'deficit model':

> ... the new focus on a crisis of 'confidence' has not entirely abandoned preconceptions about misplaced fears or public ignorance ... . On the one hand, official proposals for 'stakeholder dialogue' are put forward as a novel approach, developed from lessons learnt from past paternalistic institutional behaviour. On the other hand, they continue to frame the problem as a gap between scientific knowledge and public anxiety – presumably a gap between rational judgments and irrational concerns. 'Public debate' and 'input from society' are sought mainly as a means to

restore the legitimacy of science and technology, not as a means to reconsider innovation processes.

Therefore, 'the new rhetoric continues to be grounded in earlier misconceptions, so that tensions emerge in policy documents and governance practices'.

The Science–Society Framing and the Role of Expertise

In its documents, the European Commission leaves out, overlooks and insufficiently conceptualizes some important aspects. First of all, the overall framing of the debate is remarkable: science governance. With regard to current struggles in the United States and the EU at to the proper relationship between science and society, particularly in the field of biotechnology, sociologist of science Jasanoff (2000) speaks of a 'crisis of expertise'. She observes that while there are some similarities in diagnosis and political reactions, there are some fundamental differences between the debates in the EU and the United States: In the EU, the discussion focuses on the status of science in general, on new forms of governance and on institutional reform. The focus of the US debate, in contrast, is more narrow; it centers on the role of experts, on policies as well as on specific issues. Demands are made for more transparency, participation and new forms of expertise, above all, concerning ethics in both debates.

Secondly, in modern societies the role of scientific knowledge in policymaking is immense; policymakers have become more and more dependent on expert advise. The European Commission is no exception to the rule. Yet, along with the 'scientification' of politics, science itself has become politicized. Jasanoff (1990, p. 17) has forcefully argued that 'the idea that scientists can speak truth to power in a value-free manner has emerged as a myth without correlates in reality'. Science and expertise has lost its authoritative status: the hypothetical, uncertain and unsecured status of scientific knowledge, the inherent epistemic limits of scientific knowledge are evermore obvious (cf. Weingart 1999). The scientific and political management of uncertainty is the key challenge for the regulation of risks associated with technological development. This is most obvious at the EU level where a 'new politics of risk regulation' is coming into force particularly with regard to food safety and GMOs: the European Food Safety Authority (EFSA) established in 2002 (cf. Abels 2002, pp. 7–9; Buonanno et al. 2001).

Thirdly, in the various policy papers (and also in Levidow and Marris' critique) the focus is on science in general, yet no clear distinction between expertise and science is made – indeed the words are often used interchangeably. The European Commission thus does not focus sufficiently on the issues at stake and their relation to EU policymaking. Saretzki (1997) has emphasized that science and expertise are not the same and, therefore, that the democratization of expertise is not the same as of science in general. Expertise refers to the use of experts and their knowledge in policymaking; experts are advisers to policymakers. Hence, the democratization of expertise first of all refers to the formal and informal mechanisms of policy advising. Saretzki argues that the challenge is to 'democratise policy advice in general, in particular: to open up all those processes and institutions where scientific knowledge for advice to policymakers is collected, assessed, used and disseminated'. The task is to mediate scientific knowledge with other forms of knowledge. This mediation is necessary due to the transformation of science in addition to the various and inherent cognitive boundaries (for instance, epistemic and normative limits) of scientific knowledge.

Having said all that, my question is, whether or not the common system of scientific and technical reference proposed could encounter the structural problems and shortcomings. The European Commission seems to presume that there is or, at least could be, a body of 'pure' uncontested knowledge; there is the belief that uncertainty is just a matter of technical imprecision and of the lack of knowledge which simply requires further research ('sound science model'). The European Commission's preference for 'depoliticized', 'interest-free' and 'value-free' regulatory agencies (such as EFSA) is an institutional response to the narrow framing of the knowledge problem. This understanding of uncertainty, however, neglects the value dimension in risk assessment and risk management, because uncertainty is too often irreducible (cf. Levidow and Marris 2001, p. 350).

In the final analysis, the European Commission's explanation and political strategy is informed by two misconceptions: firstly, the European Commission employs to some extent a cover-up version of the old 'deficit model' which puts the blame on the distrustful public; it would restrict the participation of stakeholders and the public to the assessment of innovations once they are close to the market, but not permit evaluations of general trajectories in research policy. Secondly, the European Commission still regards scientific knowledge as an objective basis for policymaking. According to Levidow and Marris, this last misconception, in fact, has created the very legitimacy crisis it now tries to tackle. They demand that 'if the aim is to relegitimise decision-making, government will need to "unlearn" many institutional assumptions and to redefine the problem at stake. Rather than seeking ways to change the public, it is necessary to change the institutions responsible for promoting innovation and regulating risks.' (Levidow and Marris 2001, pp. 357 f.)

In my judgment, the strategy of creating a common system of scientific and technical reference with regulatory agencies as the institutional core is contradictory: If the negative public image of science is one of the main reasons for the crisis, as the European Commission concludes in the science–society paper, why should the public trust science-based regulation? First of all, there are the epistemic and normative limits to science itself. Secondly, not only the Member States but also the European Commission itself has used scientific expertise in an instrumental way such as in the BSE crisis and, thereby, has discredited the outcomes. The year-long political controversy over an EU regulatory agency for food safety is another example. In addition, given the strong emphasis on communication and public participation, it is striking that the European Commission does not discuss combing regulatory agencies with participatory approaches (cf. Radaelli 2002) – particularly since the concept for the EFSA management board, in fact, adopts such (yet rather corporatist) approach and includes stakeholders involvement.

The Status of Ethical Concerns

Ethical concerns are believed to be the other major problem for the social contextualization of biotechnology. Again, the framing is interesting. While ethics is now taken into consideration and often even takes center-stage, it is understood to comprise 'extra-scientific' matters. Scientific and other arguments are characterized as separable; while the former are perceived to be objective and 'value-free', the latter are attributed to the subjective realm and, therefore, of secondary importance only (Levidow and Marris 2001, p. 349). The separation between scientific and extra-scientific issues keeps the notion of 'sound science' alive; the public is still the source of the problem. However who draws the line? It is, above all, the normative dimension of biotechnology policy that has led to hot public debates and, ultimately, to the need for changes in governance practices. The difficulty is that in a pluralist society, representative democracy and majority rule are insufficient institutions for resolving conflicts over fundamental values since facts and norms are actually inseparable. Public discourse is considered the key tool.

The European Commission recommends all forms of dialogue be used at all levels. It emphasizes consensus conferences, a TA instrument so far only practiced in the nation states, also in the EU as a whole on issues emerging at the supranational level. Besides closer co-operation of ethical advisory committees, this is regarded as an important means for developing an 'area of shared values' and for involving citizens in policymaking. But are all stakeholders and prospective participants actually interested in dialogue with the public? The response, for example, from the Yeast Industry Platform (YIP) and the Industrial Platform for Microbiology (IPM) raises some doubts about their commitment and in what dialogue actually means, due to their strong belief in the 'deficit model' and in sound science: 'Opinions, cmotions, fears, expectations, preferences and religious beliefs ... ought to be respected in their diversity but they have to be taken for what they are and cannot be applied as tools in problem-solving approaches: these tools are in science and rationality, conciliation and dialogue' (YIP and IPM 2000, p. 5).

In the recent debate on FP6, the role of ethics in research policy has served as a source of disagreement between the Member States. The disagreement is not so much about abstract values such as human rights or dignity, because these are already part of the treaty preambles and, moreover, part of the EU Charter of Fundamental Rights (particularly Article 3). The struggle is over the interpretation of these values and the concrete conclusions to be drawn for research policy and research regulation based on ethical standards. The question was as to whether research on human embryonic stem cells and therapeutic cloning should be included in FP6. The regulation of this research rests within the competence of each member state. While many allow this kind of research (or at least some aspects given that more or less restrictive conditions are fulfilled), some don't. The UK and Sweden, for example, have relatively liberal regulations on embryo research in general and specifically allow so-called therapeutic cloning. Germany and Austria in general rule out embryo research and any kind of cloning by law, while Ireland, on the other hand, implicitly prohibits any kind of embryo research on constitutional grounds. What happened is that there was intense 'trilog' between the European Commission, the Council and the European Parliament as well as a much debate between the Member States in the Council. Often influential in matters of bioethics and research regulation, the European Parliament was split on this issues. In its reading of FP6, the Conservatives and the Greens explicitly wanted to exclude embryo research and cloning from funding. They defended their position: (a) by referring to the moral status of the embryo; and (b) because they feared the exploitation of women as potential egg cell donors and thereby an instrumental use of the female body (Abels 2003). Due to the divisions among the Member States, the Council finally decided in July 2002 to exclude all research involving the use of human embryos and embryonic stem cell for the time being – unless the stem cells are already existing in biobanks and the respective national law allows such research.[6]

The German and Austrian example are quite instructive: their position in the Council was ambivalent. After months of hot public and media debate, coupled with opposing statements from the National Ethics Board and the Parliamentary Inquiry Commission ('Enquete-Kommission') *Law and Ethics of Modern Medicine*, the German 'Bundestag' finally decided on 30 January 2002 that human embryonic stem cells can be imported and experimented with for research purposes – once a number of very strict conditions are fulfilled. These conditions include that there is no feasible research alternative; there has to be case-by-case approval by a special licensing body; there is a deadline as to when embryos had to be collected etc. Chancellor Schröder and the Federal Minister of Research, Bulmahn, have always favored a less

restrictive position that would even allow therapeutic cloning. In the deliberations on FP6, Germany did not really try to introduce such strict
regulations for research at the EU level (as the decision by the 'Bundestag'
demands). Yet Bulmahn claims that the restriction for EU-funded research is
a success of German intervention in the Council deliberation. In Austria,
Research Minister Gehrer requested an opinion from the National Ethics
Board, if support of embryonic stem cell research is ethically justifiable.
While the Board approved funding, the minister finally voted against it in the
Council because she personally believed that embryo research is morally
wrong.

So in the end, some research on embryonic stem cells will be funded in
FP6, but only with some very basic common guidelines. A shared ethical
framework shall be developed by the Council until the end of 2003 – this is
part of the intergovernmental compromise. Until then, if research teams apply
for EU funding, national law is applied. Practical questions remain, for example, whether German researchers are eligible to mobility funds that would
enable them to learn techniques (for example, therapeutic cloning in the UK)
that are prohibited in Germany but funded by EU money? Yet, some research
will be excluded that is all research involving reproductive cloning, the creation of embryos solely for research purposes or genetic manipulation of hu-
mans. There was no ethical disagreement about that. Commissioner Busquin
announced in a speech on 17 May 2002 that the European Commission will
append a declaration with binding character to FP6 ruling out such research –
in order to appease ethics concerns.

The example of ethics in relation to FP6 stresses the fact that shared ethi-
cal standards are not only of secondary importance, but that they sometimes
rest at the very heart of research policymaking. It further illustrates how the
European level can be used by national governments to evade unfavorable
national positions. Whether the co-operation of ethical advisory boards, the
European Commission's own advisory structure for bioethics (that is the
European Group of Ethics [EGE]; cf. Abels 2002, p. 6) or participatory TA at
European level can produce such shared interpretations of values, is so far an
open question. Since political institutions are yet not capable of producing
legitimate policies in and of themselves, it is at least worth experimenting
with different modes of governing biopolitics.

CONCLUSIONS

My article was based on the assumption that the technological innovation
process has to go hand in hand with a process of social contextualization.
Technological developments are not successful until they are socially

embedded. For some technologies such as biotechnology and its specific applications this is a very complex and complicated process. There is no logical reason to assume that biotechnology is a singular case and, hence, that no generalization is possible. Technologies still in the pipeline (for instance, nanotechnology especially concerning options for its biomedical application) may raise serious problems, too.

Over the last decade, EU research policy has become more responsive to social needs; the ERA concept and the related policy papers on science and society are an acknowledgment of this openness. The EU, particularly the European Commission, is an important policymakers in research policy and it wants to strengthen its influence in the future. If it wants to be successful, it has to consider the societal aspects of technological developments and these are much harder to influence than, for example, public expenditures for research, a harmonized EU patenting law or mobility or researchers. It was, above all, the social conflict over biotechnology that has taught EU policymakers this lesson. However the perspective defining fundamental problems is still too narrow: The top priority is to foster technological innovations as a key condition for the competitiveness of European industry in a globalized and knowledge-based economy. This is the overall aim of ERA. The European Commission employs a deterministic notion as to the potential of biotechnology; above all, it remains fully committed to the technological-market imperative. This undisputed orientation may severely restrict the European Commission's attempts to make its policy more responsive to the societal context.

A common strategy for managing the conflict over biotechnology is proceduralization and 'bioethicalization'. The same holds true for the Member States. For the supranational level this development, however, poses some difficulties, given the nature of the EU polity. Whether expert-based or participatory, procedures have to be connected to established political institutions. The system of advise to EU policymakers can be improved, but it is no substitute for difficult political decisions. To most people, policy- and decision-making in the EU is a most confusing process and it is hard to hold policymakers accountable; integrating more actors and creating new arenas may increase openness but not transparency. Ethical concerns are deeply rooted in national cultural and political traditions. The cultural and political diversity in the EU and the lack of a European public space limit the deliberative strategy so favored by the European Commission. Discourses about values have to be located in the public sphere and participatory TA are above all directed towards the public (Joss 2002). But what if there is no such public but only multiple national public spheres (cf. Kielmansegg 1996)? Furthermore, it is still very much unclear to what end this will occur and what effects this may have. Will social contextualization be limited to sheer acceptance and will dialog have merely a symbolic function? The dialogue approach is built on the condition that, last but not least, scientists and industrialists are open to, and interested in, dialogue. Without stakeholders' and participants' commitment, dialogue does simply not work.

The ERA cannot compensate for deficits that are based on the characteristics of the EU polity as a fragmented and highly sectoralized multi-level system. The ERA constitutes a sectoral approach to reforming European governance; it raises the fundamental question as to how the supranational and the national level are and should be interrelated. The contextualization of technological innovations in many social subsystems has to be resolved, first and foremost, on the national agenda. Given the assigned status of biotechnology as a 'key technology for the 21st century', there are surely some incentives for competition between national system of contextualization.

The EU can take on a very important complementary role, both as pertains to legal regulation of the common market but also to research itself. One of the most important contributions of EU research policy is to fund comparative research regarding social processes of contextualization in the Member States. The ERA concept and FP6 strengthen research in the field connecting citizens and governance in a knowledge-based economy, yet it is only one piece in the complex puzzle of embedding technological innovations.

NOTES

[1] I am grateful to Joyce Marie Mushaben for her valuable language assistance.

[2] As a result of this meeting, the European Commission established the Group of Advisers on the Ethical Implications of Biotechnology. In 1998, the group was suspended and the new European Group of Ethics in Science and New Technologies was set up. In addition, in April 2000 Research Commissioner Busquin formed a special European Group on Life Sciences. This group informs the Commissioner as to new developments in the life sciences, and it proposes ways to further the science–society dialogue.

[3] The most important ones are the regulation on the contained use of GMOs (90/219/EC) and the one on the deliberate release of GMOs (both 1990), the last one being the cornerstone of the regulatory framework (Cantley 1995; Gottweis 1998; Patterson 2000); the patenting directive from 1997 (Leskien 1998), the novel food regulation (EC) 258/97 from 1997 (Rücker 2000) and accompanying regulations for labelling.

[4] Consensus conferences are an instrument of TA known for their participatory approach; they serve as a complement to classical expert-oriented modes. Developed by the Danish Board of Technology and first put to the test in 1987, consensus conferences have been experimented with in many EU Member States, particularly on issues of biotechnology. A direct dialogue between citizens and experts on controversial technological developments lies at the very heart of the procedure. At the end of the process, the citizens' panel publishes a written report addressed to policymakers and the general public.

[5] This approach to governance as an inclusion strategy is, in addition, in line with the reform ideas for European Governance as defined in the White Paper on governance. However the European Commission applies various interpretations of governance.

[6] In September 2002 the Research Committee of the European Parliament queried the

compromise arguing that the intergovernmental bargaining represents an illegitimate restriction of its co-decision rights (Abels 2003).

REFERENCES

Abels, G. (1998), 'The European Community as an Ethical Actor? Policy-making on the Human Genome and the Role of the European Parliament', in Wheale, P., R. von Schomburg and P. Glasner (eds), *The Social Management of Genetic Engineering*, Aldershot, Brookfield, USA, Singapore and Sydney: Ashgate, pp. 45–62.

Abels, G. (2000), *Strategische Forschung in den Biowissenschaften. Der Politikprozeß zum europäischen Humangenomprogramm*, Berlin: edition sigma.

Abels, G. (2002), 'Experts, citizens, and Eurocrats: towards a policy shift in the governance of biopolitics in the EU', *European Integration online Papers (EioP)*, **6** (19), http://eiop.or.at/eiop/texte/2002-019a.htm.

Abels, G. (2003), 'Frauen und Embryonen im Policy-Frame supranationaler Biopolitik: Chancen und Grenzen eines *engendering*', *Österreichische Zeitschrift für Politikwissenschaft*, **32** (2), 177–88.

Abels, G., K. Braun and T. Kulawik (2003), 'Geschlecht und Biomedizinpolitik. Vergleichende Perspektiven', *Österreichische Zeitschrift für Politikwissenschaft*, **32** (2).

Behrens, M. (2000), 'Nationale Innovationssysteme im Gentechnikkonflikt: Ein Vergleich zwischen Deutschland, Großbritannien und den Niederlanden', in Barben, D. and G. Abels (eds), *Biotechnologie – Globalisierung – Demokratie. Politische Gestaltung transnationaler Technologieentwicklung*, Berlin: edition sigma, pp. 205–27.

Behrens, M. (2001), *Staaten im Innovationskonflikt: Vergleichende Analyse staatlicher Handlungsspielräume im gentechnischen Innovationsprozeß Deutschlands und den Niederlanden*, Frankfurt/M., Berlin, Bern, Bruxelles, New York, Oxford and Wien: Peter Lang.

Bradley, K.St.C. (1998), 'Alien Corn or the Transgenic Procedural Maze', in van Schendelen, M.P.C.M. (ed.), *EU Committees As Influential Policymakers*, Aldershot, Brookfield USA, Singapore and Sydney: Ashgate, pp. 207–22.

Buonanno, L., S. Zablotney and R. Keefer (2001), 'Politics versus science in the making of a new regulatory regime for food in Europe', *European Integration online Papers (EioP)*, **5** (12), http://eiop.or.at/eiop/texte/2001-012a.htm.

Cantley, M.F. (1995), 'The Regulation of Modern Biotechnology. A Historical and European Perspective', in Brauer, D. (ed.), *Biotechnology, vol. 12, 'Legal, Economic and Ethical Dimensions'*, second edition, Weinheim and Berlin: Wiley-VCH, pp. 505–681.

Durant, J., M.W. Bauer and G. Gaskell (1998), *Biotechnology in the Public Sphere. A European Sourcebook*, London: Science Museum.

European Commission (1991), 'Promoting the competitive environment for the industrial activities based on biotechnology within the Community, in European Industrial Policy for the 1990s', *Bulletin of the European Communities*, Supplement **3** (91), Luxembourg, 41–54.

European Commission (2000a), *Making a Reality of the European Research Area: Guidelines for EU Research Activities*, 4 October 2000, Brussels: European

Commission, COM (2000) 612.

European Commission (2000b), *Science, Society and the Citizen in Europe*, 14 November, Brussels: European Commission, Working Document, SEC (2000) 1973.

European Commission (2000c), *Towards a European Research Area*, 18 January 2000, Brussels: European Commission, COM (2000) 6.

European Commission (2001a), *Democratising Expertise and Establishing Scientific Reference Systems*, report of the Working Group 'White Paper on Governance', Work Area 1: Broadening and Enriching the Public Debate on European Matters, May 2001, Brussels: European Commission.

European Commission (2001b), *European Governance. A White Paper*, 25 July 2001, Brussels: European Commission, COM (2001) 428 final.

European Commission (2001c), *Science and Society. Action Plan*, 4 December 2001, Brussels: European Commission, COM (2001) 714 final.

European Commission (2001d), *Towards a Strategic Vision of Life Sciences and Biotechnology*, consultation document, Brussels: European Commission, COM (2001) 454 final.

European Commission (2001e): *Transgenic Plants: Breaking the Deadlock*, http://europa.eu.int./comm/research/newscentre/en/agr/019agr01d.html.

European Commission (2002), *Life Sciences and Biotechnology – a Strategy for Europe*, 23 January 2002, Brussels: European Commission, COM (2002) 17 final.

Fuchs, M. (2001), *Ethikräte im internationalen Vergleich: Modelle für Deutschland?* Arbeitspapier Nr. 12/2001, Sankt Augustin: Konrad-Adenauer-Stiftung.

Gaskell, G. and M.W. Bauer (2001), *Biotechnology 1996–2000: the Years of Controversy*, London: Science Museum.

Gaskell, G., N. Allum and S. Stares (2003), *Europeans and Biotechnology in 2002. Eurobarometer 58.0.*, 2nd edition, 21 March 2003, London.

Giesecke, S. (2000), 'The contrasting roles of government in the development of biotechnology industry in the US and Germany', *Research Policy*, **29** (2), 205–23.

Gottweis, H. (1998), 'Regulating Genetic Engineering in the European Union: a Post-structuralist Perspective', in Kohler-Koch, B. and R. Eising (eds), *The Transformation of Governance in the European Union*, London and New York: Routledge, pp. 98–141.

Grabner, P. (2003), 'Schlaglichter auf die österreichische biopolitische Debatte', *Österreichische Zeitschrift für Politikwissenschaft*, **32** (2), 201–11.

Grande, E. (2001), 'Von der Technologie- zur Innovationspolitik – Europäische Forschungs- und Technologiepolitik im Zeitalter der Globalisierung', in Simonis, G., R. Martinsen and Th. Saretzki (eds), *Politik und Technik: Analysen zum Verhältnis von technologischem, politischem und staatlichem Wandel am Anfang des 21. Jahrhunderts*, PVS special issue 31, Opladen und Wiesbaden: Westdeutscher Verlag, pp. 368–87.

Irwin, A. (2001), 'Constructing the scientific citizen: science and democracy in the biosciences', *Public Understanding of Science*, **10** (1), 1–18.

Jasanoff, S. (1990), *The Fifth Branch: Science Advisers As Policy Makers*, Cambridge, US and London: Harvard University Press.

Jasanoff, S. (2000), 'Science and governance: the US experience', *IPTS Report*, **45**, 20–23.

Joly, P.B. and G. Assouline (2001), *Assessing Public Debate and Participation in Technology Assessment in Europe (ADAPTA)*, final report, Grenoble and Theys: INRA.

Joss, S. (2002), 'Towards the public sphere reflections on the development of participatory TA', *Bulletin of Science, Technology & Society*, **22** (3), 220–31.

Joss, S. and S. Bellucci (2002), *Participatory Technology Assessment: European Perspectives*, London: University of Westminster Press.

Kielmansegg, P.G. (1996), 'Integration und Demokratie', in Jachtenfuchs, M. and B. Kohler-Koch (eds), *Europäische Integration*, Opladen: Leske + Budrich, pp. 47–71.

Kohler-Koch, B. and J. Edler (1998), 'Ideendiskurs und Vergemeinschaftung: Erschließung transnationaler Räume durch europäisches Regieren', in Kohler-Koch, B. (ed.), *Regieren in entgrenzten Räumen*, PVS special issue 29, Opladen and Wiesbaden: Westdeutscher Verlag, pp. 169–206.

Leskien, D. (1998), 'The European patent directive on biotechnology', *Biotechnology and Development Monitor*, **36**, 16–19.

Levidow, L. and C. Marris (2001), 'Science and governance in Europe: lessons from the case of agricultural biotechnology', *Science and Public Policy*, **28** (5), 345–60.

Lindsey, N., M.W. Kamaraa, E. Jelsøe and A.T. Mortensen (2001), 'Changing frames: the emergence of ethics in European policy on biotechnolgy', *Notizie di POLITEIA*, **63**, 80–93.

OECD (2001), *Biotechnology Statistics in OECD Member Countries: Compendium of Existing National Statistics*, STI Working Papers 2001/6, Paris: OECD (Organisation for Economic Co-operation and Development).

Patterson, L.A. (2000), 'Biotechnology Policy', in Wallace, H. and W. Wallace (eds), *Policy-Making in the European Union*, fourth edition, Oxford: Oxford University Press, pp. 317–43.

Peterson, J. and M. Sharp (1998), *Technology Policy in the European Union*, Houndsmills, London and New York: Macmillan and St. Martin's Press.

Radaelli, C. (2002), 'Democratising Expertise', in Grote, J.R. and B. Gbikpi (eds), *Participatory Governance. Political and Societal Implications*, Opladen: Leske + Budrich, pp. 197–212.

Rücker, A. (2000), *Die Entstehung der Novel-Food-Verordnung der EU*, Frankfurt/Main, Berlin, Bern, Brussels, New York, Oxford and Vienna: Peter Lang.

Saretzki, Th. (1997), 'Demokratisierung von Expertise? Zur politischen Dynamik der Wissensgesellschaft', in Klein, A. and R. Schmalz-Bruns (eds), *Politische Beteiligung und Bürgerengagement in Deutschland*, Bonn: Bundeszentrale für politische Bildung, pp. 277–313.

Toeller, A.E. and H.C.H. Hofmann (2000), 'Democracy and the Reform of Comitology', in Andenas, M. and A. Türk (eds), *Delegated Legislation and the Role of Committees in the EC*, The Hague, London and Boston: Kluwer Law International, pp. 25–50.

Weingart, P. (1999), 'Scientific expertise and political accountability: paradoxes of science in politics', *Science and Public Policy*, **26** (3), 151–61.

YIP (Yeast Industry Platform) and IPM (Industrial Platform for Microbiology) (2000), *Input on the Commission Proposal 'Towards a European Research Area'*, final document, 19 May 2000, http://www.cordis.lu/rtd2002/era-debate/ others.htm.

Zito, A.R. (2001), 'Epistemic communities, European Union governance and the public voice', *Science and Public Policy*, **28** (6), 465–76.

Index